Professional
Ajax

Professional
Ajax

Nicholas C. Zakas
Jeremy McPeak
Joe Fawcett

WILEY

Wiley Publishing, Inc.

Professional Ajax

Published by
Wiley Publishing, Inc.
10475 Crosspoint Boulevard
Indianapolis, IN 46256
www.wiley.com

Copyright © 2006 by Wiley Publishing, Inc., Indianapolis, Indiana

Published simultaneously in Canada

ISBN-13: 978-0-471-77778-6
ISBN-10: 0-471-77778-1

Manufactured in the United States of America

10 9 8 7 6 5 4 3 2 1

1B/RZ/QR/QW/IN

Library of Congress Cataloging-in-Publication Data

Zakas, Nicholas C.
  Professional Ajax / Nicholas C. Zakas, Jeremy McPeak, Joe Fawcett.
    p. cm.
  Includes index.
  ISBN-13: 978-0-471-77778-6 (paper/website)
  ISBN-10: 0-471-77778-1 (paper/website)
  1. JavaScript (Computer program language) 2. Asynchronous transfer mode. 3. World Wide Web. I. McPeak, Jeremy, 1979– II. Fawcett, Joe, 1962– III. Title.
  QA76.73.J39Z35 2006
  005.13'3—dc22
                         2005034274

About the Authors

Nicholas C. Zakas has a BS degree in Computer Science from Merrimack College and an MBA degree from Endicott College. He is the author of *Professional JavaScript for Web Developers* as well as several online articles. Nicholas has worked in web development for more than five years and has helped develop web solutions in use at some of the largest companies in the world. Nicholas can be reached through his web site at www.nczonline.net.

Jeremy McPeak began tinkering with web development as a hobby in 1998. Currently working in the IT department of a school district, Jeremy has experience developing web solutions with JavaScript, PHP, and C#. He has written several online articles covering topics such as XSLT, WebForms, and C#.

Joe Fawcett started programming in the 1970s and worked briefly in IT after leaving full-time education. He then pursued a more checkered career before returning to software development in 1994. In 2003, he was awarded the title Microsoft Most Valuable Professional in XML for community contributions and technical expertise. Joe currently works in London as a developer for The Financial Training Company, which provides professional certifications and business training.

Credits

Senior Acquisitions Editor
Jim Minatel

Development Editor
John Sleeva

Technical Editor
Alexei Gorkov

Production Editor
Kathryn Duggan

Copy Editor
Michael Koch

Editorial Manager
Mary Beth Wakefield

Production Manager
Tim Tate

Vice President and Executive Group Publisher
Richard Swadley

Vice President and Executive Publisher
Joseph B. Wikert

Graphics and Production Specialists
Carrie A. Foster
Lauren Goddard
Joyce Haughey
Jennifer Heleine
Barbara Moore
Melanee Prendergast
Alicia B. South

Quality Control Technician
John Greenough

Proofreading and Indexing
TECHBOOKS Production Services

To my family and Emily, whose love and support have been invaluable over the past couple of years.

—Nicholas C. Zakas

To my parents, Sheila and William, who instilled in me a love of reading. Thank you!

—Jeremy McPeak

Contents

Contents

Contents

Contents

Acknowledgments

It takes many people to create a book such as this, and we'd like to thank some people for their contributions to this work.

First and foremost, thanks to everyone at Wiley for their support: Jim Minatel for starting the process, Gabrielle Nabi for helping with the first few chapters, and John Sleeva for finishing where Gabrielle left off. Also, a big thanks to our technical editor, Alexei Gorkov, for doing a fantastic job of keeping us honest.

Last, a big thanks to those who provided pre-publication feedback, including Martin Honnen, Peter Frueh, Mike Shaffer, Brad Neuberg, Steven Peterson, and Eric Miraglia.

Introduction

With recent advances in JavaScript, web developers have been able to create an unprecedented user experience in web applications. Breaking free of the "click-and-wait" paradigm that has dominated the web since its inception, developers can now bring features formerly reserved for desktop applications onto the web using a technique called Ajax.

Ajax is an all-encompassing term surrounding the use of asynchronous HTTP requests initiated by JavaScript for the purpose of retrieving information from the server without unloading the page. These requests may be executed in any number of ways and using any number of different data transmission formats. Combining this remote data retrieval with the interactivity of the Document Object Model (DOM) has bred a new generation of web applications that seem to defy all the traditional rules of what can happen on the web. Big companies such as Google, Yahoo!, and Microsoft have devoted resources specifically towards the goal of creating web applications that look and behave like desktop applications.

This book covers the various aspects of Ajax, including the different ways you can initiate HTTP requests to the server and the different formats that can be used to carry data back and forth. You will learn different Ajax techniques and patterns for executing client-server communication on your web site and in web applications.

Whom This Book Is For

This book is aimed at two groups of readers:

❑ Web application developers looking to enhance the usability of their web sites and web applications.

❑ Intermediate JavaScript developers looking to further understand the language.

In addition, familiarity with the following related technologies is a strong indicator that this book is for you:

❑ XML

❑ XSLT

❑ Web Services

❑ PHP

❑ C#

❑ HTML

❑ CSS

This book is not aimed at beginners without a basic understanding of the aforementioned technologies. Also, a good understanding of JavaScript is vitally important to understanding this book. Readers who do not have this knowledge should instead refer to books such as *Beginning JavaScript, Second Edition* (Wiley Publishing, ISBN 0-7645-5587-1) and *Professional JavaScript for Web Developers* (Wiley Publishing, ISBN 0-7645-7908-8).

What This Book Covers

Professional Ajax provides a developer-level tutorial of Ajax techniques, patterns, and use cases.

The book begins by exploring the roots of Ajax, covering how the evolution of the Web and new technologies directly led to the development of Ajax techniques. A detailed discussion of how frames, JavaScript, cookies, XML, and XMLHttp related to Ajax is included.

After this introduction, the book moves on to cover the implementation of specific Ajax techniques. Request brokers such as hidden frames, dynamic iframes, and XMLHttp are compared and contrasted, explaining when one method should be used over another. To make this discussion clearer, a brief overview of HTTP requests and responses is included.

Once a basic understanding of the various request types is discussed, the book moves on to provide in-depth examples of how and when to use Ajax in a web site or web application. Different data transmission formats—including plain text, HTML, XML, and JSON—are discussed for their advantages and disadvantages. Also included is a discussion on web services and how they may be used to perform Ajax techniques.

The last part of the book walks you through the creation of a full-fledged Ajax web application called AjaxMail, which incorporates many of the techniques discussed throughout the book, and introduces you to several Ajax libraries designed to make Ajax communication easier on developers.

How This Book Is Structured

This book begins by providing background about the origins of Ajax before moving into actual implementation. Next, the various ways to accomplish client-server communication are discussed, setting the stage for the rest of the book. It is recommended that you read the book straight through, as each chapter builds on information in the previous chapters.

The chapter-level breakdown is as follows:

❑ **Chapter 1: "What Is Ajax?"** This chapter explains the origins of Ajax and the technologies involved. It describes how Ajax developed as the Web developed and who, if anyone, can claim ownership of the term and techniques.

❑ **Chapter 2: "Ajax Basics."** This chapter introduces the various ways to accomplish Ajax communication, including the hidden frame technique and XMLHttp. The advantages and disadvantages of each approach are discussed, as well as guidelines as to when each should be used.

❑ **Chapter 3: "Ajax Patterns."** This chapter focuses on design patterns using Ajax. There are a variety of ways to incorporate Ajax into web sites and web applications; these have been organized into a handful of design patterns that describe best practices for Ajax incorporation.

❑ **Chapter 4: "XML, XPath, and XSLT."** This chapter introduces XML, XPath, and XSLT as complementary technologies to Ajax. The discussion centers on using XML as a data transmission format and using XPath and XSLT to access and display information.

❑ **Chapter 5: "Syndication with RSS/Atom."** This chapter deals with using Ajax together with the data syndication formats RSS and Atom to create a web-based news aggregator.

❑ **Chapter 6: "Web Services."** This chapter brings web services into the Ajax picture. Examples of how to call web services from the client are explained, as well as how to create server-side proxies to work around browser security restrictions.

❑ **Chapter 7: "JSON."** This chapter introduces JavaScript Object Notation (JSON) as an alternate data transmission format for Ajax communications. Advantages and disadvantages over using XML and plain text are discussed.

❑ **Chapter 8: "Web Site Widgets."** This chapter brings the techniques from the previous chapters into focus by creating Ajax widgets that can be included in your web site.

❑ **Chapter 9: "AjaxMail."** This chapter walks you through the development of a complete web application, AjaxMail. This application is an Ajax-based e-mail system that uses many of the techniques described earlier in the book.

❑ **Chapter 10: "Ajax Frameworks."** This chapter covers three Ajax frameworks: JPSPAN for PHP, DWR for Java and JSP, and Ajax.NET for the .NET framework. Each of these frameworks attempts to automate some part of the Ajax development process.

What You Need to Use This Book

To run the samples in the book, you will need the following:

❑ Windows 2000, Windows Server 2003, Windows XP, or Mac OS X

❑ Internet Explorer 5.5 or higher (Windows), Mozilla 1.0 or higher (all platforms), Opera 7.5 or higher (all platforms), or Safari 1.2 or higher (Mac OS X).

The complete source code for the samples is available for download from www.wrox.com.

Conventions

To help you get the most from the text and keep track of what's happening, we've used a number of conventions throughout the book.

> **Boxes like this one hold important, not-to-be forgotten information that is directly relevant to the surrounding text.**

Tips, hints, tricks, and asides to the current discussion are offset and placed in italics like this.

As for styles in the text:

❑ We *highlight* new terms and important words in italic when we introduce them.

❑ We show keyboard strokes like this: Ctrl+A.

❑ We show file names, URLs, and code within the text like so: `persistence.properties`.

❑   We present code in two different ways:

```
In code examples we highlight new and important code with a gray background.
```

> The gray highlighting is not used for code that's less important in the present context, or has been shown before.

Source Code

As you work through the examples in this book, you may choose either to type all the code manually or to use the source code files that accompany the book. All of the source code used in this book is available for download at www.wrox.com. When at the site, locate the book's title (either by using the Search box or by using one of the title lists) and click the Download Code link on the book's detail page to obtain all the source code for the book.

> *Because many books have similar titles, you may find it easiest to search by ISBN; this book's ISBN is 0-471-77778-1.*

After you have downloaded the code, decompress it with your favorite compression tool. Alternately, you can go to the main Wrox code download page at www.wrox.com/dynamic/books/download.aspx to see the code available for this book and all other Wrox books.

Errata

We make every effort to ensure that there are no errors in the text or in the code. However, no one is perfect, and mistakes do occur. If you find an error in one of our books, like a spelling mistake or faulty piece of code, we would be very grateful for your feedback. By sending in errata you may save another reader hours of frustration and at the same time you will be helping us provide even higher quality information.

To find the errata page for this book, go to www.wrox.com and locate the title using the Search box or one of the title lists. Then, on the book details page, click the Book Errata link. On this page you can view all errata that has been submitted for this book and posted by Wrox editors. A complete book list including links to each's book's errata is also available at www.wrox.com/misc-pages/booklist.shtml.

If you don't spot "your" error on the Book Errata page, go to www.wrox.com/contact/techsupport.shtml and complete the form there to send us the error you have found. We'll check the information and, if appropriate, post a message to the book's errata page and fix the problem in subsequent editions of the book.

p2p.wrox.com

For author and peer discussion, join the P2P forums at p2p.wrox.com. The forums are a Web-based system for you to post messages relating to Wrox books and related technologies and interact with other readers and technology users. The forums offer a subscription feature to e-mail you topics of interest of your choosing when new posts are made to the forums. Wrox authors, editors, other industry experts, and your fellow readers are present on these forums.

At http://p2p.wrox.com you will find a number of different forums that will help you not only as you read this book, but also as you develop your own applications. To join the forums, just follow these steps:

1. Go to p2p.wrox.com and click the Register link.

2. Read the terms of use and click Agree.

3. Complete the required information to join as well as any optional information you would like to provide and click Submit.

4. You will receive an e-mail with information describing how to verify your account and complete the joining process.

> *You can read messages in the forums without joining P2P but in order to post your own messages, you must join.*

After you've joined the forum, you can post new messages and respond to messages other users post. You can read messages at any time on the Web. If you would like to have new messages from a particular forum e-mailed to you, click the Subscribe to this Forum icon next to the forum name in the forum listing.

For more information about how to use the Wrox P2P, be sure to read the P2P FAQs for answers to questions about how the forum software works as well as many common questions specific to P2P and Wrox books. To read the FAQs, click the FAQ link on any P2P page.

1

What Is Ajax?

From 2001 to 2005, the World Wide Web went through a tremendous growth spurt in terms of the technologies and methodologies being used to bring this once-static medium to life. Online brochures and catalogs no longer dominated the Web as web applications began to emerge as a significant portion of online destinations. Web applications differed from their web site ancestors in that they provided an instant service to their users. Whether for business process management or personal interests, developers were forced to create new interaction paradigms as users came to expect richer functionality.

Spurred on by little-known and lesser-used technologies that had been included in web browsers for some time, the Web took a bold step forward, shattering the traditional usage model that required a full page load every time new data or a new part of the application's logic was accessed. Companies began to experiment with dynamic reloading of portions of web pages, transmitting only a small amount of data to the client, resulting in a faster, and arguably better, user experience.

At the forefront of this movement was Google. After the search giant went public, new experiments conducted by Google engineers began popping up through a special part of the site called Google Labs. Many of the projects at Google Labs, such as Google Suggest and Google Maps, involved only a single web page that was never unloaded but was constantly updated nevertheless. These innovations, which began to bring the affordances of desktop software interfaces into the confines of the browser screen, were praised around the Web as ushering in a new age in web development. And indeed they did.

Numerous open source and commercial products began development to take advantage of this new web application model. These projects explained their technology using a variety of terms such as JavaScript remoting, web remote procedure calls, and dynamic updating. Soon, however, a new term would emerge.

Ajax Is Born

In February 2005, Jesse James Garrett of Adaptive Path, LLC published an online article entitled, "Ajax: A New Approach to Web Applications" (still available at www.adaptivepath.com/publications/ essays/archives/000385.php). In this essay, Garrett explained how he believed web applications were closing the gap between the Web and traditional desktop applications. He cited new technologies and several of the Google projects as examples of how traditionally desktop-based user interaction models were now being used on the Web. Then came the two sentences that would ignite a firestorm of interest, excitement, and controversy:

> *Google Suggest and Google Maps are two examples of a new approach to web applications that we at Adaptive Path have been calling Ajax. The name is shorthand for Asynchronous JavaScript + XML, and it represents a fundamental shift in what's possible on the Web.*

From that point forward, a tidal wave of Ajax articles, code samples, and debates began popping up all over the Web. Developers blogged about it, technology magazines wrote about it, and companies began hitching their products to it. But to understand what Ajax is, you first must understand how the evolution of several web technologies led to its development.

The Evolution of the Web

When Tim Berners-Lee crafted the first proposal for the World Wide Web in 1990, the idea was fairly simple: to create a "web" of interconnected information using hypertext and Uniform Resource Identifiers (URIs). The ability to link disparate documents from all around the world held huge potential for scholarly endeavors, where people would be able to access referenced material almost instantly. Indeed, the first version of the HyperText Markup Language (HTML) featured little more than formatting and linking commands, a platform not for building rich interactive software but rather for sharing the kinds of textual and illustrative information that dominated the late age of print. It was from these static web pages that the Web grew.

As the Web evolved, businesses soon saw potential in the ability to distribute information about products and services to the masses. The next generation of the Web saw an increased ability to format and display information as HTML also evolved to meet the needs and match the expectations of these new media-savvy users. But a small company called Netscape would soon be ready to push the evolution of the Web forward at a much faster pace.

JavaScript

Netscape Navigator was the first successful mainstream web browser, and as such, moved web technologies along quickly. However, Netscape often was ridiculed by standards organizations for implementing new technologies and extensions to existing technologies before the standards were in place (much like Microsoft is being chastised today for ignoring existing standards in its development of Internet Explorer). One such technology was JavaScript.

Originally named LiveScript, JavaScript was created by Brendan Eich of Netscape and included in version 2.0 of the browser (released in 1995). For the first time, developers were able to affect how a web page could interact with the user. Instead of making constant trips to the server and back for simple tasks such as data validation, it became possible to transfer this small bit of processing to the browser.

This ability was very important at a time when most Internet users were connected through a 28.8 Kbps modem, turning every request to the server into a waiting game. Minimizing the number of times that the user had to wait for a response was the first major step toward the Ajax approach.

Frames

The original version of HTML intended for every document to be standalone, and it wasn't until HTML 4.0 that frames were officially introduced. The idea that the display of a web page could be split up into several documents was a radical one, and controversy brewed as Netscape chose to implement the feature before HTML 4.0 was completed. Netscape Navigator 2.0 was the first browser to support frames and JavaScript together. This turned out to be a major step in the evolution of Ajax.

When the browser wars of the late 1990s began between Microsoft and Netscape, both JavaScript and frames became formalized. As more features were added to both, creative developers began experimenting using the two together. Because a frame represented a completely separate request to the server, the ability to control a frame and its contents with JavaScript opened the door to some exciting possibilities.

The Hidden Frame Technique

As developers began to understand how to manipulate frames, a new technique emerged to facilitate client-server communication. The hidden frame technique involved setting up a frameset where one frame was set to a width or height of 0 pixels, and its sole purpose was to initiate communication with the server. The hidden frame would contain an HTML form with specific form fields that could be dynamically filled out by JavaScript and submitted back to the server. When the frame returned, it would call another JavaScript function to notify the original that data had been returned. The hidden frame technique represented the first asynchronous request/response model for web applications.

While this was the first Ajax communication model, another technological advance was just around the corner.

Dynamic HTML and the DOM

Up to about 1996, the Web was still mainly a static world. Although JavaScript and the hidden frame technique livened up the user interaction, there was still no way to change the display of a page without reloading it. Then came Internet Explorer 4.0.

At this point, Internet Explorer had caught up with the technology of market leader Netscape Navigator and even one-upped it in one important respect through the introduction of Dynamic HTML (DHTML). Although still in the development phase, DHTML represented a significant step forward from the days of static web pages, enabling developers to alter any part of a loaded page by using JavaScript. Along with the emergence of cascading style sheets (CSS), DHTML reinvigorated web development, despite deep disparities between the paths Microsoft and Netscape followed during the early years of each discipline. Excitement in the developer community was justified, however, because combining DHTML with the hidden frame technique meant that any part of a page could be refreshed with server information at any time. This was a genuine paradigm shift for the Web.

DHTML never made it to a standards body, although Microsoft's influence would be felt strongly with the introduction of the Document Object Model (DOM) as the centerpiece of the standards effort. Unlike DHTML, which sought only to modify sections of a web page, the DOM had a more ambitious purpose: to provide a structure for an entire web page. The manipulation of that structure would then allow DHTML-like modifications to the page. This was the next step forward for Ajax.

Iframes

Although the hidden frame technique became incredibly popular, it had a downside—one had to plan ahead of time and write a frameset anticipating the usage of hidden frames. When the `<iframe/>` element was introduced as an official part HTML 4.0 in 1997, it represented another significant step in the evolution of the Web.

Instead of defining framesets, developers could place iframes anywhere on a page. This enabled developers to forego framesets altogether and simply place invisible iframes (through the use of CSS) on a page to enable client-server communication. And when the DOM was finally implemented in Internet Explorer 5 and Netscape 6, it introduced the ability to dynamically create iframes on the fly, meaning that a JavaScript function could be used to create an iframe, make a request, and get the response—all without including any additional HTML in a page. This led to the next generation of the hidden frame technique: the hidden iframe technique.

XMLHttp

The browser developers at Microsoft must have realized the popularity of the hidden frame technique and the newer hidden iframe technique, because they decided to provide developers with a better tool for client-server interaction. That tool came in the form of an ActiveX object called XMLHttp, introduced in 2001.

One of the Microsoft extensions to JavaScript allowed the creation of ActiveX controls, Microsoft's proprietary programming objects. When Microsoft began supporting XML through a library called MSXML, the XMLHttp object was included. Although it carried the XML name, this object was more than just another way of manipulating XML data. Indeed, it was more like an ad hoc HTTP request that could be controlled from JavaScript. Developers had access to HTTP status codes and headers, as well as any data returned from the server. That data might be structured XML, pre-formatted swaths of HTML, serialized JavaScript objects, or data in any other format desired by the developer. Instead of using hidden frames or iframes, it was now possible to access the server programmatically using pure JavaScript, independent of the page load/reload cycle. The XMLHttp object became a tremendous hit for Internet Explorer developers.

With popularity mounting, developers at the open source Mozilla project began their own port of XMLHttp. Instead of allowing access to ActiveX, the Mozilla developers replicated the object's principal methods and properties in a native browser objectXMLHttpRequest. With both of the major browsers supporting some form of XMLHttp, the development of Ajax-type interfaces really took off and forced the fringe browsers, Opera and Safari, to support some form of XMLHttp as well (both chose to do so natively with an XMLHttpRequest object, mimicking Mozilla).

The Real Ajax

Despite the frequently asked questions attached to the end of Garrett's essay, some confusion still exists as to what Ajax really is. Put simply, Ajax is nothing more than an approach to web interaction. This approach involves transmitting only a small amount of information to and from the server in order to give the user the most responsive experience possible.

Instead of the traditional web application model where the browser itself is responsible for initiating requests to, and processing requests from, the web server, the Ajax model provides an intermediate layer — what Garrett calls an *Ajax engine* — to handle this communication. An Ajax engine is really just a JavaScript object or function that is called whenever information needs to be requested from the server. Instead of the traditional model of providing a link to another resource (such as another web page), each link makes a call to the Ajax engine, which schedules and executes the request. The request is done asynchronously, meaning that code execution doesn't wait for a response before continuing.

The server — which traditionally would serve up HTML, images, CSS, or JavaScript — is configured to return data that the Ajax engine can use. This data can be plain text, XML, or any other data format that you may need. The only requirement is that the Ajax engine can understand and interpret the data

When the Ajax engine receives the server response, it goes into action, often parsing the data and making several changes to the user interface based on the information it was provided. Because this process involves transferring less information than the traditional web application model, user interface updates are faster, and the user is able to do his or her work more quickly. Figure 1-1 is an adaptation of the figure in Garrett's article, displaying the difference between the traditional and Ajax web application models.

Traditional Web Application Model

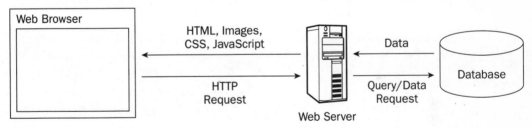

Ajax Web Application Model

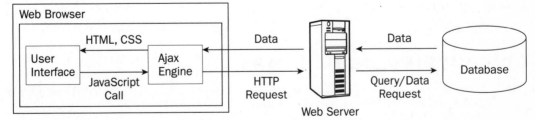

Figure 1-1

Ajax Principles

As a new web application model, Ajax is still in its infancy. However, several web developers have taken this new development as a challenge. The challenge is to define what makes a good Ajax web application versus what makes a bad or mediocre one. Michael Mahemoff (http://mahemoff.com/), a software developer and usability expert, identified several key principles of good Ajax applications that are worth repeating:

❑ **Minimal traffic:** Ajax applications should send and receive as little information as possible to and from the server. In short, Ajax can minimize the amount of traffic between the client and the server. Making sure that your Ajax application doesn't send and receive unnecessary information adds to its robustness.

❑ **No surprises:** Ajax applications typically introduce different user interaction models than traditional web applications. As opposed to the web standard of click-and-wait, some Ajax applications use other user interface paradigms such as drag-and-drop or double-clicking. No matter what user interaction model you choose, be consistent so that the user knows what to do next.

❑ **Established conventions:** Don't waste time inventing new user interaction models that your users will be unfamiliar with. Borrow heavily from traditional web applications and desktop applications so there is a minimal learning curve.

❑ **No distractions:** Avoid unnecessary and distracting page elements such as looping animations, and blinking page sections. Such gimmicks distract the user from what he or she is trying to accomplish.

❑ **Accessibility:** Consider who your primary and secondary users will be and how they most likely will access your Ajax application. Don't program yourself into a corner so that an unexpected new audience will be completely locked out. Will your users be using older browsers or special software? Make sure you know ahead of time and plan for it.

❑ **Avoid entire page downloads:** All server communication after the initial page download should be managed by the Ajax engine. Don't ruin the user experience by downloading small amounts of data in one place, but reloading the entire page in others.

❑ **User first:** Design the Ajax application with the users in mind before anything else. Try to make the common use cases easy to accomplish and don't be caught up with how you're going to fit in advertising or cool effects.

The common thread in all these principles is usability. Ajax is, primarily, about enhancing the web experience for your users; the technology behind it is merely a means to that end. By adhering to the preceding principles, you can be reasonably assured that your Ajax application will be useful and usable.

Technologies Behind Ajax

Garrett's article mentions several technologies that he sees as parts of an Ajax solution. These are:

❑ **HTML/XHTML:** Primary content representation languages

❑ **CSS:** Provides stylistic formatting to XHTML

❑ **DOM:** Dynamic updating of a loaded page

- ❑ **XML:** Data exchange format
- ❑ **XSLT:** Transforms XML into XHTML (styled by CSS)
- ❑ **XMLHttp:** Primary communication broker
- ❑ **JavaScript:** Scripting language used to program an Ajax engine

In reality, all these technologies are available to be used in Ajax solutions, but only three are required: HTML/XHTML, DOM, and JavaScript. XHTML is obviously necessary for the display of information, while the DOM is necessary to change portions of an XHTML page without reloading it. The last part, JavaScript, is necessary to initiate the client-server communication and manipulate the DOM to update the web page. The other technologies in the list are helpful in fine-tuning an Ajax solution, but they aren't necessary.

There is one major component that Garrett neglected to mention in his article: the necessity of server-side processing. All of the previously listed technologies relate directly to the client-side Ajax engine, but there is no Ajax without a stable, responsive server waiting to send content to the engine. For this purpose you can use the application server of your choice. Whether you choose to write your server-side components as PHP pages, Java servlets, or .NET components, you need only ensure the correct data format is being sent back to the Ajax engine.

The examples in this book make use of as many server-side technologies as possible to give you enough information to set up Ajax communication systems on a variety of servers.

Who Is Using Ajax?

A number of commercial web sites use Ajax techniques to improve their user experience. These sites are really more like web applications than traditional brochureware web sites that just display information because you visit it to accomplish a specific goal. The following are some of the more well-known and well-executed web applications that use Ajax.

Google Suggest

One of the first examples that developers cite when talking about Ajax is Google Suggest (`www.google.com/webhp?complete=1`). The interface is simply a clone of the main Google interface, which prominently features a text box to enter search terms. Everything appears to be the same until you start typing in the textbox. As you type, Google Suggest requests suggestions from the server, showing you a drop-down list of search terms that you may be interested in. Each suggestion is displayed with a number of results available for the given term to help you decide (see Figure 1-2).

This simple client-server interaction is very powerful and effective without being obtrusive to the user. The interface is responsive beyond what you may have learned to expect from a web application; it updates no matter how quickly you type and, as with autocomplete features in desktop software, you can use the up and down arrows to highlight and select each item in the suggestions list. Although still in beta, expect to see this approach make its way into the main Google page eventually.

Figure 1-2

Gmail

Gmail, Google's free e-mail service, has been raved about as a marvel of client-server interaction in the age of Ajax. When you first log in to Gmail, a user interface engine is loaded into one of the few iframes the application uses. All further requests back to the server occur through this user interface engine through an XMLHttp object. The data being transferred back and forth is JavaScript code, which makes for fast execution once downloaded by the browser. These requests serve as instructions to the user interface engine as to what should be updated on the screen.

Additionally, the Gmail application uses several frames and iframes to manage and cache big user interface changes. The extremely complicated use of frames enables Gmail to function properly with the Back and Forward buttons, which is one of the advantages of using frames or iframes instead of or in conjunction with XMLHttp.

The biggest win for Gmail is its usability. The user interface, as shown in Figure 1-3, is simple and uncluttered. Interaction with the user and communication with the server is all seamless. Once again, Google used Ajax to improve on an already simple concept to provide an exceptional user experience.

Google Maps

The latest addition to Google's dominant Ajax web applications is Google Maps (http://maps .google.com). Designed to compete with well-established mapping sites, Google Maps uses Ajax to avoid reloading its main page at all (see Figure 1-4).

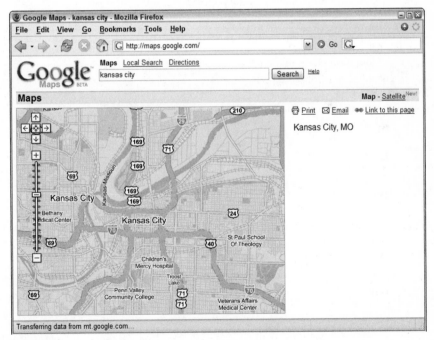

Figure 1-3

Figure 1-4

Unlike other mapping web applications, Google Maps enables you to drag the map to move it in various directions. The dragging code is nothing new to JavaScript developers, but the tiling of the map and seemingly endless scrolling effect are another story. The map is broken up into a series of images that are tiled together to make the appearance of a contiguous image. The number of images used to display the map is finite, as creating new images every time the user moves the map would quickly lead to memory problems. Instead, the same images are used over and over to display different segments of the map.

The client-server communication is done through a hidden iframe. Whenever you do a search or ask for new directions, this information is submitted and returned within that iframe. The data returned is in XML format and is passed to a JavaScript function (the Ajax engine) to handle. This XML is then used in a variety of different ways: some is used to call the correct map images, and some is transformed using XSLT into HTML and displayed in the main window. The bottom line is that this is another complex Ajax application that has an incredibly bright future.

A9

Amazon.com is world famous for being an online marketplace for just about anything, but when it released a search engine, it did so with little fanfare and attention. The introduction of A9 (www.a9.com) showed off enhanced searching, enabling you to search different types of information simultaneously. For web and image searches it uses Google to fetch results. It performs searches of books on Amazon.com and movies on IMDb (Internet Movie Database). Searches for Yellow Pages, Wikipedia, and Answers.com debuted in mid-2005.

What makes A9 unique is how its user interface works. When you perform a search, the different types of results are displayed in different areas of the page (see Figure 1-5).

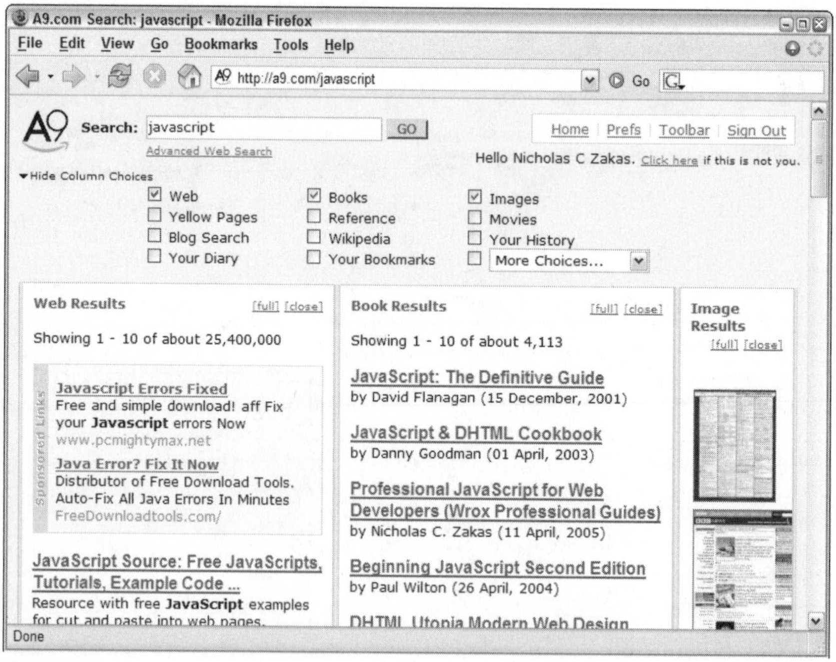

Figure 1-5

On the search results page, you have the option of selecting other searches to perform using the same criteria. When you select a check box corresponding to a type of search, the search is performed behind the scenes using a combination of hidden iframes and XMLHttp. The user interface shifts to allow room for the extra search results, which are loaded as soon as they are received from the server. The result is a more responsive search results page that doesn't need to be reloaded when you want to search on different types of information.

Yahoo! News

Also introduced in 2005 was a new design for the Yahoo! News site (http://news.yahoo.com). The new design features an interesting enhancement: when you move your mouse over a particular headline, a small box pops up with a summary and, optionally, a photo associated with that story (see Figure 1-6).

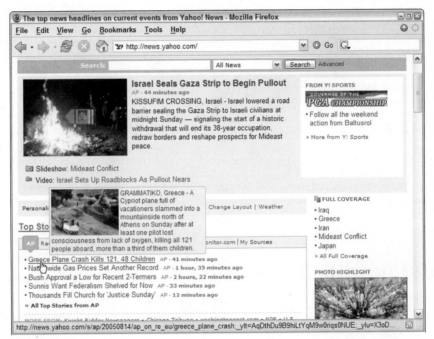

Figure 1-6

The photo information and summary are retrieved from the server using XMLHttp and inserted into the page dynamically. This is a perfect example of how Ajax can be used to enhance a web page. Rather than making Ajax the primary usage mode, the Yahoo! News site is completely usable without Ajax; the Ajax functionality is used only to add a more responsive user experience in browsers that support it. Underneath is a semantically correct HTML page that is laid out logically even without CSS formatting.

Bitflux Blog

Another great example of using Ajax only as an enhancement is Bitflux Blog (http://blog.bitflux .ch/), which features a technology called LiveSearch. LiveSearch works in conjunction with the search box on the site. As you type into the box, a list of possible search results is displayed immediately below (see Figure 1-7).

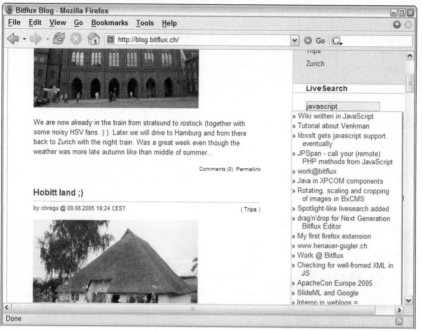

Figure 1-7

The search results are retrieved using XMLHttp as an HTML string that is then inserted into the page. You can search the site the old-fashioned way as well: by filling in the text box and pressing Enter. The LiveSearch Ajax functionality is just an enhancement to the overall site and isn't required to search.

Confusion and Controversy

Despite the popularity of the term *Ajax*, it has been met with its fair share of dissenters and controversy. Some believe that Ajax is an aberration of what the Web was moving toward before Ajax entered the picture. The proponents of semantic HTML design, accessibility, and the separation of content and presentation were gaining ground and acceptance among web developers, and some believe that the popularity of Ajax has pushed that movement into the background. The belief of these detractors is that Ajax promotes creating presentation within JavaScript, thus turning it into a messy mix similar to the early days of server-side scripting. Many believe that accessibility will suffer if more developers turn to Ajax solutions.

Others have spent a significant amount of time dissecting Garrett's article and disproving several assumptions that he makes. For instance, the article mentions using XML and XMLHttp repeatedly as being the core of the Ajax model, but many of the examples he lists don't use them. Gmail and Google Maps don't use either of these technologies; Google Suggest uses only XMLHttp and uses JavaScript arrays instead of XML for data exchange. Critics also point out that the technical explanation of Ajax in the article is completely misleading, citing several technologies that are not only unnecessary (such as XML and XMLHttp) but unlikely to be used in many cases (such as XSLT).

Another big argument surrounding Ajax and Garrett's Adaptive Path article is that it's merely a new name for a technique that has already been used for some time. Although this type of data retrieval could be enacted in Netscape Navigator 2.0, it really became more prominent in 2001–2002, especially with the publication of an article on Apple's Developer Connection site entitled, "Remote Scripting With IFRAME" (available at `http://developer.apple.com/internet/webcontent/iframe.html`). This article is widely believed to be the first mainstream article published on Ajax-like methodologies. The term *remote scripting* never caught on with quite the staying power as Ajax.

Still others scoff at the term *Ajax* and Garrett's article, believing that its creation was little more than a marketing gimmick for Garrett's company, Adaptive Path, LLC. Some believe that creating a name for a technique that already existed is disingenuous and a clear sign of ill intent. Regardless of this and other controversies surrounding Ajax, the approach now has a name that developers are quickly becoming familiar with, and with that comes a need for a deeper understanding and explanation so that it may be used in the best possible ways.

Summary

This chapter introduced you to the basic premise of Ajax. Short for Asynchronous JavaScript + XML, the term *Ajax* was coined by Jesse James Garrett in an article posted on the Adaptive Path, LLC web site. The article introduced Ajax as a new user interaction model for web applications in which full page loads are no longer necessary.

This chapter also explored the evolution of the Web in relation to the development of technologies that enable Ajax to be a reality today. Ajax owes its existence to the introduction of both JavaScript and frames into web browsers, which made asynchronous data retrieval using JavaScript theoretically possible in Netscape Navigator 2.0. Throughout the evolution of new web technologies, Ajax methodologies such as the hidden frame technique developed. The introduction of iframes and XMLHttp really pushed Ajax development forward.

Although Ajax can be used to accomplish many things, it is best used to enhance the user experience rather than providing cool effects. This chapter discussed several Ajax principles, all circling back to the requirements of the user being paramount to anything else in web application development.

Several of the most popular Ajax applications were also discussed, including Google Suggest, Gmail, Google Maps, Yahoo! News, and the Bitflux Blog.

Finally, the chapter covered the controversy surrounding Ajax, Garrett's article, and Ajax's place on the Web. Some feel that the popularization of Ajax will lead to an overall lack of accessibility, whereas others question Garrett's motive for writing the now-famous article. As with all approaches, Ajax is at its best when used in a logical enhancement to a well-designed web application.

2

Ajax Basics

The driving force behind Ajax is the interaction between the client (web browser) and the server. Previously, the understanding of this communication was limited to those who developed purely on the server-side using languages such as Perl and C. Newer technologies such as ASP.NET, PHP, and JSP encouraged more of a mix of client- and server-side techniques for software engineers interested in creating web applications, but they often lacked a full understanding of all client-side technologies (such as JavaScript). Now the pendulum has swung in the other direction, and client-side developers need to understand more about server-side technology in order to create Ajax solutions.

HTTP Primer

Central to a good grasp of Ajax techniques is hypertext transmission protocol (HTTP), the protocol to transmit web pages, images, and other types of files over the Internet to your web browser and back. Whenever you type a URL into the browser, an "http://" is prepended to the address, indicating that you will be using HTTP to access the information at the given location. (Most browsers support a number of different protocols as well, most notably FTP.)

Note that this section covers only those aspects of HTTP that are of interest to Ajax developers. It does constitute an HTTP reference guide or tutorial.

HTTP consists of two parts: a request and a response. When you type a URL in a web browser, the browser creates and sends a request on your behalf. This request contains the URL that you typed in as well as some information about the browser itself. The server receives this request and sends back a response. The response contains information about the request as well as the data located at the URL (if any). It's up to the browser to interpret the response and display the web page (or other resource).

HTTP Requests

The format of an HTTP request is as follows:

```
<request-line>
<headers>
<blank line>
[<request-body>]
```

In an HTTP request, the first line must be a request line indicating the type of request, the resource to access, and the version of HTTP being used. Next, a section of headers indicate additional information that may be of use to the server. After the headers is a blank line, which can optionally be followed by additional data (called the *body*).

There are a large number of request types defined in HTTP, but the two of interest to Ajax developers are GET and POST. Anytime you type a URL in a web browser, the browser sends a GET request to the server for that URL, which basically tells the server to get the resource and send it back. Here's what a GET request for www.wrox.com might look like:

```
GET / HTTP/1.1
Host: www.wrox.com
User-Agent: Mozilla/5.0 (Windows; U; Windows NT 5.1; en-US; rv:1.7.6)
            Gecko/20050225 Firefox/1.0.1
Connection: Keep-Alive
```

The first part of the request line specifies this as a GET request. The second part of that line is a forward slash (/), indicating that the request is for the root of the domain. The last part of the request line specifies to use HTTP version 1.1 (the alternative is 1.0). And where is the request sent? That's where the second line comes in.

The second line is the first header in the request, Host. The Host header indicates the target of the request. Combining Host with the forward slash from the first line tells the server that the request is for www.wrox.com/. (The Host header is a requirement of HTTP 1.1; the older version 1.0 didn't require it.) The third line contains the User-Agent header, which is accessible to both server- and client-side scripts and is the cornerstone of most browser-detection logic. This information is defined by the browser that you are using (in this example, Firefox 1.0.1) and is automatically sent on every request. The last line is the Connection header, which is typically set to Keep-Alive for browser operations (it can also be set to other values, but that's beyond the scope of this book). Note that there is a single blank line after this last header. Even though there is no request body, the blank line is required.

If you were to request a page under the www.wrox.com domain, such as http://www.wrox.com/books, the request would look like this:

```
GET /books/ HTTP/1.1
Host: www.wrox.com
User-Agent: Mozilla/5.0 (Windows; U; Windows NT 5.1; en-US; rv:1.7.6)
            Gecko/20050225 Firefox/1.0.1
Connection: Keep-Alive
```

Note that only the first line changed, and it contains only the part that comes after www.wrox.com in the URL.

Sending parameters for a GET request requires that the extra information be appended to the URL itself. The format looks like this:

```
URL ? name1=value1&name2=value2&..&nameN=valueN
```

This information, called a *query string*, is duplicated in the request line of the HTTP request, as follows:

```
GET /books/?name=Professional%20Ajax HTTP/1.1
Host: www.wrox.com
User-Agent: Mozilla/5.0 (Windows; U; Windows NT 5.1; en-US; rv:1.7.6)
          Gecko/20050225 Firefox/1.0.1
Connection: Keep-Alive
```

Note that the text "Professional Ajax" had to be encoded, replacing the space with %20, in order to send it as a parameter to the URL. This is called *URL encoding* and is used in many parts of HTTP. (JavaScript has built-in functions to handle URL encoding and decoding; these are discussed later in the chapter). The name-value pairs are separated with an ampersand. Most server-side technologies will decode the request body automatically and provide access to these values in some sort of logical manner. Of course, it is up to the server to decide what to do with this data.

> **Browsers often send many more headers than the ones discussed in this section. The examples here have been kept short for simplicity.**

The POST request, on the other hand, provides additional information to the server in the request body. Typically, when you fill out an online form and submit it, that data is being sent through a POST request.

Here's what a typical POST request looks like:

```
POST / HTTP/1.1
Host: www.wrox.com
User-Agent: Mozilla/5.0 (Windows; U; Windows NT 5.1; en-US; rv:1.7.6)
          Gecko/20050225 Firefox/1.0.1
Content-Type: application/x-www-form-urlencoded
Content-Length: 40
Connection: Keep-Alive
```

```
name=Professional%20Ajax&publisher=Wiley
```

You should note a few differences between a POST request and a GET request. First, the request line begins with POST instead of GET, indicating the type of request. You'll notice that the Host and User-Agent headers are still there, along with two new ones. The Content-Type header indicates how the request body is encoded. Browsers always encode post data as application/x-www-form-urlencoded, which is the MIME type for simple URL encoding. The Content-Length header indicates the byte length of the request body. After the Connection header and the blank line is the request body. As with most browser POST requests, this is made up of simple name-value pairs, where name is Professional Ajax and publisher is Wiley. You may recognize that this format is the same as that of query string parameters on URLs.

As mentioned previously, there are other HTTP request types, but they follow the same basic format as GET and POST. The next step is to take a look at what the server sends back in response to an HTTP request.

HTTP Responses

The format of an HTTP response, which is very similar to that of a request, is as follows:

```
<status-line>
<headers>
<blank line>
[<response-body>]
```

As you can see, the only real difference in a response is that the first line contains status information instead of request information. The status line tells you about the requested resource by providing a status code. Here's a sample HTTP response:

```
HTTP/1.1 200 OK
Date: Sat, 31 Dec 2005 23:59:59 GMT
Content-Type: text/html;charset=ISO-8859-1
Content-Length: 122

<html>
    <head>
        <title>Wrox Homepage</title>
    </head>
    <body>
        <!-- body goes here -->
    </body>
</html>
```

In this example, the status line gives an HTTP status code of 200 and a message of OK. The status line always contains the status code and the corresponding short message so that there isn't any confusion. The most common status codes are:

- ❑ **200 (OK):** The resource was found and all is well.

- ❑ **304 (NOT MODIFIED):** The resource has not been modified since the last request. This is used most often for browser cache mechanisms.

- ❑ **401 (UNAUTHORIZED):** The client is not authorized to access the resource. Often, this will cause the browser to ask for a user name and password to log in to the server.

- ❑ **403 (FORBIDDEN):** The client failed to gain authorization. This typically happens if you fail to log in with a correct user name and password after a 401.

- ❑ **404 (NOT FOUND):** The resource does not exist at the given location.

Following the status line are some headers. Typically, the server will return a Date header indicating the date and time that the response was generated. (Servers typically also return some information about themselves, although this is not required.) The next two headers should look familiar as well, as they are the same Content-Type and Content-Length headers used in POST requests. In this case, the Content-Type header specifies the MIME type for HTML (text/html) with an encoding of ISO-8859-1 (which is standard for the United States English resources). The body of the response simply contains the HTML source of the requested resource (although it could also contain plain text or binary data for other types of resources). It is this data that the browser displays to the user.

Note that there is no indication as to the type of request that asked for this response; however, this is of no consequence to the server. It is up to the client to know what type of data should be sent back for each type of request and to decide how that data should be used.

Ajax Communication Techniques

Now that you understand the basics of how HTTP communication works, it's time to look into enacting such communication from within a web page. As you know, there are a lot of requests going back and forth between the browser and server while you are surfing the Web. Initially, all these requests happened because the user made an overt action that required such a step. Ajax techniques free developers from waiting for the user to make such an action, allowing you to create a call to the server at any time.

As discussed in Chapter 1, Ajax communication supports a number of different techniques. Each of these techniques has advantages and disadvantages, so it's important to understand which one to use in which situation.

The Hidden Frame Technique

With the introduction of HTML frames, the hidden frame technique was born. The basic idea behind this technique is to create a frameset that has a hidden frame that is used for client-server communication. You can hide a frame by setting its width or height to 0 pixels, effectively removing it from the display. Although some early browsers (such as Netscape 4) couldn't fully hide frames, often leaving thick borders, this technique still gained popularity among developers.

The Pattern

The hidden frame technique follows a very specific, four-step pattern (see Figure 2-1). The first step always begins with the visible frame, where the user is interacting with a web page. Naturally, the user is unaware that there is a hidden frame (in modern browsers, it is not rendered) and goes about interacting with the page as one typically would. At some point, the user performs an action that requires additional data from the server. When this happens, the first step in the process occurs: a JavaScript function call is made to the hidden frame. This call can be as simple as redirecting the hidden frame to another page or as complicated as posting form data. Regardless of the intricacy of the function, the result is the second step in the process: a request made to the server.

The third step in the pattern is a response received from the server. Because you are dealing with frames, this response must be another web page. This web page must contain the data requested from the server as well as some JavaScript to transfer that data to the visible frame. Typically, this is done by assigning an onload event handler in the returned web page that calls a function in the visible frame after it has been fully loaded (this is the fourth step). With the data now in the visible frame, it is up to that frame to decide what to do with the data.

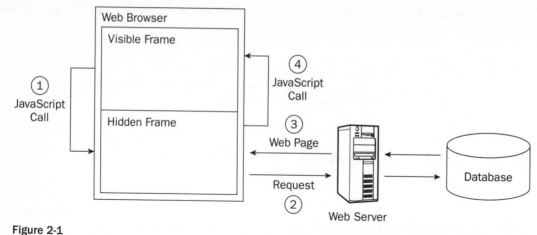

Figure 2-1

Hidden Frame GET Requests

Now that the hidden frame technique has been explained, it's time to learn more about it. As with any new technique, the best way to learn is to work through an example. For this example, you'll be creating a simple lookup page where a customer service representative can look up information about a customer. Since this is the first example in the book, it is very simple: The user will enter a customer ID and receive in return information about the customer. Since this type of functionality will most often be used with a database, it is necessary to do some server-side programming as well. This example uses PHP, an excellent open source server-side language, and MySQL (available at www.mysql.org), an open source database that ties together very well with PHP.

> Although this example is intended to be used with MySQL, you should be able to run it on other databases with little or no modification.

First, before customer data can be looked up, you must have a table to contain it. You can create the customer table by using the following SQL script:

```
CREATE TABLE `Customers` (
  `CustomerId` int(11) NOT NULL auto_increment,
  `Name` varchar(255) NOT NULL default '',
  `Address` varchar(255) NOT NULL default '',
  `City` varchar(255) NOT NULL default '',
  `State` varchar(255) NOT NULL default '',
  `Zip` varchar(255) NOT NULL default '',
  `Phone` varchar(255) NOT NULL default '',
  `E-mail` varchar(255) NOT NULL default '',
  PRIMARY KEY  (`CustomerId`)
) TYPE=MyISAM COMMENT='Sample Customer Data';
```

The most important field in this table is `CustomerId`, which is what you will use to look up the customer information.

You can download this script, along with some sample data, from www.wrox.com.

With the database table all set up, it's time to move on to the HTML code. To use the hidden frame technique, you must start with an HTML frameset, such as this:

```
<frameset rows="100%,0" frameborder="0">
    <frame name="displayFrame" src="display.htm" noresize="noresize" />
    <frame name="hiddenFrame" src="about:blank" noresize="noresize" />
</frameset>
```

The important part of this code is the `rows` attribute of the `<frameset/>` element. By setting it to `100%,0`, browsers know not to display the body of the second frame, whose name is `hiddenFrame`. Next, the `frameborder` attribute is set to 0 to make sure that there isn't a visible border around each frame. The final important step in the frameset declaration is to set the `noresize` attributes on each frame so that the user can't inadvertently resize the frames and see what's in the hidden one; the contents of the hidden frame are never meant to be part of the displayed interface.

Next up is the page to request and display the customer data. This is a relatively simple page, consisting of a text box to enter the customer ID, a button to execute the request, and a `<div/>` element to display the retrieved customer information:

```
<p>Enter customer ID number to retrieve information:</p>
<p>Customer ID: <input type="text" id="txtCustomerId" value="" /></p>
<p><input type="button" value="Get Customer Info"
          onclick="requestCustomerInfo()" /></p>
<div id="divCustomerInfo"></div>
```

You'll notice that the button calls a function named `requestCustomerInfo()`, which interacts with the hidden frame to retrieve information. It simply takes the value in the text box and adds it to the query string of `getcustomerdata.php`, creating a URL in the form of `getcustomerdata.php?id=23`. This URL is then assigned to the hidden frame. Here's the function:

```
function requestCustomerInfo() {
    var sId = document.getElementById("txtCustomerId").value;
    top.frames["hiddenFrame"].location = "getcustomerdata.php?id=" + sId;
}
```

The first step in this function is to retrieve the customer identification number (`"txtCustomerId"`) from the text box. To do so, `document.getElementById()` is called with the text box ID, `"txtCustomerId"`, and the `value` property is retrieved. (The `value` property holds the text that is inside the text box.) Then, this ID is added to the string `"getcustomerdata.php?id="` to create the full URL. The second line creates the URL and assigns it to the hidden frame. To get a reference to the hidden frame, you first need to access the topmost window of the browser using the `top` object. That object has a `frames` array, within which you can find the hidden frame. Since each frame is just another window object, you can set its location to the desired URL.

That's all it takes to request the information. Note that because this is a GET request (passing information in the query string), it makes the request very easy. (You'll see how to execute a POST request using the hidden frame technique shortly.)

In addition to the `requestCustomerInfo()` function, you'll need another function to display the customer information after it is received. This function, `displayCustomerInfo()`, will be called by the hidden frame when it returns with data. The sole argument is a string containing the customer data to be displayed:

```
function displayCustomerInfo(sText) {
    var divCustomerInfo = document.getElementById("divCustomerInfo");
    divCustomerInfo.innerHTML = sText;
}
```

In this function, the first line retrieves a reference to the `<div/>` element that will display the data. In the second line, the customer info string (`sText`) is assigned into the `innerHTML` property of the `<div/>` element. Using `innerHTML` makes it possible to embed HTML into the string for formatting purposes. This completes the code for the main display page. Now it's time to create the server-side logic.

The basic code for `getcustomerdata.php` is a very basic HTML page with PHP code in two places:

```
<html>
    <head>
        <title>Get Customer Data</title>
<?php

    //php code

?>
    </head>
    <body>
        <div id="divInfoToReturn"><?php echo $sInfo ?></div>
    </body>
</html>
```

In this page, the first PHP block will contain the logic to retrieve customer data (which is discussed shortly). The second PHP block outputs the variable `$sInfo`, containing customer data, into a `<div/>`. It is from this `<div/>` that you will read out the data and send it to the display frame. To do so, you need to create a JavaScript function that is called when the page has loaded completely:

```
window.onload = function () {
    var divInfoToReturn = document.getElementById("divInfoToReturn");
    top.frames["displayFrame"].displayCustomerInfo(divInfoToReturn.innerHTML);
};
```

This function is assigned directly to the `window.onload` event handler. It first retrieves a reference to the `<div/>` that contains the customer information. Then, it accesses the display frame using the `top.frames` array and calls the `displayCustomerInfo()` function defined earlier, passing in the `innerHTML` of the `<div/>`. That's all the JavaScript it takes to send the information where it belongs. But how does the information get there in the first place? Some PHP code is needed to pull it out of the database.

The first step in the PHP code is to define all of the pieces of data you'll need. In this example, those pieces of data are the customer ID to look up, the `$sInfo` variable to return the information, and the information necessary to access the database (the database server, the database name, a user name, a password, and the SQL query string):

```php
<?php

    $sID = $_GET["id"];
    $sInfo = "";

    $sDBServer = "your.databaser.server";
    $sDBName = "your_db_name";
    $sDBUsername = "your_db_username";
    $sDBPassword = "your_db_password";
    $sQuery = "Select * from Customers where CustomerId=".$sID;


    //More here
?>
```

This code begins with retrieving the id argument from the query string. PHP organizes all query string arguments into the $_GET array for easy retrieval. This id is stored in $sID and is used to create the SQL query string stored in $sQuery. The $sInfo variable is also created here and set to be an empty string. All the other variables in this code block contain information specific to your particular database configuration; you'll have to replace these with the correct values for your implementation.

Having captured the user's input and set up the foundation for the connection to the database, the next step is to invoke that database connection, execute the query, and return the results. If there is a customer with the given ID, $sInfo is filled with an HTML string containing all the data, including the creation of a link for the e-mail address. If the customer ID is invalid, $sInfo is filled with an error message that will be passed back to the display frame:

```php
<?php

    $sID = $_GET["id"];
    $sInfo = "";

    $sDBServer = "your.databaser.server";
    $sDBName = "your_db_name";
    $sDBUsername = "your_db_username";
    $sDBPassword = "your_db_password";
    $sQuery = "Select * from Customers where CustomerId=".$sID;

    $oLink = mysql_connect($sDBServer,$sDBUsername,$sDBPassword);
    @mysql_select_db($sDBName) or $sInfo="Unable to open database";

    if($oResult = mysql_query($sQuery) and mysql_num_rows($oResult) > 0) {
        $aValues = mysql_fetch_array($oResult,MYSQL_ASSOC);
        $sInfo = $aValues['Name']."<br />".$aValues['Address']."<br />".
                 $aValues['City']."<br />".$aValues['State']."<br />".
                 $aValues['Zip']."<br /><br />Phone: ".$aValues['Phone']."<br />".
                 "<a href=\"mailto:".$aValues['E-mail']."\">".
                 $aValues['E-mail']."</a>";
    } else {
        $sInfo = "Customer with ID $sID doesn't exist.";
    }


    mysql_close($oLink);
?>
```

The first two lines in the highlighted section contain the calls to connect to a MySQL database from PHP. Following that, the `mysql_query()` function is called to execute the SQL query. If that function returns a result and the result has at least one row, then the code continues to get the information and store it in `$sInfo`; otherwise, `$sInfo` is filled with an error message. The last two lines clean up the database connection.

> *It's beyond the scope of this book to explain the intricacies of PHP and MySQL programming. If you'd like to learn more, consider picking up Beginning PHP, Apache, MySQL Web Development (Wiley Press, ISBN 0-7645-5744-0).*

Now when `$sInfo` is output into the `<div/>`, it will contain the appropriate information. The `onload` event handler reads that data out and sends it back up to the display frame. If the customer was found, the information will be displayed, as shown in Figure 2-2.

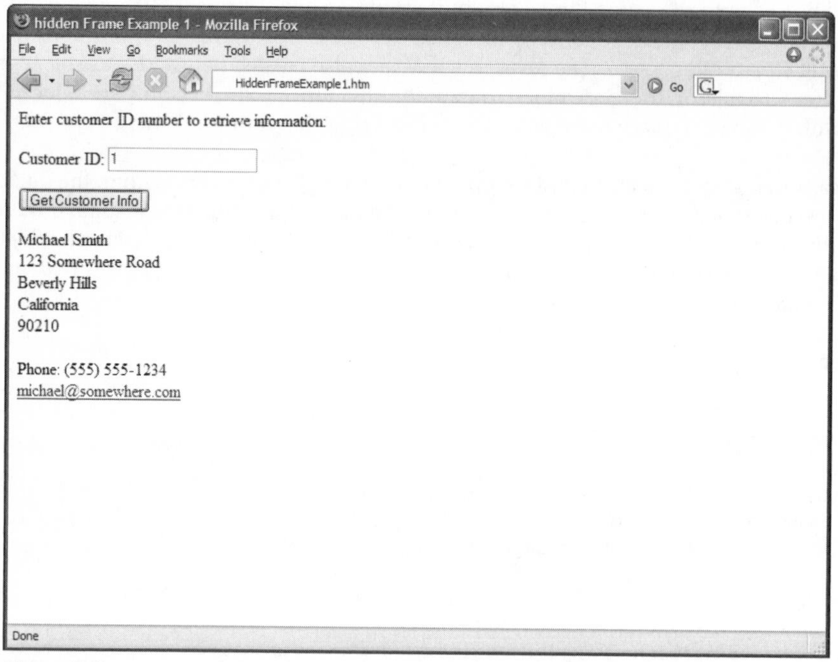

Figure 2-2

If, on the other hand, the customer doesn't exist, an error message will be displayed in that same location on the screen. Either way, the customer service representative will have a nice user experience. This completes your first Ajax example.

Hidden Frame POST Requests

The previous example used a GET request to retrieve information from a database. This was fairly simple because the customer ID could just be appended to the URL in a query string and sent on its way. But what if you need to send a POST request? This, too, is possible using the hidden frame technique, although it takes a little extra work.

A POST request is typically sent when data needs to be sent to the server as opposed to a GET, which merely requests data from the server. Although GET requests can send extra data through the query string, some browsers can handle only up to 512KB of query string information. A POST request, on the other hand, can send up to 2GB of information, making it ideal for most uses.

Traditionally, the only way to send POST requests was to use a form with its method attribute set to post. Then, the data contained in the form was sent in a POST request to the URL specified in the action attribute. Further complicating matters was the fact that a typical form submission navigates the page to the new URL. This completely defeats the purpose of Ajax. Thankfully, there is a very easy workaround in the form of a little-known attribute called target.

The target attribute of the <form/> element is used in a similar manner to the target attribute of the <a/> element: it specifies where the navigation should occur. By setting the target attribute on a form, you effectively tell the form page to remain behind while the result of the form submission is displayed in another frame or window (in this case, a hidden frame).

To begin, define another frameset. The only difference from the previous example is that the visible frame contains an entry form for customer data:

```
<frameset rows="100%,0" frameborder="0">
    <frame name="displayFrame" src="entry.htm" noresize="noresize" />
    <frame name="hiddenFrame" src="about:blank" noresize="noresize" />
</frameset>
```

The body of the entry form is contained within a <form/> element and has text boxes for each of the fields stored in the database (aside from customer ID, which will be autogenerated). There is also a <div/> that is used for status messages relating to the client-server communication:

```
<form method="post" action="SaveCustomer.php" target="hiddenFrame">
    <p>Enter customer information to be saved:</p>
    <p>Customer Name: <input type="text" name="txtName" value="" /><br />
    Address: <input type="text" name="txtAddress" value="" /><br />
    City: <input type="text" name="txtCity" value="" /><br />
    State: <input type="text" name="txtState" value="" /><br />
    Zip Code: <input type="text" name="txtZipCode" value="" /><br />
    Phone: <input type="text" name="txtPhone" value="" /><br />
    E-mail: <input type="text" name="txtEmail" value="" /></p>
    <p><input type="submit" value="Save Customer Info" /></p>
</form>
<div id="divStatus"></div>
```

Note also that the target of the <form/> element is set to hiddenFrame so that when the user clicks the button, the submission goes to the hidden frame.

In this example, only one JavaScript function is necessary in the main page: saveResult(). This function will be called when the hidden frame returns from saving the customer data:

```
function saveResult(sMessage) {
    var divStatus = document.getElementById("divStatus");
    divStatus.innerHTML = "Request completed: " + sMessage;
}
```

It's the responsibility of the hidden frame to pass a message to this function that will be displayed to the user. This will either be a confirmation that the information was saved or an error message explaining why it wasn't.

Next is SaveCustomer.php, the file that handles the POST request. As in the previous example, this page is set up as a simple HTML page with a combination of PHP and JavaScript code. The PHP code is used to gather the information from the request and store it in the database. Since this is a POST request, the $_POST array contains all the information that was submitted:

```php
<?php
    $sName = $_POST["txtName"];
    $sAddress = $_POST["txtAddress"];
    $sCity = $_POST["txtCity"];
    $sState = $_POST["txtState"];
    $sZipCode = $_POST["txtZipCode"];
    $sPhone = $_POST["txtPhone"];
    $sEmail = $_POST["txtEmail"];

    $sStatus = "";

    $sDBServer = "your.database.server";
    $sDBName = "your_db_name";
    $sDBUsername = "your_db_username";
    $sDBPassword = "your_db_password";

    $sSQL = "Insert into Customers(Name,Address,City,State,Zip,Phone,`E-mail`) ".
            " values ('$sName','$sAddress','$sCity','$sState', '$sZipCode'".
            ", '$sPhone', '$sEmail')";

    //more here
?>
```

This code snippet retrieves all the POST information about the customer; moreover, it defines a status message ($sStatus) and the required database information (same as in the previous example). The SQL statement this time is an INSERT, adding in all the retrieved information.

The code to execute the SQL statement is very similar to that of the previous example:

```php
<?php
    $sName = $_POST["txtName"];
    $sAddress = $_POST["txtAddress"];
    $sCity = $_POST["txtCity"];
    $sState = $_POST["txtState"];
    $sZipCode = $_POST["txtZipCode"];
    $sPhone = $_POST["txtPhone"];
    $sEmail = $_POST["txtEmail"];

    $sStatus = "";

    $sDBServer = "your.database.server";
```

```php
$sDBName = "your_db_name";
$sDBUsername = "your_db_username";
$sDBPassword = "your_db_password";

$sSQL = "Insert into Customers(Name,Address,City,State,Zip,Phone,`E-mail`) ".
        " values ('$sName','$sAddress','$sCity','$sState', '$sZipCode'".
        ", '$sPhone', '$sEmail')";


$oLink = mysql_connect($sDBServer,$sDBUsername,$sDBPassword);
@mysql_select_db($sDBName) or $sStatus = "Unable to open database";

if($oResult = mysql_query($sSQL)) {
    $sStatus = "Added customer; customer ID is ".mysql_insert_id();
} else {
    $sStatus = "An error occurred while inserting; customer not saved.";
}


mysql_close($oLink);
?>
```

Here, the result of the `mysql_query()` function is simply an indicator that the statement was executed successfully. In that case, the `$sStatus` variable is filled with a message indicating that the save was successful and returning the customer ID assigned to the data. The `mysql_insert_id()` function always returns the last auto-incremented value of the most recent INSERT statement. If for some reason the statement didn't execute successfully, the `$sStatus` variable is filled with an error message.

The `$sStatus` variable is output into a JavaScript function that is run when the window loads:

```html
<script type="text/javascript">

    window.onload = function () {
        top.frames["displayFrame"].saveResult("<?php echo $sStatus ?>");
    }

</script>
```

This code calls the `saveResult()` function defined in the display frame, passing in the value of the PHP variable `$sStatus`. Because this variable contains a string, you must enclose the PHP `echo` statement in quotation marks. When this function executes, assuming the customer data was saved, the entry form page resembles the one shown in Figure 2-3.

After this code has executed, you are free to add more customers to the database using the same form because it never disappeared.

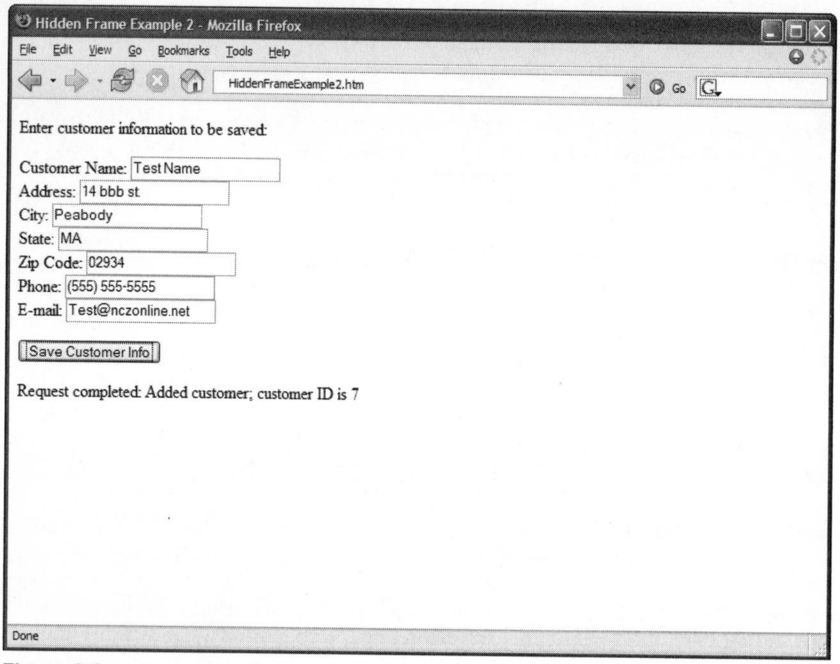

Figure 2-3

Hidden iFrames

The next generation of behind-the-scenes client-server communication was to make use of iframes, which were introduced in HTML 4.0. Basically, an iframe is the same as a frame with the exception that it can be placed inside of a non-frameset HTML page, effectively allowing any part of a page to become a frame. The iframe technique can be applied to pages not originally created as a frameset, making it much better suited to incremental addition of functionality; an iframe can even be created on-the-fly in JavaScript, allowing for simple, semantic HTML to be supplied to the browser with the enhanced Ajax functionality serving as a progressive enhancement (this is discussed shortly). Because iframes can be used and accessed in the same way as regular frames, they are ideal for Ajax communication.

There are two ways to take advantage of iframes. The easiest way is to simply embed an iframe inside of your page and use that as the hidden frame to make requests. Doing this would change the first example display page to:

```
<p>Enter customer ID number to retrieve information:</p>
<p>Customer ID: <input type="text" id="txtCustomerId" value="" /></p>
<p><input type="button" value="Get Customer Info"
        onclick="requestCustomerInfo()" /></p>
<div id="divCustomerInfo"></div>
<iframe src="about:blank" name="hiddenFrame" width="0" height="0"
        frameborder="0"></iframe>
```

Note that the iframe has its `width`, `height`, and `frameborder` attributes set to 0; this effectively hides it from view. Since the name of the iframe is `hiddenFrame`, all the JavaScript code in this page will continue to work as before. There is, however, one small change that is necessary to the

`GetCustomerData.php` page. The JavaScript function in that page previously looked for the `displayCustomerInfo()` function in the frame named `displayFrame`. If you use this technique, there is no frame with that name, so you must update the code to use `parent` instead:

```
window.onload = function () {
    var divInfoToReturn = document.getElementById("divInfoToReturn");
    parent.displayCustomerInfo(divInfoToReturn.innerHTML);
};
```

Now this example will work just as the first example in this chapter did.

The second way to use hidden iframes is to create them dynamically using JavaScript. This can get a little bit tricky because not all browsers implement iframes in the same way, so it helps to simply go step-by-step in creating a hidden iframe.

The first step is easy; you create the iframe using the `document.createElement()` method and assign the necessary attributes:

```
function createIFrame() {
    var oIFrameElement = document.createElement("iframe");
    oIFrameElement.width=0;
    oIFrameElement.height=0;
    oIFrameElement.frameBorder=0;
    oIFrameElement.name = "hiddenFrame";
    oIFrameElement.id = "hiddenFrame";
    document.body.appendChild(oIFrameElement);

    //more code
}
```

The last line of this code is very important because it adds the iframe to the document structure; an iframe that isn't added to the document can't perform requests. Also note that both the `name` and `id` attributes are set to `hiddenFrame`. This is necessary because some browsers access the new frame by its `name` and some by its `id` attribute.

Next, define a global variable to hold a reference to the frame object. Note that the frame object for an iframe element isn't what is returned from `createElement()`. In order to get this object, you must look into the frames collection. This is what will be stored in the global variable:

```
var oIFrame = null;

function createIFrame() {
    var oIFrameElement = document.createElement("iframe");
    oIFrameElement.width=0;
    oIFrameElement.height=0;
    oIFrameElement.frameBorder=0;
    oIFrameElement.name = "hiddenFrame";
    oIFrameElement.id = "hiddenFrame";
    document.body.appendChild(oIFrameElement);

    oIFrame = frames["hiddenFrame"];
}
```

If you place this code into the previous iframe example, you can then make the following modifications to requestCustomerInfo():

```
function requestCustomerInfo() {
    if (!oIFrame) {
        createIFrame();
        setTimeout(requestCustomerInfo, 10);
        return;
    }

    var sId = document.getElementById("txtCustomerId").value;
    oIFrame.location = "GetCustomerData.php?id=" + sId;
}
```

With these changes, the function now checks to see if oIFrame is null or not. If it is, then it calls createIFrame() and then sets a timeout to run the function again in 10 milliseconds. This is necessary because only the Internet Explorer (IE) browser recognizes the inserted iframe immediately; most other browsers take a couple of milliseconds to recognize it and allow requests to be sent. When the function executes again, it will go on to the rest of the code, where the last line has been changed to reference the oIFrame object.

Although this technique works fairly easily with GET requests, POST requests are a different story. Only some browsers will enable you to set the target of a form to a dynamically created iframe; IE is not one of them. So, to use the hidden iframe technique with a POST request requires a bit of trickery.

Hidden IFrame POST Requests

To accomplish a POST request using hidden iframes, the approach is to load a page that contains a form into the hidden frame, populate that form with data, and then submit the form. When the visible form (the one you are actually typing into) is submitted, you need to cancel that submission and forward the information to the hidden frame. To do so, you'll need to define a function that handles the creation of the iframe and the loading of the hidden form:

```
function checkIFrame() {
    if (!oIFrame) {
        createIFrame();
    }
    setTimeout(function () {
        oIFrame.location = "ProxyForm.htm";
    }, 10);
}
```

This function, checkIFrame(), first checks to see if the hidden iframe has been created. If not, createIFrame() is called. Then, a timeout is set before setting the location of the iframe to ProxyForm.htm, which is the hidden form page. Because this function may be called several times, it's important that this page be loaded each time the form is submitted.

The ProxyForm.htm file is very simple. It contains only a small bit of JavaScript to notify the main page that it has been loaded:

```
<html>
  <head>
    <title>Proxy Form</title>
    <script type="text/javascript">

        window.onload = function () {
            parent.formReady();
        }

    </script>
  </head>
  <body>
    <form method="post"></form>
  </body>
</html>
```

As you can see, the body of this page contains only an empty form and the head contains only an `onload` event handler. When the page is loaded, it calls `parent.formReady()` to let the main page know that it is ready to accept a request. The `formReady()` function is contained in the main page itself and looks like this:

```
function formReady() {
    var oHiddenForm = oIFrame.document.forms[0];
    var oForm = document.forms[0];

    for (var i=0 ; i < oForm.elements.length; i++) {
        var oHidden = oIFrame.document.createElement("input");
        oHidden.type = "hidden";
        oHidden.name = oForm.elements[i].name;
        oHidden.value = oForm.elements[i].value;
        oHiddenForm.appendChild(oHidden);
    }

    oHiddenForm.action = oForm.action;
    oHiddenForm.submit();
};
```

The first step in this function is to get a reference to the form in the hidden iframe, which you can do by accessing the `document.forms` collection of that frame. Because there is only one form on the page, you can safely get the first form in the collection (at index 0); this is stored in `oHiddenForm`. Following that, a reference to the form on the main page is saved into `oForm`. Next, a `for` loop iterates through the form elements on the main page (using the `elements` collection). For each form element, a new hidden input element is created in the hidden frame (note that you must use `oIFrame.document.createElement()` instead of just `document.createElement()`). This hidden input element is assigned the name and value of the form element and added to the hidden form using the `appendChild()` function.

After each form element has been added, the hidden form is assigned the same `action` as the main page form. By reading the `action` out of the form instead of hard coding it, you can use `formReady()` on any number of pages. The last step in the function is to submit the hidden form.

The only thing left to do is to make sure the main page form doesn't submit itself in the normal way. To do this, assign an `onsubmit` event handler that calls `checkIFrame()` and returns `false`:

```
<form method="post" action="SaveCustomer.php"
    onsubmit="checkIFrame();return false">
    <p>Enter customer information to be saved:</p>
    <p>Customer Name: <input type="text" name="txtName" value="" /><br />
    Address: <input type="text" name="txtAddress" value="" /><br />
    City: <input type="text" name="txtCity" value="" /><br />
    State: <input type="text" name="txtState" value="" /><br />
    Zip Code: <input type="text" name="txtZipCode" value="" /><br />
    Phone: <input type="text" name="txtPhone" value="" /><br />
    E-mail: <input type="text" name="txtEmail" value="" /></p>
    <p><input type="submit" value="Save Customer Info" /></p>
</form>
<div id="divStatus"></div>
```

By returning `false` in this way, you are preventing the default behavior of the form (to submit itself to the server). Instead, the `checkIFrame()` method is called and the process of submitting to the hidden iframe begins.

With this complete, you can now use this example the same way as the hidden frame POST example; the `SaveCustomer.php` page handles the data and calls `saveResult()` in the main page when completed.

> Note that the examples in this section have been simplified in order to focus on the Ajax techniques involved. If you were to use these in a real web application, you would need to provide more user feedback, such as disabling the form while a request is being made.

Advantages and Disadvantages of Hidden Frames

Now that you have seen the powerful things that you can do using hidden frames, it's time to discuss the practicality of using them. As mentioned previously, this technique has been around for many years and is still used in many Ajax applications.

One of the biggest arguments for using hidden frames is that you can maintain the browser history and thus enable users to still use the Back and Forward buttons in the browser. Because the browser doesn't know that a hidden frame is, in fact, hidden, it keeps track of all the requests made through it. Whereas the main page of an Ajax application may not change, the changes in the hidden frame mean that the Back and Forward buttons will move through the history of that frame instead of the main page. This technique is used in both Gmail and Google Maps for this very reason.

> Be careful, because iframes don't always store browser history. Whereas IE always stores the history of iframes, Firefox does so only if the iframe was defined using HTML (that is, not created dynamically using JavaScript). Safari never stores browser history for iframes, regardless of how they are included in the page.

The downside of hidden frames is that there is very little information about what's going on behind the scenes. You are completely reliant on the proper page being returned. The examples in this section all had the same problem: If the hidden frame page failed to load, there is no notification to the user that a problem has occurred; the main page will continue to wait until the appropriate JavaScript function is called. You may be able to provide some comfort to a user by setting a timeout for a long period of time, maybe five minutes, and displaying a message if the page hasn't loaded by then, but that's just a workaround. The main problem is that you don't have enough information about the HTTP request that is happening behind the scenes. Fortunately, there is another option.

XMLHttp Requests

When Microsoft Internet Explorer 5.0 introduced a rudimentary level of XML support, an ActiveX library called MSXML was also introduced (discussed at length in Chapter 4). One of the objects provided in this library quickly became very popular: XMLHttp.

The XMLHttp object was created to enable developers to initiate HTTP requests from anywhere in an application. These requests were intended to return XML, so the XMLHttp object provided an easy way to access this information in the form of an XML document. Since it was an ActiveX control, XMLHttp could be used not only in web pages but also in any Windows-based desktop application; however, its popularity on the Web has far outpaced its popularity for desktop applications.

Picking up on that popularity, Mozilla duplicated the XMLHttp functionality for use in its browsers, such as Firefox. Shortly thereafter, both the Safari (as of version 1.2) and Opera (version 7.6) browsers had duplicated Mozilla's implementation. Today, all four browsers support XMLHttp to some extent. (Safari and Opera still have incomplete implementations, supporting GET and POST but no other request types.)

Creating an XMLHttp Object

The first step to using an XMLHttp object is, obviously, to create one. Because Microsoft's implementation is an ActiveX control, you must use the proprietary ActiveXObject class in JavaScript, passing in the XMLHttp control's signature:

```
var oXmlHttp = new ActiveXObject("Microsoft.XMLHttp");
```

This line creates the first version of the XMLHttp object (the one shipped with IE 5.0). The problem is that there have been several new versions released with each subsequent release of the MSXML library. Each release brings with it better stability and speed, so you want to make sure you are always using the most recent version available on the user's machine. The signatures are:

❏   Microsoft.XMLHttp

❏   MSXML2.XMLHttp

❏   MSXML2.XMLHttp.3.0

❏   MSXML2.XMLHttp.4.0

❏   MSXML2.XMLHttp.5.0

Unfortunately, the only way to determine the best version to use is to try to create each one. Because this is an ActiveX control, any failure to create an object will throw an error, which means that you must enclose each attempt within a try...catch block. The end result is a function such as this:

```
function createXMLHttp() {
    var aVersions = [ "MSXML2.XMLHttp.5.0",
        "MSXML2.XMLHttp.4.0","MSXML2.XMLHttp.3.0",
        "MSXML2.XMLHttp","Microsoft.XMLHttp"
    ];

    for (var i = 0; i < aVersions.length; i++) {
        try {
            var oXmlHttp = new ActiveXObject(aVersions[i]);
            return oXmlHttp;
        } catch (oError) {
            //Do nothing
        }
    }
    throw new Error("MSXML is not installed.");
}
```

The `createXMLHttp()` function stores an array of `XMLHttp` signatures, with the most recent one first. It iterates through this array and tries to create an `XMLHttp` object with each signature. If the creation fails, the `catch` statement prevents a JavaScript error from stopping execution; then the next signature is attempted. When an object is created, it is returned. If the function completes without creating an `XMLHttp` object, an error is thrown indicating that the creation failed.

Fortunately, creating an `XMLHttp` object is much easier in other browsers. Mozilla Firefox, Safari, and Opera all use the same code:

```
var oXmlHttp = new XMLHttpRequest();
```

Naturally, it helps to have a cross-browser way of creating `XMLHttp` objects. You can create such a function by altering the `createXMLHttp()` function defined previously:

```
function createXMLHttp() {

    if (typeof XMLHttpRequest != "undefined") {
        return new XMLHttpRequest();
    } else if (window.ActiveXObject) {
        var aVersions = [ "MSXML2.XMLHttp.5.0",
            "MSXML2.XMLHttp.4.0","MSXML2.XMLHttp.3.0",
            "MSXML2.XMLHttp","Microsoft.XMLHttp"
        ];

        for (var i = 0; i < aVersions.length; i++) {
            try {
                var oXmlHttp = new ActiveXObject(aVersions[i]);
                return oXmlHttp;
            } catch (oError) {
                //Do nothing
            }
        }
    }
    throw new Error("XMLHttp object could be created.");
}
```

Now this function first checks to see if an XMLHttpRequest class is defined (by using the typeof operator). If XMLHttpRequest is present, it is used to create the XMLHttp object; otherwise, it checks to see if the ActiveXObject class is present and, if so, goes through the same process of creating an XMLHttp object for IE. If both of these tests fail, an error is thrown.

The other option for creating cross-browser XMLHttp objects is to use a library that already has cross-browser code written. The zXml library, written by two of your authors, is one such library and is available for download at www.nczonline.net/downloads/. This library defines a single function for the creation of XMLHttp objects:

```
var oXmlHttp = zXmlHttp.createRequest();
```

The createRequest() function, and the zXml library itself, will be used throughout this book to aid in cross-browser handling of Ajax technologies.

Using XMLHttp

After you have created an XMLHttp object, you are ready to start making HTTP requests from JavaScript. The first step is to call the open() method, which initializes the object. This method accepts the following three arguments:

❑ **Request Type:** A string indicating the request type to be made — typically, GET or POST (these are the only ones currently supported by all browsers).

❑ **URL:** A string indicating the URL to send the request to.

❑ **Async:** A Boolean value indicating whether the request should be made asynchronously.

The last argument, async, is very important because it controls how JavaScript executes the request. When set to true, the request is sent asynchronously, and JavaScript code execution continues without waiting for the response; you must use an event handler to watch for the response to the request. If async is set to false, the request is sent synchronously, and JavaScript waits for a response from the server before continuing code execution. That means if the response takes a long time, the user cannot interact with the browser until the response has completed. For this reason, best practices around the development of Ajax applications favor the use of asynchronous requests for routine data retrieval, with synchronous requests reserved for short messages sent to and from the server.

To make an asynchronous GET request to info.txt, you would start by doing this:

```
var oXmlHttp = zXmlHttp.createRequest();
oXmlHttp.open("get", "info.txt", true);
```

Note that the case of the first argument, the request type, is irrelevant even though technically request types are defined as all uppercase.

Next, you need to define an onreadystatechange event handler. The XMLHttp object has a property called readyState that changes as the request goes through and the response is received. There are five possible values for readyState:

- ❏ **0 (Uninitialized):** The object has been created but the `open()` method hasn't been called.
- ❏ **1 (Loading):** The `open()` method has been called but the request hasn't been sent.
- ❏ **2 (Loaded):** The request has been sent.
- ❏ **3 (Interactive).** A partial response has been received.
- ❏ **4 (Complete):** All data has been received and the connection has been closed.

Every time the `readyState` property changes from one value to another, the `readystatechange` event fires and the `onreadystatechange` event handler is called. Because of differences in browser implementations, the only reliable `readyState` values for cross-browser development are 0, 1, and 4. In most cases, however, you will check only for 4 to see when the request has returned:

```
var oXmlHttp = zXmlHttp.createRequest();
oXmlHttp.open("get", "info.txt", true);
oXmlHttp.onreadystatechange = function () {
    if (oXmlHttp.readyState == 4) {
        alert("Got response.");
    }
};
```

The last step is to call the `send()` method, which actually sends the request. This method accepts a single argument, which is a string for the request body. If the request doesn't require a body (remember, a GET request doesn't), you must pass in `null`:

```
var oXmlHttp = zXmlHttp.createRequest();
oXmlHttp.open("get", "info.txt", true);
oXmlHttp.onreadystatechange = function () {
    if (oXmlHttp.readyState == 4) {
        alert("Got response.");
    }
};
oXmlHttp.send(null);
```

That's it! The request has been sent and when the response is received, an alert will be displayed. But just showing a message that the request has been received isn't very useful. The true power of `XMLHttp` is that you have access to the returned data, the response status, and the response headers.

To retrieve the data returned from the request, you can use the `responseText` or `responseXML` properties. The `responseText` property returns a string containing the response body, whereas the `responseXML` property is an XML document object used only if the data returned has a content type of `text/xml`. (XML documents are discussed in Chapter 4.) So, to get the text contained in `info.txt`, the call would be as follows:

```
var sData = oXmlHttp.responseText;
```

Note that this will return the text in `info.txt` only if the file was found and no errors occurred. If, for example, `info.txt` didn't exist, then the `responseText` would contain the server's 404 message. Fortunately, there is a way to determine if any errors occurred.

The `status` property contains the HTTP status code sent in the response, and `statusText` contains the text description of the status (such as "OK" or "Not Found"). Using these two properties, you can make sure the data you've received is actually the data you want or tell the user why the data wasn't retrieved:

```
if (oXmlHttp.status == 200) {
    alert("Data returned is: " + oXmlHttp.responseText;
} else {
    alert("An error occurred: " + oXmlHttp.statusText;
}
```

Generally, you should always ensure that the status of a response is `200`, indicating that the request was completely successful. The `readyState` property is set to 4 even if a server error occurred, so just checking that is not enough. In this example, the `responseText` property is shown only if the `status` is `200`; otherwise, the error message is displayed.

> The `statusText` property isn't implemented in Opera and sometimes returns an inaccurate description in other browsers. You should never rely on `statusText` alone to determine if an error occurred.

As mentioned previously, it's also possible to access the response headers. You can retrieve a specific header value using the `getResponseHeader()` method and passing in the name of the header that you want to retrieve. One of the most useful response headers is `Content-Type`, which tells you the type of data being sent:

```
var sContentType = oXmlHttp.getResponseHeader("Content-Type");
if (sContentType == "text/xml") {
    alert("XML content received.");
} else if (sContentType == "text/plain") {
    alert("Plain text content received.");
} else {
    alert("Unexpected content received.");
}
```

This code snippet checks the content type of the response and displays an alert indicating the type of data returned. Typically, you will receive only XML data (content type of `text/xml`) or plain text (content type of `text/plain`) from the server, because these content types are the easiest to work with using JavaScript.

If you'd prefer to see all headers returned from the server, you can use the `getAllResponseHeaders()` method, which simply returns a string containing all of the headers. Each heading in the string is separated by either a new line character (`\n` in JavaScript) or a combination of the carriage return and new line (`\r\n` in JavaScript), so you can deal with individual headers as follows:

```
var sHeaders = oXmlHttp.getAllResponseHeaders();
var aHeaders = sHeaders.split(/\r?\n/);

for (var i=0; i < aHeaders.length; i++) {
    alert(aHeaders[i]);
}
```

This example splits the header string into an array of headers by using the JavaScript `split()` method for strings and passing in a regular expression (which matches either a carriage return/new line couple or just a new line). Now you can iterate through the headers and do with them as you please. Keep in mind that each string in `aHeaders` is in the format *headername: headervalue*.

It's also possible to set headers on the request before it's sent out. You may want to indicate the content type of data that you'll be sending, or you may just want to send along some extra data that the server may need to deal with the request. To do so, use the `setRequestHeader()` method before calling `send()`:

```
var oXmlHttp = zXmlHttp.createRequest();
oXmlHttp.open("get", "info.txt", true);
oXmlHttp.onreadystatechange = function () {
    if (oXmlHttp.readyState == 4) {
        alert("Got response.");
    }
};
oXmlHttp.setRequestHeader("myheader", "myvalue");
oXmlHttp.send(null);
```

In this code, a header named `myheader` is added to the request before it's sent out. The header will be added to the default headers as `myheader: myvalue`.

Up to this point, you've been dealing with asynchronous requests, which are preferable in most situations. Sending synchronous requests means that you don't need to assign the `onreadystatechange` event handler because the response will have been received by the time the `send()` method returns. This makes it possible to do something like this:

```
var oXmlHttp = zXmlHttp.createRequest();
oXmlHttp.open("get", "info.txt", false);
oXmlHttp.send(null);

if (oXmlHttp.status == 200) {
    alert("Data returned is: " + oXmlHttp.responseText;
} else {
    alert("An error occurred: " + oXmlHttp.statusText;
}
```

Sending the request synchronously (setting the third argument of `open()` to `false`) enables you to start evaluating the response immediately after the call to `send()`. This can be useful if you want the user interaction to wait for a response or if you're expecting to receive only a very small amount of data (for example, less than 1K). In the case of average or larger amounts of data, it's best to use an asynchronous call.

XMLHttp GET Requests

It's time to revisit the hidden frame GET example to see how the process could be improved using `XMLHttp`. The first change will be to `GetCustomerData.php`, which must be changed from an HTML page to simply return an HTML snippet. The entire file now becomes streamlined:

```
<?php
    header("Content-Type: text/plain");

    $sID = $_GET["id"];
```

```php
$sInfo = "";

$sDBServer = "your.databaser.server";
$sDBName = "your_db_name";
$sDBUsername = "your_db_username";
$sDBPassword = "your_db_password";
$sQuery = "Select * from Customers where CustomerId=".$sID;

$oLink = mysql_connect($sDBServer,$sDBUsername,$sDBPassword);
@mysql_select_db($sDBName) or $sInfo="Unable to open database";

if($oResult = mysql_query($sQuery) and mysql_num_rows($oResult) > 0) {
    $aValues = mysql_fetch_array($oResult,MYSQL_ASSOC);
    $sInfo = $aValues['Name']."<br />".$aValues['Address']."<br />".
            $aValues['City']."<br />".$aValues['State']."<br />".
            $aValues['Zip']."<br /><br />Phone: ".$aValues['Phone']."<br />".
            "<a href=\"mailto:".$aValues['E-mail']."\">".
            $aValues['E-mail']."</a>";
} else {
    $sInfo = "Customer with ID $sID doesn't exist.";
}


mysql_close($oLink);

    echo $sInfo;
?>
```

As you can see, there are no visible HTML or JavaScript calls in the page. All the main logic remains the same, but there are two additional lines of PHP code. The first occurs at the beginning, where the `header()` function is used to set the content type of the page. Even though the page will return an HTML snippet, it's fine to set the content type as `text/plain`, because it's not a complete HTML page (and therefore wouldn't validate as HTML). You should always set the content type in any page that is sending non-HTML to the browser. The second added line is towards the bottom, where the `$sInfo` variable is output to the stream by using the `echo` command.

In the main HTML page, the basic setup is this:

```html
<p>Enter customer ID number to retrieve information:</p>
<p>Customer ID: <input type="text" id="txtCustomerId" value="" /></p>
<p><input type="button" value="Get Customer Info"
        onclick="requestCustomerInfo()" /></p>
<div id="divCustomerInfo"></div>
```

The `requestCustomerInfo()` function previously created a hidden iframe but now must be changed to use `XMLHttp`:

```javascript
function requestCustomerInfo() {
    var sId = document.getElementById("txtCustomerId").value;
    var oXmlHttp = zXmlHttp.createRequest();
    oXmlHttp.open("get", "GetCustomerData.php?id=" + sId, true);
    oXmlHttp.onreadystatechange = function () {
        if (oXmlHttp.readyState == 4) {
```

```
            if (oXmlHttp.status == 200) {
                displayCustomerInfo(oXmlHttp.responseText);
            } else {
                displayCustomerInfo("An error occurred: " + oXmlHttp.statusText);
            }
        }
    };
    oXmlHttp.send(null);
}
```

Note that the function begins the same way, by retrieving the ID the user entered. Then, an XMLHttp object is created using the zXml library. The open() method is called, specifying an asynchronous GET request for GetCustomerData.php (which has the aforementioned ID added to its query string). Next comes the assignment of the event handler, which checks for a readyState of 4 and then checks the status of the request. If the request was successful (status of 200), the displayCustomerInfo() function is called with the response body (accessed via responseText). If there was an error (status is not 200), then the error information is passed to displayCustomerInfo().

There are several differences between this and the hidden frame/iframe example. First, no JavaScript code is required outside of the main page. This is important because any time you need to keep code in two different places there is the possibility of creating incompatibilities; in the frame-based examples, you relied on separate scripts in the display page and the hidden frames to communicate with one another. By changing GetCustomerInfo.php to return just the data you're interested in, you have eliminated potential problems with JavaScript calling between these locations. The second difference is that it's much easier to tell if there was a problem executing the request. In previous examples, there was no mechanism by which you could identify and respond to a server error in the request process. Using XMLHttp, all server errors are revealed to you as a developer, enabling you to pass along meaningful error feedback to the user. In many ways, XMLHttp is a more elegant solution than hidden frames for in-page HTTP requests.

XMLHttp POST Requests

Now that you've seen how XMLHttp can simplify GET requests, it's time to take a look at POST requests. First, you need to make the same changes to SaveCustomer.php as you did for GetCustomerInfo.php, which means you need to remove extraneous HTML and JavaScript, add the content type information, and output the text:

```php
<?php

header("Content-Type: text/plain");

$sName = $_POST["txtName"];
$sAddress = $_POST["txtAddress"];
$sCity = $_POST["txtCity"];
$sState = $_POST["txtState"];
$sZipCode = $_POST["txtZipCode"];
$sPhone = $_POST["txtPhone"];
$sEmail = $_POST["txtEmail"];

$sStatus = "";

$sDBServer = "your.database.server";
```

```php
$sDBName = "your_db_name";
$sDBUsername = "your_db_username";
$sDBPassword = "your_db_password";

$sSQL = "Insert into Customers(Name,Address,City,State,Zip,Phone,`E-mail`) ".
        " values ('$sName','$sAddress','$sCity','$sState', '$sZipCode'".
        ", '$sPhone', '$sEmail')";


$oLink = mysql_connect($sDBServer,$sDBUsername,$sDBPassword);
@mysql_select_db($sDBName) or $sStatus = "Unable to open database";

if($oResult = mysql_query($sSQL)) {
    $sStatus = "Added customer; customer ID is ".mysql_insert_id();
  } else {
    $sStatus = "An error occurred while inserting; customer not saved.";
}


mysql_close($oLink);

echo $sStatus;
?>
```

This now represents the entirety of `SaveCustomer.php`. Note that the `header()` function is called to set the content type, and `echo` is used to output `$sStatus`.

In the main page, the simple form that was set up to allow entry of new customer info is the following:

```html
<form method="post" action="SaveCustomer.php"
    onsubmit="sendRequest(); return false">
  <p>Enter customer information to be saved:</p>
  <p>Customer Name: <input type="text" name="txtName" value="" /><br />
  Address: <input type="text" name="txtAddress" value="" /><br />
  City: <input type="text" name="txtCity" value="" /><br />
  State: <input type="text" name="txtState" value="" /><br />
  Zip Code: <input type="text" name="txtZipCode" value="" /><br />
  Phone: <input type="text" name="txtPhone" value="" /><br />
  E-mail: <input type="text" name="txtEmail" value="" /></p>
  <p><input type="submit" value="Save Customer Info" /></p>
</form>
<div id="divStatus"></div>
```

You'll note that the `onsubmit` event handler has now changed to call the function `sendRequest()` (although the event handler still returns `false` to prevent actual form submission). This method first assembles the data for the POST request and then creates the `XMLHttp` object to send it. The data must be sent in the format as a query string:

```
name1=value1&name2=value2&name3=value3
```

Both the name and value of each parameter must be URL-encoded in order to avoid data loss during transmission. JavaScript provides a built-in function called `encodeURIComponent()` that can be used to perform this encoding. To create this string, you'll need to iterate over the form fields, extracting and encoding the name and value. The `getRequestBody()` function handles this:

```
function getRequestBody(oForm) {
    var aParams = new Array();

    for (var i=0 ; i < oForm.elements.length; i++) {
        var sParam = encodeURIComponent(oForm.elements[i].name);
        sParam += "=";
        sParam += encodeURIComponent(oForm.elements[i].value);
        aParams.push(sParam);
    }

    return aParams.join("&");
}
```

This function assumes that you will supply a reference to the form as an argument. An array (aParams) is created to store each individual name-value pair. Then, the elements of the form are iterated over, building up a string and storing it in sParam, which is then added to the array. Doing this prevents multiple string concatenation, which can lead to slower code execution in some browsers. The last step is to call join() on the array, passing in the ampersand character. This effectively combines all the name-value pairs with ampersands, creating a single string in the correct format.

String concatenation in most browsers is an expensive process because strings are immutable, meaning that once created, they cannot have their values changed. Thus, concatenating two strings involves first allocating a new string and then copying the contents of the two other strings into it. Repeating this process over and over causes a severe slowdown. For this reason, it's always best to keep string concatenations at a minimum and use the array's join() *method to handle longer string concatenation.*

The sendRequest() function calls getRequestBody() and sets up the request:

```
function sendRequest() {
    var oForm = document.forms[0];
    var sBody = getRequestBody(oForm);

    var oXmlHttp = zXmlHttp.createRequest();
    oXmlHttp.open("post", oForm.action, true);
    oXmlHttp.setRequestHeader("Content-Type", "application/x-www-form-urlencoded");

    oXmlHttp.onreadystatechange = function () {
        if (oXmlHttp.readyState == 4) {
            if (oXmlHttp.status == 200) {
                saveResult(oXmlHttp.responseText);
            } else {
                saveResult("An error occurred: " + oXmlHttp.statusText);
            }
        }
    };
    oXmlHttp.send(sBody);
}
```

As with previous examples, the first step in this function is to get a reference to the form and store it in a variable (oForm). Then, the request body is generated and stored in sBody. Next comes the creation and setup of the XMLHttp object. Note that the first argument of open() is now post instead of get, and the second is set to oForm.action (once again, so this script can be used on multiple pages). You'll also notice that a request header is being set. When a form is posted from the browser to a server, it sets the content type of the request as application/x-www-form-urlencoded. Most server-side languages look for this encoding in order to parse the incoming POST data properly, so it is very important for it to be set.

The onreadystatechange event handler is very similar to that of the GET example; the only change is the call to saveResult() instead of displayCustomerInfo(). The last line is very important, as the sBody string is passed to send() so that it will become part of the request body. This effectively mimics what the browser does, so all server-side logic should work as expected.

Advantages and Disadvantages of XMLHttp

Undoubtedly, you can see the advantage of using XMLHttp for client-server communication instead of hidden frames. The code you write is much cleaner and the intent of the code is much more apparent than using numerous callback functions with hidden frames. You have access to request and response headers as well as HTTP status codes, enabling you to determine if your request was successful.

The downside is that, unlike hidden frames, there is no browser history record of the calls that were made. The Back and Forward buttons do not tie in to XMLHttp requests, so you have effectively cut off their use. It is for this reason that many Ajax applications use a mixture of XMLHttp and hidden frames to make a truly usable interface.

Another disadvantage, which applies to Internet Explorer only, is that you depend on ActiveX controls being enabled. If the user has your page set up in a particular security zone that doesn't allow ActiveX controls, you cannot access the XMLHttp object. In that case, you may have to default to using hidden frames.

Further Considerations

Whether you decide to use hidden frames or XMLHttp, there are several things you'll need to consider when building an Ajax application. Expanding the role of JavaScript into the realm of server-side logic brings with it a lot of power, but also several pitfalls that require vigilance on the part of web developers.

The Same Origin Policy

Because web browsers run on a user's computer, browser manufacturers craft important security restrictions to prevent malicious coders from doing damage to users' machines. The most important security restriction in the JavaScript paradigm is called the *same origin policy*, which determines the servers a certain page is allowed to communicate with.

An *origin* is considered a single domain, such as www.wrox.com, accessed through a single protocol, most often HTTP. The same origin policy states that any page loaded from this origin may access, download, and interact with (using JavaScript) any other resource from the same origin. This is what enables the hidden frame technique to work: both frames load a page from the same origin; thus, they are allowed to communicate using JavaScript. If you try to load a frame with a page from another origin, you will not be able to interact with that page or access any scripting features of it. The intent is to prevent malicious programmers from getting your information out of a legitimate web page.

The same origin policy also affects how XMLHttp works. Using XMLHttp, you cannot access any resource that is not from the same origin as the page running the code. This means that, by default, you cannot use a URL beginning with http:// in the open() method; you can use only absolute or relative URLs from within the same domain. If you need to access a URL located in a different origin, you must create a server-side proxy to handle the communication (see Figure 2-4).

Server-Side Proxies

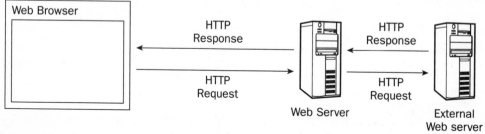

Figure 2-4

Using a server-side proxy, the browser makes a request to the web server. The web server then contacts another web server outside of the domain to request the appropriate information. When your web server receives the response, it is forwarded back to the browser. The result is a seamless transmission of external data. You'll be using server-side proxies later in this book.

> Internet Explorer doesn't have an explicit same origin policy. Instead, it relies on its own security zones to determine what can and cannot be accessed. Those pages belonging to the Internet security zone typically follow rules similar to the same origin policy, whereas those in the Trusted zone may be exempt.

Cache Control

Whenever you are dealing with repeat calls to the same page, you should be concerned about browser caching. For those unaware, web browsers tend to cache certain resources to improve the speed with which sites are downloaded and displayed. This can result in a tremendous speed increase on frequently visited web sites, but can also cause problems for pages that change frequently. If you are making several Ajax calls, you need to be aware that caching may cause you problems.

The best way to deal with caching is to include a no-cache header on any data being sent from the server to the browser. This can be done using the Cache-Control header, which should be set up as follows:

```
Cache-Control: no-cache
```

This tells the browser not to cache the data coming from the specific URL. Instead, the browser always calls a new version from the server instead of a saved version from its own cache.

Summary

This chapter introduced you to several Ajax techniques for client-server communication. It began with an HTTP primer, exploring HTTP requests and responses. You learned about the format of HTTP messages and the differences between a GET request and a POST request. The concepts of headers and message bodies were introduced.

The first Ajax technique you learned was the hidden frame technique, which uses a frame with a width or height of zero, effectively hiding it from the user. This technique uses JavaScript calls to and from the hidden frame to facilitate the client-server communication. Using the hidden frame technique, you learned how to send both GET and POST requests.

Next, you learned about replacing hidden frames with hidden iframes. Because iframes can be created dynamically using JavaScript, this may be a preferable way to initiate client-server communication in modern browsers. The same techniques were used as with hidden frames, although iframes provide a bit more flexibility in the design of your pages.

The chapter also introduced the use of XMLHttp for client-server communication. You learned that Internet Explorer, Mozilla Firefox, Safari, and Opera all support some form of XMLHttp object, and some extra coding is necessary to detect these differences. The differences between asynchronous and synchronous requests were explained, and you learned how to make GET and POST requests using XMLHttp. You also learned how to use request and response headers along with HTTP status codes to better handle requests.

Lastly, considerations when initiating client-server communication were discussed. You learned about the same origin policy and how it affects the ability to communicate with other servers. The various security restrictions were discussed along with a brief introduction to server-side proxies. You also learned about the importance of cache control when creating Ajax functionality.

3

Ajax Patterns

Design patterns describe programming techniques to solve common problems. Given that programming has been around for several decades, chances are that many of the problems you face every day have already been solved by someone else. Since the mid-1990s, a lot of attention has been drawn to design patterns as a way to cut development time.

Even though the term *Ajax* has been around only since early 2005, the techniques that Ajax describes have been used since the late 1990s, giving rise to several Ajax patterns that solve specific problems. You've already seen some of these patterns in action, namely the hidden frame technique and asynchronous XMLHttp calls. These are *communication patterns* between the client and server using JavaScript. As you may have expected, there are many more types of patterns.

Author and programmer Michael Mahemoff was the first to attempt to document Ajax design patterns at his web site, www.ajaxpatterns.org. The patterns presented in this chapter are a mixture of Mahemoff's and others that your authors have identified. Note that design patterns, whether described on a web site or in a book, can never be official, only accepted. Design patterns are not standards to be followed, merely designs of solutions that have worked previously. It is up to the development community to generate a "collective wisdom" around specific patterns; it's up to the individual developer to decide whether to implement a given pattern in his or her own application.

Communication Control Patterns

You already know, from Chapter 2, how to communicate with the server from JavaScript. The real question is: What is the best way to initiate and continue to make requests back to the server? In some cases, it may be best to preload information from the server so that it is available immediately upon some user action. In other cases, you may want to send data to, or receive data from, the server in varying intervals. Perhaps everything shouldn't be downloaded at once, and instead should be downloaded in a particular sequence. Ajax affords you fine granularity in controlling the communication between client and server to achieve your desired behavior.

Predictive Fetch

In a traditional web solution, the application has no idea what is to come next. A page is presented with any number of links, each one leading to a different part of the site. This may be termed "fetch on demand," where the user, through his or her actions, tells the server exactly what data should be retrieved. While this paradigm has defined the Web since its inception, it has the unfortunate side effect of forcing the start-and-stop model of user interaction upon the user. With the help of Ajax, however, this is beginning to change.

The Predictive Fetch pattern is a relatively simple idea that can be somewhat difficult to implement: the Ajax application guesses what the user is going to do next and retrieves the appropriate data. In a perfect world, it would be wonderful to always know what the user is going to do and make sure that the next data is readily available when needed. In reality, however, determining future user action is just a guessing game depending on your intentions.

There are simple use cases where predicting user actions is somewhat easier. Suppose you are reading an online article that is separated into three pages. It is logical to assume that if you are interested in reading the first page, you're also interested in reading the second and third page. So if the first page has been loaded for a few seconds (which can easily be determined by using a timeout), it is probably safe to download the second page in the background. Likewise, if the second page has been loaded for a few seconds, it is logical to assume that the reader will continue on to the third page. As this extra data is being loaded and cached on the client, the reader continues to read and barely even notices that the next page comes up almost instantaneously after clicking the Next Page link.

Another simple use case happens during the writing of an e-mail. Most of the time, you'll be writing an e-mail to someone you know, so it's logical to assume that the person is already in your address book. To help you out, it may be wise to preload your address book in the background and offer suggestions. This approach is taken by many web-based e-mail systems, including Gmail and AOL Webmail. The key, once again, is the "logical-to-assume" criterion. By anticipating and pre-loading information related to the user's most likely next steps, you can make your application feel lighter and more responsive; by using Ajax to fetch information related to any possible next step, you can quickly overload your server and make the browser bog down with extra processing. As a rule of thumb, only pre-fetch information when you believe it's logical to assume that information will be requisite to completing the user's next request.

Page Preloading Example

As mentioned previously, one of the simplest and most logical uses of the Predictive Fetch pattern is in the preloading of pages in an online article. With the advent of weblogs, or blogs for short, everyone seems to have been bitten by the publishing bug, writing their own articles on their own web sites. Reading long articles online is very difficult on the eyes, so many sites split them into multiple pages. This is better for reading, but takes longer to load because each new page brings with it all of the formatting, menus, and ads that were on the original page. Predictive Fetch eases the load on both the client and server by loading only the text for the next page while the reader is still reading the first page.

To begin, you'll need a page that handles the server-side logic for page preloading. The file `ArticleExample.php` contains code for displaying an article online:

```php
<?php
    $page = 1;
    $dataOnly = false;
    if (isset($_GET["page"])) {
        $page = (int) $_GET["page"];
    }

    if (isset($_GET["data"]) && $_GET["dataonly"] == "true") {
        $dataOnly = true;
    }

    if (!$dataOnly) {
?>
<!DOCTYPE html PUBLIC "-//W3C//DTD XHTML 1.0 Transitional//EN"
     "http://www.w3.org/TR/xhtml1/DTD/xhtml1-transitional.dtd">
<html xmlns="http://www.w3.org/1999/xhtml" xml:lang="en" lang="en">
    <head>
        <title>Article Example</title>
        <script type="text/javascript" src="zxml.js"></script>
        <script type="text/javascript" src="Article.js"></script>
        <link rel="stylesheet" type="text/css" href="Article.css" />
    </head>
    <body>
        <h1>Article Title</h1>
        <div id="divLoadArea" style="display:none"></div>
<?php
        $output = "<p>Page ";

        for ($i=1; $i < 4; $i++) {
            $output .= "<a href=\"ArticleExample.php?page=$i\" id=\"aPage$i\"";
            if ($i==$page) {
                $output .= "class=\"current\"";
            }
            $output .= ">$i</a> ";
        }
        echo $output;
    }

    if ($page==1) {
        echo $page1Text;
    } else if ($page == 2) {
        echo $page2Text;
    } else if ($page == 3) {
        echo $page3Text;
    }

    if (!$dataOnly) {
?>
    </body>
</html>
<?php
    }
?>
```

By default, this file displays the first page of text for the article. If the `page` query string parameter is specified, such as `page=2`, then it shows the given page of the article. When the query string contains `dataonly=true`, the page outputs only a `<div/>` element containing the article text for the given page. Combining this with the `page` parameter enables you to retrieve just any page of the article that you need.

The HTML in this page has a space for the article title as well as a `<div/>` element used for loading extra pages. This `<div/>` element has its display property set to `none` to ensure that its contents are not displayed accidentally. The PHP code immediately following contains logic to output a list of pages available for the article. In this example, there will be three pages of content, so there are three links output at the top (see Figure 3-1).

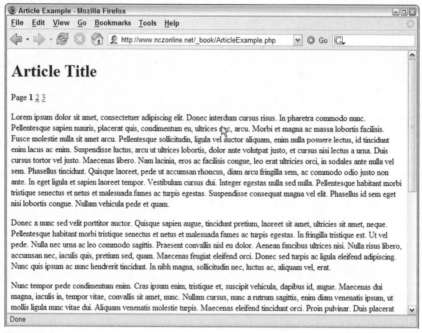

Figure 3-1

The current page is assigned a CSS class of `current` so that the user knows which page he or she is viewing. This class is defined in `Article.css` as:

```
a.current {
    color: black;
    font-weight: bold;
    text-decoration: none;
}
```

When the reader is viewing a particular page, the link for that page becomes black, bold, and is no longer underlined, providing a clear indication of the page that he or she is reading. By default, these links simply load the same page and change the `page` parameter of the query string; this is the way that most web sites handle multipage articles. Using Predictive Fetch, however, will improve the user's experience and the speed with which the data is available.

Several global JavaScript variables are required to implement Predictive Fetch for this example:

```
var oXmlHttp = null;          //The XMLHttp object
var iPageCount = 3;           //The number of pages
var iCurPage = -1;            //The currently displayed page
var iWaitBeforeLoad = 5000;   //The time (in ms) before loading new page
var iNextPageToLoad = -1;     //The next page to load
```

The first variable is a global XMLHttp object that is used to make all requests for more information. The second, iPageCount, is the number of pages used in this article. (This is hard coded here, but in actual practice this would have to be generated.) The iCurPage variable stores the page number currently being displayed to the user. The next two variables deal directly with the preloading of data: iWaitBeforeLoad is the number of milliseconds to wait before loading the next page, and iNextPageToLoad contains the page number that should be loaded once the specified amount of time has passed. For this example, a new page is loaded behind the scenes every 5 seconds (5000 milliseconds), which should be long enough for someone to read the first few sentences of an article to determine if it's worth reading the rest. If the reader leaves before 5 seconds are up, chances are they have no intention of reading the rest of the article.

To begin the process, you'll need a function to determine the URL for retrieving a particular page. This function, getURLForPage(), accepts a single argument that specifies the page number you want to retrieve. Then, the current URL is extracted and the page parameter is appended to the end:

```
function getURLForPage(iPage) {
    var sNewUrl = location.href;
    if (location.search.length > 0) {
        sNewUrl = sNewUrl.substring(0, sNewUrl.indexOf("?"))
    }
    sNewUrl += "?page=" + iPage;
    return sNewUrl;
}
```

This function begins by extracting the URL from location.href, which gives the complete URL for the page, including the query string. Then, the URL is tested to see if there is a query string specified by determining if the length of location.search is greater than 0 (location.search returns just the query string, including the question mark, if there is one specified). If there is a query string, it is stripped off using the substring() method. The page parameter is then appended to the URL and returned. This function will come in handy in a number of different places.

The next function is called showPage(), and as you may have guessed, it is responsible for displaying the next page of the article:

```
function showPage(sPage) {

    var divPage = document.getElementById("divPage" + sPage);

    if (divPage) {
        for (var i=0; i < iPageCount; i++) {
            var iPageNum = i+1;
            var divOtherPage = document.getElementById("divPage" + iPageNum);
            var aOtherLink = document.getElementById("aPage" + iPageNum);
```

```
            if (divOtherPage && sPage != iPageNum) {
                divOtherPage.style.display = "none";
                aOtherLink.className = "";
            }
        }
        divPage.style.display = "block";
        document.getElementById("aPage" + sPage).className = "current";
    } else {
        location.href = getURLForPage(parseInt(sPage));
    }
}
```

This function first checks to see whether the given page has a <div/> element already loaded. The <div/> element would be named divPage plus the page number (for example, divPage1 for the first page, divPage2 for the second, and so on). If this <div/> element exists, the page has been prefetched already, so you can just switch the currently visible page. This is done by iterating through the pages and hiding all pages except the one indicated by the argument sPage. At the same time, the links for each page are given an empty string for their CSS class. Then, the <div/> element for the current page has its display property set to block in order to show it, and the link for the page has its CSS class set to current.

If, on the other hand, the <div/> element doesn't exist, the page navigates to the next page in the article the old-fashioned way, by getting the URL (using the getURLForPage() function defined previously) and assigning it to location.href. This is a fallback functionality so that if the user clicks a page link before 5 seconds are up, the experience falls back to the traditional web paradigm.

The loadNextPage() function is used to load each new page behind the scenes. This function is responsible for ensuring that requests are made only for valid pages and that pages are retrieved in order and in the specified intervals:

```
function loadNextPage() {

    if (iNextPageToLoad <= iPageCount) {

        if (!oXmlHttp) {
            oXmlHttp = zXmlHttp.createRequest();
        } else if (oXmlHttp.readyState != 0) {
            oXmlHttp.abort();
        }

        oXmlHttp.open("get", getURLForPage(iNextPageToLoad)
                                    + "&dataonly=true", true);
        oXmlHttp.onreadystatechange = function () {

            //more code here
        };
        oXmlHttp.send(null);
    }
}
```

The function begins by ensuring that the page number stored in `iNextPageToLoad` is valid by comparing it to `iPageCount`. Passing this test, the next step is to see if the global XMLHttp object has been created yet. If not, it is created using the zXml library's `createRequest()` method. If it has already been instantiated, the `readyState` property is checked to ensure that it's 0. If `readyState` is not 0, the `abort()` method must be called to reset the XMLHttp object.

Next, the `open()` method is called, specifying that the request will get an asynchronous GET request. The URL is retrieved by using the `getURLForPage()` function and then appending the string `"&dataonly=true"` to ensure that only the page text is returned. With all of that set, it's time to move on to the `onreadystatechange` event handler.

In this case, the `onreadystatechange` event handler is responsible for retrieving the article text as well as creating the appropriate DOM structure to represent it:

```
function loadNextPage() {

    if (iNextPageToLoad <= iPageCount) {

        if (!oXmlHttp) {
            oXmlHttp = zXmlHttp.createRequest();
        } else if (oXmlHttp.readyState != 0) {
            oXmlHttp.abort();
        }

        oXmlHttp.open("get", getURLForPage(iNextPageToLoad)
                                        + "&dataonly=true", true);
        oXmlHttp.onreadystatechange = function () {

            if (oXmlHttp.readyState == 4) {
                if (oXmlHttp.status == 200) {
                    var divLoadArea = document.getElementById("divLoadArea");
                    divLoadArea.innerHTML = oXmlHttp.responseText;
                    var divNewPage = document.getElementById("divPage"
                                                        + iNextPageToLoad);
                    divNewPage.style.display = "none";
                    document.body.appendChild(divNewPage);
                    divLoadArea.innerHTML = "";
                    iNextPageToLoad++;
                    setTimeout(loadNextPage, iWaitBeforeLoad);
                }

            }
        };
        oXmlHttp.send(null);
    }
}
```

As discussed in the previous chapter, the `readyState` property is checked to see when it is equal to 4, and the `status` property is checked to make sure there was no error. Once you've passed those two conditions, the real processing begins. First, a reference to the load area `<div/>` element is retrieved and stored in `divLoadArea`. Then, the `responseText` from the request is assigned to the load area's `innerHTML` property. Since the text coming back is an HTML snippet, it will be parsed and the appropriate DOM objects will be created. Next, a reference to the `<div/>` element that contains the next page is retrieved (you know the ID will be `divPage` plus `iNextPageToLoad`) and its `display` property is set to `none` to ensure it remains invisible when it is moved outside of the load area. The next line appends `divNewPage` to the document's body, putting it into the regular viewing area for usage. Then the load area's `innerHTML` property is set to an empty string to prepare for another page to be loaded. After that, the `iNextPageToLoad` variable is incremented and a new timeout is set to call this function again after the specified period of time. This function will continue to be called every 5 seconds until all pages have been loaded.

Because this page should be functional without JavaScript, all this code is attached at runtime after determining if the browser is capable of using XMLHttp. Fortunately, the `zXmlHttp` object in the zXml library has a function, `isSupported()`, that can be used to determine this:

```
window.onload = function () {
    if (zXmlHttp.isSupported()) {
        //begin Ajax code here
    }
};
```

Inside this code block is where all the Predictive Fetch code will go, ensuring that browsers without XMLHttp support will not have their usability adversely affected by half-functioning code.

The first step in the process of setting up Predictive Fetch for the article is to determine which page the user is currently viewing. To do so, you must look into the URL's query string to see if the page parameter is specified. If it is, you can extract the page number from there; otherwise, you can assume that the page number is 1 (the default):

```
window.onload = function () {
    if (zXmlHttp.isSupported()) {

        if (location.href.indexOf("page=") > -1) {
          var sQueryString = location.search.substring(1);
          iCurPage = parseInt(sQueryString.substring(sQueryString.indexOf("=")+1));
        } else {
          iCurPage = 1;
        }

        iNextPageToLoad = iCurPage+1;

        //more code here
    }
};
```

In this section of code, the page's URL (accessible through `location.href`) is tested to see if page= has been specified. If so, the query string is retrieved by using `location.search` (which returns only the query string, including the question mark, that the call to `substring(1)` strips out). The next line retrieves just the part of the query string after the equals sign (which should be the page number), converts it to an integer using `parseInt()`, and stores the result in `iCurPage`. If, on the other hand, the page parameter isn't specified in the query string, the page is assumed to be the first one, and 1 is assigned to `iCurPage`. The last line in this section sets the `iNextPageToLoad` variable to the current page plus one, ensuring that you don't end up reloading data that is already available.

The next step is to override the functionality of the page links. Remember, by default, these links reload the same page with a different query string to specify which page should be displayed. If XMLHttp is supported, you need to override this behavior and replace it with function calls to the Ajax functionality:

```
window.onload = function () {
    if (zXmlHttp.isSupported()) {

        if (location.href.indexOf("page=") > -1) {
          var sQueryString = location.search.substring(1);
          iCurPage = parseInt(sQueryString.substring(sQueryString.indexOf("=")+1));
        } else {
           iCurPage = 1;
        }

        iNextPageToLoad = iCurPage+1;

        var colLinks = document.getElementsByTagName("a");
        for (var i=0; i < colLinks.length; i++) {
            if (colLinks[i].id.indexOf("aPage") == 0) {
                colLinks[i].onclick = function (oEvent) {
                    var sPage = this.id.substring(5);
                    showPage(sPage);

                    if (oEvent) {
                        oEvent.preventDefault();
                    } else {
                        window.event.returnValue = false;
                    }
                }
            }
        }

        setTimeout(loadNextPage, iWaitBeforeLoad);

    }
};
```

Here, a collection of links (`<a/>` elements) is retrieved using `getElementsByTagName()`. If the link has an ID beginning with `aPage`, it is a page link and needs to be addressed; this is determined by using `indexOf()` and checking for a value of 0, which indicates that `aPage` is the first part of the string. Next, an `onclick` event handler is assigned to the link. Within this event handler, the page number is extracted by using the ID of the link (accessible through `this.id`) and using `substring()` to return everything after `aPage`. Then, this value is passed into the `showPage()` function defined earlier in this section, which displays the appropriate page. After that point, you need only worry about canceling the default behavior of the link, which is to navigate to a new page. Because of differences in the Internet Explorer (IE) and DOM event models, an `if` statement is necessary to determine the appropriate course of action. If the `event` object was passed in to the function (the argument `oEvent`), then this is a DOM-compliant browser and the `preventDefault()` method is called to block the default behavior. If, however, `oEvent` is `null`, that means it's IE and so the `event` object is accessible as `window.event`. The `returnValue` property is then set to `false`, which is the way IE cancels default event actions.

After the links have been properly handled, a timeout is created for the initial call to `loadNextPage()`. This first call will take place after 5 seconds and will automatically load the second page at that point.

When you test this functionality yourself, try clicking the page links at different points in time. If you click it before 5 seconds have passed, you will see the page navigate to a new URL with the query string changed. The next time, wait about ten seconds and click a page link. You should see that the text changes while the URL does not (it is also noticeably faster than navigating to a URL).

Submission Throttling

Predictive Fetch is one pattern for retrieving data from the server; the other side of an Ajax solution is the sending of data to the server. Since you want to avoid page refreshes, the question of when to send user data is important. In a traditional web site or web application, each click makes a request back to the server so that the server is always aware of what the client is doing. In the Ajax model, the user interacts with the site or application without additional requests being generated for each click.

One solution would be to send data back to the server every time a user action occurs, similar to that of a traditional web solution. Thus, when the user types a letter, that letter is sent to the server immediately. The process is then repeated for each letter typed. The problem with this approach is that it has the possibility to create a large number of requests in a short amount of time, which may not only cause problems for the server but may cause the user interface to slow down as each request is being made and processed. The Submission Throttling design pattern is an alternative approach to this problematic issue.

Using Submission Throttling, you buffer the data to be sent to the server on the client and then send the data at predetermined times. The venerable Google Suggest feature does this brilliantly. It doesn't send a request after each character is typed. Instead, it waits for a certain amount of time and sends all the text currently in the text box. The delay from typing to sending has been fine-tuned to the point that it doesn't seem like much of a delay at all. Submission Throttling, in part, gives Google Suggest its speed.

Submission Throttling typically begins either when the web site or application first loads or because of a specific user action. Then, a client-side function is called to begin the buffering of data. Every so often, the user's status is checked to see if he or she is idle (doing so prevents any interference with the user interface). If the user is still active, data continues to be collected. When the user is idle, which is to say he or she is not performing an action, it's time to decide whether to send the data. This determination varies depending on your use case; you may want to send data only when it reaches a certain size, or you may want to send it every time the user is idle. After the data is sent, the application typically continues to gather data until either a server response or some user action signals to stop the data collection. Figure 3-2 outlines this process.

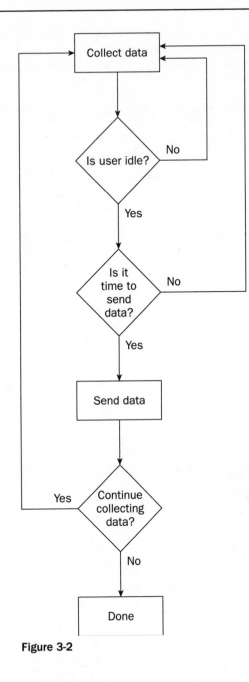

Figure 3-2

> The Submission Throttling pattern should never be used for mission-critical data. If information must be posted to the server within a specific amount of time, you are better off using a traditional form to ensure the correct and timely delivery of the information.

Incremental Form Validation Example

As mentioned previously, Submission Throttling can be achieved through various user interactions. When using forms, it's sometimes useful to upload data incrementally as the form is being filled out. The most common usage is to validate data as the user is filling in the form instead of waiting until the end to determine any errors. In this case, you would most likely use the onchange event handler of each form element to determine when to upload the data.

The change event fires for a <select/> element whenever a different option is selected; it fires for other controls when its value has changed and it has lost focus. For example, if you typed a couple of letters into a text box and then clicked elsewhere on the screen (causing the text box to lose focus), the change event fires and the onchange event handler is called. If you click in the text box again, and then click elsewhere (or press the Tab key), the text box will lose focus but the change event will not fire because no changes have been made. Using this event handler for Submission Throttling can prevent extraneous requests.

Normally, the form validation is simply a precursor to submission. The form's submit button starts out disabled, becoming enabled only when all fields in the form have been validated by the server. For example, suppose you are running a web site where users must sign up to gain access to certain features. This may be a shopping site that requires sign-in to purchase items or a site that requires membership to access the message board. The items you'll want to be sure of when creating this new account are:

❑ The user name must not be taken.

❑ The e-mail address must be valid.

❑ The birthday must be a valid date.

Of course, the type of data required will differ depending on your usage, but these items provide a good starting point for most applications.

The first step in creating such interaction is to define the HTML form that will collect the data. This form should stand alone so that it can be used even if Ajax calls aren't possible:

```
<form method="post" action="Success.php">
    <table>
        <tr>
            <td><label for="txtFirstName">First Name</label></td>
            <td><input type="text" id="txtFirstName" name="txtFirstName" /></td>
        </tr>
        <tr>
            <td><label for="txtLastName">Last Name</label></td>
            <td><input type="text" id="txtLastName" name="txtLastName" /></td>
        </tr>
```

```
        <tr>
            <td><label for="txtEmail">E-mail</label></td>
            <td><input type="text" id="txtEmail" name="txtEmail" /><img
src="error.gif" alt="Error" id="imgEmailError" style="display:none" /></td>
        </tr>
        <tr>
            <td><label for="txtUsername">Username</label></td>
            <td><input type="text" id="txtUsername" name="txtUsername" /><img
src="error.gif" alt="Error" id="imgUsernameError" style="display:none" /></td>
        </tr>
        <tr>
            <td><label for="txtBirthday">Birthday</label></td>
            <td><input type="text" id="txtBirthday" name="txtBirthday" /><img
src="error.gif" alt="Error" id="imgBirthdayError" style="display:none" />
(m/d/yyyy)</td>
        </tr>
        <tr>
            <td><label for="selGender">Gender</label></td>
            <td><select id="selGender"
name="selGender"><option>Male</option></option>Female</option></select></td>
        </tr>
    </table>
    <input type="submit" id="btnSignUp" value="Sign Up!" />
</form>
```

You should note a few things about this form. First, not all fields will be validated using Ajax calls. The fields for first and last name as well as gender (represented by a combo box) don't require validation. The other fields — for e-mail, user name, and birthday — will make use of Ajax validation. Second, you'll note that these fields have a hidden image after the text box. This image is used only in the event that there is a validation error. Initially the images are hidden, because those browsers without Ajax capabilities should never see them. There is absolutely no JavaScript on this form; all the appropriate functions and event handlers are defined in a separate file.

A single function called `validateField()` is used to validate each form field. This is possible because each field uses the same validation technique (call the server and wait for a response). The only differences are the types of data being validated and which image to show if validation is unsuccessful.

The server-side functionality is stored in a file named `ValidateForm.php`. This file expects a name-value pair to be passed in the query string. The name should be the name of the control whose value is being checked, and the value should be the value of that control. Depending on the name of the control, this page runs the appropriate validation tests on the value. Then, it outputs a simple string in the following format:

```
<true|false>||<error message>
```

The first part of this string indicates whether the value is valid (`true` if it is; `false` if not). The second part, after the double pipes (||), is an error message that is provided only when the value is invalid. Here are a couple of examples of what the returned string might look like:

```
true||
false||Invalid date.
```

The first line represents a valid value; the second represents an invalid date.

> This is a plain-text message, although later in the book you will learn about using other data formats, such as XML and JSON for this same purpose.

The code that does the validation is as follows:

```php
<?php
    $valid = "false";
    $message = "An unknown error occurred.";

    if (isset($_GET["txtUsername"])) {

        //load array of usernames
        $usernames = array();
        $usernames[] = "SuperBlue";
        $usernames[] = "Ninja123";
        $usernames[] = "Daisy1724";
        $usernames[] = "NatPack";

        //check usernames
        if (in_array($_GET["txtUsername"], $usernames)) {
            $message = "This username already exists. Please choose another.";
        } else if (strlen($_GET["txtUsername"]) < 8) {
            $message = "Username must be at least 8 characters long.";
        } else {
            $valid = "true";
            $message = "";
        }

    } else if (isset($_GET["txtBirthday"])) {

        $date = strtotime($_GET["txtBirthday"]);
        if ($date < 0) {
            $message = "This is not a valid date.";
        } else {
            $valid = "true";
            $message = "";
        }

    } else if (isset($_GET["txtEmail"])) {

        if(!eregi(
            "^[_a-z0-9-]+(\.[_a-z0-9-]+)*@[a-z0-9-]+(\.[a-z0-9-]+)*(\.[a-z]{2,3})$",
            $_GET["txtEmail"])) {
            $message = "This e-mail address is not valid";
        } else {
            $valid = "true";
            $message = "";
        }
    }

    echo "$valid||$message"; ?>
```

In this file, the first step is to determine which field to validate. This is done using the `isset()` function to test the `$_GET` array for a value. If there is a value for a particular field, then the validation commences. For the user name, the value is checked to see if it already exists in an array of user names and then checked to ensure that it is at least eight characters long. The birthday is passed directly into PHP's built-in `strto time()` function, which converts a date string in any number of U.S. formats into a UNIX timestamp (the number of seconds since January 1, 1970). If there is an error, this function returns –1, indicating that the string passed in was not a valid date. The e-mail address is checked against a regular expression to ensure that it is in the correct format. This regular expression was devised by John Coggeshall in his article, "E-mail validation with PHP 4," available online at `www.zend.com/zend/spotlight/ev12apr.php`.

> Note that the user names in this example are stored in a simple array and hard-coded into the page. In an actual implementation, the user names should be stored in a database and the database should be queried to determine whether the user name already exists.

The `$valid` and `$message` variables are initialized to `false` and `An unknown error occurred`. This ensures that if the file is used incorrectly (passing in an unrecognized field name, for example), a negative validation will always be returned. When a positive validation occurs, however, this requires that both variables be reset to appropriate values (`true` for `$valid`, an empty string for `$message`). In the case of a negative validation, only the `$message` variable has to be set since `$valid` is already `false`. The very last step in this page is to output the response string in the format mentioned previously.

Next, the JavaScript to perform the validation must be created. A single function, `validateField()`, can be used to validate each field so long as it knows which field it should be validating. This takes a little bit of work to counteract cross-browser compatibility issues:

```
function validateField(oEvent) {
    oEvent = oEvent || window.event;
    var txtField = oEvent.target || oEvent.srcElement;

    //more code to come
}
```

The first two lines of code inside this function equalize the differences between event models in IE and DOM-compliant browsers (such as Mozilla Firefox, Opera, and Safari). DOM-compliant browsers pass in an `event` object to each event handler; the control that caused the event is stored in the `event` object's `target` property. In IE, the `event` object is a property of `window`; therefore, the first line inside the function assigns the correct value to the `oEvent` variable. Logical OR (`||`) returns a non-null value when used with an object and a `null` object. If you are using IE, `oEvent` will be `null`; thus, the value of `window.event` is assigned to `oEvent`. If you are using a DOM-compliant browser, `oEvent` will be reassigned to itself. The second line does the same operation for the control that caused the event, which is stored in the `srcElement` property in IE. At the end of these two lines, the control that caused the event is stored in the `txtField` variable. The next step is to create the HTTP request using XMLHttp:

```
function validateField(oEvent) {
    oEvent = oEvent || window.event;
    var txtField = oEvent.target || oEvent.srcElement;
```

```
        var oXmlHttp = zXmlHttp.createRequest();
        oXmlHttp.open("get", "ValidateForm.php?" + txtField.name + "="
                                    + encodeURIComponent(txtField.value), true);
        oXmlHttp.onreadystatechange = function () {
            //more code to come
        };
        oXmlHttp.send(null);
    }
```

As in Chapter 2, you are using the zXml library for cross-browser XMLHttp support. The XMLHttp object is created and stored in oXmlHttp. Next, the connection is initialized to a GET request using open(). Note that the query string for ValidateForm.php is created by combining the name of the field, an equals sign, and the value of the field (which is URL encoded using encodeURIComponent()). Also note that this is an asynchronous request. This is extremely important for this use case, because you don't want to interfere with the user filling out the rest of the form while you are checking the validity of a single field; remember that synchronous requests made using XMLHttp objects freeze most aspects of the user interface (including typing and clicking) during their execution.. The last part of this function is to handle the response from the server:

```
function validateField(oEvent) {
    oEvent = oEvent || window.event;
    var txtField = oEvent.target || oEvent.srcElement;
    var oXmlHttp = zXmlHttp.createRequest();
    oXmlHttp.open("get", "ValidateForm.php?" + txtField.name + "="
                                + encodeURIComponent(txtField.value), true);
    oXmlHttp.onreadystatechange = function () {
        if (oXmlHttp.readyState == 4) {
            if (oXmlHttp.status == 200) {
                var arrInfo = oXmlHttp.responseText.split("||");
                var imgError = document.getElementById("img"
                                        + txtField.id.substring(3) + "Error");
                var btnSignUp = document.getElementById("btnSignUp");

                if (!eval(arrInfo[0])) {
                    imgError.title = arrInfo[1];
                    imgError.style.display = "";
                    txtField.valid = false;
                } else {
                    imgError.style.display = "none";
                    txtField.valid = true;
                }

                btnSignUp.disabled = !isFormValid();
            } else {
                alert("An error occurred while trying to contact the server.");
            }
        }
    };
    oXmlHttp.send(null);
}
```

After checking for the correct `readyState` and `status`, the `responseText` is split into an array of strings (arrInfo) using the JavaScript `split()` method. The value in the first slot of `arrInfo` will be the value of the PHP variable `$valid`; the value in the second slot will be the value of the PHP variable `$message`. Also, a reference to the appropriate error image and the Sign Up button is returned. The error image is gained by dissecting the field name, removing the "txt" from the front (using `substring()`), prepending "img" and appending "Error" to the end (so for the field "txtBirthday", the error image name is constructed as "imgBirthdayError").

The value in `arrInfo[0]` must be passed into `eval()` in order to get a true Boolean value out of it. (Remember, it's a string: either `true` or `false`.) If this value is `false`, the error image's `title` property is assigned the error message from `arrInfo[1]`, the image is displayed, and the custom `valid` property of the text box is set to `false` (this will come in handy later). When a value is invalid, the error image appears, and when the user moves the mouse over it, the error message appears (see Figure 3-3). If the value is valid, however, the error image is hidden and the custom `valid` property is set to `true`.

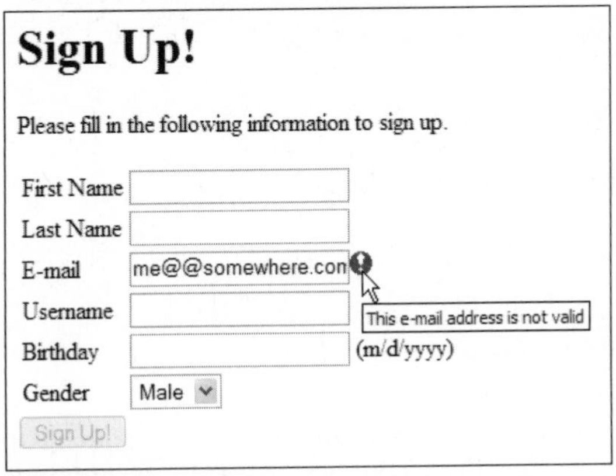

Figure 3-3

You'll also notice that the Sign Up button is used in this function. The Sign Up button should be disabled if there is any invalid data in the form. To accomplish this, a function called `isFormValid()` is called. If this function returns `false`, the Sign Up button's `disabled` property is set to `true`, disabling it. The `isFormValid()` function simply iterates through the form fields and checks the `valid` property:

```
function isFormValid() {
    var frmMain = document.forms[0];
    var blnValid = true;

    for (var i=0; i < frmMain.elements.length; i++) {
        if (typeof frmMain.elements[i].valid == "boolean") {
            blnValid = blnValid && frmMain.elements[i].valid;
        }
    }

    return blnValid;
}
```

For each element in the form, the `valid` property is first checked to see if it exists. This is done by using the `typeof` operator, which will return `boolean` if the property exists and has been given a Boolean value. Because there are fields that aren't being validated (and thus won't have the custom `valid` property), this check ensures that only validated fields are considered.

The last part of the script is to set up the event handlers for the text boxes. This should be done when the form has finished loading, but only if XMLHttp is supported (because that is how the Ajax validation is being performed here):

```
//if Ajax is enabled, disable the submit button and assign event handlers
window.onload = function () {
    if (zXmlHttp.isSupported()) {
        var btnSignUp = document.getElementById("btnSignUp");
        var txtUsername = document.getElementById("txtUsername");
        var txtBirthday = document.getElementById("txtBirthday");
        var txtEmail = document.getElementById("txtEmail");

        btnSignUp.disabled = true;
        txtUsername.onchange = validateField;
        txtBirthday.onchange = validateField;
        txtEmail.onchange = validateField;
        txtUsername.valid = false;
        txtBirthday.valid = false;
        txtEmail.valid = false;

    }
};
```

This `onload` event handler assigns the `onchange` event handlers for each text box as well as initializes the custom `valid` property to `false`. Additionally, the Sign Up button is disabled from the start to prevent invalid data from being submitted. Note, however, that the button will be disabled only if XMLHttp is supported; otherwise, the form will behave as a normal web form and the validation will have to be done when the entire form is submitted.

When you load this example, each of the three validated text fields will make a request to the server for validation whenever their values change and you move on to another field. The user experience is seamless using the Submission Throttling pattern, but the form remains functional even if JavaScript is turned off or XMLHttp is not supported.

> **Even when using this type of validation, it is essential that all the data be validated again once the entire form is submitted. Remember, if the user turns off JavaScript, you still need to be sure the data is valid before performing operations using it.**

Incremental Field Validation Example

Whereas the previous example validated each field when its value changed, the other popular form of the Submission Throttling design pattern involves submitting a single field periodically as changes are made. This is the version of Submission Throttling used for both Bitflux LiveSearch and Google Suggest, where data is repeatedly sent to the server as the user types. In both of these cases, the submission activates a search on the server; however, the same method can be used to validate a single field repeatedly as the user types.

Suppose that instead of asking you to fill in a whole form, sign-up for a given site requires you first to select a user name (maybe as step 1 of a multistep sign-up process). In this case, you'd want to ensure that only a non-existent user name be used. Instead of waiting for the form to be submitted, you can periodically upload the data to the server for validation, making sure that the data can't be submitted until a valid user name is entered.

> Note that this example is for demonstration purposes. If you were to use the technique described in a production environment, you would have to protect against spam bots that may use this feature to harvest user names and passwords.

The form for this example is much simpler, made up of a single text box and a Next button:

```
<form method="post" action="Success.php">
    <table>
        <tr>
            <td><label for="txtUsername">Username</label></td>
            <td><input type="text" id="txtUsername" name="txtUsername" />
                <img src="error.gif" alt="Error" id="imgUsernameError"
                    style="display:none" /></td>
        </tr>
    </table>
    <input type="submit" id="btnNext" value="Next" />
</form>
```

Note that the same basic format of the previous example has been kept, including the hidden error image. Next, the validateField() function from the previous example is used, with a few changes:

```
var oXmlHttp = null;
var iTimeoutId = null;

function validateField(oEvent) {
    oEvent = oEvent || window.event;
    var txtField = oEvent.target || oEvent.srcElement;

    var btnNext = document.getElementById("btnNext");
    btnNext.disabled = true;

    if (iTimeoutId != null) {
        clearTimeout(iTimeoutId);
        iTimeoutId = null;
    }

    if (!oXmlHttp) {
        oXmlHttp = zXmlHttp.createRequest();
    } else if (oXmlHttp.readyState != 0) {
        oXmlHttp.abort();
    }

    oXmlHttp.open("get", "ValidateForm.php?" + txtField.name + "="
```

```
                                    + encodeURIComponent(txtField.value), true);
        oXmlHttp.onreadystatechange = function () {

            if (oXmlHttp.readyState == 4) {
                if (oXmlHttp.status == 200) {
                    var arrInfo = oXmlHttp.responseText.split("||");
                    var imgError = document.getElementById("img"
                                               + txtField.id.substring(3) + "Error");

                    if (!eval(arrInfo[0])) {
                        imgError.title = arrInfo[1];
                        imgError.style.display = "";
                        txtField.valid = false;
                    } else {
                        imgError.style.display = "none";
                        txtField.valid = true;
                    }

                    btnNext.disabled = !txtField.valid;
                } else {
                    alert("An error occurred while trying to contact the server.");
                }
            }
        };

        iTimeoutId = setTimeout(function () {
            oXmlHttp.send(null);
        }, 500);
    };
```

The first thing to note about this updated function is the inclusion of two global variables: oXmlHttp and iTimeoutId. The first, oXmlHttp, holds a global reference to an XMLHttp object that is used repeatedly (as opposed to being used just once in the previous example); the second, iTimeoutId, holds a timeout identifier used to delay sending a request. Inside the function, the first new part sets the Next button to be disabled right away. This is important because a request may not be sent out immediately following a call to this function. The next block after that clears the timeout identifier if it's not null, which prevents the sending of too many requests in succession. (If there is a pending request, this cancels it.)

Next, the global oXmlHttp object is tested to see if it is null. If so, a new XMLHttpobject is created and assigned to it. If an XMLHttp object already exists, its readyState is checked to see if it's ready for a request. As mentioned in the previous chapter, the readyState changes from 0 to 1 when the open() method is called; therefore, any readyState other than 0 indicates that a request has already been started, so the abort() method must be called before attempting to send a new request. Note that the same ValidateForm.php page is used for validation purposes.

Inside of the onreadystatechange event handler, the only new line is one that changes the Next button's disabled state based on the validity of user name. Toward the end of the function, the setTimeout() function is called to delay the sending of the request by half a second (500 milliseconds). The identifier from this call is saved in iTimeoutId, so it is possible to cancel the request the next time the function is called. By using the timeout functionality of JavaScript in this way, you are ensuring that the user hasn't typed anything for at least half a second. If the user types something quickly, the timeout will repeatedly be cleared and the request aborted. It's only when there is a pause that the request will finally be sent.

The only part left now is to set up the event handler. Since this method uploads information as the user types, you can't rely on the onchange event handler alone (although it is still needed). In this case, you need to use the onkeyup event handler, which is called every time a key is pressed and then released:

```
window.onload = function () {
    if (zXmlHttp.isSupported()) {
        var btnNext = document.getElementById("btnNext");
        var txtUsername = document.getElementById("txtUsername");

        btnNext.disabled = true;
        txtUsername.onkeyup = validateField;
        txtUsername.onchange = validateField;
        txtUsername.valid = false;
    }
};
```

Once again, this is very similar to the previous example. The only changes are the name of the button (which is now btnNext) and the assignment of validateField() to the onkeyup event handler. As the user types, the user name will be checked for validity. Every time a valid user name is entered, the Next button becomes enabled. Whenever a request is being made, the button is first disabled to accommodate a specific situation. It is possible that the user will continue typing even after a valid user name has been entered. As a side effect, the extra characters may cause the user name to become invalid, and you don't want to allow invalid data to be submitted.

> **Although a nice feature, incremental field validation should be used sparingly because it creates a high volume of requests. Unless your server configuration is set up specifically to handle an increased amount of requests, it is best to forego this approach.**

Periodic Refresh

The Periodic Refresh design pattern describes the process of checking for new server information in specific intervals. This approach, also called *polling*, requires the browser to keep track of when another request to the server should take place.

This pattern is used in a variety of different ways on the Web:

❑ ESPN uses Periodic Refresh to update its online scoreboards automatically. For example, the NFL Scoreboard, located at http://sports.espn.go.com/nfl/scoreboard, shows up-to-the-minute scores and drive charts for every NFL game being played at the time. Using XMLHttp objects and a little bit of Flash, the page repeatedly updates itself with new information.

❑ Gmail (http://gmail.google.com) uses Periodic Refresh to notify users when new mail has been received. As you are reading an e-mail or performing other operations, Gmail repeatedly checks the server to see if new mail has arrived. This is done without notification unless there is new mail, at which point the number of new e-mails received is displayed in parentheses next to the Inbox menu item.

❑ XHTML Live Chat (www.plasticshore.com/projects/chat/) uses Periodic Refresh to implement a chat room using simple web technologies. The chat room text is updated automatically every few seconds by checking the server for new information. If there is a new message, the page is updated to reflect it, thus creating a traditional chat room experience.

❑ The Magnetic Ajax demo (www.broken-notebook.com/magnetic/) re-creates online the experience of magnetic poetry (using single word magnets that can be rearranged to make sentences). The full version polls the server for new arrangements every few seconds, so if you and someone else are rearranging words at the same time, you will see the movement.

Clearly, there are many different ways that Period Refresh can increase user experience, but the basic purpose remains the same: to notify users of updated information.

New Comment Notifier Example

A feature that has been creeping into blogs across the Web since the beginning of 2005 is a New Comment Notifier. A New Comment Notifier does exactly what it says it does: it alerts the user when a new comment has been added. This can take the form of a simple text message displayed on the page or an animated message that slides in from out of view, but the basic idea is the same. In this example, Periodic Refresh is used to check a database table containing comments to see which is the newest.

Suppose you have a simple MySQL table, defined as follows:

```
CREATE TABLE `BlogComments` (
`CommentId` INT NOT NULL AUTO_INCREMENT ,
`BlogEntryId` INT NOT NULL ,
`Name` VARCHAR( 100 ) NOT NULL ,
`Message` VARCHAR( 255 ) NOT NULL ,
`Date` DATETIME NOT NULL ,
PRIMARY KEY (`CommentId`)
) COMMENT = 'Blog Comments';
```

The SQL query to run this is:

```
select CommentId,Name,LEFT(Message, 50)
from BlogComments order by Date desc
limit 0,1
```

This query returns the comment ID (which is autogenerated), the name of the person who left the comment, and the first 50 characters of the message text (using the LEFT() function) for the most recent comment. The 50 characters are used as a preview of the actual comment (you probably don't want to get the entire message because it could be long).

The page that runs this query is called CheckComments.php, and it outputs a string in the following format:

```
<comment ID>||<name>||<message>
```

This format allows the JavaScript Array.split() method to be used in order to extract the individual pieces of information with little effort. If there are no comments or there is an error, the comment ID will be -1 and the other parts of the string will be blank. Here is the complete code listing for CheckComments.php:

```php
<?php
    header("Cache-control: No-Cache");
    header("Pragma: No-Cache");

    //database information
    $sDBServer = "your.database.server";
    $sDBName = "your_db_name";
    $sDBUsername = "your_db_username";
    $sDBPassword = "your_db_password";

    //create the SQL query string
    $sSQL = "select CommentId,Name,LEFT(Message, 50) as ShortMessage from
BlogComments order by Date desc limit 0,1";

    $oLink = mysql_connect($sDBServer,$sDBUsername,$sDBPassword);
    @mysql_select_db($sDBName) or die("-1|| || ");

    if($oResult = mysql_query($sSQL) and mysql_num_rows($oResult) > 0) {
        $aValues = mysql_fetch_array($oResult,MYSQL_ASSOC);
        echo $aValues['CommentId']."||".$aValues['Name']."||".
            $aValues['ShortMessage'];
    } else {
        echo "-1|| || ";
    }

    mysql_free_result($oResult);
    mysql_close($oLink);
?>
```

Perhaps the most important parts of this file are the two headers included at the top. By setting Cache-control and Pragma to No-Cache, you are telling the browser to always retrieve this file from the server and not from the client cache. Without this, some browsers would return the same information repeatedly, effectively nullifying this functionality altogether. The rest of this file should look very familiar, as it uses essentially the same algorithm as previous examples that make use of MySQL database calls.

> *You can also avoid caching problems by changing the query string every time a request is made to this file. This is often done by assigning a timestamp into the query string to trick the browser into getting a fresh copy from the server.*

Next comes the JavaScript that calls this file. To start, you'll need a few global variables once again:

```javascript
var oXmlHttp = null;         //The XMLHttp object
var iInterval = 1000;        //The interval to check (in milliseconds)
var iLastCommentId = -1;     //The ID of the last comment received
var divNotification = null;  //The layer to display the notification
```

As usual, the first global variable is an XMLHttp object called oXmlHttp, which will be used for all requests. The second variable, iInterval, specifies the number of milliseconds that should occur between each check for new comments. In this case it is set to 1000 milliseconds, or 1 second, although this can and should be customized based on your needs. Next, the iLastCommentId variable is used to store the last comment ID in the database. It is by comparing this value to the most recently retrieved comment ID that you can determine whether a new comment has been added. The last variable, divNotification, holds a reference to the <div/> element that is used to display a notification to the user about new comments.

When a new comment is detected, divNotification is filled with information about the new comment, including the name of the person making the comment, a summary of the message, and a link to view the entire comment. If the <div/> element hasn't yet been created, it must be created and assigned the appropriate style information:

```
function showNotification(sName, sMessage) {
    if (!divNotification) {
        divNotification = document.createElement("div");
        divNotification.className = "notification";
        document.body.appendChild(divNotification);
    }

    divNotification.innerHTML = "<strong>New Comment</strong><br />" + sName
                 + " says: " + sMessage + "...<br /><a href=\"ViewComment.php?id="
                 + iLastCommentId + "\">View</a>";
    divNotification.style.top = document.body.scrollTop + "px";
    divNotification.style.left = document.body.scrollLeft + "px";
    divNotification.style.display = "block";
    setTimeout(function () {
        divNotification.style.display = "none";
    }, 5000);
}
```

As you can see, the showNotification() function accepts two arguments: a name and a message. However, before this information is used, you must ensure that divNotification is not null. If necessary, a new <div/> element is created and its CSS class set to notification before being added to the document's body. After that, the innerHTML property is used to set the notification HTML, which says "New Comment" in bold, followed by the name, the message, and the link to view the comment. The link points to ViewComment.php and assigns a query string parameter id the value of iLastCommentId, which indicates the comment to view. Then, the position of the notification is set by using the scrollTop and scrollLeft properties of document.body. This ensures that the notification is always visible at the upper-left corner of the page regardless of the scroll position (if you have scrolled down or right). Following that, the display property is set to block to make the notification visible.

The last part of this function is a timeout that hides the notification after 5 seconds (5000 milliseconds). It's not a good idea to leave the notification up unless you have a spot specifically designated for such a purpose in your design; otherwise, you could be covering up important information.

In this example, the notification CSS class is defined as follows:

```
div.notification {
    border: 1px solid red;
    padding: 10px;
    background-color: white;
    position: absolute;
    display: none;
    top: 0px;
    left: 0px;
}
```

This creates a white box with a red border around it. Of course, you'll want to style this in a manner that's appropriate for the site or application in which it is used. The important parts for this example are that `position` is set to `absolute` and `display` is set to `none`. Setting both properties ensures that when the `<div/>` element is added to the page, it won't interrupt the normal page flow or move any elements around. The result is a notification area, as displayed in Figure 3-4.

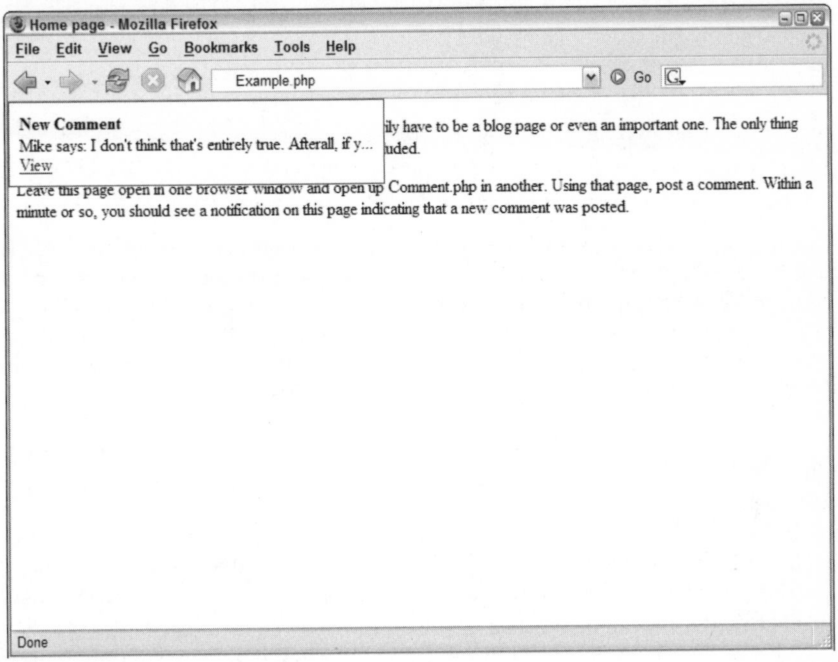

Figure 3-4

Back to the JavaScript. The function that does the most work is `checkComments()`, which is responsible for checking the server for updates. The code is very similar to the previous examples:

```
function checkComments() {
    if (!oXmlHttp) {
        oXmlHttp = zXmlHttp.createRequest();
    } else if (oXmlHttp.readyState != 0) {
        oXmlHttp.abort();
    }

    oXmlHttp.open("get", "CheckComments.php", true);
    oXmlHttp.onreadystatechange = function () {

        if (oXmlHttp.readyState == 4) {
            if (oXmlHttp.status == 200) {

                var aData = oXmlHttp.responseText.split("||");
                if (aData[0] != iLastCommentId) {

                    if (iLastCommentId != -1) {
```

```
                        showNotification(aData[1], aData[2]);
                }

                iLastCommentId = aData[0];
        }

        setTimeout(checkComments, iInterval);
    }
};

oXmlHttp.send(null);

}
```

This function creates an XMLHttp object and calls CheckComments.php asynchronously. The important part of this code is highlighted (the rest is almost exactly the same as the previous examples). In this section, the responseText is split into an array using the split() method. The first value in the array, aData[0], is the comment ID that was added last. If it isn't equal to the last comment ID stored, then a notification may be needed. Next, if the last comment ID is -1, no comment IDs have been retrieved and thus a notification should not be shown. If the last comment ID is not -1, at least one comment ID has been retrieved and since it's different from the one just received from the server, the notification should be displayed. After that, the new ID is assigned to iLastCommentId for future use. The very last step in the event handler is to set another timeout for checkComments(), to continue checking for more comments.

The final step in the process is to initiate a call to checkComments() once the page has loaded. This will retrieve the most recent comment ID in the database but won't display a notification (because iLastCommentId will be equal to –1 initially). When the next call is made to checkComments(), the ID retrieved from the database can be checked against the one stored in iLastCommentId to determine if a notification must be displayed. As usual, this functionality should be initiated only if the browser supports XMLHttp:

```
window.onload = function () {
    if (zXmlHttp.isSupported()) {
        checkComments();
    }
};
```

That's all it takes to create this Periodic Refresh solution. You need only remember to include the necessary JavaScript and CSS files in any page that you would like this functionality on.

> The files for this example are available for download at www.wrox.com. Along with those files are other pages you can use to add and view comments for the purpose of testing.

Multi-Stage Download

One of the lasting problems on the Web has been the speed at which pages download. When everyone was using 56 Kbps modems, web designers were much more aware of how much their pages "weighed" (the size of the page in total bytes). With the popularity of residential broadband Internet solutions, many sites have upgraded, including multimedia, more pictures, and more content. This approach, while giving the user more information, also leads to slower download times as everything is loaded in seemingly random order. Fortunately, there is an Ajax solution for this problem.

Multi-Stage Download is an Ajax pattern wherein only the most basic functionality is loaded into a page initially. Upon completion, the page then begins to download other components that should appear on the page. If the user should leave the page before all of the components are downloaded, it's of no consequence. If, however, the user stays on the page for an extended period of time (perhaps reading an article), the extra functionality is loaded in the background and available when the user is ready. The major advantage here is that you, as the developer, get to decide what is downloaded and at what point in time.

This is a fairly new Ajax pattern and has been popularized by Microsoft's start.com. When you first visit start.com, it is a very simple page with a search box in the middle. Behind the scenes, however, a series of requests is being fired off to fill in more content on the page. Within a few seconds, the page jumps to life as content from several different locations is pulled in and displayed.

Although nice, Multi-Stage Download does have a downside: the page must work in its simplest form for browsers that don't support Ajax technologies. This means that all the basic functionality must work without any additional downloads. The typical way of dealing with this problem is to provide *graceful degradation*, meaning that those browsers that support Ajax technologies will get the more extensive interface while other browsers get a simple, bare-bones interface. This is especially important if you are expecting search engines to crawl your site; since these bots don't support JavaScript, they rely solely on the HTML in the page to determine your site's value.

Additional Information Links Example

When reading through an article online, frequently there are Additional Information links included for further reading on the topic. The key question here is this: What is the main content? Clearly the article text is the main content on the page, so it should be downloaded when the page is initially loaded. The additional links aren't as important, so they can be loaded later. This example walks you through the creation of such a solution.

First, you'll need to lay out a page to hold the article. For this example, it's a very simple layout:

```
<!DOCTYPE html PUBLIC "-//W3C//DTD XHTML 1.0 Transitional//EN"
    "http://www.w3.org/TR/xhtml1/DTD/xhtml1-transitional.dtd">
<html xmlns="http://www.w3.org/1999/xhtml" xml:lang="en" lang="en">
    <head>
        <title>Article Example</title>
        <script type="text/javascript" src="zxml.js"></script>
        <script type="text/javascript" src="Article.js"></script>
        <link rel="stylesheet" type="text/css" href="Article.css" />
    </head>
    <body>
        <h1>Article Title</h1>
        <div id="divAdditionalLinks"></div>
        <div id="divPage1">
            <!-- article content here -->
        </div>
    </body>
</html>
```

The important part of the HTML is the `<div/>` with the ID of `divAdditionalLinks`. This is the container for the additional links that will be downloaded for the article. By default, it is styled to be right aligned and invisible:

```css
#divAdditionalLinks {
    float: right;
    padding: 10px;
    border: 1px solid navy;
    background-color: #cccccc;
    display: none;
}
```

It's very important that the CSS `display` property be set to `none` so that the empty `<div/>` element doesn't take up any space in the page layout. Without this, you would see a small empty box to the right of the article.

Unlike the previous examples, the content to download is just plain text contained in a text file containing links and a header. This file, `AdditionalLinks.txt`, contains some simple HTML code:

```html
<h4>Additional Information</h4>
<ul>
    <li><a href="http://www.wrox.com">Wrox</a></li>
    <li><a href="http://www.nczonline.net">NCZOnline</a></li>
    <li><a href="http://www.wdonline.com">XWeb</a></li>
</ul>
```

This file could just as well be created dynamically using server-side logic, but for the purposes of this example, static content works just as well.

The JavaScript that makes this work is very simple and quite similar to all the previous examples in this chapter:

```javascript
function downloadLinks() {
    var oXmlHttp = zXmlHttp.createRequest();

    oXmlHttp.open("get", "AdditionalLinks.txt", true);
    oXmlHttp.onreadystatechange = function () {
        if (oXmlHttp.readyState == 4) {
            if (oXmlHttp.status == 200) {
                var divAdditionalLinks =
                                document.getElementById("divAdditionalLinks");
                divAdditionalLinks.innerHTML = oXmlHttp.responseText;
                divAdditionalLinks.style.display = "block";
            }
        }
    }
    oXmlHttp.send(null);
}

window.onload = function () {
    if (zXmlHttp.isSupported()) {
        downloadLinks();
    }
};
```

The function that does the work is `downloadLinks()`, which is called only if the browser supports XMLHttp and only once the page is completely loaded. The code inside of `downloadLinks()` is the standard XMLHttp algorithm that you've used before. After the content from `AdditionalLinks.txt` has been retrieved, it is set into the placeholder `<div/>` using the `innerHTML` property. The last step in the process is to set the `<div/>` element's `display` property to `block` so it can be seen. The end result is displayed in Figure 3-5.

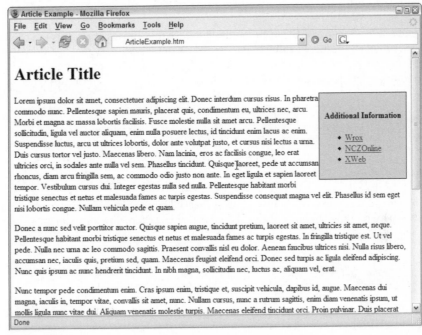

Figure 3-5

If XMLHttp isn't supported in the browser, the block containing the additional links will never appear and so the first paragraph will stretch all the way across the top.

This technique can be done numerous times for any number of sections of a page; you certainly aren't restricted to having only one section that is loaded after the initial page is complete. You can create new XMLHttp objects for each request and then send them off one after the other, or you can do it sequentially, waiting until a response has been received before sending off the next request. The choice is completely up to you and your desired functionality.

Fallback Patterns

The previous section dealt with when to send or receive data from the server, which presupposes that everything goes according to plan on the server-side: the request is received, the necessary changes are made, and the appropriate response is sent to the client. But what happens if there's an error on the server? Or worse yet, what if the request never makes it to the server? When developing Ajax applications, it is imperative that you plan ahead for these problems and describe how your application should work if one of these should occur.

Cancel Pending Requests

If an error occurs on the server, meaning a status of something other than 200 is returned, you need to decide what to do. Chances are that if a file is not found (404) or an internal server error occurred (302), trying again in a few minutes isn't going to help since both of these require an administrator to fix the problem. The simplest way to deal with this situation is to simply cancel all pending requests. You can set a flag somewhere in your code that says, "don't send any more requests." This clearly has the highest impact on solutions using the Periodic Refresh pattern.

The comment notification example can be modified to take this into account. This is a case where the Ajax solution provides additional value to the user but is not the primary focus of the page. If a request fails, there is no reason to alert the user; you can simply cancel any future requests to prevent any further errors from occurring. To do so, you must add a global variable that indicates whether requests are enabled:

```
var oXmlHttp = null;
var iInterval = 1000;
var iLastCommentId = -1;
var divNotification = null;
var blnRequestsEnabled = true;
```

Now, the `blnRequestsEnabled` variable must be checked before any request is made. This can be accomplished by wrapping the body of the `checkComments()` function inside of an `if` statement:

```
function checkComments() {

    if (blnRequestsEnabled) {
        if (!oXmlHttp) {
            oXmlHttp = zXmlHttp.createRequest();
        } else if (oXmlHttp.readyState != 0) {
            oXmlHttp.abort();
        }

        oXmlHttp.open("get", "CheckComments.php", true);
        oXmlHttp.onreadystatechange = function () {
            if (oXmlHttp.readyState == 4) {
                if (oXmlHttp.status == 200) {
                    var aData = oXmlHttp.responseText.split("||");
                    if (aData[0] != iLastCommentId) {
                        if (iLastCommentId != -1) {
                            showNotification(aData[1], aData[2]);
                        }
                        iLastCommentId = aData[0];
                    }
                    setTimeout(checkComments, iInterval);
                }
            }
        };

        oXmlHttp.send(null);
    }
}
```

But that isn't all that must be done; you must also detect the two different types of errors that may occur: server errors that give status codes and a failure to reach the server (either the server is down or the Internet connection is lost).

To begin, wrap everything inside of the initial `if` statement inside a `try...catch` block. Different browsers react at different times when a server can't be reached, but they all throw errors. Wrapping the entire request block in a `try...catch` ensures you catch any error that is thrown, at which point you can set `blnRequestsEnabled` to `false`. Next, for server errors, you can throw a custom error whenever the status is not equal to `200`. This will be caught by the `try...catch` block and have the same effect as if the server couldn't be reached (setting `blnRequestsEnabled` to `false`):

```
function checkComments() {

    if (blnRequestsEnabled) {
        try {
            if (!oXmlHttp) {
                oXmlHttp = zXmlHttp.createRequest();
            } else if (oXmlHttp.readyState != 0) {
                oXmlHttp.abort();
            }

            oXmlHttp.open("get", "CheckComments.php", true);
            oXmlHttp.onreadystatechange = function () {

                if (oXmlHttp.readyState == 4) {
                    if (oXmlHttp.status == 200) {

                        var aData = oXmlHttp.responseText.split("||");
                        if (aData[0] != iLastCommentId) {

                            if (iLastCommentId != -1) {
                                showNotification(aData[1], aData[2]);
                            }

                            iLastCommentId = aData[0];
                        }

                        setTimeout(checkComments, iInterval);
                    } else {
                        throw new Error("An error occurred.");
                    }
                }
            };

            oXmlHttp.send(null);
        } catch (oException) {
            blnRequestsEnabled = false;
        }
    }
}
```

Now, when either of the two error types occurs, an error will be thrown (either by the browser or by you) and the `blnRequestsEnabled` variable will be set to `false`, effectively canceling any further requests if `checkComments()` is called again.

> You may also have noticed that a timeout for another request is created only if the status is 200, which prevents another request from occurring for any other status. That works fine for server errors, but it doesn't do anything for communication errors. It's always better to have more than one way to handle errors when they occur.

Try Again

Another option when dealing with errors is to silently keep trying for either a specified amount of time or a particular number of tries. Once again, unless the Ajax functionality is key to the user's experience, there is no need to notify him or her about the failure. It is best to handle the problem behind the scenes until it can be resolved.

To illustrate the Try Again pattern, consider the Multi-Stage Download example. In that example, extra links were downloaded and displayed alongside the article. If an error occurred during the request, an error message would pop up in most browsers. The user would have no idea what the error was or what caused it, so why bother displaying a message at all? Instead, it would make much more sense to continue trying to download the information a few times before giving up.

To track the number of failed attempts, a global variable is necessary:

```
var iFailed = 0;
```

The `iFailed` variable starts at 0 and is incremented every time a request fails. So, if `iFailed` is ever greater than a specific number, you can just cancel the request because it is clearly not going to work. If, for example, you want to try ten times before canceling all pending requests, you can do the following:

```
function downloadLinks() {
    var oXmlHttp = zXmlHttp.createRequest();

    if (iFailed < 10) {
        try {
            oXmlHttp.open("get", "AdditionalLinks.txt", true);
            oXmlHttp.onreadystatechange = function () {
                if (oXmlHttp.readyState == 4) {
                    if (oXmlHttp.status == 200) {
                        var divAdditionalLinks =
                                    document.getElementById("divAdditionalLinks");
                        divAdditionalLinks.innerHTML = oXmlHttp.responseText;
                        divAdditionalLinks.style.display = "block";
                    } else {
                        throw new Error("An error occurred.");
                    }
                }
```

```
            }

        oXmlHttp.send(null);
    } catch (oException) {
        iFailed++;
        downloadLinks();
    }
  }
}
```

This code is constructed similarly to the previous example. The `try...catch` block is used to catch any errors that may occur during the communication, and a custom error is thrown when the `status` isn't `200`. The main difference is that when an error is caught, the `iFailed` variable is incremented and `downloadLinks()` is called again. As long as `iFailed` is less than 10 (meaning it's failed less than ten times), another request will be fired off to attempt the download.

In general, the Try Again pattern should be used only when the request is intended to occur only once, as in a Multi-Stage Download. If you try to use this pattern with interval-driven requests, such as Periodic Refresh, you could end up with an ever-increasing number of open requests taking up memory.

Summary

In this chapter, you learned about various design patterns for Ajax solutions. You first learned about how to use Predictive Fetch to improve the user experience through preloading information that is likely to be used in the future. You created an example using Predictive Fetch to preload pages in an article after a few seconds, when it is likely that the user intends to read the entire article.

Next, you learned about Submission Throttling, which is a way of incrementally sending data to the server instead of doing it all at once. You learned how to use this pattern for data validation in a form. It's sibling pattern, Periodic Refresh, was also discussed, which periodically receives information from the server. You built an example using Periodic Refresh that displays a notification when a new comment has been posted to a blog or message board.

This chapter also introduced you to the Multi-Stage Download pattern, which is a way of continuing to download extra information after the page has loaded. You learned that this would lead to faster initial download time for pages and that you can control the frequency and sequence of requests in any way you see fit.

The last section discussed fallback patterns that are used to handle errors in client-server communication. You learned that there are two types of errors you may encounter: server errors (such as 404 not found) or communication errors (where the server cannot be contacted). Two patterns, Cancel Pending Requests and Try Again, were discussed as ways of dealing with these errors.

XML, XPath, and XSLT

As the popularity of XML grew, web developers wanted to use the technology on both the server- and client-side, but only the former initially offered XML functionality. Starting with Internet Explorer 5.0 and Mozilla 1.0, Microsoft and Mozilla began to support XML through JavaScript in their browsers. Recently, Apple and Opera added some XML support to their browsers, albeit not to the extent that Microsoft and Mozilla have. Browser makers continue to broaden the availability of XML support with new features, giving web developers powerful tools akin to those formerly found only on the server.

In this chapter, you will learn how to load and manipulate XML documents in an XML DOM object, use XPath to select XML nodes that meet certain criteria, and transform XML documents into HTML using XSLT.

XML Support in Browsers

Many web browsers are available today, but few have as complete support for XML and its related technologies as Internet Explorer (IE) and Mozilla Firefox. Although other browsers are starting to catch up, with Safari and Opera now able to open XML documents, the functionality is either incomplete or incorrect. Because of these issues, this chapter focuses primarily on the implementations in IE and Firefox.

XML DOM in IE

When Microsoft added XML support to IE 5.0, they did so by incorporating the MSXML ActiveX library, a component originally written to parse Active Channels in IE 4.0. This original version wasn't intended for public use, but developers became aware of the component and began using it. Microsoft responded with a fully upgraded version of MSXML, which was included in IE 4.01.

MSXML was primarily an IE-only component until 2001 when Microsoft released MSXML 3.0, a separate distribution available through the company's web site. Later that year, version 4.0 was released and MSXML was renamed Microsoft XML Core Services Component. Since its inception, MSXML has gone from a basic, non-validating XML parser to a full-featured component that can validate XML documents, perform XSL transformations, support namespace usage, the Simple API for XML (SAX), and the W3C XPath and XML Schema standards, all while improving performance with each new version.

To create an ActiveX object in JavaScript, Microsoft implemented a new class called `ActiveXObject` that can be used to instantiate a number of ActiveX objects. Its constructor takes one argument, a string containing the version of the ActiveX object to create; in this case, it is the version of the XML document. The first XML DOM ActiveX object was called `Microsoft.XmlDom`, whose creation looks like this:

```
var oXmlDom = new ActiveXObject("Microsoft.XmlDom");
```

The newly created XML DOM object behaves like any other DOM object, enabling you to traverse the DOM tree and manipulate DOM nodes.

At the time of this writing, there are five different versions of the MSXML DOM document, and their version strings are as follows:

❑ Microsoft.XmlDom

❑ MSXML2.DOMDocument

❑ MSXML2.DOMDocument.3.0

❑ MSXML2.DOMDocument.4.0

❑ MSXML2.DOMDocument.5.0

> **MSXML is an ActiveX implementation; therefore, it is available only on Windows platforms. IE 5 on the Mac has no XML DOM support.**

Because there are five different versions, and you presumably always want to use the latest, it is helpful to use a function to determine which version to use. Doing so ensures you the most up-to-date support and the highest performance. The following function, `createDocument()`, enables you to create the correct MSXML DOM document:

```
function createDocument() {
    var aVersions = [ "MSXML2.DOMDocument.5.0",
        "MSXML2.DOMDocument.4.0","MSXML2.DOMDocument.3.0",
        "MSXML2.DOMDocument","Microsoft.XmlDom"
    ];

    for (var i = 0; i < aVersions.length; i++) {
        try {
            var oXmlDom = new ActiveXObject(aVersions[i]);
            return oXmlDom;
        } catch (oError) {
            //Do nothing
```

```
        }
    }
    throw new Error("MSXML is not installed.");
}
```

This function iterates through the aVersions array, which contains the version strings of MSXML DOM documents. It starts with the latest version, MSXML2.DOMDocument.5.0, and attempts to create the DOM document. If the object creation is successful, it is returned and createDocument() exits; if it fails, an error is thrown and then caught by the try...catch block, so the loop continues and the next version is tried. If the creation of an MSXML DOM document fails, a thrown error states that MSXML is not installed. This function is not a class, so its usage looks like any other function that returns a value:

```
var oXmlDom = createDocument();
```

Using createDocument() will ensure that the most up-to-date DOM document is used. Now that you have an XML document at your disposal, it is time to load some XML data.

Loading XML Data in IE

MSXML supports two methods to load XML: load() and loadXML(). The load() method loads an XML file at a specific location on the Web. As with XMLHttp, the load() method enables you to load the data in two modes: asynchronously or synchronously. By default, the load() method is asynchronous; to use synchronous mode, the MSXML object's async property must be set to false, as follows:

```
oXmlDom.async = false;
```

When in asynchronous mode, the MSXML object exposes the readyState property, which has the same five states as the XMLHttp readyState property.

Additionally, the DOM document supports the onreadystatechange event handler, enabling you to monitor the readyState property. Because asynchronous mode is the default, setting the async property to true is optional:

```
oXmlDom.async = true;

oXmlDom.onreadystatechange = function () {
    if (oXmlDom.readyState == 4) {
        //Do something when the document is fully loaded.
    }
};

oXmlDom.load("myxml.xml");
```

In this example, the fictitious XML document named myxml.xml is loaded into the XML DOM. When the readyState reaches the value of 4, the document is fully loaded and the code inside the if block will execute.

The second way to load XML data, loadXML(), differs from the load() method in that the former loads XML from a string. This string must contain well-formed XML, as in the following example:

```
var sXml = "<root><person><name>Jeremy McPeak</name></person></root>";

oXmlDom.loadXML(sXml);
```

Here, the XML data contained in the variable sXml is loaded into the oXmlDom document. There is no reason to check the readyState property or to set the async property when using loadXML() because it doesn't involve a server request.

Traversing the XML DOM in IE

Navigating an XML DOM is much like navigating an HTML DOM: it is a hierarchical node structure. At the top of the tree is the documentElement property, which contains the root element of the document. From there, you can access any element or attribute in the document using the properties listed in Table 4-1.

Table 4-1 XML DOM Properties

Property	Description
attributes	Contains an array of attributes for this node.
childNodes	Contains an array of child nodes.
firstChild	Refers to the first direct child of the node.
lastChild	Refers to the last child of the node.
nextSibling	Returns the node immediately following the current node.
nodeName	Returns the qualified name of the node.
nodeType	Specifies the XML DOM node type of the node.
nodeValue	Contains the text associated with the node.
ownerDocument	Returns the root element of the document.
parentNode	Refers to the parent node of the current node.
previousSibling	Returns the node immediately before the current node.
text	Returns the content of the node or the concatenated text of the current node and its descendants. It is an IE-only property.
xml	Returns the XML of the current node and its children as a string. It is an IE-only property.

Traversing and retrieving data from the DOM is a straight-forward process. Consider the following XML document:

```
<?xml version="1.0" encoding="utf-8"?>

<books>
    <book isbn="0471777781">Professional Ajax</book>
    <book isbn="0764579088">Professional JavaScript for Web Developers</book>
    <book isbn="0764557599">Professional C#</book>
    <book isbn="1861002025">Professional Visual Basic 6 Databases</book>
</books>
```

This simple XML document includes a root element, <books/>, with four child <book/> elements. Using this document as a reference, you can explore the DOM. The DOM tree is based on the relationships nodes have with other nodes. One node may contain other nodes, or child nodes. Another node may share the same parent as other nodes, which are siblings.

Perhaps you want to retrieve the first <book/> element in the document. This is easily achieved with the firstChild property:

```
var oRoot = oXmlDom.documentElement;

var oFirstBook = oRoot.firstChild;
```

The assignment of the documentElement to oRoot will save space and typing, although it is not necessary. Using the firstChild property, the first <book/> element is referenced and assigned to the variable oFirstBook because it is the first child element of the root element <books/>.

You can also use the childNodes collection to achieve the same results:

```
var oFirstBook2 = oRoot.childNodes[0];
```

Selecting the first item in the childNodes collection returns the first child of the node. Because childNodes is a NodeList in JavaScript, you can retrieve the amount of children a node has by using the length property, as follows:

```
var iChildren = oRoot.childNodes.length;
```

In this example, the integer 4 is assigned to iChildren because there are four child nodes of the document element.

As already discussed, nodes can have children, which means they can have parents, too. The parentNode property selects the parent of the current node:

```
var oParent = oFirstBook.parentNode;
```

You saw oFirstBook earlier in this section, but as a quick refresher, it is the first <book/> element in the document. The parentNode property of this node refers to the <books/> element, the documentElement of the DOM.

What if your current node is a book element and you want to select another book element? The <book/> elements are siblings to each other because they share the same direct parent. Two properties, nextSibling and previousSibling, exist to select adjacent nodes to the current node. The nextSibling property references the next occurring sibling, whereas the previousSibling property selects the preceding sibling:

```
var oSecondBook = oFirstBook.nextSibling;

oFirstBook2 = oSecondBook.previousSibling;
```

In this code, the second <book/> element is referenced and assigned to oSecondBook. The oFirstBook2 variable is then reassigned to reference the oSecondBook sibling immediately before it, resulting in oFirstBook2 to contain the same value as it did before. If a node has no siblings after it, then nextSibling is null. The same holds true for previousSibling; if there is no sibling immediately before the current node, previousSibling is null.

Now that you know how to traverse through the document hierarchy, you should know how to retrieve data from nodes in the tree. For example, to retrieve the text contained within the third <book/> element, you could use the text property, as follows:

```
var sText = oRoot.childNodes[2].text;
```

The text property retrieves all the text nodes contained within this node and is a Microsoft proprietary property, but it is extremely helpful. Without the text property, you would have to access the text node as follows:

```
var sText = oRoot.childNodes[2].firstChild.nodeValue;
```

This code achieves the same results as using the text property. Like the previous example, the third <book/> element is referenced using the childNodes collection; the text node of the <book/> element is then referenced with the use of firstChild because a text node is still a node in the DOM. The text is then retrieved by using the nodeValue property that retrieves the value of the current node.

The results from these two examples are identical; however, the text property behaves in a different way than using the nodeValue property on a text node. The text property retrieves the value of all text nodes contained within the element and its children, whereas the nodeValue property gets only the value of the current node. It is a helpful property, but it has the potential to return more text than desired. For example, consider this modified XML document:

```
<?xml version="1.0" encoding="utf-8"?>

<books>

    <book isbn="0471777781">
        <title>Professional Ajax</title>
        <author>Nicholas C. Zakas, Jeremy McPeak, Joe Fawcett</author>
    </book>
    <book isbn="0764579088">Professional JavaScript for Web Developers</book>
    <book isbn="0764557599">Professional C#</book>
    <book isbn="1861002025">Professional Visual Basic 6 Databases</book>
</books>
```

This new XML document adds two new children to the first `<book/>` element: the `<title/>` element, which contains the title of the book, and the `<author/>` element, which holds the author data. Once again, use the `text` property:

```
alert(oFirstChild.text);
```

There is nothing new in this code, as you have already seen it. However, look at the results, as shown in Figure 4-1.

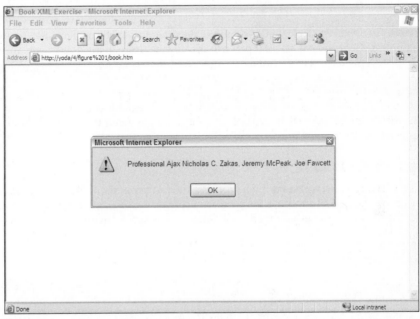

Figure 4-1

Notice that the text nodes from the `<title/>` and `<author/>` elements are retrieved and concatenated. This is how `text` differs from `nodeValue`. The `nodeValue` property retrieves only the value of the current node, whereas the `text` property retrieves all text nodes contained in the current node and its children.

MSXML also provides a number of methods to retrieve specific nodes or values; the two most often used are `getAttribute()` and `getElementsByTagName()`.

The `getAttribute()` method takes a string argument containing the name of the attribute and returns that attribute's value. If the attribute does not exist, the value returned is `null`. Using the same XML document introduced earlier in this section, consider the following code:

```
var sAttribute = oFirstChild.getAttribute("isbn");

alert(sAttribute);
```

This code retrieves the value of the `isbn` attribute of the first `<book/>` element and assigns it to the `sAttribute` variable. This value is then used in the `alert()` method to display the value.

The `getElementsByTagName()` method returns a `NodeList` of child elements with the name specified by its argument. This method searches for elements within the given node only, so the returned `NodeList` does not include any external elements. For example:

```
var cBooks = oRoot.getElementsByTagName("book");

alert(cBooks.length);
```

This code retrieves all `<book/>` elements within the document and returns the `NodeList` to `cBooks`. With the sample XML document, an alert box will display that four `<book/>` elements were found. To retrieve all child elements, pass `"*"` as the parameter to `getElementsByTagName()`, as follows:

```
var cElements = oRoot.getElementsByTagName("*");
```

Because the example XML document contains only `<book/>` elements, the resulting `NodeList` of this code sample matches that of the previous example.

Retrieving XML Data in IE

Retrieving XML data is as simple as using a property, the `xml` property. This property serializes the XML data of the current node. *Serialization* is the process of converting objects into an easily storable or transmittable format. The `xml` property converts XML into a string representation, complete with tag names, attributes, and text:

```
var sXml = oRoot.xml;

alert(sXml);
```

This code serializes the XML data starting with the document element, which is then passed to the `alert()` method. A portion of the serialized XML looks like this:

```
<books><book isbn="0471777781">Professional Ajax</book></books>
```

You can load serialized data into another XML DOM object, send to a server application, or pass to another page. The serialized XML data returned by the `xml` property depends on the current node. Using the `xml` property at the `documentElement` node returns the XML data of the entire document, whereas using it on a `<book/>` element returns only the XML data contained in that `<book/>` element.

The `xml` property is read-only. If you want to add elements to the document, you will have to use DOM methods to do so.

Manipulating the DOM in IE

Until this point, you have learned how to traverse the DOM, extract information from it, and convert XML into string format. You also have the ability to add to, delete from, and replace nodes in the DOM.

Creating Nodes

You can create a variety of nodes using DOM methods, the first of which is an element with the `createElement()` method. This method takes one argument, a string containing the tag name of the element to create, and returns an `XMLDOMElement` reference:

```
var oNewBook = oXmlDom.createElement("book");

oXmlDom.documentElement.appendChild(oNewBook);
```

This code creates a new `<book/>` element and appends it to `documentElement` with the `appendChild()` method. The `appendChild()` method appends the new element, specified by its argument, as the last child node. This code, however, appends an empty `<book/>` element to the document, so the element needs some text:

```
var oNewBook = oXmlDom.createElement("book");


var oNewBookText = oXmlDom.createTextNode("Professional .NET 2.0 Generics");

oNewBook.appendChild(oNewBookText);

oXmlDom.documentElement.appendChild(oNewBook);
```

This code creates a text node with the `createTextNode()` method and appends it to the newly created `<book/>` element with `appendChild()`. The `createTextNode()` method takes a string argument specifying the value applied to the text node.

At this point, you have programmatically created a new `<book/>` element, provided it a text node, and appended it to the document. One last piece of information is required to get this new element on par with its other siblings, the `isbn` attribute. Creating an attribute is as simple as using the `setAttribute()` method, which is available on every element node:

```
var oNewBook = oXmlDom.createElement("book");

var oNewBookText = oXmlDom.createTextNode("Professional .NET 2.0 Generics");
oNewBook.appendChild(oNewBookText);

oNewBook.setAttribute("isbn","0764559885");

oXmlDom.documentElement.appendChild(oNewBook);
```

The new line of code in this example creates an `isbn` attribute and assigns it the value of `0764559885`. The `setAttribute()` method takes two string arguments: the first is the name of the attribute, and the second is the value to assign to the attribute. IE also provides other methods to add attributes to an element; however, they hold no real advantage over `setAttribute()` and require much more coding.

Removing, Replacing, and Inserting Nodes

If you can add nodes to a document, it seems only natural to be able to remove them as well. The `removeChild()` method does just that. This method has one argument: the node to remove. Suppose, for example, that you want to remove the first `<book/>` element from the document. You could use the following code:

```
var oRemovedChild = oRoot.removeChild(oRoot.firstChild);
```

The `removeChild()` method returns the removed child node, so `oRemoveChild` now references the removed `<book/>` element. You now have a reference to the old node, so you can place it anywhere else into the document.

Perhaps you want to replace the third `<book/>` element with `oRemovedChild`. The `replaceChild()` does that and returns the replaced node:

```
var oReplacedChild = oRoot.replaceChild(oRemovedChild, oRoot.childNodes[2]);
```

The `replaceChild()` method accepts two arguments: the node to add and the node to replace. In this code, the node referenced by `oRemovedChild` replaces the third `<book/>` element, and the replaced node is now referenced by `oReplacedChild`.

Because `oReplacedChild` references the replaced node, you can easily insert it into the document. You could use `appendChild()` to add the node to the end of the child list, or you can use the `insertBefore()` method to insert the node before another sibling:

```
oRoot.insertBefore(oReplacedChild, oRoot.lastChild);
```

This code inserts the previously replaced node before the last `<book/>` element. You'll notice the use of the `lastChild` property, which retrieves the last child node, much like `firstChild` selects the first child node. The `insertBefore()` method takes two arguments: the node to insert and the node to insert before. This method also returns the value of the inserted node, but it is not necessary for this example.

As you have seen, the DOM is a powerful interface from which you can retrieve, remove, and add data.

Error Handling in IE

When XML data is loaded, errors can be thrown for a variety of reasons. For example, the external XML file may not be found or the XML may not be well formed. To handle these occasions, MSXML provides the `parseError` object, which contains the error information. This object is a property of every XML DOM document MSXML creates.

To check for errors, the `parseError` object exposes the `errorCode` property, which can be compared to the integer 0; if `errorCode` does not equal 0, an error has occurred. The following example is designed specifically to cause an error:

```
var sXml = "<root><person><name>Jeremy McPeak</name></root>";
var oXmlDom = createDocument();
oXmlDom.loadXML(sXml);

if (oXmlDom.parseError.errorCode != 0) {
    alert("An Error Occurred: " + oXmlDom.parseError.reason);
} else {
    //Code to do for successful load.
}
```

In the highlighted line, notice that the `<person/>` element is not closed. Because the XML being loaded is not well formed, an error occurs. The `errorCode` is then compared to 0; if they do not match (and they don't in this example), an alert will display what caused the error. To do this, it uses the `reason` property of the `parseError` object, which describes the reason for the error.

The `parseError` object provides the following properties to enable you to better understand an error:

- ❑ `errorCode`: The error code as a long integer
- ❑ `filePos`: A long integer specifying the position in the file where the error occurred
- ❑ `line`: The line number that contains the error as a long integer
- ❑ `linePos`: The character position in the line where the error occurred (long integer)
- ❑ `reason`: A string specifying why the error happened
- ❑ `srcText`: The text of the line where the error happened
- ❑ `url`: The URL of the XML document as a string

Although all of these properties provide information about each error, it is up to you which ones make the most sense given your needs.

> The `errorCode` **property can be positive or negative; only when** `errorCode` **is 0 can you be sure that no error occurred.**

XML DOM in Firefox

When it came time to implement the XML DOM in Mozilla Firefox, the developers took a more standards-centric approach in making it a part of the JavaScript implementation. In doing so, Mozilla ensured XML DOM support on all platforms in all Gecko-based browsers.

To create an XML DOM in Firefox, the `createDocument()` method of the `document.implementation` object is called. This method takes three arguments: the first is a string containing the namespace URI for the document to use, the second is a string containing the qualified name of the document's root element, and the third is the type of document (also called *doctype*) to create. To create an empty DOM document, you can do this:

```
var oXmlDom = document.implementation.createDocument("", "", null);
```

By passing in an empty string for the first two arguments, and `null` for the last, you ensure a completely empty document. In fact, there is currently no JavaScript support for doctypes in Firefox, so the third argument must always be `null`. To create an XML DOM with a document element, specify the tag name in the second argument:

```
var oXmlDom = document.implementation.createDocument("", "books", null);
```

This code creates an XML DOM whose `documentElement` is `<books/>`. You can take it a step further and specify a namespace in the creation of the DOM by specifying the namespace URI in the first argument:

```
var oXmlDom = document.implementation.createDocument("http://www.site1.com",
        "books", null);
```

When a namespace is specified in the createDocument() method, Firefox automatically assigns the prefix a0 to represent the namespace URI:

```
<a0:books xmlns:a0="http://www.site1.com" />
```

From here, you can populate the XML document programmatically; generally, however, you will want to load preexisting XML documents into a blank XML DOM object.

Loading XML Data in Firefox

Loading XML into an XML DOM is similar to Microsoft's approach with one glaring difference: Firefox supports only the load() method. Therefore, you can use the same code to load external XML data in both browsers:

```
oXmlDom.load("books.xml");
```

Also like Microsoft, Firefox implemented the async property, and its behavior matches that of Microsoft's: setting async to false forces the document to be loaded in synchronous mode; otherwise, the document is loaded asynchronously.

Another difference between the Firefox and Microsoft XML DOM implementations is that Firefox does not support the readyState property or the onreadystatechange event handler. Instead, it supports the load event and the onload event handler. The load event fires after the document is completely loaded:

```
oXmlDom.load("books.xml");
oXmlDom.onload = function () {
    //Do something when the document is fully loaded.
};
```

As mentioned previously, the loadXML() method does not exist in the Firefox implementation; however, it is possible to emulate the loadXML() behavior through the Firefox DOMParser class. This class has a method called parseFromString(), which loads a string and parses it into a document:

```
var sXml = "<root><person><name>Jeremy McPeak</name></person></root>";
var oParser = new DOMParser();
var oXmlDom = oParser.parseFromString(sXml,"text/xml");
```

In this code, a string of XML is created to pass to the DOMParser parseFromString() method. The two arguments for parseFromString() are the XML string and the content type of the data (typically set to "text/xml"). The parseFromString() method returns an XML DOM object, so you can treat oXmlDom in this code as one.

Retrieving XML Data in Firefox

Despite all their differences, IE and Firefox do share many properties and methods used to retrieve XML data contained in the document. As in IE, you can retrieve the root element of the document by using the documentElement property, as follows:

```
var oRoot = oXmlDom.documentElement;
```

Firefox also supports the W3C standards properties of attributes, childNodes, firstChild, lastChild, nextSibling, nodeName, nodeType, nodeValue, ownerDocument, parentNode, and previousSibling. Unfortunately, Firefox does not support the Microsoft-proprietary text and xml properties, but thanks to its flexibility, you can emulate their behavior.

As a quick recap, the text property returns the content of the node or the concatenated text of the current node and its descendants. Therefore, not only does it return the text of the existing node, but also the text of all child nodes; this is easy enough to emulate. A simple function that takes a node as an argument can provide the same result:

```
function getText(oNode) {
    var sText = "";
    for (var i = 0; i < oNode.childNodes.length; i++) {
        if (oNode.childNodes[i].hasChildNodes()) {
            sText += getText(oNode.childNodes[i]);
        } else {
            sText += oNode.childNodes[i].nodeValue;
        }
    }
    return sText;
}
```

In getText(), sText is used to store every piece of text that is retrieved. As the for loop iterates through the oNode children, each child is checked to see if it contains children. If it does, the childNode is passed through getText() and goes through the same process. If no children exist, then the nodeValue of the current node is added to the string (for text nodes, this is just the text string). After all children have been processed, the function returns sText.

The IE xml property serializes all XML contained in the current node. Firefox accomplishes the same result by providing the XMLSerializer object. This object has a single method that is accessible using JavaScript called serializeToString(). Using this method, XML data is serialized:

```
function serializeXml(oNode) {
    var oSerializer = new XMLSerializer();
    return oSerializer.serializeToString(oNode);
}
```

The serializeXml() function takes an XML node as an argument. An XMLSerializer object is created, and the node is passed to the serializeToString() method. The result of this method, a string representation of the XML data, is returned to the caller.

Firefox shares the same DOM methods for manipulating nodes as IE. Refer to the "Manipulating the DOM in IE" section for a refresher.

Error Handling in Firefox

Firefox, unsurprisingly, handles errors differently from IE. When IE runs into an error, it populates the `parseError` object; when Firefox runs into an error, it loads an XML document containing the error into the XML DOM document. Consider the following example:

```
var sXml = "<root><person><name>Jeremy McPeak</name></root>";
var oParser = new DOMParser();
var oXmlDom = oParser.parseFromString(sXml,"text/xml");

if (oXmlDom.documentElement.tagName != "parsererror") {
    //No error occurred. Do something here.
} else {
    alert("An Error Occurred");
}
```

In the highlighted line, you'll see what will cause the error: a malformed XML string (because the `person/>` element is not closed). When the malformed XML is loaded, the XML DOM object loads an error document with a `documentElement` of `<parsererror/>`. You can easily determine if an error occurred by checking the `documentElement` `tagName` property; if it's not `parsererror`, you can be assured that an error did not occur.

The error document created in this example looks like this:

```
<parsererror xmlns="http://www.mozilla.org/newlayout/xml/parsererror.xml">XML
Parsing Error: mismatched tag. Expected: </person>.
Location: http://yoda/fooreader/test.htm
Line Number 1, Column 43:<sourcetext><root><person><name>Jeremy
McPeak</name></root>
---------------------------------------^</sourcetext></parsererror>
```

All of the information about the error is available as text in the error document. If you want to use this information programmatically, you have to parse it first. The easiest way to do so is to use a rather lengthy regular expression:

```
var reError = />([\s\S]*?)Location:([\s\S]*?)Line Number (\d+), Column
    (\d+):<sourcetext>([\s\S]*?)(?:\-*\^)/;
```

This regular expression divides the error document into five sections: the error message, the file name where the error happened, the line number, the position in the line where the error occurred, and the source code that caused the error. Using the `test()` method of the regular expression object will enable you to use these pieces of data:

```
if (oXmlDom.firstChild.tagName != "parsererror") {
    //No error occurred. Do something here.
} else {
    var oXmlSerializer = new XMLSerializer();
    var sXmlError = oXmlSerializer.serializeToString(oXmlDom);
    var reError = />([\s\S]*?)Location:([\s\S]*?)Line Number (\d+), Column
        (\d+):<sourcetext>([\s\S]*?)(?:\-*\^)/;

    reError.test(sXmlError);
```

The first chunk of data captured by the regular expression is error message, the second is the file name, the third is the line number, the fourth is the position in the line, and the fifth is source code. You can now use this parsed information to create your own error message:

```
var str = "An error occurred!!\n" +
    "Description: " + RegExp.$1 + "\n" +
    "File: " + RegExp.$2 + "\n" +
    "Line: " + RegExp.$3 + "\n" +
    "Line Position: " + RegExp.$4 + "\n" +
    "Source Code: " + RegExp.$5;

alert(str);
```

If an error occurs, an alert box will display the relevant error information in an easy-to-read fashion.

Cross-Browser XML

In an Ajax application, and most JavaScript code, you always need to consider cross-browser differences. When using an XML-based solution in IE and Firefox, you have two options: create your own functions that use the correct code based on the browser, or use a ready-made library. Most of the time it's easiest to use a pre-existing library, such as the zXml library introduced in Chapter 2. Along with XMLHttp support, zXml also has common interfaces for XML operations.

For example, to create an XML DOM document, you can use zXmlDom.createDocument():

```
var oXmlDom = zXmlDom.createDocument();
```

This single line of code can be used instead of doing separate browser-dependent code each time a DOM document is needed. Additionally, zXml adds a host of IE functionality to the standard Firefox DOM document.

One of the major things zXml does for convenience is to add support for the readyState property and the onreadystatechange event handler. Instead of needing to use the separate onload event handler in Firefox, you can write one set of code without browser detection, such as:

```
oXmlDom.onreadystatechange = function () {
    if (oXmlDom.readyState == 4) {
        //Do something when the document is fully loaded.
    }
};
```

The zXml library also adds the xml and text attributes to all nodes in Firefox. Instead of using an XMLSerializer or a standalone function to get these values, you can use them the same way as in IE:

```
var oRoot = oXmlDom.documentElement;

var sFirstChildText = oRoot.firstChild.text;

var sXml = oRoot.xml;
```

zXml also provides a `loadXML()` method for the Firefox DOM document, eliminating the need to use a `DOMParser` object.

```
var oXmlDom2 = zXmlDom.createDocument();

oXmlDom2.loadXML(sXml);
```

Last, the zXml library adds a `parseError` object to the Firefox implementation. This object emulates fairly closely the corresponding object in IE. The one major difference is the `errorCode` property, which is simply set to a non-zero number when an error occurs. Therefore, you shouldn't use this property to look for a specific error, only to see if an error has occurred. Other than that, you can use the other properties as you would in IE:

```
if (oXmlDom.parseError.errorCode != 0) {
    var str = "An error occurred!!\n" +
        "Description: " + oXmlDom.parseError.reason + "\n" +
        "File: " + oXmlDom.parseError.url + "\n" +
        "Line: " + oXmlDom.parseError.line + "\n" +
        "Line Position: " + oXmlDom.parseError.linePos + "\n" +
        "Source Code: " + oXmlDom.parseError.srcText;
    alert(str);
} else {
    //Code to do for successful load.
}
```

You certainly aren't required to use a cross-browser XML library for your solutions, but it can definitely help. The following section develops an example using the zXml library.

A Basic XML Example

XML is a semantic, describing language. Generally, the elements contained in any given XML document describe the data of that document, thus making it a decent data store for static information, or information that doesn't change often.

Imagine you run an online bookstore and have a list of Best Picks whose information is stored in an XML document, `books.xml`. You need to display this information to the user, but you want to do so without using a server component, so you turn to a JavaScript solution. You are going to write a JavaScript solution using the zXml library that will load the XML file, parse through it, and display the information in a web page using DOM methods.

The `books.xml` file contains the following XML data:

```
<?xml version="1.0" encoding="utf-8"?>

<bookList>
    <book isbn="0471777781">
        <title>Professional Ajax</title>
        <author>Nicholas C. Zakas, Jeremy McPeak, Joe Fawcett</author>
        <publisher>Wrox</publisher>
    </book>
    <book isbn="0764579088">
```

```
        <title>Professional JavaScript for Web Developers</title>
        <author>Nicholas C. Zakas</author>
        <publisher>Wrox</publisher>
    </book>
    <book isbn="0764557599">
        <title>Professional C#</title>
        <author>Simon Robinson, et al</author>
        <publisher>Wrox</publisher>
    </book>
    <book isbn="1861006314">
        <title>GDI+ Programming: Creating Custom Controls Using C#</title>
        <author>Eric White</author>
        <publisher>Wrox</publisher>
    </book>
    <book isbn="1861002025">
        <title>Professional Visual Basic 6 Databases</title>
        <author>Charles Williams</author>
        <publisher>Wrox</publisher>
    </book>
</bookList>
```

As you can see, the document element `<bookList/>` contains a few `<book/>` elements, which include information about a given book.

Loading XML Data

The first step is to create an XML DOM document and load the XML data into it. Because `books.xml` will be loaded asynchronously, you need to set the `onreadystatechange` event handler:

```
var oXmlDom = zXmlDom.createDocument();
oXmlDom.onreadystatechange = function () {
    if (oXmlDom.readyState == 4) {


    }
};
```

When the `readystatechange` event fires and the event handler is called, you check the `readyState` property; a value of 4 lets you know that the document is completely loaded and the DOM is ready to use.

The next step is to check for errors because even though the document is loaded, that is not necessarily a sign that everything works as it should:

```
var oXmlDom = zXmlDom.createDocument();
oXmlDom.onreadystatechange = function () {
    if (oXmlDom.readyState == 4) {
        if (oXmlDom.parseError.errorCode == 0) {
            parseBookInfo(oXmlDom);
        } else {
            var str = "An error occurred!!\n" +
                "Description: " + oXmlDom.parseError.reason + "\n" +
                "File: " + oXmlDom.parseError.url + "\n" +
                "Line: " + oXmlDom.parseError.line + "\n" +
                "Line Position: " + oXmlDom.parseError.linePos + "\n" +
```

```
                    "Source Code: " + oXmlDom.parseError.srcText;
              alert(str);
          }
      }
   };
```

If no error occurred, the XML DOM document is passed to `parseBookInfo()`, the function that parses the book list. If an error did occur, the error information collected in the `parseError` object is displayed in an alert.

With the `onreadystatechange` event handler written, the `load()` method is used to load the XML data:

```
oXmlDom.load("books.xml");
```

The XML document is now loaded. The next step in the process is to parse the XML data.

Parsing the Book List

The `parseBookInfo()` function is in charge of parsing the DOM document. This function accepts one argument, which is the DOM document itself:

```
function parseBookInfo(oXmlDom) {
    var oRoot = oXmlDom.documentElement;
    var oFragment = document.createDocumentFragment();
```

The variable `oRoot` is set to the `documentElement` of the XML document. This is merely a convenience, because it is far easier and faster to type `oRoot` than `oXmlDom.documentElement`. You also create a document fragment. The `parseBookInfo()` function generates many HTML elements and thus, many changes to the HTML DOM loaded in the browser. Adding each element to the HTML DOM individually is an expensive process in terms of the time it takes to display the changes. Instead, each element is added to a document fragment, which will be added to the document once all HTML elements are created. Doing so allows the HTML DOM to be updated only once instead of multiple times, resulting in faster rendering.

You know that only `<book/>` elements are children of the document element, so you can iterate through the `childNodes` collection:

```
var aBooks = oRoot.getElementsByTagName("book");

for (var i = 0; i < aBooks.length; i++) {
    var sIsbn = aBooks[i].getAttribute("isbn");
    var sAuthor, sTitle, sPublisher;
```

Inside the `for` loop, the actual parsing begins. To start, the `isbn` attribute of the `<book/>` element is retrieved with `getAttribute()` and stored in `sIsbn`. This value is used to display the book cover as well as the actual ISBN value to the user. The variables `sAuthor`, `sTitle`, and `sPublisher` are also declared; these variables will hold the values of the `<author/>`, `<title/>`, and `<publisher/>` elements, respectively.

Next, you retrieve the book's data, which can be done in a number of different ways. You could use the `childNodes` collection and loop through the children, but this example uses a different approach. You can accomplish the same result using a `do...while` loop, which makes use of the `firstChild` and `nextSibling` properties:

```
var oCurrentChild = aBooks[i].firstChild;

do {
    switch (oCurrentChild.tagName) {
        case "title":
            sTitle = oCurrentChild.text;
        break;
        case "author":
            sAuthor = oCurrentChild.text;
        break;
        case "publisher":
            sPublisher = oCurrentChild.text;
        break;
        default:
        break;
    }
    oCurrentChild = oCurrentChild.nextSibling;
} while (oCurrentChild = oCurrentChild.nextSibling);
```

In the first line, the variable `oCurrentChild` is assigned the first child of the current `<book/>` element. (Remember, this occurs inside of the `for` loop.) The child `tagName` is used in a `switch` block to determine what should be done with its data. The `switch` block then does its work assigning the data variable of the corresponding `tagName` of the current node. To retrieve this data, you use the node's `text` property, which retrieves all text nodes within the element. The `oCurrentChild` variable is assigned the node immediately following the current node by using the `nextSibling` property. If a next sibling exists, the loop continues; if not, `oCurrentChild` is `null` and the loop exits.

When all data variables contain the needed data, you can start generating HTML elements to display that data. The HTML structure of the elements you create programmatically looks like this:

```
<div class="bookContainer">
    <img class="bookCover" alt="Professional Ajax" src="0471777781.png" />
    <div class="bookContent">
        <h3>Professional Ajax</h3>
        Written by: Nicholas C. Zakas, Jeremy McPeak, Joe Fawcett<br />
        ISBN #0471777781
        <div class="bookPublisher">Published by Wrox</div>
    </div>
</div>
```

To add some readability to the list, the containing `<div/>` element will have alternating background colors. Books that are an odd number in the list will have a grayish background color and a class name of `bookContainer-odd`, whereas even books will have a white background defined by the `bookContainer` CSS class.

Generating this coding through DOM methods is an easy but lengthy process. The first step is to create the containing `<div/>`, the `<img/>`, and the content `<div/>` elements, which is done through the `createElement()` DOM method:

```
var divContainer = document.createElement("div");
var imgBookCover = document.createElement("img");
var divContent = document.createElement("div");

var sOdd = (i % 2)?"":"-odd";
divContainer.className = "bookContainer" + sOdd;
```

Along with the element creation, the differing class names are processed here as well. The current book is judged to be odd or even by the use of the modulus (%) operator. The `sOdd` variable is assigned the appropriate appendix, an empty string for even and `"-odd"` for odd, and used in the `className` assignment.

You can then assign the properties of the book cover image. These PNG images use the ISBN number as their file names:

```
imgBookCover.src = "images/" + sIsbn + ".png";
imgBookCover.className = "bookCover";
divContainer.appendChild(imgBookCover);
```

Here, the `src` and `className` properties are assigned and the image is appended to `divContainer`. With the image finished, you can add the content. The first piece of information to be added is the book's title, which is a heading level 3 element (`<h3/>`). Again, this element is created with `createElement()`:

```
var h3Title = document.createElement("h3");
h3Title.appendChild(document.createTextNode(sTitle));
divContent.appendChild(h3Title);
```

To create a text node containing the title, you use the `createTextNode()` method, which is appended to the `<h3/>` element, and then append the completed heading to `divContent`.

The author and ISBN information are next to be added. These two pieces of information are text nodes and have no parent element other than `divContent`. There is, however, one breaking element in between the two text nodes:

```
divContent.appendChild(document.createTextNode("Written by: " + sAuthor));
divContent.appendChild(document.createElement("br"));
divContent.appendChild(document.createTextNode("ISBN: #" + sIsbn));
```

This code creates this information. First, the text node containing the author information is appended to `divContent`, followed by the creation and appending of the breaking element (`<br/>`). Last, you append the text node containing the ISBN information.

The last piece of information to add is the publisher:

```
var divPublisher = document.createElement("div");
divPublisher.className = "bookPublisher";
divPublisher.appendChild(document.createTextNode("Published by: " + sPublisher));
divContent.appendChild(divPublisher);
```

The publisher is displayed in a `<div/>` element. After its creation, the `className` is assigned `"bookPublisher"` and the text node containing the publisher's name is appended to the element. The `divPublisher` element is complete, so you can append it to `divContent`.

At this point, all data operations are complete. However, `divContent` still lacks its class name and must be appended to `divContainer`, which in turn must be appended to the document fragment. The following three lines of code do this:

```
divContent.className = "bookContent";
divContainer.appendChild(divContent);
oFragment.appendChild(divContainer);
```

The last step is to append the document fragment to the page body after the book nodes are iterated through:

```
document.body.appendChild(oFragment);
```

This code doesn't actually append the document fragment itself; instead, it appends all the child nodes of the document fragment, making all the changes to the HTML DOM at once. With this final line of code, `parseBookInfo()` is complete.

Tying It Together

The body of this web page is generated entirely by JavaScript. Because of this, the element creation and insertion code must execute after the document is loaded. Remember, `parseBookInfo()` is called after `books.xml` is loaded, so the XML DOM object creation code needs to execute at the page load. Create a function called `init()` to house the XML DOM creation code:

```
function init() {
    var oXmlDom = zXmlDom.createDocument();
    oXmlDom.onreadystatechange = function () {
        if (oXmlDom.readyState == 4) {
            if (oXmlDom.parseError.errorCode == 0) {
                parseBookInfo(oXmlDom);
            } else {
                alert("An Error Occurred: " + oXmlDom.parseError.reason);
            }
        }
    };
    oXmlDom.load("book.xml");
}
```

You'll use `init()` to handle the `window.onload` event. This will help ensure that the JavaScript-generated elements are added to the page without causing errors.

This mini application houses itself in an HTML document. All that is required are two `<script/>` elements, a `<link/>` element for the CSS, and the assignment of the `onload` event handler:

```
<!DOCTYPE html PUBLIC "-//W3C//DTD XHTML 1.1//EN"
                      "http://www.w3.org/TR/xhtml11/DTD/xhtml11.dtd">

<html xmlns="http://www.w3.org/1999/xhtml" >
```

```
<head>
    <title>Book XML Exercise</title>
    <link rel="stylesheet" type="text/css" href="books.css" />
    <script type="text/javascript" src="zxml.js"></script>
    <script type="text/javascript" src="books.js"></script>
</head>
<body onload="init()">

</body>
</html>
```

When you run this code, you will see the result shown in Figure 4-2.

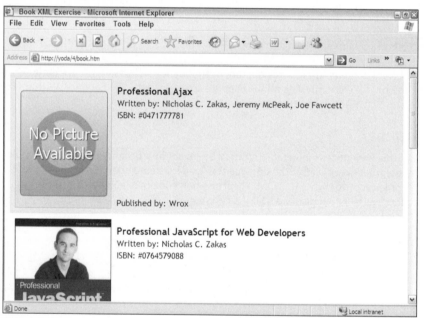

Figure 4-2

XPath Support in Browsers

As XML grew in popularity, the need to access specific pieces of data directly became apparent. In July 1999, XML Path Language (XPath) was introduced in the Extensible Stylesheet Language (XSL) specification as a means to find any node within an XML document. XPath uses a non-XML syntax that closely resembles the path syntax of a file system. The language consists of location paths and expressions, as well as a few helpful functions to aid in retrieving specific data.

Introduction to XPath

An XPath expression consists of two parts: a context node and a selection pattern. The context node is the context from which the selection pattern begins. Referring to `books.xml` from the previous section, consider this XPath expression:

```
book/author
```

If this expression were executed at the root level (its context), all `<author/>` nodes would be returned because the `<book/>` element is a child of the document element and contains an `<author/>` element. This expression is not very specific, so all `<author/>` elements are returned.

What if you want to retrieve only the `<book/>` element that has a specific ISBN? The XPath expression would look like this:

```
book[@isbn='0471777781']
```

The `book` part of the expression describes which element to retrieve. Inside of the square brackets is a condition that this element must match. The `@isbn` part represents the `isbn` attribute (@ being short for attribute). So, this expression reads "find the book elements that have an `isbn` attribute of `'041777781'`."

XPath expressions can also be very complex. Consider the following expression:

```
book[author[contains(text(),'McPeak')]]
```

This expression reads, "find the book elements that have author elements whose text contains the string 'McPeak'." Since this is a more complicated expression, it helps to break it down, working from the outside towards the inside. Removing all conditions, you have this expression:

```
book[...]
```

First, you know that a `<book/>` element will be returned since it is the outermost element; next come the conditions. Inside the first set of brackets, you notice the `<author/>` element:

```
author[...]
```

You now know you are looking for a book element with a child `<author/>` element. However, the children of the `<author/>` element need to be checked as well because the expression doesn't end there:

```
contains(text(),'McPeak')
```

The `contains()` function takes two arguments and returns `true` if the first string argument contains the second string argument. The `text()` function returns all the text in the given context, so the text contents of the `<author/>` element are passed as the first argument in `contains()`. The second argument passed to `contains()` is the search text, in this case `'McPeak'`.

> Note that the `contains()` function, like all XPath functions, is case-sensitive.

The resulting node set is one `<book/>` element, because there is only one book with an author (or co-author) whose name is McPeak.

As you can see, XPath is a useful language that makes finding specific nodes in XML data rather simple. It is no wonder Microsoft and Mozilla implemented XPath in their browsers for client-side use.

XPath in IE

Microsoft's implementation of XPath is a part of MSXML 3.0 and later. If you are using any version of Windows XP, or have IE 6.0 or higher installed, then your computer has this capability. If not, you will need to download and install the latest MSXML package.

Microsoft chose to implement two methods that select nodes based on XPath expressions. The first, `selectSingleNode()`, returns the first node within its context that matches the expression. For example:

```
var oFirstAuthor = oXmlDom.documentElement.selectSingleNode("book/author");
```

This code returns the first `<author/>` element that is a child of a `<book/>` element in the context of `documentElement`. The result of this is the following node:

```
<author>Nicholas C. Zakas, Jeremy McPeak, Joe Fawcett</author>
```

The second method in Microsoft's XPath implementation is `selectNodes()`. This method returns a `NodeList`, a collection of all nodes that match the pattern in the XPath expression:

```
var cAuthors = oXmlDom.documentElement.selectNodes("book/author");
```

As you may have guessed, all `<author/>` elements with a parent of `<book/>` in the context of the document element are returned. If the pattern cannot be matched in the document, a `NodeList` is still returned but it has a `length` of 0. It is a good idea to check the length of a returned `NodeList` before attempting to use it:

```
var cAuthors = oXmlDom.documentElement.selectNodes("book/author");

if (cAuthors.length > 0) {
    //Do something
}
```

Working with Namespaces

The *X* in XML stands for *eXtensible*. There are no predefined elements in an XML document; a developer created every element in any given XML document. This extensibility is part of what makes XML so popular, but it also inherently causes a problem: naming conflicts. For example, consider the following XML document:

```
<?xml version="1.0" encoding="utf-8"?>

<addresses>
    <address>
        <number>12345</number>
```

```
            <street>Your Street</street>
            <city>Your City</city>
            <state>Your State</state>
            <country>USA</country>
        </address>
    </addresses>
```

There is nothing out of the ordinary in this document. It simply describes an address located in the USA. But what if the following lines were added:

```
<?xml version="1.0" encoding="utf-8"?>

<addresses>
    <address>
        <number>12345</number>
        <street>Your Street</street>
        <city>Your City</city>
        <state>Your State</state>
        <country>USA</country>
    </address>

    <address>
        <ip>127.0.0.1</ip>
        <hostname>localhost</hostname>
    </address>
</addresses>
```

This document now describes two types of addresses: a physical mailing address and a computer address. While both addresses are legitimate addresses, handling this information requires different approaches, especially since both `<address/>` elements contain completely different child elements. An XML processor will not distinguish the difference between these two `<address/>` elements, so it is up to you to do it. This is where namespaces come into play.

Namespaces consists of two parts: a *namespaceURI* and a *prefix*. The namespaceURI identifies the namespace. Generally, namespaceURIs are web site URLs, because they must be unique to access different web sites. The prefix is a local name in the XML document for the namespace. Every tag name in the namespace uses the namespace prefix. The syntax of namespace declarations are as follows:

```
xmlns:namespace-prefix="namespaceURI"
```

The `xmlns` keyword tells the XML parser that a namespace declaration is taking place. The `namespace-prefix` is the local name used in the elements that fall under this namespace, and `namespaceURI` is the universal resource locator that the prefix represents.

Namespace declarations must appear before the namespace is used in the XML document. In the example, the root element contains the namespaces declarations:

```
<?xml version="1.0" encoding="utf-8"?>

<addresses xmlns:mail="http://www.wrox.com/mail"
           xmlns:comp="http://www.wrox.com/computer">

    <mail:address>
```

```
            <mail:number>12345</mail:number>
            <mail:street>Your Street</mail:street>
            <mail:city>Your City</mail:city>
            <mail:state>Your State</mail:state>
            <mail:country>USA</mail:country>
        </mail:address>
        <comp:address>
            <comp:ip>127.0.0.1</comp:ip>
            <comp:hostname>localhost</comp:hostname>
        </comp:address>
    </addresses>
```

This newly edited XML document defines two namespaces: one with the prefix `mail` to represent a mailing address, and the other with a prefix of `comp` to represent a computer address. Probably the first thing you noticed was the usage of the prefixes. Every element associated with a certain address type is associated with the corresponding namespace, so every element associated as a mailing address has the `mail` prefix while every computer-based address has the `comp` prefix.

The use of namespaces avoids naming conflicts, and XML processors now understand the difference between the two address types.

Namespaces in XPath add a slight complication when using `selectSingleNode()` and `selectNodes()`. Consider the following modified version of `books.xml`:

```
<?xml version="1.0" encoding="utf-8"?>
<bookList xmlns="http://site1.com" xmlns:pub="http://site2.com">

    <book isbn="0471777781">
        <title>Professional Ajax</title>
        <author>Nicholas C. Zakas, Jeremy McPeak, Joe Fawcett</author>

        <pub:name>Wrox</pub:name>

    </book>
    <book isbn="0764579088">
        <title>Professional JavaScript for Web Developers</title>
        <author>Nicholas C. Zakas</author>

        <pub:name>Wrox</pub:name>

    </book>
    <book isbn="0764557599">
        <title>Professional C#</title>
        <author>Simon Robinson, et al</author>

        <pub:name>Wrox</pub:name>

    </book>
    <book isbn="1861006314">
        <title>GDI+ Programming: Creating Custom Controls Using C#</title>
        <author>Eric White</author>
```

```
          <pub:name>Wrox</pub:name>

      </book>
      <book isbn="1861002025">
          <title>Professional Visual Basic 6 Databases</title>
          <author>Charles Williams</author>

          <pub:name>Wrox</pub:name>

      </book>
  </bookList>
```

This newly revised document has two namespaces in use: the default namespace specified by `xmlns="http://site1.com"`, followed by the `pub` namespace specified as `xmlns:pub="http://site2.com"`. A default namespace does not have a prefix; therefore, all non-prefixed elements in the document use the default namespace. Notice that the `<publisher/>` elements are replaced by `<pub:name/>` elements.

When dealing with an XML document that contains namespaces, these namespaces must be declared in order to use XPath expressions. The MSXML DOM document exposes a method called `setProperty()` which is used to set second-level properties for the object. The specific property `SelectionNamespaces` should be set with an alias namespace for any default or external namespace. Aside from using the `setProperty()` method, namespace declarations are assigned just as they are in XML documents:

```
var sNameSpace = "xmlns:na='http://site1.com' xmlns:pub='http://site2.com'";
oXmlDom.setProperty("SelectionNamespaces", sNameSpace);
```

The namespaces `na` and `pub` represent the namespaces used in the XML document. Notice that the namespace prefix `na` is defined for the default namespace. MSXML will not recognize a default namespace when selecting nodes with XPath, so the declaration of an alias prefix is necessary. Now that the `SelectionNamespace` property is set, you can select nodes within the document:

```
var oRoot = oXmlDom.documentElement;
var sXPath = "na:book/pub:name";
var cPublishers = oRoot.selectNodes(sXPath);

if (cPublishers.length > 0) {
    alert(cPublishers.length + " <pub:name/> elements found with " + sXPath);
}
```

The XPath expression uses the namespaces specified in the `SelectionNamespaces` property and selects all `<pub:name/>` elements. In the case of this example, a NodeList consisting of five elements is returned, which you can then use.

XPath in Firefox

The Firefox XPath implementation follows the DOM standard, which is quite different from the IE implementation. The Firefox implementation allows XPath expressions to be run against HTML and XML documents alike. At the center of this are two primary objects: `XPathEvaluator` and `XPathResult`.

The `XPathEvaluator` class evaluates a given XPath expression using the `evaluate()` method, which takes five arguments: the XPath expression string to be evaluated, the context node that the expression should be run against, a namespace resolver (which is a function that will handle the namespaces in the expression), the result type you want (ten different result types are available), and an `XPathResult` object to contain the results (if this argument is `null`, then a new `XPathResult` object is returned).

Before moving on, it's important to understand the various result types that can be returned from `evaluate()`. These are:

❑ `XPathResult.ANY_TYPE`, which returns no specific type. The method returns the type that naturally results from the evaluation of the expression.

❑ `XPathResult.ANY_UNORDERED_NODE_TYPE`, which returns a node set of one node that is accessed through the `singleNodeValue` property; `null` is returned if there are no matching nodes. The returned node may or may not be the first occurring node.

❑ `XPathResult.BOOLEAN_TYPE`, which returns a Boolean value.

❑ `XPathResult.FIRST_ORDERED_NODE_TYPE`, which returns a node set consisting of one node. This node is accessed with the `singleNodeValue` property of the `XPathResult` class. The node returned is the first occurring one in the document.

❑ `XPathResult.NUMBER_TYPE`, which returns a number value.

❑ `XPathResult.ORDERED_NODE_ITERATOR_TYPE`, which returns a document-ordered node set that can be iterated through using the `iterateNext()` method; therefore, you can easily access each individual node in the set.

❑ `XPathResult.ORDERED_NODE_SNAPSHOT_TYPE`, which returns a document-ordered node set that is a snapshot of the result set. Any modifications made to the nodes in the document do not affect the retrieved results.

❑ `XPathResult.STRING_TYPE`, which returns a string value.

❑ `XPathResult.UNORDERED_NODE_ITERATOR_TYPE`, which returns a node set that can be iterated through; however, the results may or may not be in the same order as they appear in the document.

❑ `XPathResult.UNORDERED_NODE_SNAPSHOT_TYPE`, which returns an unordered snapshot node set. Any modifications made to the nodes in the document do not affect the result set.

The most common result type is `XPathResult.ORDERED_NODE_ITERATOR_TYPE`:

```
var oEvaluator = new XPathEvaluator();
var sXPath = "book/author";
var oResult = oEvaluator.evaluate(sXPath,oXmlDom.documentElement,null,
        XPathResult.ORDERED_NODE_ITERATOR_TYPE, null);

var aNodes = new Array;

if (oResult != null) {
    var oElement;
    while (oElement = oResult.iterateNext()) {
        aNodes.push(oElement);
    }
}
```

In this code, an XPathEvaluator object is created and used to evaluate the XPath expression book/author in the context of the document's root element. Because the result type is ORDERED_NOE_ITERATOR_TYPE, the evaluation returns a node set that you can iterate through using the iterateNext().

The iterateNext() method resembles the nextSibling property of a DOM node in that it selects the next node in the result set and returns null when the end of the result set is reached. This function enables you to use it in a while loop as in the previous example; as long as oElement is not null, it is added to the aNodes array through the push() method. Populating an array gives you IE-like functionality; therefore, you can use it in a for loop or access separate array elements easily.

Working with Namespace Resolver

In the syntax of the evaluate() method, you saw a reference to a namespace resolver. A *namespace resolver* is a function that resolves any namespace prefixes appearing in the XPath expression to a namespace URI. The namespace resolver function can be named any name you want, but it requires that a string argument be accepted (which is the prefix to check).

The resolver checks for the prefix provided by the argument and should return the namespace URI associated with it. To use the values from the IE example, you can write the following resolver:

```
function nsResolver(sPrefix) {
    switch (sPrefix) {
        case "na":
            return "http://site1.com";
            break;
        case "pub":
            return "http://site2.com";
            break;
        default:
            return null;
            break;
    }
}
```

With the resolver written, you can use the following XPath expression on the modified books.xml document from the IE namespace example:

```
var sXPath = "na:book/pub:name";

var oEvaluator = new XPathEvaluator();

var oResult = oEvaluator.evaluate(sXPath,oXmlDom.documentElement,nsResolver,
        XPathResult.ORDERED_NODE_ITERATOR_TYPE, null);


var aNodes = new Array;

if (oResult != null) {
    var oElement;
    while (oElement = oResult.iterateNext()) {
        aNodes.push(oElement);
    }
}
```

This example resembles the last evaluation code. However, notice the addition to the `evaluate()` method: the pointer to the `nsResolver()` function, written earlier, is passed to the `evaluate()` method to handle the namespaces in the XPath expression. The remainder of the code should look familiar to you. The resulting `NodeList` is converted to an array by using the `iterateNext()` method of the `XPathResult` class to iterate through the result.

As you can see, the Firefox XPath implementation is quite different from the Microsoft approach; so it is helpful to use a cross-browser library that enables you to perform XPath evaluations easily.

Cross-Browser XPath

The zXml library created by the authors provides cross-browser XPath functionality through a common interface. The object responsible for providing XPath functionality is `zXPath`, which has two methods.

The first method is `selectSingleNode()`. This method, like the IE method of the same name, returns the first node that matches a pattern. Unlike the IE implementation, this method accepts three arguments: the context node, the XPath expression string, and a string containing the namespace declarations. The namespace string should be in the following format:

```
"xmlns:na='http://site1.com' xmlns:pub='http://site2.com'
    xmlns:ns='http://site3.com'"
```

If you are not working with namespaces, then the first two arguments of `selectSingleNode()` are the only required arguments.

The returned result of `selectSingleNode()` is the selected XML node, or `null` if a match cannot be found. If the browser does not support XPath, an error is thrown stating that the browser does not have an XPath engine installed. The following example evaluates an XPath expression against the document element:

```
var oRoot = oXmlDom.documentElement;
var oNode = zXPath.selectSingleNode(oRoot, "book/author", null);

if (oNode) {
    alert(oNode.xml);
}
```

This example searches for the first `<author/>` element contained in a `<book/>` element in the context of the document root. If found, the serialized form of the XML data is displayed to the user in an alert box.

The second method of `zXPath` is `selectNodes()`, which returns a node set much like the IE `selectNodes()` method. The syntax closely resembles that of the `selectSingleNode()` method above, and the arguments are exactly the same, and the same namespace rules apply. Also like `selectSingleNode()` an error is thrown in the event the browser does not have an XPath engine installed. The next example demonstrates the `selectNodes()` method:

```
var sNameSpace = "xmlns:na='http://site1.com' xmlns:pub='http://site2.com'";
var oRoot = oXmlDom.documentElement;
var sXPath = "na:book/pub:name";
```

```
var oNodes = zXPath.selectNodes(oRoot, sXPath, sNameSpace);

if (oNodes.length > 0) {
    alert(oNodes.length);
}
```

This example, much like the `selectSingleNode()` example, searches for all author elements of a document that incorporates namespaces. If the result set has a length greater than 0, the length of the result is displayed to the user.

XPath is a powerful tool to navigate through and select certain nodes in an XML document, although it was never intended to be used as a standalone tool. Instead, it was created for use in XSL Transformations.

XSL Transformation Support in Browsers

Extensible Stylesheet Language (XSL) is a family of languages that are designed to transform XML data. XSL refers to three main languages: XSL Transformations (XSLT), which is a language that transforms XML documents into other XML documents; XPath, which was discussed in the previous section; and XSL Formatting Objects (XSL-FO), which describes how the transformed data should be rendered when presented. Since no browser currently supports XSL-FO, any transformations must be accomplished through the use of XSLT.

Introduction to XSLT

XSLT is an XML-based language designed to transform an XML document into another data form. This definition may make XSLT to be a not-so-useful technology, but the truth is far from the matter. The most popular use of XSLT is to transform XML documents into HTML documents, which is precisely what this introduction covers.

XSLT documents are nothing more than specialized XML documents, so they must conform to the same rules as all XML documents: they must contain an XML declaration, they must have a single root element, and they must be well formed.

As an example, you'll once again be using `books.xml`. The information contained in this file can be transformed into HTML using XSLT, without the need to build the DOM structure manually. For starters, you need an XSLT document, `books.xsl`, which begins with an XML declaration and a root element:

```
<?xml version="1.0" encoding="UTF-8" ?>

<xsl:stylesheet version="1.0" xmlns:xsl="http://www.w3.org/1999/XSL/Transform">
<xsl:output method="html" omit-xml-declaration="yes" indent="yes" />

</xsl:stylesheet>
```

The document element of an XSLT document is `<xsl:stylesheet/>`. In this element, the XSL version is specified, and the `xsl` namespace is declared. This required information determines the behavior of the XSLT processor; without it, an error will be thrown. The `xsl` prefix is also important, as this allows all XSL directives to be visibly and logically separate from other code in the document.

The `<xsl:output/>` element defines the format of the resulting output. In this example, the resulting transformation results in HTML data, with the XML declaration omitted, and the elements indented. You can specify the format to be plain text, XML, or HTML data.

Just like any application, a transformation must have an entry point. XSLT is a template-based language, and the processor works on an XML document by matching template rules. In this example, the first element to match is the root of the XML document. This is done by using the `<xsl:template/>` directive. *Directives* tell the processor to execute a specific function. The `<xsl:template/>` directive creates a template that is used when the pattern in the `match` attribute is matched:

```xml
<?xml version="1.0" encoding="UTF-8" ?>

<xsl:stylesheet version="1.0" xmlns:xsl="http://www.w3.org/1999/XSL/Transform">

<xsl:template match="/">

<html>
    <head>
        <link rel="stylesheet" type="text/css" href="books.css" />
        <title>XSL Transformations</title>
    </head>
    <body>
        <xsl:apply-templates />
    </body>
</html>

</xsl:template>

</xsl:stylesheet>
```

The `match` attribute takes an XPath expression as its value to select the proper XML node. In this case, it is the root element of `books.xml` (the XPath expression / always selects the document element). Inside of the template, you'll notice HTML elements. These elements are a part of the transformation's output. Inside of the `<body/>` element, another XSL directive is found. The `<xsl:apply-templates />` element tells the processor to start parsing all templates within the context of the document element, which brings the next template into play:

```xml
<?xml version="1.0" encoding="UTF-8" ?>

<xsl:stylesheet version="1.0" xmlns:xsl="http://www.w3.org/1999/XSL/Transform">
<xsl:output method="html" omit-xml-declaration="yes" indent="yes" />

<xsl:template match="/">

<html>
    <head>
        <link rel="stylesheet" type="text/css" href="books.css" />
```

```
            <title>XSL Transformations</title>
        </head>
        <body>
            <xsl:apply-templates />
        </body>
    </html>

</xsl:template>
```

```
<xsl:template match="book">
    <div class="bookContainer">
        <xsl:variable name="varIsbn" select="@isbn" />
        <xsl:variable name="varTitle" select="title" />
        <img class="bookCover" alt="{$varTitle}" src="{$varIsbn}.png" />
        <div class="bookContent">
            <h3><xsl:value-of select="$varTitle" /></h3>
            Written by: <xsl:value-of select="author" /><br />
            ISBN #<xsl:value-of select="$varIsbn" />
            <div class="bookPublisher"><xsl:value-of select="publisher" /></div>
        </div>
    </div>
</xsl:template>
```

```
</xsl:stylesheet>
```

This new template matches all `<book/>` elements, so when the processor reaches each `<book/>` in the XML document, this template is used. The first two XSL directives in this template are `<xsl:variable/>`, which define variables.

Variables in XSL are primarily used in XPath expressions or attributes (where elements cannot be used without breaking XML syntax). The `<xsl:variable/>` element has two attributes: `name` and `select`. As you may have guessed, the `name` attribute sets the name of the variable. The `select` attribute specifies an XPath expression and stores the matching value in the variable. After the initial declaration, variables are referenced to with the $ sign (so the variable defined as `varIsbn` is later referenced as `$varIsbn`).

The first variable, `$varIsbn`, is assigned the value of the `<book/>` element's `isbn` attribute. The second, `$varTitle`, is assigned the value of the `<title/>` element. These two pieces of information are used in the attributes of the HTML `<img/>` element. To output variables in attributes, you surround the variable name in braces:

```
<img class="bookCover" alt="{$title}" src="{$isbn}.png" />
```

Without the braces, the output would use the string literals `"$varTitle"` and `"$varIsbn"` instead.

> **Using variables in attributes of XSL directives, like `select`, are the exception to this rule. Using curly braces in these types of attributes will cause an error, and the document transformation will fail.**

The remainder of XSL directives in this example are `<xsl:value-of/>` elements. These elements retrieve the value of the matched variable or node according to the `select` attribute. The `select` attribute behaves in the same way as the `select` attributes of `<xsl:variable/>` do: they take an XPath expression and select the node or variable that matches that expression. The first instance of `<xsl:value-of/>` in this template references the `$varTitle` variable (notice the lack of braces), so the value of the variable is used. Next, the value of the `<author/>` element is used; the same with `$varTitle` and `<publisher/>`.

In order for an XML document to transform in the browser, it must have a stylesheet specified. In `books.xml`, add the following line immediately after the XML declaration:

```
<?xml-stylesheet type="text/xsl" href="books.xsl"?>
```

This tells the XML processor to apply the stylesheet `books.xsl` to this document. Viewing this modified XML document in a web browser will no longer show the XML structure, but it will show the resulting transformation to HTML. However, using this directive won't work through JavaScript. For that, you'll need to use some special objects.

XSLT in IE

There are two ways to transform an XML document in IE, both of which require the use of MSXML. Starting with version 3.0, MSXML has full support for XSLT 1.0. If you don't have Windows XP or IE 6, it is time to upgrade. You can find the latest MSXML downloads at `http://msdn.microsoft.com/XML/XMLDownloads/`.

The first and easiest method loads both the XML and XSLT documents into separate XML DOM objects:

```
var oXmlDom = zXmlDom.createDocument();
var oXslDom = zXmlDom.createDocument();

oXmlDom.async = false;
oXslDom.async = false;

oXmlDom.load("books.xml");
oXslDom.load("books.xsl");
```

When both documents are loaded, you call the `transformNode()` method to start the transformation:

```
var sResults = oXmlDom.transformNode(oXslDom);
```

The `transformNode()` method takes an XML DOM object as an argument (in this case, the XSL document) and returns the transformed data as a string. But you don't have to call `transformNode()` at the document level; it can be called from any element in the XML document:

```
var sResults = oXmlDom.documentElement.firstChild.transformNode(oXslDom);
```

The `transformNode()` method will transform only the element it was called from and its children. In this example, the first `<book/>` element is transformed, as shown in Figure 4-3. This is because you transformed only one node by calling `transformNode()` on an element with no children.

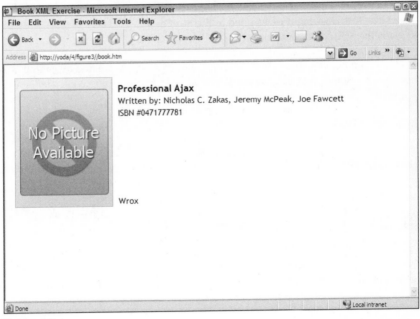

Figure 4-3

The second method of transformations in IE is a bit more involved, but it also gives you more control and features. This process involves creating multiple objects in the MSXML library. The first step in this somewhat lengthy process is to create a thread-safe XML DOM object, which the XSL stylesheet is loaded into:

```
var oXmlDom = zXmlDom.createDocument();
oXmlDom.async = false;
oXmlDom.load("books.xml");
```

```
var oXslDom = new ActiveXObject("Msxml2.FreeThreadedDOMDocument.3.0");
oXslDom.async = false;
oXslDom.load("books.xsl");
```

The `FreeThreadedDOMDocument` class is yet another ActiveX class and a part of the MSXML library. You must use the `FreeThreadedDomDocument` class to create `XSLTemplate` objects, which this example does (the next example shows the creation of a `XSLTemplate` object). In early versions of MSXML, every call to the `transformNode()` method forced a recompile of the XSL stylesheet slowing the transformation process considerably. With a `FreeThreadedDOMDocument`, the compiled stylesheet is cached and ready to use until it's removed from memory.

After the XML DOM object creation, you must create another ActiveX object, an XSL template:

```
var oXslTemplate = new ActiveXObject("Msxml2.XSLTemplate.3.0");
oXslTemplate.stylesheet = oXslDom;
```

The XSLTemplate class is used to cache XSL stylesheets and create an XSLProcessor; so after the template is created, the XSL document is assigned to the XSLTemplate class's stylesheet property, which caches and loads the XSL stylesheet.

The next step in this process is to create an XSLProcessor, which is created by calling the createProcessor() method of the XSLTemplate class:

```
var oXslProcessor = oXslTemplate.createProcessor();
oXslProcessor.input = oXmlDom;
```

After creation of the processor, its input property is assigned oXmlDom, the XML DOM object containing the XML document to transform. At this point, everything the processor requires is in place, so all that remains is the actual transformation and the retrieval of the output:

```
oXslProcessor.transform();
document.body.innerHTML = oXslProcessor.output;
```

Unlike transformNodes(), the transform() method does not return the resulting output as a string. To retrieve the output of the transformation, use the output property of the XSLProcessor object. This entire process requires much more coding than the transformNode() method and yields the same result. So why use this process?

MSXML provides a few extra methods that can be used in these transformations. The first is addObject(). This method adds a JavaScript object to the stylesheet, and can even call methods and output property values in the transformed document. Consider the following object:

```
var oBook = {
    propertyOne : "My Current Books",
    methodOne   : function () {
        alert("Welcome to my Book List");
        return "";
    }
};
```

What if you wanted to use this information in the transformation? Using the addObject() method, you can pass this information into the XSLT stylesheet passing in two arguments: the oBook object and a namespace URI to identify it. So, to add this object with a namespace URI of "http://my-object", you could do the following:

```
var oXmlDom = zXmlDom.createDocument();
oXmlDom.async = false;
oXmlDom.load("books.xml");

var oXslDom = new ActiveXObject("Msxml2.FreeThreadedDOMDocument.3.0");
oXslDom.async = false;
oXslDom.load("books.xsl");

var oXslTemplate = new ActiveXObject("Msxml2.XSLTemplate.3.0");
oXslTemplate.stylesheet = oXslDom;

var oXslProcessor = oXslTemplate.createProcessor();
```

```
oXslProcessor.input = oXmlDom;

oXslProcessor.addObject(oBook, "http://my-object");


oXslProcessor.transform();
document.body.innerHTML = oXslProcessor.output;
```

The `oBook` object is now passed to the `XSLProcessor`, meaning that the XSLT stylesheet can use it. Now the XSL document must be changed to look for this object and use its information. The first requirement is to add a new namespace to the root element, `<xsl:stylesheet/>`. This namespace will match the one used in `addObject()`:

```
<xsl:stylesheet version="1.0" xmlns:xsl="http://www.w3.org/1999/XSL/Transform"

        xmlns:bookObj="http://my-object">
```

The prefix `bookObj` will be used to access this information. Now that the namespace and prefix are ready to go, some `<xsl:value-of/>` elements should be added to the document to retrieve the object's members:

```
<xsl:template match="/">

<html>
    <head>
        <link rel="stylesheet" type="text/css" href="books.css" />
    </head>
    <body>

        <xsl:value-of select="bookObj:methodOne()" />
        <div align="center">
            <b><xsl:value-of select="bookObj:get-propertyOne()" /></b>
        </div>
        <xsl:apply-templates />
    </body>
</html>

</xsl:template>
```

Remember that the `<xsl:value-of/>` XSL directive retrieves the value of an element, or in this case, an object. The first `<xsl:value-of/>` directive retrieves (or calls) `methodOne()`, which sends an alert welcoming the user to the page. The second `<xsl:value-of/>` directive is similar to the first, except that it retrieves the value of the `propertyOne` property of the `oBook` object. When the transformed output is displayed in the browser, the user will see the phrase My Current Books at the top of the page.

> **When using an object in transformations, all properties and methods must return a value that the `XSLProcessor` can understand. String, number, and Boolean values all work as expected; returning any other value will throw a JavaScript error when the transformation executes.**

The next useful feature of the XSLProcessor is the addParameter() method. Unlike sending an object into a transformation, parameters are a standard part of XSLT. Parameters are passed to the XSL stylesheet and used as variables. To specify a parameter, pass the name and its value, like this:

```
var oXslProcessor = oXslTemplate.createProcessor();
oXslProcessor.input = oXmlDom;
oXslProcessor.addParameter("message", "My Book List");
```

This code adds the "message" parameter to the XSLProcessor. When the XSL transformation executes, the processor uses the value of the parameter, "My Book List", and places it in the according location. Parameters in XSL use the <xsl:param/> directive:

```
<xsl:param name="message" />
```

Notice that the name attribute matches the name passed in addParameter(). This parameter receives the value "My Book List" which is retrieved using the variable syntax you learned earlier:

```
<xsl:value-of select="$message" />
```

In this example, the <xsl:value-of/> directive retrieves the parameters value. The updated XSL stylesheet would look like this:

```
<xsl:stylesheet version="1.0" xmlns:xsl="http://www.w3.org/1999/XSL/Transform">


<xsl:param name="message" />


<xsl:template match="/">

<html>
    <head>
        <link rel="stylesheet" type="text/css" href="books.css" />
    </head>
    <body>


        <xsl:value-of select="$message" />


        <xsl:apply-templates />
    </body>
</html>

</xsl:template>
```

The updated stylesheet adds two new lines of code. The first is the addition of the <xsl:param/> directive, and the second is the <xsl:value-of/> directive that retrieves the value of the parameter. Parameter declarations can exist anywhere in the XSL document. This code shows the parameter declaration at the top of the document, but you are not limited to this location.

One final feature of using an XSLProcessor is its speed; it compiles the XSL stylesheet, so subsequent transformations using the same stylesheet result in faster transformations (compared to using transformNodes()). To do this, use the reset() method of the XSLProcessor object. This method clears the `input` and `output` properties but not the `stylesheet` property. This readies the processor for the next transformation with the same stylesheet.

XSLT in Firefox

Like XML and XPath, the Firefox implementation of XSLT transformations varies from the IE implementation. Firefox does implement an `XSLTProcessor` class to perform transformations, but the similarities end there.

The first step in performing a transformation in Firefox is to load the XML and XSL documents into a DOM object:

```
var oXmlDom = zXmlDom.createDocument();
var oXslDom = zXmlDom.createDocument();

oXmlDom.async = false;
oXslDom.async = false;

oXmlDom.load("books.xml");
oXslDom.load("books.xsl");
```

The `XSLTProcessor` class exposes the `importStylesheet()` method, which takes an XML DOM object containing the XSLT document as an argument:

```
var oXsltProcessor = new XSLTProcessor();
oXsltProcessor.importStylesheet(oXslDom);
```

Last, the transformation methods are called. There are two of these methods: `transformToDocument()` and `transformToFragment()`. The `transformToDocument()` method takes an XML DOM object as an argument and returns a new XML DOM document containing the transformation. Normally, this is the method you want to use:

```
var oNewDom = oXsltProcessor.transformToDocument(oXmlDom);
```

The resulting DOM object can be used like any other XML DOM object. You can select certain nodes with XPath, traverse the node structure with properties and methods, or even use it in another transformation.

The `transformToFragment()` method returns a document fragment, as its name suggests, to append to another DOM document. This method takes two arguments: the first is the XML DOM object you want to transform, and the second is the DOM object you intend to append the result to:

```
var oFragment = oXsltProcessor.transformToFragment(oXmlDom, document);
document.body.appendChild(oFragment);
```

In this example, the resulting document fragment is appended to the body of the `document` object. Note that you can append the resulting fragment to any node within the DOM object passed to the `transformToFragment()` method.

But what if you wanted a string returned as the result of transformation like the `transformNode()` method implemented by Microsoft? You could use the `XMLSerializer` class you learned of earlier. Just pass the transformation result to the `serializeToString()` method:

```
var oSerializer = new XMLSerializer();
var str = oSerializer.serializeToString(oNewDom);
```

If using the zXml library, this is simplified by using the `xml` property:

```
var str = oFragment.xml;
```

The `XSLTProcessor` class also enables you to set parameters to pass to the XSL stylesheet. The `setParameter()` method facilitates this functionality; it accepts three arguments: the namespace URI, the parameter name, and the value to assign the parameter. For example:

```
oXsltProcessor.importStylesheet(oXslDom);

oXsltProcessor.setParameter(null, "message", "My Book List");

var oNewDom = oXsltProcessor.transformToDocument(oXmlDom);
```

In this example, the parameter message is assigned the value `"My Book List"`. The value of `null` is passed for the namespace URI, which allows the parameter to be used without having to specify a prefix and corresponding namespace URI in the stylesheet:

```
<xsl:param name="message" />
```

The `setParameter()` method must be called before the calling of `transformToDocument()` or `transformToFragment()`, or else the parameter value will not be used in the transformation.

Cross-Browser XSLT

In the previous sections, you've seen how the zXml library makes handling XML data across both main platforms easier. Now you will use the library to perform XSLT transformations. There is only one method for XSLT in the library: `transformToText()`. This method, which returns text from a transformation, takes two arguments: the XML document to transform and the XSL document:

```
var sResult = zXslt.transformToText(oXmlDom, oXslDom);
```

As the name of the method suggests, the returned result is a string. You can then add the result of the transformation (`sResult`) to an HTML document:

```
var oDiv = document.getElementById("transformedData");
oDiv.innerHTML = sResult;
```

This is perhaps the simplest object in the zXml library.

Best Picks Revisited

Imagine once again that you run an online bookstore. Your visitors like the Best Picks feature you implemented, but you start to receive feedback that they want the picks of the previous week as well. You decide to roll with an Ajax solution.

Using XMLHttp, the browser retrieves the book list and the request's responseText is loaded into an XML DOM object. The stylesheet also is loaded into its own XML DOM object, and the XML data from the book list is transformed into HTML, which is then written to the page. To provide some usability, you provide a link in the upper right-hand corner to change from one list to another.

The first step in this solution is to retrieve the XML file with XMLHttp. This is the beginning of the code and the entry point for the mini application, so you'll encapsulate the code in a function called init():

```
function init(sFilename) {
    var oReq = zXmlHttp.createRequest();
    oReq.onreadystatechange = function () {
        if (oReq.readyState == 4) {
            // only if "OK"
            if (oReq.status == 200) {
                transformXml(oReq.responseText);
            }
        }
    };
    oReq.open("GET", sFilename, true);
    oReq.send();
}
```

The init() function accepts one argument: the file name of the XML file to load. For cross-browser compatibility (not to mention easier coding for you) you create an XMLHttp object using the zXml library. This is an asynchronous request, so the readyState property must be checked using the onreadystatechange event handler. When the request returns as OK, the responseText is sent to the transformXml() function:

```
function transformXml(sResponseText) {
    var oXmlDom = zXmlDom.createDocument();
    oXmlDom.async = false;
    oXmlDom.loadXML(sResponseText);

    var oXslDom = zXmlDom.createDocument();
    oXslDom.async = false;
    oXslDom.load("books.xsl");

    var str = zXslt.transformToText(oXmlDom, oXslDom);
    document.getElementById("divBookList").innerHTML = str;
}
```

Calling transformXml() loads the passed response text into an XML DOM object using the loadXML() method. The XSL stylesheet is also loaded, and both objects are passed to the transformToText() method in the zXml library. The transformation's result, a string, is then added to an element in the document via the innerHTML property. As a result of this function, this week's book list is visible to the user.

A good portion of the code is written, but you still lack the list-changing feature. To facilitate this ability, another function needs writing, but first, the application needs to know what list to load as the user clicks the link. This is easily handled by Boolean variable called bIsThisWeek. When this week's book list is loaded, bIsThisWeek becomes true, otherwise it's false. Since this week's list is already loaded, bIsThisWeek is set to true:

```
var bIsThisWeek = true;
```

The link that the user clicks to change the list uses the onclick event, so the next function will handle that event:

```
function changeList() {
    var aChanger = document.getElementById("aChanger");

    if (bIsThisWeek) {
        aChanger.innerHTML = "This Week's Picks";
        init("lastweekbooks.xml");
        bIsThisWeek = false;
    } else {
        aChanger.innerHTML = "Last Week's Picks";
        init("thisweekbooks.xml");
        bIsThisWeek = true;
    }
    return false;
}
```

In this code, the link (aChanger) is retrieved with the getElementById() method. The variable bIsThisWeek is checked. According to its value, the proper list is loaded by sending the file name to the init() function. This retrieves the new list, transforms the data, and writes it to the page. Also, note that the link text changes to cue users of what happens the next time they click the link. The bIsThisWeek variable also changes so that the correct list is loaded the next time the user clicks the link. Last, the function returns false. Since this function is an event handler for a link, returning any other value would cause the link to behave as a link and could take the user away from the application.

Finally, you can complete the mini application with the HTML, and here is the entire document:

```
<!DOCTYPE html PUBLIC "-//W3C//DTD XHTML 1.1//EN"
            "http://www.w3.org/TR/xhtml11/DTD/xhtml11.dtd">
<html xmlns="http://www.w3.org/1999/xhtml" >
<head>
    <title>Book XML Exercise</title>
    <link rel="stylesheet" type="text/css" href="books.css" />
    <script type="text/javascript" src="zxml.js"></script>
    <script type="text/javascript">
        function init(sFilename) {
            var oReq = zXmlHttp.createRequest();
            oReq.onreadystatechange = function () {
                if (oReq.readyState == 4) {
                    // only if "OK"
                    if (oReq.status == 200) {
                        transformXml(oReq.responseText);
                    }
```

```
                }
            };
            oReq.open("GET", sFilename, true);
            oReq.send();
        }

        function transformXml(sResponseText) {
            var oXmlDom = zXmlDom.createDocument();
            oXmlDom.async = false;
            oXmlDom.loadXML(sResponseText);

            var oXslDom = zXmlDom.createDocument();
            oXslDom.async = false;
            oXslDom.load("books.xsl");

            var str = zXslt.transformToText(oXmlDom,oXslDom);
            document.getElementById("divBookList").innerHTML = str;
        }

        var bIsThisWeek = true;

        function changeList() {
            var aChanger = document.getElementById("aChanger");
            if (bIsThisWeek) {
                aChanger.innerHTML = "This Week's Picks";
                init("lastweekbooks.xml");
                bIsThisWeek = false;
            } else {
                aChanger.innerHTML = "Last Week's Picks";
                init("thisweekbooks.xml");
                bIsThisWeek = true;
            }
            return false;
        }
    </script>
</head>
<body onload="init('thisweekbooks.xml')">
    <a id="aChanger" href="#" onclick="changeList();">Last Week's Picks</a>
    <div id="divBookList"></div>
</body>
</html>
```

To run this mini application, you must run it from a web server because XMLHttp is used. Any web server software will work fine. Just place this HTML file, the zXml library, and the CSS file into a directory called `booklists` on your web server. Then fire up your browser and point it to `http://local host/booklists/book.htm`.

Summary

In this chapter, you learned how to create and traverse the XML DOM objects in both Internet Explorer and Firefox, as well as the differences between the two browser implementations. You once again used the cross-browser XML library zXml, which enables you to create, traverse, and manipulate XML DOM objects easily using a single interface. You also learned how to load XML data using JavaScript and output it to the page.

In the second section, a brief introduction to XPath showed you the power the language offers for XML documents. You learned the IE and Firefox ways of supporting XPath and namespaces, which are quite different from one another. To ease this difficulty, the zXPath object of the zXml library was introduced, again providing one interface to select desired nodes easily for both browsers.

Finally, you learned about XSLT transformations, and how to perform them using MSXML and the Firefox XSLTProcessor class. Although the two interfaces have a few things in common, another cross-browser object of the zXml library was introduced to smooth out the wrinkles: the zXslt object, which allows XSLT transformations to be performed on both platforms with one method call.

Syndication with RSS/Atom

The introduction of XML ushered in a new era of sharing information. Previously, data sharing was difficult at best. Companies often had their own proprietary transmission protocols and data formats, and neither was available to the public. The idea of transmitting information on a web site using anything other than HTML was a strange, if unheard of, idea. But this changed in 1998 when Microsoft introduced Internet Explorer 4.0 with a new feature called Active Channels. Built upon the Microsoft-developed Channel Definition Format (CDF), Active Channels allowed web site content to be transmitted (or *syndicated*) to users' desktops using the bundled Active Desktop. The problem with Active Channels, however, was its poor support for the everyday user. Anyone could make a channel, but the industry lacked tools to create and manage CDF files easily. The primary users of Active Channels, big media companies, pushed users away with excessive ads that increased the amount of bandwidth the channel used. Additionally, there was little demand or perceived value in using Active Channels. The whole concept of syndication seemed to have died with Active Channels and the failure of CDF to reach recommendation status from the World Wide Web Consortium. And then came RSS.

RSS

In March of 1999, Netscape launched the My Netscape portal, a single place for users to visit for all their news. The idea was simple: to pull information from any number of news sources and display them on My Netscape. To facilitate this idea, Dan Libby of Netscape Communications developed RDF Site Summary (RSS), an XML data format based on the Resource Description Framework (RDF). It would later become known as RSS 0.9.

Shortly after the introduction of RSS 0.9, Dave Winer of Userland Software contacted Libby regarding the RSS 0.9 format. Winer had developed an XML format to use with his site, ScriptingNews, and believed that it and RSS 0.9 could be combined and simplified to make a better, more usable, format. In July of 1999, Libby released a prototype of the new Rich Site Summary (also RSS), which became RSS 0.91. My Netscape then began using RSS 0.91 and continued to do so until 2001, when support for external RSS feeds was dropped. Netscape soon lost interest in RSS and left it without an owner. What would follow splintered the RSS format into two different versions.

A mailing list of developers and other interested parties formed in order to continue the development of RSS. This group, called RSS-DEV (http://groups.yahoo.com/group/rss-dev/), produced a specification called RSS 1.0, in December 2000. RSS 1.0 was based on the original RDF Site Summary (RSS 0.9) and sought to extend it by modularizing the original 0.9 version. These modules are namespaces that can be created by anyone, allowing new functionality to be added without changing the specification. It's important to note that RSS 1.0 is a descendant of RSS 0.9 but not related to RSS 0.91.

At the same time, Winer declared himself the owner of RSS and continued to develop his own version, releasing what he deemed RSS 2.0 (Really Simple Syndication). This new RSS format was based on RSS 0.91, the version that Winer and Libby developed together. The emphasis for RSS 2.0 was the simplicity of the format. When Winer ended up working at Harvard, he assigned ownership of RSS 2.0 to Harvard's Berkman Center for the Internet & Society, which now manages and publishes the specification at http://blogs.law.harvard.edu/tech/rss. RSS 2.0 is the most widely used RSS format today.

Today, the term RSS encompasses three different versions of the RSS format: RSS 0.91, RSS 1.0, and RSS 2.0.

RSS 0.91

RSS 0.91 is based upon Document Type Declarations (DTDs) and was possibly the most popular RSS version until the release of RSS 2.0. Some statistics show RSS 0.91 capturing 52 percent of the syndication market in 2001, with a steady increase until the introduction of 2.0. It owes its popularity to its drop-dead simplicity. Only a handful of 0.91 feeds are in use today, but RSS 2.0 owes much of its current success to RSS 0.91.

RSS 0.91's DTD lists 24 elements (14 more than RSS 0.9); it is easily read by humans and machines alike.

Take a peek at this 0.91 example:

```
<?xml version="1.0" encoding="UTF-8" ?>

<!DOCTYPE rss PUBLIC "-//Netscape Communications//DTD RSS 0.91//EN"
     "http://my.netscape.com/publish/formats/rss-0.91.dtd">

<rss version="0.91">
    <channel>
        <title>My Revenge</title>
        <link>http://sithboys.com</link>
        <description>Dedicated to having our revenge</description>
        <item>
            <title>At last!</title>
            <link>http://sithboys.com/atlast.htm</link>
            <description>
                At last we will reveal ourselves to the Jedi. At last we will have
                our revenge.
            </description>
        </item>
    </channel>
</rss>
```

A defining feature of RSS 0.91 (and 2.0, for that matter) is the inclusion of all data inside the <channel/> element. All defining site information, as well as the <item/> elements, are contained by <channel/>. This is in stark contrast to the next RSS version: RSS 1.0.

RSS 1.0

RSS 1.0 is a departure from the then 0.91 standard and follows the RDF format of 0.9. RSS 1.0 is far more verbose than previous versions, and its extensibility makes it an attractive format, especially for developers of RDF-based applications.

RSS 1.0, although it maintains some resemblance to RSS 0.91, is structurally different and is akin to RSS 0.9.

```
<?xml version="1.0"?>

<rdf:RDF xmlns:rdf="http://www.w3.org/1999/02/22-rdf-syntax-ns#"
    xmlns="http://purl.org/rss/1.0/">

    <channel rdf:about="http:// sithboys.com/about.htm">
        <title>My Revenge</title>
        <link> http://sithboys.com</link>
        <description>
            Dedicated to having our revenge
        </description>
        <image rdf:resource="http://sithboys.com/logo.jpg" />
        <items>
            <rdf:Seq>
                <rdf:li resource="http://sithboys.com/atlast.htm" />
            </rdf:Seq>
        </items>
        <textinput rdf:resource="http://sithboys.com/search/" />
    </channel>

    <image rdf:about="http://sithboys.com/logo.jpg">
        <title>The Logo of the Sith</title>
        <link>http://sithboys.com/</link>
        <url>http://sithboys.com/logo.jpg</url>
    </image>

    <item rdf:about="http://sithboys.com/atlast.htm">
        <title>At last!</title>
        <link>http://sithboys.com/atlast.htm</link>
        <description>
            At last we will reveal ourselves to the Jedi. At last we will have
            our revenge.
        </description>
    </item>
</rdf:RDF>
```

Notice that the <item/> elements are outside the <channel/> element. The <items/> element inside of the <channel/> element contains a list of values, the <rdf:Seq/> element, of the included items outside of <channel/>. As you can see, it is far more complex than RSS 0.91, and although RSS 1.0 has gained a following, it does not compare to the popularity the other formats enjoy.

RSS 1.0 is not DTD-based like version 0.91, so it is not necessary to have one in the document.

RSS 2.0

RSS 2.0 almost exactly mirrors RSS 0.91. Version 2.0 brings many new elements to the table, like the `<author/>` element in the following example, while allowing modularized extensions like RSS 1.0. Because of the simplicity inherited from RSS 0.91, and the extensibility similar to RSS 1.0, it is no wonder that RSS 2.0 is the most used RSS format today.

The following is an example of a basic RSS 2.0 document:

```
<?xml version="1.0" encoding="UTF-8" ?>

<rss version="2.0">
    <channel>
        <title>My Revenge</title>
        <description>Dedicated to having our revenge</description>
        <link>http://sithboys.com</link>
        <item>
            <title>At last!</title>
            <link>http://sithboys.com/atlast.htm</link>
            <author>DarthMaul@sithboys.com</author>
            <description>
                At last we will reveal ourselves to the Jedi. At last we will have
                our revenge.
            </description>
        </item>
    </channel>
</rss>
```

RSS 2.0's popularity makes it a sought-after format to support. The application that this chapter covers supports one RSS format, and it is RSS 2.0.

Atom

Atom is the newest entry to the syndication scene. Since its inception, Atom has received quite a bit of coverage and usage. Atom, unlike RSS, is a strict specification. One of the problems of the RSS spec is the lack of information on how a developer handles HTML markup in its elements. Atom's specification addresses this issue and gives developers strict rules they must follow, as well as a host of new features, enabling developers to choose the content type of an element and specify attributes that designate how a specific element should be handled. With such features, it is no wonder powerhouses like Google and Movable Type are getting behind Atom.

Atom resembles RSS somewhat; aside from the different element names, the document structure is also different:

```
<?xml version="1.0" encoding="iso-8859-1"?>

<feed version="0.3" xmlns="http://www.w3.org/2005/Atom" xml:lang="en">
    <title>My Revenge</title>
```

```
<link rel="alternate" type="text/html" href="http://sithboys.com" />
<modified>2005-06-30T15:51:21-06:00</modified>
<tagline>Dedicated to having our revenge</tagline>
<id>tag:sithboys.com</id>
<copyright>Copyright (c) 2005</copyright>
<entry>
    <title>At last!</title>
    <link rel="alternate" type="text/html" href="
        http://sithboys.com/atlast.htm" />
    <modified>2005-06-30T15:51:21-06:00</modified>
    <issued>2005-06-30T15:51:21-06:00</issued>
    <id>tag:sithboys.com/atlast</id>
    <author>
        <name>Darth Maul</name>
    </author>
    <content type="text/html" xml:lang="en" xml:base="http://sithboys.com">
        At last we will reveal ourselves to the Jedi. At last we will have
        our revenge.
    </content>
</entry>
</feed>
```

FooReader.NET

Syndication with RSS and Atom is about the sharing of information. In order to view information from several different sources, an application called an *aggregator* is used to assimilate the different feeds into one location. An aggregator makes it easier and faster to stay up-to-date with information collected from around the Web (much easier than visiting several web sites each day). The rest of this chapter focuses on the design and development of such an aggregator.

FooReader.NET is a web-based, .NET RSS/Atom aggregator ported from ForgetFoo's ColdFusion-based FooReader (`http://reader.forgetfoo.com/`). With many conventional applications filling the aggregator void, including popular e-mail applications, why build a web-based RSS/Atom aggregator? Consider the following reasons:

- ❑ **The Web is cross-platform.** Building a web-based aggregator ensures that anyone with a modern browser can access it.

- ❑ **The Web is centrally located.** One of the problems with conventional aggregators that are installed on the computer is the upkeep of data in many locations. If you like to read syndicated feeds at work and at home, you must install an aggregator on each computer and load it with the appropriate feeds. A web-based aggregator eliminates this problem because any change made to the feed list is seen regardless of the user's location.

The next sections explain how FooReader.NET is built using Ajax. As with any web application, there are two main components: client-side and server-side.

Client-Side Components

As described earlier, the client-side components of an Ajax solution are in charge of presenting the data to the user and communicating with the server. For FooReader.NET, several client-side components are necessary to manage the overall user experience.

❑ XParser, the JavaScript class responsible for requesting information and parses it when the data is received.

❑ The user interface ties the user to their data. Because the user interface is essentially a web page, the usual suspects of web browser technologies are used: HTML, CSS, and JavaScript.

❑ The JavaScript code that takes the information XParser received and displays it to the UI.

Although JavaScript has no formal definition of classes, it does have the logical equivalent. To aid in your understanding, this text refers to functions that create objects as classes.

XParser

The first component in FooReader.NET is XParser, a JavaScript class that parses RSS and Atom feeds into JavaScript objects that can be easily used in web applications. The primary goal of XParser is to provide an interface for developers to easily access the most important elements. Not only does this save lines of code (not to mention download time), but extra, unnecessary work for the client as well.

The class-centric .NET Framework primarily inspires its design: with three classes comprising the main XParser class: XParserItem, XParserElement, and XParserAttribute.

Starting with the simplest class in XParser, XParserAttribute is a representation of an element's attribute. Attributes tend to have only one desired piece of data: its value, and that is the only property of XParserAttribute.

```
function XParserAttribute(oNode) {
    this.value = oNode.nodeValue;
}
```

The XParserAttribute constructor takes one argument, the DOM attribute node. From this node, the attribute's value is accessed and stored to the value property by the node's nodeValue property. Simple, eh?

The XParserElement class represents an XML element and is responsible for accessing and retrieving the element's value and attributes. The class's constructor accepts two arguments: the XML element's node and the value of that node.

```
function XParserElement(oNode,sValue) {
    this.node = oNode || false;
    this.value = sValue || (this.node && this.node.text) || false;
```

In these first few lines, two of the four class properties are set according to the values of the parameters. Notice the use of the OR (||) operator in the assignment.

In the assignment of node, using the OR operator is a shorthand version of the ternary operator and produces the same results as this.node = (oNode)?oNode:false;. The assignment of value works more like an if...else if block.

```
    if (sValue) {
        this.value = sValue;
    } else if (this.node && this.node.text) {
        this.value = this.node.text;
    } else {
        this.value = false;
    }
```

The shorthand version removes over half of the characters of the `if...else if` block, and cutting excess characters is always good.

> *There is no `text` property for an element in the Firefox DOM. To gain this functionality, `XParser` uses the `zXml` library introduced in previous chapters, which extends the Firefox DOM to include the `text` and `xml` properties.*

The next few lines build the `attributes` collection, a collection of `XParserAttribute` objects.

```
    if (this.node) {
        this.attributes = [];
        var oAtts = this.node.attributes;
        for (var i = 0; i < oAtts.length; i++) {
            this.attributes[i] = new XParserAttribute(oAtts[i]);
            this.attributes[oAtts[i].nodeName] = new
                XParserAttribute(oAtts[i]);
        }
    } else {
        this.attributes = false;
    }
    this.isNull = (!this.node && !this.value && !this.attributes);
```

The existence of the node is checked first. (There's no sense in creating a collection of attributes of a node that doesn't exist.) Then an array is created, and the element's attributes are collected through the DOM property `attributes`. Using a `for` loop, the attribute node is used in the creation of `XParserAttribute` objects; one using an integer key, and one using the attribute's name as a key that is retrieved with the `nodeName` property. The latter is to allow easy access to specific attributes where the name of the attribute is known.

If the element's node does not exist, `attributes` is set to `false`. (You can't divide by 0, and you can't get attributes from a node that doesn't exist.) Last, `isNull` is assigned. The `isNull` property enables you to check if the resulting object is `null` or not. If the `node`, `value`, and `attributes` properties are all `false`, then the `XParserElement` object is considered to be `null`.

The `XParserItem` class represents an `<rss:item/>` or an `<atom:entry/>` element (from now on, these elements will be referred to as simply *items*). Items consist of several elements, so naturally there will be quite a bit of parsing. The `XParserItem` constructor takes one argument called `itemNode`, which represents the item's DOM node.

```
    function XParserItem(itemNode) {
        this.title=this.link=this.author=this.description=this.date =
            new XParserElement();
```

This first line of this class is important. Even though RSS and Atom are standards, it does not necessarily mean that everyone follows the given standards. An RSS feed may leave out the `<author/>` element in one or all items, or an Atom feed may disregard the `<content/>` tag in favor of the `<summary/>` tag. Because of these discrepancies, it is important that the XParserItem properties have a default value in order to avoid errors down the road. This default value is a null XParserElement. Now it is time to start parsing the child elements.

```
for (var i = 0; i < itemNode.childNodes.length; i++) {
    var oNode = itemNode.childNodes[i];
    if (oNode.nodeType == 1) {
        switch (oNode.tagName.toLowerCase()) {
```

To begin, a `for` loop cycles through the child elements. The node's type is then checked; if nodeType is 1, then the current node is an element. Checking a node's type may seem like an odd thing to do, but it is necessary. Mozilla can count white space between elements as children; therefore, checking the nodeType avoids errors when the node is sent to XParserElement. When it is confirmed that the current node is indeed an element, the tag name is used in a `switch...case` block and the item's properties are assigned according to their tag name counterparts.

```
//Shared Tags
case "title":
    this.title = new XParserElement(oNode);
break;
case "link":
    if (oNode.getAttribute("href")) {
        this.link = new XParserElement(oNode,oNode.getAttribute("href"));
    } else {
        this.link = new XParserElement(oNode);
    }
break;
case "author":
    this.author = new XParserElement(oNode);
break;
```

Although different in many ways, RSS and Atom do have a few elements in common. In this code these like elements are the `<title/>`, `<link/>`, and `<author/>` elements. The only difference is in the `<link/>` element; in an Atom feed the desired value is located in the `href` attribute. The RSS value is simply the element's value.

```
//RSS Tags
case "description":
    this.description = new XParserElement(oNode);
break;
case "pubdate":
    this.date = new XParserElement(oNode);
break;
```

Following the shared elements are the RSS-specific elements, where the `<description/>` and `<pubdate />` elements are matched and sent to XParserElement.

```
//Atom Tags
case "content":
    this.description = new XParserElement(oNode);
```

```
        break;
    case "issued":
        this.date = new XParserElement(oNode);
        break;
```

In this code, the Atom-specific elements `<content/>` and `<issued/>` are matched. The last elements checked are extensions:

```
    //Extensions
    case "dc:date":
        this.date = new XParserElement(oNode);
        break;
    default:
        break;
```

This code checks for the `<dc:date/>` element, a part of the Dublin Core extension (`http://dublin core.org/documents/dcmi-terms/`). This extension is widely used, so it is a good idea to check for it and use its value.

If for some reason a feed does not have an element in the `switch` block, the property representing the element defaults to a blank `XParserElement` object (from the first line of the `XParserItem` class). Because `XParser` is a JavaScript class, not every element needs to be parsed. However, the use of `switch` easily allows for the addition of other elements, if needed.

The `XParser` class is the main class that encompasses all the previous classes discussed. Its constructor accepts an argument `sFileName` and an optional argument called `bIsXml`. For maximum flexibility, `XParser` is designed either to make its own XMLHttp requests or to have the `responseText` of an external request passed to the constructor. If `bIsXml` is `false` or `undefined`, then `sFileName` is treated as a URL and `XParser` will make its own request; otherwise, `sFileName` is treated as an XML string and will be loaded into an XML DOM object.

```
    var oThis = this;
    this.title=this.link=this.description=this.copyright=this.generator=this.modified=
        this.author = new XParserElement();
    this.onload = null;
```

It may seem strange to assign a variable to contain the object's reference, but this technique comes in handy when dealing with the `onreadystatechange()` event handler of an XMLHttp object, which will be seen later. The next line of code is similar in idea and function to the first line in `XParserItem`. It sets the object's properties that represent important elements with a default value. The following line declares `onload`, an event handler, which fires when the feed is completely loaded.

`XParser`'s `load()` method is called when the XML data is retrieved. When XML is passed to the constructor, the `load()` method is immediately called and the XML data contained in `sFileName` is passed to the method.

```
    if (bIsXml) {
        this.load(sFileName);
    }
```

However, when a URL is passed to the constructor (and `bIsXml` is `false` or `undefined`), `XParser` makes its own request.

```
    else {
        var oReq = zXmlHttp.createRequest();
        oReq.onreadystatechange = function () {
            if (oReq.readyState == 4) {
                //only if "OK"
                if (oReq.status == 200) {
                    oThis.load(oReq.responseText);
                }
            }
        };
        oReq.open("GET", sFileName, true);
        oReq.send(null);
    }
}
```

Note that this code uses the zXmlHttp cross-browser factory introduced earlier in the book using the onreadystatechange() event, the status of the request is checked and the responseText is passed to the load() method when the request is successful. This is where the oThis variable comes into play. Had this.load(oReq.responseText) been used, an error would have been thrown stating this.load() is not a function. This particular error is thrown because while inside the onreadystate change event handler, the this keyword references the event handler, not the XParser object.

Finally, the request is sent via the send() method.

The load() method is called only when XML data is ready to parse. It takes one argument, sXml, which is the XML data to parse.

```
XParser.prototype.load = function (sXml) {
    var oXmlDom = zXmlDom.createDocument();
    oXmlDom.loadXML(sXml);
```

In this code, the XML data is loaded into an XMLDOM object created from the cross-browser XML DOM factory discussed in Chapter 4. Now that the DOM is ready to go, the parsing can begin.

```
this.root = oXmlDom.documentElement;
```

The first step is to parse the simple properties of the file. Using the root property, which references the XML document element, it's possible to determine what type of feed is being parsed.

```
this.isRss = (this.root.tagName.toLowerCase() == "rss");
if (this.isRss && parseInt(this.root.getAttribute("version")) < 2) {
    throw new Error("RSS version is less than 2");
}
this.isAtom = (this.root.tagName.toLowerCase() == "feed");
this.type = (this.isRss)?"RSS":"Atom";
```

To find out what type of feed it is, the document's root element is checked. If the tag name is rss, then a version of RSS is being used. If the document's root element is feed, then it is an Atom feed. The Boolean properties isRss and isAtom are assigned their values according to the feed type. Last, the type property is set to reflect the feed type. This particular property is displayed to the user.

If the feed is RSS, it is important to check the version of the feed. XParser was written to parse RSS 2.x feeds, and if the version is less than 2, an error is thrown and all parsing is stopped.

Both RSS and Atom have elements that contain information about the feed itself, but they are located in different parts of the document. In RSS, this information is contained in a <channel /> element that encloses all other elements in the feed. Atom, on the other hand, uses its root element to enclose the information. This similarity can be used to parse the feed easily:

```
var oChannel = (this.isRss)?this.root.getElementsByTagName("channel")[0]:this.root;
```

If the feed is RSS, the oChannel variable is set to the <channel/> element; otherwise, it's set to the document element of the feed. After this common starting point, parsing the non-items can begin:

```
for (var i = 0; i < oChannel.childNodes.length; i++) {
    var oNode = oChannel.childNodes[i];
    if (oNode.nodeType == 1) {
```

A for loop is used to loop through the children of the channel. Once again, the nodeType property of the current node is checked. If confirmed to be an element, parsing continues. Just like XParserItem, a switch block is used.

```
switch (oNode.tagName.toLowerCase()) {
    //Shared Tags
    case "title":
        this.title = new XParserElement(oNode);
    break;
    case "link":
        if (this.isAtom) {
            if (oNode.getAttribute("href")) {
                this.link = new XParserElement(oNode,oNode.getAttribute("href"));
            }
        } else {
            this.link = new XParserElement(oNode);
        }
    break;
    case "copyright":
        this.copyright = new XParserElement(oNode);
    break;
    case "generator":
        this.generator = new XParserElement(oNode);
    break;
```

RSS and Atom have quite a few elements in this part of their specifications that are similar, and this makes life easier (and keeps the amount of code down). The main difference in these few elements is the <link/> element (just like in XParserItem). Atom feeds contain a <link/> element, but the value you want to use is an attribute. Using the getAttribute() method, the href attribute's value is retrieved and is included in the XParserElement constructor. Next are the RSS-specific elements.

```
    //RSS Tags
    case "description":
        this.description = new XParserElement(oNode);
    break;
    case "lastbuilddate":
        this.modified = new XParserElement(oNode);
    break;
```

```
case "managingeditor":
    this.author = new XParserElement(oNode);
break;
```

And then the Atom-specific elements.

```
//Atom Tags
case "tagline":
    this.description = new XParserElement(oNode);
break;
case "modified":
    this.modified = new XParserElement(oNode);
break;
case "author":
    this.author = new XParserElement(oNode);
break;
default:
break;
```

The feed's informational elements are parsed, and then it is time to create and populate the `items` array. As the name implies, the `items` array is a collection is of `XParserItem` objects. The `<rss:item/>` and `<atom:entry/>` elements will be looped through and sent to the `XParserItem` constructor:

```
var oItems = null;
if (this.isRss) {
    oItems = oChannel.getElementsByTagName("item");
} else {
    try {
        oXmlDom.setProperty('SelectionLanguage', 'XPath');
        oXmlDom.setProperty("SelectionNamespaces",
            "xmlns:atom='http://www.w3.org/2005/Atom'");
        oItems = oXmlDom.selectNodes("/atom:feed/atom:entry");
    } catch (oError) {
        oItems = oChannel.getElementsByTagName("entry");
    }
}
```

Since the Microsoft XML DOM version 4, the `getElementsByTagName()` method has changed somewhat. In version 3 and below, qualified names were ignored when using `getElementsByTagName()`, so retrieving any element was as simple as passing the tag name to the method.

In version 4 and later, however, selecting an element with a default namespace requires the use of the `selectNodes()` method, which takes an XPath expression. The `setProperty()` method, which sets additional properties for the XML DOM parser, is used to set the namespace in order make selections with `selectNode()` possible. In the previous example, a `try...catch` block is used to discern which method should be used. The newer `selectNodes()` method is tried; if it fails, then `getElementsByTagName()` is used to retrieve the elements.

>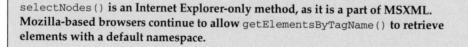
> `selectNodes()` is an Internet Explorer-only method, as it is a part of MSXML. Mozilla-based browsers continue to allow `getElementsByTagName()` to retrieve elements with a default namespace.

After the retrieval of the `<rss:item/>` and `<atom:entry/>` elements, each individual node is passed to the `XParserItem` class constructor to create the `items` array:

```
for (var i = 0; i < oItems.length; i++) {
    this.items[i] = new XParserItem(oItems[i]);
}
```

At this point, all of the important elements are parsed and contained in their corresponding properties. The only thing left to do is fire the `onload` event:

```
if (typeof this.onload == "function") {
    this.onload();
}
```

When `onload` was first declared, it was assigned the value of `null`. Because of this, it is important to check the `onload` type. If it is a function (meaning that the event now has a handler), then the `onload()` method is called. Use of this event will be seen later in the chapter.

The User Experience

The user interface may be the most important part of any application; if the user cannot use the application, there is no reason for the application to exist. FooReader.NET was designed to be easily used and understood by the user. In fact, it borrows heavily from the Microsoft Outlook 2003 user interface. It has a three-pane interface where the first two panes are a fixed width while the third pane is fluid (see Figure 5-1).

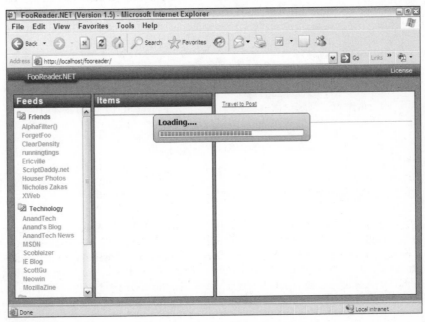

Figure 5-1

The first pane, called the *feeds pane*, displays the different feeds as links that the user can click on. A `<div/>` element with an `id` of `divFeedList` in the feeds pane allows the feeds list to be written to the document. Because this pane is populated dynamically, only the containing elements are statically written:

```
<div id="divFeedsPane">
    <div class="paneheader">Feeds</div>
    <div id="divFeedList"></div>
</div>
```

When the user clicks on a feed, the feed items are loaded into the middle pane: the *items pane*. This second pane has two elements that are used to display information. The first is a `<div/>` element with an `id` of `divViewingItem`. This element displays two things to the user: which feed they are currently reading and the feed document type (RSS or Atom). The second element is another `<div/>` element whose `id` attribute is set to `divItemList`. This element will contain a list of `<item/>` RSS elements or `<entry/>` Atom elements. Like the feeds pane, only the containing elements are statically written to the page:

```
<div id="divItemPane">
    <div class="paneheader">Items</div>
    <div id="divViewingItem"></div>
    <div id="divItemList"></div>
</div>
```

If the user single-clicks an item, it loads the item into the last pane: the *reading pane*. This pane has three elements that display the item's information. The first, whose `id` is `divMessageTitle`, is where the `<title/>` element of RSS and Atom feeds is displayed. The second element has an `id` of `aMessageLink` whose `href` attribute is changed dynamically. Finally, the last element is `divMessageBody`, where the `<rss:description/>` and `<atom:content/>` elements are displayed:

```
<div id="divReadingPane">
    <div class="contentcontainer">
        <div class="messageheader">
            <div id="divMessageTitle"></div>
            <a href="" id="aMessageLink" title="Click to goto posting."
                target="_new">Travel to Post</a>
        </div>
        <div id="divMessageBody"></div>
    </div>
</div>
```

Usability

There are a few usability issues that you should be concerned with. For one, users expect web applications to function like any other application. In Outlook 2003, from which this application borrows heavily, double-clicking an item in the items pane pulled up the specific e-mail message in a new window. Since FooReader.NET is based on that model, double-clicking an item opens a new window and takes the user to the specific blog post or article. To achieve this, the `ondblclick` event on the items is assigned the `doubleClick()` handler (you'll see this assignment later):

```
function doubleClick() {
    var oItem = oFeed.items[this.getAttribute("frFeedItem")];
    var oWindow = window.open(oItem.link.value);
}
```

Second, the user needs to know when the application is working to fill a request. The only time a request is made to the server is when a feed is loaded, so some type of visual cue needs to show the user that something is happening. For this purpose, a loading screen is shown when a feed is requested and is hidden when the feed is loaded. Figure 5-2 shows this user interface cue in action.

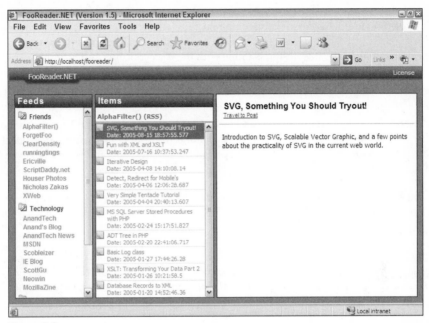

Figure 5-2

This loading cue is controlled by a JavaScript function called `toggleLoadingDiv()`. It takes one argument, a Boolean value that determines whether the cue is shown:

```
function toggleLoadingDiv(bShow) {
    var oToggleDiv = document.getElementById("loadingDiv");
    oToggleDiv.style.display = (bShow)?"block":"none";
}
```

Server-Side Components

In a perfect world, a simple application such as FooReader.NET would be strictly client-side. JavaScript would be able to retrieve XML feeds across domains with XMLHttp, and there would be no need to make any calls to a server component. Because of the Internet Explorer and Firefox security restrictions, however, it is not possible to retrieve data from a different domain; thus, a server-side component is required.

Possible Paradigms

The server's job in FooReader.NET is to retrieve the remote XML feeds for the client to use. Following this model, there are two possible design paths for the server; both have their pros and cons.

The first method is a cached feed architecture. The server program would act as a service, fetching a list of feeds at a certain time interval, caching them, and serving the cached feeds to the client when requested. This option potentially saves bandwidth, but it also risks the reader not having up-to-date feeds. More user action would be required to display the current, up-to-date feeds, which goes against the Ajax ideology.

The second method is a delivery on demand architecture, where the server would retrieve any given feed when the user requests it. This may use more bandwidth, but it ensures the reader will have up-to-date information; moreover, this design is inline with the Ajax concepts and is what the user would expect.

Implementation

FooReader.NET uses the delivery on demand model, with the exception that a feed is cached when it is fetched. The cached version is used only in the event that the remote host cannot be contacted and an up-to-date feed cannot be retrieved. This ensures that the user has something to read, even though it is older data.

Because the server is responsible only for pulling and caching remote feeds, it makes sense to have one ASP.NET page responsible for these operations. This page, called xml.aspx, will have a code-behind file where a good deal of ASP.NET code is contained.

> *Code-behind is a method for authoring web pages for the ASP.NET platform. Unlike inline program-ming models, where the server-side code is interspersed with HTML markup (like PHP and ASP), code-behind enables you to remove all logic from the HTML code and place it in a separate class file. This results in a clean separation of HTML and your .NET programming language of choice.*

The entry point for the server-side is the Page_Load event handler, where a method called StartFooReader() is called. It is in StartFooReader() where your code will be contained.

The language of choice for this project is C#, which is the language created specifically for the .NET Framework.

Setting the Headers

For this application, you must set a few headers. Settings headers in ASP.NET is a simple task:

```
Response.ContentType = "text/xml";
Response.CacheControl = "No-cache";
```

Headers are set with the Response object, which encapsulates HTTP response information. Setting the MIME content type is imperative to the operation of the application. Mozilla-based browsers will not load an XML file as XML unless the MIME specifies an XML document, and "text/xml" is one of many types that do this.

It is also important to make sure that the XML data retrieved with XMLHttp is not cached. Internet Explorer (IE) caches all data retrieved with XMLHttp unless explicitly told not to with the CacheControl header. If this header is not set, IE will use the cached data until the browser's cache is dumped.

Getting the Remote Data

To determine the feeds to display, FooReader.NET uses a proprietary XML document, `feeds.xml`, which contains a list of feeds that are available for the user to request. This file contains a set of `<link/>` elements divided into sections by `<section/>` elements. Each `<link/>` element has a `filename` attribute which is similar to an `id` attribute in HTML; it must be unique, and it is an identifier for the `<link/>` element:

```xml
<?xml version="1.0" encoding="utf-8"?>
<feeds>
    <section name="News">
        <link name="Yahoo! Top Stories" filename="yahoo_topstories"
href="http://rss.news.yahoo.com/rss/topstories" />
    </section>
</feeds>
```

The example shows a basic feeds list. A typical list can contain as many `<section/>` and `<link/>` elements as you desire. Note that `<section/>` elements can only be children of the root element, and `<link/>` elements can only be contained in `<section/>` elements.

The name *attribute of the* `<section/>` *and* `<link/>` *elements is displayed to the user in the feeds pane and is not used in any other operation.*

When requesting a feed, the value of the `filename` attribute is assigned to the `xml` variable in the query string.

```
xml.aspx?xml=fileName
```

In ASP.NET, the `Request` object contains a `NameValueCollection` called `QueryString`. Using this collection, you can extract the value of the `xml` variable in the query string:

```
if (Request.QueryString["xml"] != null)
{
    string xml = Request.QueryString["xml"];
    FeedsFile feedsFile = new FeedsFile(Server.MapPath("feeds.xml"));
```

In the first line, the existence of the `xml` variable in the query string is checked. That value is then assigned to the `xml` variable, and a `FeedsFile` object is then instantiated.

The `FeedsFile` class contains a method called `GetLinkByFileName`, which returns a `FeedsFileLink` object and contains the information of a specific `<link/>` element. A string variable, `fileName`, is assigned the value of the cached feed's path that is used later.

```
FeedsFileLink link = feedsFile.GetLinkByFileName(xml);
string fileName = string.Format(
    @"{0}\xml\{1}.xml",Server.MapPath(String.Empty),link.FileName);
```

`String.Format()`, *as its name implies, formats strings (duh!). The first argument passed to the method is the string to format. This string most likely contains characters called format items that look like {0}, {1}, {2}, and so on. These format items are replaced with the corresponding arguments passed to the method. In the example above, {0} is replaced with the resulting string that* `Server.MapPath(String.Empty)` *returns.*

The @ operator before a string tells the compiler not to process escape strings. The string in the above example could have been written like `"{0}\\xml\\{1}.xml"` *with the same results.*

The .NET Framework provides the `HttpWebRequest` class, contained in the `System.Net` namespace, to request data from remote web hosts. The .NET Framework provides a few classes to perform this task (such as the generic `WebRequest` class), but the `HttpWebRequest` class provides HTTP-specific functionality, so it is best suited for this application. To create an `HttpWebRequest` object, you call the `Create()` method of the `WebRequest` class and cast it as `HttpWebRequest`:

```
HttpWebRequest getFeed = (HttpWebRequest) WebRequest.Create(link.Url);
getFeed.UserAgent = "FooReader.NET (http://reader.wdonline.com)";
string feedXml = String.Empty;
```

One HTTP-specific member, `HttpWebRequest`, provides is the `UserAgent` property. It is not completely necessary to use this property, but it accurately documents what is hitting the remote server. Many conventional aggregators have their own user agent string; so too does FooReader.NET. The variable `feedXml` is created as an empty string. This variable will later be assigned the contents of the remote feed. The next step in this process is to make the request and get the remote host's response:

```
//Get the response.
using (HttpWebResponse responseFeed = (HttpWebResponse) getFeed.GetResponse())
{
    //Create a stream reader.
    using (StreamReader reader = new
            StreamReader(responseFeed.GetResponseStream()))
    {
        //Read the contents.
        feedXml = reader.ReadToEnd();
    }
}
```

An `HttpWebResponse` object is created when the `GetResponse()` method of the `HttpWebRequest` class is invoked. The server's response is then read by creating a `StreamReader` object through the `GetResponseStream()` method, a member of the `HttpWebResponse` class. That stream is "read" to the `feedXml` variable, which was declared earlier. Since the `using` statement is used for the creation of the `HttpWebResponse` and `StreamReader` objects, they will be properly disposed of and do not require closing.

Caching the Feed

Although not entirely necessary, caching the feed is beneficial to the user in case the remote server cannot be reached. FooReader.NET is a newsreader, and it is desirable for the user to have something to read, even if it is an older version. There is primarily only one instance when the cached version is served to the user: when the remote host cannot be contacted because of Internet traffic or the route to the remote host is down.

A `StreamWriter` is perfect for this job for its ease of use and its default UTF-8 encoding:

```
using (StreamWriter strmWriter = new StreamWriter(fileName))
{
    strmWriter.Write(feedXml);
}
```

The `fileName` variable, which was created earlier, is passed to the constructor of the `StreamWriter`. This creates the file or overwrites an existing one with the same name. The XML data contained in `feedXml` is then written to the file using the `Write()` method.

The feed is cached; now the XML data is written to the page using `Response.Write()`.

```
Response.Write(feedXml);
```

Error Handling

There are two main areas where an error takes place. The first is when the `xml` variable cannot be found in the query string. Without this variable, the application doesn't know what feed to locate in `feeds.xml`; an error document, which is a static RSS document, is loaded using the `GetLocalFile()` method (which is discussed later) and is written to the page.

```
if (Request.QueryString["xml"] != null)
{
    //Code goes here
}
else
{
    Response.Write(GetLocalFile(Server.MapPath("error.xml")));
}
```

Because the error document is an RSS document, the reader displays the error message like it would a feed.

The second area where an error can be thrown is when the remote host cannot be contacted. To catch this error, the request and response code is placed within a `try...catch` block.

```
try
{
    //Web request code here
}
catch (WebException webEx)
{
    string fileToUse = File.Exists(fileName)?fileName:Server.MapPath("error.xml");
    Response.Write(GetLocalFile(fileToUse));
}
```

Catching only a `WebException` forces other errors to not be handled. ASP.NET error reporting is very informational; if an `UnauthorizedAccessException` is thrown (which can happen in the `try...catch` block because of the caching operations) then permissions are not correctly set, and the error message can be helpful in deciding upon a solution.

This is where the cached file comes into play. When the error is caught, the application needs to know what file to write to the page: either the cached feed or the error document. It first checks to see if there is a cached copy using `File.Exists()`. If the cached file exists, the resulting file is retrieved with `GetLocalFile()` and written to the page. The `GetLocalFile()` method, which has been used a few times already, is a simple file-reading function. It opens the designated file, reads it, and returns the contents as a string:

```
public string GetLocalFile(string path)
{
    string contents = string.Empty;
    using (StreamReader file = File.OpenText(path))
    {
        contents = file.ReadToEnd();
    }
    return contents;
}
```

This really is just a convenience function since the application requires a great deal of file reading.

Parsing the Feeds File

The FeedsFile class opens the feeds file into an XmlDocument that can be used to retrieve any element desired through the DOM.

```
private XmlDocument _doc;
public FeedsFile(string path)
{
    _doc = new XmlDocument();
    _doc.Load(path);
}
```

FeedsFile exposes the GetLinkByFileName() method. This method takes one argument, fileName, and returns a FeedsFileLink object.

```
public FeedsFileLink GetLinkByFileName(string fileName)
{
    string pathToNode =
String.Format("/feeds/section/link[@filename='{0}']",fileName);
    XmlNode linkNode = _doc.SelectSingleNode(pathToNode);
    return new FeedsFileLink(linkNode);
}
```

The XmlDocument SelectSingleNode() method selects a specific XmlNode according to the XPath expression passed to it. The XPath expression used in this particular instance is formatted using String.Format() and selects a specific <link/> with a specific filename attribute. The selected XmlNode is then passed to the FeedsFileLink constructor and the object reference is returned.

FeedsFileLink takes an XmlNode and retrieves the information required from that node and assigns it to private members.

```
private string _name;
private string _filename;
private Uri _uri;

public FeedsFileLink(XmlNode myNode)
{
    _name = myNode.Attributes["name"].Value;
    _filename = myNode.Attributes["filename"].Value;
    _uri = new Uri(myNode.Attributes["href"].Value);
}
```

_name holds the value of the node's name attribute, _filename is assigned the filename attribute's value, and a System.Uri object is created and assigned to _uri.

Yes, a string *could be used instead of an* Uri *object, as most .NET classes and methods that take* Uri objects *are also overloaded to take a* string, *but* Uri *objects are so much cooler.*

The members mentioned above are private. Without an *accessor*, a private member cannot be accessed outside of the class. Accessors in C# allow read and/or write access to private members, among many other things:

```
public string Name
{
    get
    {
        return _name;
    }
}

public string FileName
{
    get
    {
        return _filename;
    }
}

public Uri Url
{
    get
    {
        return _uri;
    }
}
```

The accessors in FeedsFileLink provide read-only access to the private members. These particular accessors, called *getters*, return the value of the private members. This ensures that the data contained in the class is not mistakenly overwritten or corrupted.

Tying the Client to the Server

The glue of FooReader.NET is the JavaScript code that uses the data retrieved by XParser and the JavaScript FeedsFile class and sends it to the user interface to be displayed. This code is contained in feedsfileparser.js and fooreader.js.

Parsing the Feeds File — Client Style

The FeedsFile class, located in feedsfileparser.js, closely resembles its server-side counterpart; it is responsible for parsing feeds.xml into JavaScript objects.

The FeedsFileElement class represents an element in feeds.xml. Because only two different elements are used in the document, the class is fairly simple. It takes one argument: the element's node.

```
function FeedsFileElement(oNode) {
    if (oNode.tagName.toLowerCase() == "section") {
        this.links = [];
        var linkNodes = oNode.getElementsByTagName("link");
        for (var i = 0; i < linkNodes.length; i++) {
            this.links[i] = new FeedsFileElement(linkNodes[i]);
        }
    }
```

If oNode is a <section/> element, then an array of the contained <link/> elements must be made. The links array is populated by passing the <link/> elements through the FeedsFileElement constructor. When oNode is a <link/> element, the fileName property is assigned the value of the <link/> element's filename attribute by using the getAttribute() method:

```
    else {
        this.fileName = oNode.getAttribute("filename");
    }
    this.name = oNode.getAttribute("name");
```

Because both <section/> and <link/> elements have a name attribute, the name property it is assigned the value of the name attribute after all logic is complete.

The feeds file is loaded using the cross-browser XML library introduced in Chapter 4. The XML DOM is used instead of XMLHttp for a variety of reasons. For one, feeds.xml is a static XML file. Using XMLHttp in IE would require more back-end coding to specify the no-cache header; IE would continue to load its cached version of feeds.xml even after changes were made to the file.

```
function FeedsFile() {
    var oThis = this;
    this.sections = [];
    this.onload = null;

    var oXmlDom = zXmlDom.createDocument();
    oXmlDom.load("feeds.xml");
```

Even though the feeds file is loaded using the XML DOM, you should still use the asynchronous abilities (the default behavior) of the XML DOM object. Had the file been loaded synchronously, the application would wait until the document is fully loaded before continuing, which could appear to the user that the application has frozen. The onreadystatechange event is used to monitor the loading status:

```
    oXmlDom.onreadystatechange = function () {
        if (oXmlDom.readyState == 4) {
            var oSections = oXmlDom.documentElement.getElementsByTagName("section");

            for (var i = 0; i < oSections.length; i++) {
                oThis.sections[i] = new FeedsFileElement(oSections[i]);
            }
        }
    }

    oXmlDom = null;

    if (typeof oThis.onload == "function") {
```

```
            oThis.onload();
        }
    };
```

The `<section/>` elements are retrieved with the `getElementsByTagName()` DOM method, and the sections array is populated with `FeedsFileElement` objects. Once all DOM operations are complete, the document is released from memory by setting `oXmlDom` to `null`, and the `onload` event is fired.

The `FeedsFile` class has one method called `getLinkByFileName()` (which you should remember from the C# version). This method searches the `links` array of each `section` and returns the link object with the matching file name. Again, file names are unique (they have to be), so this is the identifier of a link:

```
this.getLinkByFileName = function (sFileName) {
    for (var i = 0; i < this.sections.length; i++) {
        var section = this.sections[i];
        for (var j = 0; j < section.links.length; j++) {
            var link = section.links[j];
            if (sFileName.toLowerCase() == link.fileName.toLowerCase()) {
                return link;
            }
        }
    }
    alert("Cannot fine the specified feed information.");
    return this.sections[0].link[0];
};
```

When a match cannot be found, an error message is displayed via the `alert()` method, and the first `<link/>` element in the feeds list is returned.

Drawing the User Interface Elements

The code within `fooreader.js` is responsible for generating the dynamic elements required to display the data to the user. The feeds list in the feeds pane and the items in the item pane are all dynamically generated according to the data they receive. This dynamic content is generated by both DOM methods and `innerHTML`. Elements created via the DOM are primarily created at the page load and when a new feed is loaded.

The contents of the message pane are displayed using `innerHTML`. This is necessary because many feeds include CDATA sections, which contain HTML formatting; using DOM methods to display the text could generate some confusing results (for example, text that is supposed to be bold could look like `<b>text goes here</b>`).

init()

The entry point for the client-side components is the `init()` function, which is responsible for populating the feeds pane and loading the first feed. A clean, easy-to-follow layout is key for the feeds pane, and to that end, unordered lists are used to format the data.

```
var divFeedList = document.getElementById("divFeedList");
var oFragment = document.createDocumentFragment();

for (var i = 0; i < oFeedsFile.sections.length; i++) {
    var oSection = oFeedsFile.sections[i];
```

The destination element for the feeds list is retrieved via `getElementById()` and stored in `divFeedList`. Creating the feed list updates the page constantly, which can lower the performance of the UI (and annoy the user). To correct this problem, the feeds list is first appended to a document fragment. When all append operations are complete, the fragment is then appended to the document (which appends all of the fragment's child nodes).

As mentioned earlier, sections should be easily and plainly defined in the UI, and having an icon next to the section's name is a good way to do this:

```
var oIcon = document.createElement("img");
oIcon.src = "img/category_icon.gif";
oIcon.border = "0";
oIcon.alt = "";

var oSpan = document.createElement("span");
oSpan.appendChild(document.createTextNode(section.name));
oSpan.className = "navheading";
```

The DOM method `createElement()` allows the creation of the icon, an image, and the section's name, which is encapsulated in a `<span/>` element. The creation of the section heading is complete so they are appended to the document fragment; an unordered list is also created to contain the section's feeds:

```
oFragment.appendChild(oIcon);
oFragment.appendChild(oSpan);
var oUl = document.createElement("UL");
oUl.className = "navlist";
```

The individual feeds are displayed as links, so `<a/>` and `<li/>` elements are created:

```
for (var j = 0; j < section.links.length; j++) {
    var oLink = oSection.links[j];
    var oLi = document.createElement("li");

    var oA = document.createElement("a");
    oA.appendChild(document.createTextNode(oLink.name));
    oA.href = "#";
    oA.onclick = loadFeed;
    oA.className = "navlinks";
    oA.title="Load " + oLink.name;
    oA.setAttribute("frFileName",link.fileName);

    oLi.appendChild(oA);
    oUl.appendChild(oLi);
}
```

The `<a/>` elements have an attribute called `frFileName`, which will contain the file name associated with the feed. When all links and sections are created, the unordered list is appended to the document fragment:

```
oFragment.appendChild(oUl);
```

And the document fragment is then appended to divFeedList, and the first feed is loaded in the user interface.

```
divFeedList.appendChild(oFragment);
loadFeed(feedsFile.sections[0].links[0].fileName);
```

The application is almost fully loaded at this point. The feeds list is completely populated, but the items pane is empty. Control is passed to loadFeed().

loadFeed()

The loadFeed() function is responsible for loading a specified feed in an XParser object and populating the items pane. This function also doubles as an onclick event handler for the links in the feeds pane. It takes one argument, sFileName, which corresponds with the filename attribute of a <link/> element in feeds.xml. If loadFeed() is fired because of an event, sFileName is changed to the value of the frFileName attribute mentioned earlier:

```
function loadFeed(sFileName) {
    sFileName = (typeof sFileName == "string")?sFileName:
        this.getAttribute("frFileName");
```

There are two elements in the user interface that must first be found and referenced in order to display the items list and feed information, divItemList and divViewingItem:

```
var divItemList = document.getElementById("divItemList");
var divViewingItem = document.getElementById("divViewingItem");
```

The list of items will appear to divItemList, and divViewingItem will contain the feed's name and type.

```
var sName = feedsFile.getLinkByFileName(sFileName).name;
toggleLoadingDiv(true);
```

The feed's name is retrieved via the getListByFileName() method of the feedsFile object. The toggleLoadingDiv() function is then called to cue the user that the application is working to fill the request.

The item list is nothing more than <a/> elements created by DOM methods. But first, any existing items must be removed from the document to be replaced with the new list. This is easily handled in a while loop:

```
while (divItemList.hasChildNodes()) {
    divItemList.removeChild(divItemList.lastChild);
}
```

Since the only children in divItemList are items, it is safe to remove every child. With all old items removed, it is time to create the XParser object:

```
sFileName = "xml.aspx?xml=" + sFileName;
oFeed = new XParser(sFileName);
```

The sFileName variable is changed to reflect the URL of the server application and is passed to the XParser constructor.

Performing an XMLHttp request can take several moments, and errors can be thrown if this is not taken into account. To solve this issue, XParser exposes an event called onload, which is fired when the XMLHttp request reaches a status of OK (status code 200). In FooReader.NET, the XParser onload event is used to write the items to divItemList, load the first item into the reading pane, and hide the loading user interface cue.

```
oFeed.onload = function () {
    var oFragment = document.createDocumentFragment();
    divViewingItem.innerHTML = sTitle + " (" + oFeed.type + ")";
```

Just as in init(), a document fragment is created here to reduce the load on the user interface. As stated earlier, divViewItem will display the feed's name and type by using the innerHTML property. This type of user feedback is critical to creating a good Ajax application. Although the information may not be necessary for the application to function properly, it gives the user an understanding of what he or she is doing.

The innerHTML property is used for simplicity's sake. In this situation, it takes fewer characters and less space to change the contents of the element with innerHTML than to use DOM methods. The innerText property would be ideal; Firefox, however, doesn't support the property.

Now it is time to create the items. Items are block style <a/> elements that contain two <div/> elements: one <div/> encloses the item's title, whereas the other houses the item's date. Like the list in the feed pane, the elements making up the items are created using the createElement() DOM method.

```
for (var i = 0; i < oFeed.items.length; i++) {
    var oItem = oFeed.items[i];
    var oA = document.createElement("a");
    oA.className = "itemlink";
    oA.href = "#";
    oA.onclick = itemClick;
    oA.ondblclick = doubleClick;
    oA.id = "oA" + i;
    oA.setAttribute("frFeedItem",i);
```

The first element created is the <a/> element. The anchor's attributes are typical: the class attribute is set to the CSS class itemlink, href is set to "#", onclick is set to itemClick, the ondbclick event, which fires when the anchor is double clicked, is handled by doubleClick(), and the id attribute is set to contain the string oAx, where x is the item's number.

The itemClick() function is covered in the next section.

The first <div/> element is then created. This element will contain the item's title:

```
var divTitle = document.createElement("div");
divTitle.className = "itemheadline";
divTitle.innerHTML = oItem.title.value;
```

You'll notice the use of `innerHTML` again instead of `createTextNode()`. This is due to the use of HTML formatting some use in their titles (be they HTML entities or elements). This leaves one more `<div/>` element to hold the date:

```
var divDate = document.createElement("div");
divDate.className = "itemdate";
divDate.appendChild(document.createTextNode("Date: " + oItem.date.value));
```

Creating the element for the date is much like the one for the title, except you'll notice the use of `createTextNode()` to append the text to the element (this is done because there shouldn't be any HTML formatting in the date).

Both `<div/>` elements are appended to the `<a/>` element which is, in turn, appended to the document fragment:

```
oA.appendChild(divTitle);
oA.appendChild(divDate);
oFragment.appendChild(oA);
```

After the loop is exited and all items are created, the document fragment is appended to the document, or more specifically, the item list:

```
divItemList.appendChild(oFragment);
```

`itemClick()` is then called to load the first item into the reading pane, and the loading user interface cue is hidden from view:

```
itemClick(0);
toggleLoadingDiv();
```

The items pane is now fully populated. All that remains is to load the first item into the reading pane, which is done by calling `itemClick()`.

itemClick()

The `itemClick()` function is called when the user clicks a link in the item pane (like `loadFeed()`, `itemClick()` also doubles as an event handler); it takes one parameter, `iItem`, which is an integer representing the item to display. It is also responsible for showing the user the last link that was clicked by changing its background color. This change of background color is achieved by changing the CSS class of the element to `itemlink-selected`. Making the style differences with CSS allows easy customization of the application.

For this user interface feature to work properly, a global variable is used to keep track of the selected item. This variable is called `oSelected` and will be assigned the selected element's reference:

```
iItem = (typeof iItem == "number")?iItem:this.getAttribute("frFeedItem");
var oEl = document.getElementById("oA"+iItem);
if (oSelected != oEl) {
    if (oSelected) oSelected.className = "itemlink";
    oEl.className += "-selected";
    oSelected = oEl;
```

The clicked link's object reference is retrieved with `getElementById()` and is assigned to `oEl`. `oEl` is then compared to `oSelected` to determine if it is a new link that was clicked. If the two objects are the same reference, nothing happens because the link that was clicked is the link that is currently selected. If the references do not match, then the `oSelected` class is set back to `itemlink`, the new link's class is set to `itemlink-selected`, and `oSelected` is set to the new link's reference.

To display the item in the reading pane, a few elements' references must be retrieved.

```
var divTitle = document.getElementById("divMessageTitle");
var aLink = document.getElementById("aMessageLink");
var divBody = document.getElementById("divMessageBody");
```

The `divTitle` element, as its name implies, is where the item's title will be displayed. The `aLink` element provides the user a link to click that loads the actual news item. The `divBody` element is where the `<rss:description/>` or `<atom:content/>` element is displayed:

```
var oItem = oFeed.items[iItem];
divTitle.innerHTML = oItem.title.value;
aLink.href = oItem.link.value;
divBody.innerHTML = oItem.description.value;
```

The item object is then assigned to `oItem` and is used to retrieve the data from `oFeed`. The item's title is then displayed in `divTitle`, and the link's `href` attribute is changed to reflect the new value. The item's description is displayed in `divBody` via `innerHTML`. Using `innerHTML` for `divBody` ensures that the item is displayed in a readable fashion for the user. HTML entities like `&amp;` will correctly be displayed as "&".

Setup

Generally, web applications are simple to set up and use. .NET web applications, however, require a few extra steps during setup.

The first requirement in installing FooReader.NET is to make sure that Internet Information Services (IIS) is installed on the machine. IIS is Microsoft's web server and is only available for owners of Windows 2000 Professional, Windows 2000 Server, Windows XP Professional, and Windows Server 2003. Installing IIS requires the Windows CD and can be done in the Add/Remove Windows Components section of the Add/Remove Programs Control Panel applet (see Figure 5-3).

You also must install the .NET Framework in order to run FooReader.NET. You need version 1.1 or greater. It is freely available at `http://msdn.microsoft.com/netframework/downloads/updates/default.aspx` for users of Windows 98 and later versions.

When IIS and the .NET Framework are installed, create a folder called FooReader in the IIS `wwwroot` directory, located at `c:\Inetpub\`, and move all FooReader.NET files and folders to the newly created `FooReader` folder. After the files have been placed in the FooReader directory, you need to register the application in IIS, which you can do in the IIS Management Console (see Figure 5-4). In the computer's Control Panel (Start⇨Control Panel), double-click Administrative Tools, and then double-click the Internet Information Services icon.

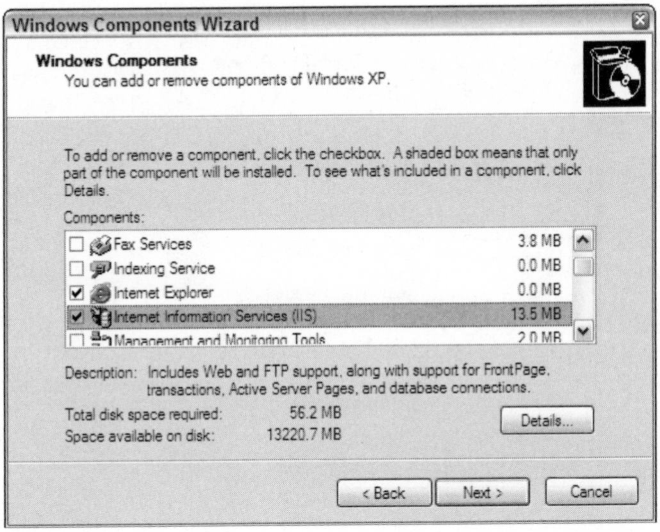

Figure 5-3

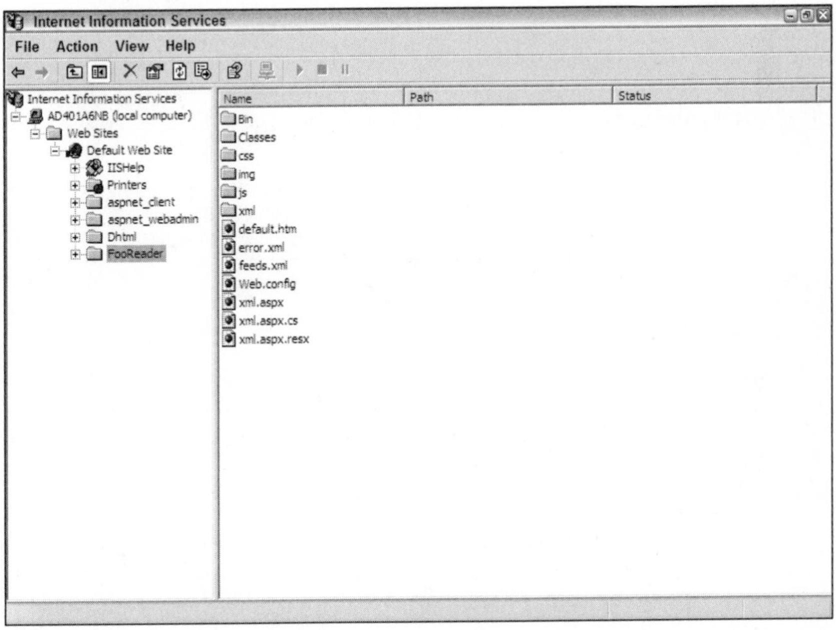

Figure 5-4

In the console, you will see a list of files and folders. These items are contained in the IIS root folder. In the left-hand pane, locate the FooReader folder. Right-click the folder and choose Properties from the context menu. You are now looking at the web properties of the FooReader folder (see Figure 5-5).

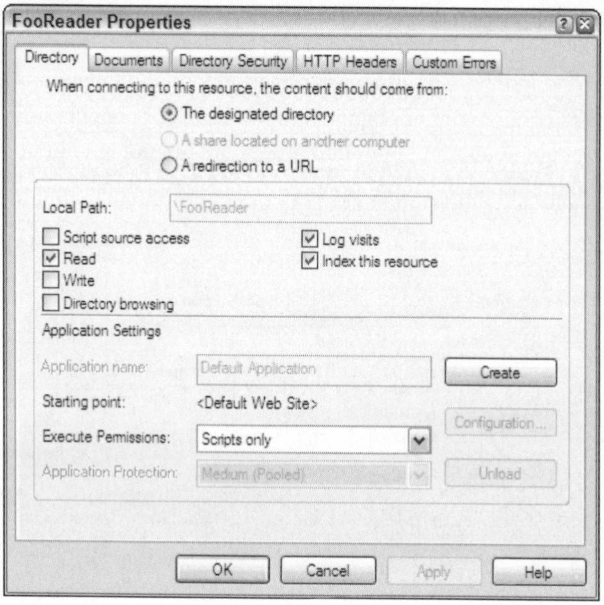

FooReader Properties

Directory | Documents | Directory Security | HTTP Headers | Custom Errors

When connecting to this resource, the content should come from:

- ◉ The designated directory
- ◯ A share located on another computer
- ◯ A redirection to a URL

Local Path: \FooReader

- ☐ Script source access   ☑ Log visits
- ☑ Read   ☑ Index this resource
- ☐ Write
- ☐ Directory browsing

Application Settings

Application name: Default Application   [Create]

Starting point: <Default Web Site>

Execute Permissions: Scripts only ▼   [Configuration...]

Application Protection: Medium (Pooled) ▼   [Unload]

[OK]   [Cancel]   [Apply]   [Help]

Figure 5-5

On the Directory tab, you see an Application Settings section in the bottom part of the window. Click the Create button, and the Properties window is displayed (see Figure 5-6).

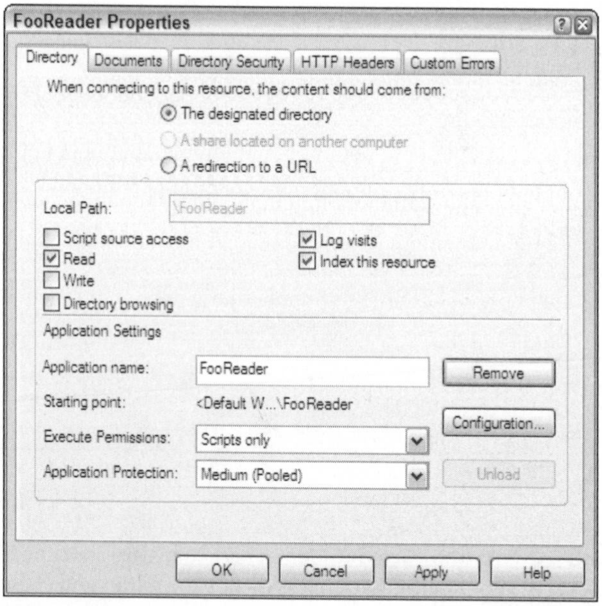

FooReader Properties

Directory | Documents | Directory Security | HTTP Headers | Custom Errors

When connecting to this resource, the content should come from:

- ◉ The designated directory
- ◯ A share located on another computer
- ◯ A redirection to a URL

Local Path: \FooReader

- ☐ Script source access   ☑ Log visits
- ☑ Read   ☑ Index this resource
- ☐ Write
- ☐ Directory browsing

Application Settings

Application name: FooReader   [Remove]

Starting point: <Default W...\FooReader

Execute Permissions: Scripts only ▼   [Configuration...]

Application Protection: Medium (Pooled) ▼   [Unload]

[OK]   [Cancel]   [Apply]   [Help]

Figure 5-6

Click OK. IIS now knows to treat the FooReader folder as an application, and will run it as one. The FooReader.NET application is now installed.

Testing

Before deploying any web application, it is always a good idea to test the installation. For testing purposes, `feeds.xml` contains only one feed: Yahoo! News.

Open your browser and navigate to `http://localhost/fooreader/xml.aspx?xml=yahoo_topstories`.

This tests to make sure that the server-side component is able to retrieve an external news feed properly. If everything is working correctly, you should see the XML feed displayed in your browser (see Figure 5-7).

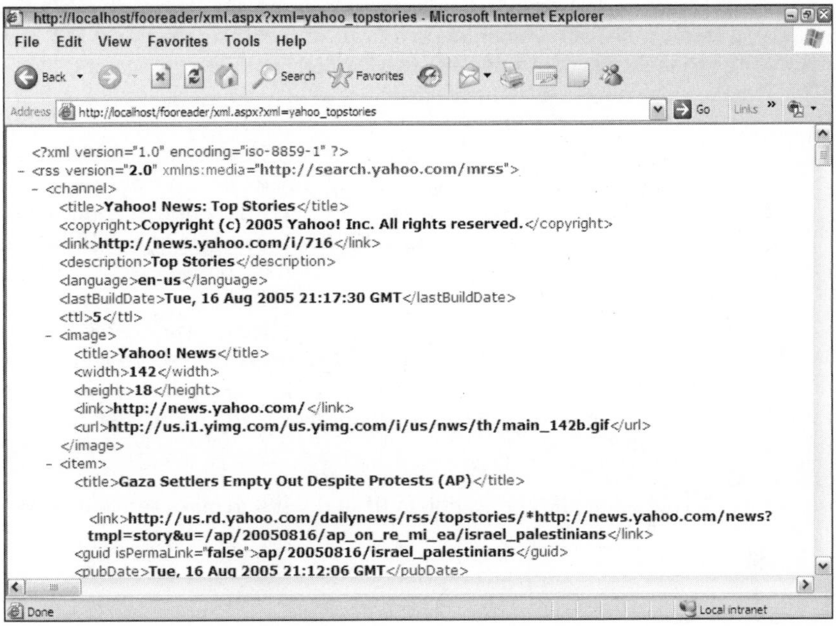

Figure 5-7

If for some reason you see an ASP.NET error, the error message will tell you what you should do. The most common error is an Access Denied error, in which case the proper modify rights should be given to the ASP.NET user account (or NETWORK SERVICE for Windows 2003).

If you do not have access to set permissions for the web server, such as when you rent web space from a provider, you may be able to solve Access Denied errors by turning on impersonation. The impersonation settings are located in the `web.config` file.

The `web.config` file is an XML-based configuration file for a web application. The root element of `web.config` is `<configuration/>`, which is usually followed by the `<system.web/>` element. You can add the following line to the `<system.web/>` element:

```
<identity impersonate="true"/>
```

Bear in mind that this solution is highly situational and depends on the web server's settings. However, it may solve unauthorized access errors you may encounter in a rented server environment.

Once the application is tested and is confirmed to work, you can edit `feeds.xml` to contain whatever feeds you desire.

Summary

In this chapter, you learned the history of online syndication, including the rise of RSS and Atom as the two dominant XML formats for syndication. You also learned how RSS aggregators, such as FooReader.NET, make using news feeds much easier.

This chapter walked through the creation and implementation of a web-based RSS/Atom aggregator, FooReader.NET. Starting with the client components, you learned how to create `XParser`, a JavaScript RSS/Atom parser that provides an easy to use interface for developers of web applications based on RSS and Atom. You also learned how `XParser` uses the XML DOM present in Microsoft Internet Explorer and Mozilla-based browsers.

You learned that while the client-side components of a web application are a necessity to properly display data to the user, server-side components are needed to retrieve the necessary data. Using C# and the .NET Framework, you learned how to retrieve remote XML feeds, cache them, and output them to a page. You also learned how to set HTTP headers so that browsers will know what to expect, and remote servers will know what is hitting them.

Finally, you learned how to set up the application in IIS and test it to make sure it was properly installed.

6

Web Services

When XML use began to take off just after the year 2000, businesses, developers, and others looked for new ways to use it. The promise of separating content and presentation had been met, but how could this capability be capitalized on? The answer came in the form of web services.

Web services provide a way to exchange data between applications and servers. To facilitate this communication, web services use the Internet to send messages composed of XML data back and forth between a *consumer* (the application that uses the data) and a *provider* (the server that contains the data). This is not unlike traditional distributed computing models, such as CORBA, DCOM, and RMI, where method calls are executed over a network connection. The major difference with web services is that the data being transmitted is XML text instead of a binary format.

The promise behind web services is that of having software components available, on demand, to any application in the world. Whether that be a web application or a traditional desktop application, it is possible to use the same service to perform the same task.

Related Technologies

Web services aren't a single technology or platform; in fact, they are a mixture of several protocols, languages, and formats. And although several different platforms have incorporated web services into their current offerings, there are still some basic parts that remain consistent.

SOAP

SOAP is a combination of an XML-based language and any number of common protocols for transmitting this data. The SOAP specification describes an intricate language with numerous elements and attributes, intended to describe most types of data. This information can be transported over any number of protocols, but is most commonly sent over HTTP along with other web traffic.

> Originally an acronym for Simple Object Access Protocol, the specification now simply goes by SOAP.

There are two main ways of using SOAP, the *remote procedure call* (*RPC*) style and the *document* style.

RPC-Style SOAP

The RPC style of SOAP treats the web service as though it were an object containing one or more methods (in much the same way you would use a local class to establish communication with a database). A request is made to the service detailing the method name to call and the parameters, if any, to pass. The method is executed on the server, and an XML response is dispatched containing the return value, if any, or an error message if something went awry. Imagine a web service that provides simple arithmetic operations: addition, subtraction, multiplication, and division. Each method takes two numbers and returns a result. An RPC-style request for the add operation would look something like this:

```
<?xml version="1.0" encoding="utf-8" ?>
<soap:Envelope xmlns:soap="http://schemas.xmlsoap.org/soap/envelope/"
                soap:encodingStyle="http://schemas.xmlsoap.org/soap/encoding/">
  <soap:Body>
    <w:add xmlns:w="http://www.wrox.com/services/math">
      <w:op1>4.5</w:op1>
      <w:op2>5.4</w:op2>
    </w:add>
  </soap:Body>
</soap:Envelope>
```

Whenever you are dealing with non-trivial XML documents, for example documents that are to be shared across businesses and applications, namespaces come into play. Namespaces are especially important in SOAP because these documents need to be produced and read by different systems. The SOAP namespace, specified in this example as `http://schemas.xmlsoap.org/soap/envelope/`, is for version 1.1, and can vary depending on which version you are using. The version 1.2 namespace is `http://www.w3.org/2003/05/soap-envelope`.

The `<w:add/>` element specifies the name of the method to call (`add`) and contains the other namespace in the example, `http://www.wrox.com/services/math`. This namespace is specific to the service that is being called and can be defined by the developer. The `soap:encodingStyle` attribute points to a URI indicating how the data is encoded in the request. There are a variety of other encoding styles available as well, such as the type system employed in XML schemas.

> An optional `<soap:Header/>` element can be used to contain additional information, such as security credentials. If used, this element comes immediately before `<soap:Body/>`.

If the request to add two numbers executed successfully, the response message would look like this:

```
<?xml version="1.0" encoding="utf-8" ?>
<soap:Envelope xmlns:soap="http://schemas.xmlsoap.org/soap/envelope/"
                soap:encodingStyle="http://schemas.xmlsoap.org/soap/encoding/">
```

```
      <soap:Body>
        <w:addResponse xmlns:w="http://www.wrox.com/services/math">
          <w:addResult>9.9</w:addResult>
        </w:addResponse>
      </soap:Body>
    </soap:Envelope>
```

As you can see, the format is similar to the initial request. The standard way of supplying the result is to create an element with the name of the method followed by the word "Response." In this case, the element is `<w:addResponse/>`, and has the same namespace as the `<w:add/>` element in the request. The actual result is returned in the `<w:addResult/>` element. Note that the web service developer can define all these element names.

Were there a problem processing the SOAP request on the server, assuming the request actually reached that far, then a `<soap:Fault>` element will be returned. For instance, if the first operand in the example had been wrongly entered as a letter instead of the number, you might receive the following:

```
    <?xml version="1.0" encoding="utf-8" ?>
    <soap:Envelope xmlns:soap="http://schemas.xmlsoap.org/soap/envelope/">
      <soap:Body>
        <soap:Fault>
          <faultcode>soap:Client</faultcode>
          <faultstring>Server was unable to read request.
                       Input string was not in a correct format.
                       There is an error in XML document (4, 13).
          </faultstring>
          <detail/>
        </soap:Fault>
      </soap:Body>
    </soap:Envelope>
```

The `<soap:Fault>` element, of which there can be only one, gives a clue as to the problem encountered. The most telling information is that contained in `<faultcode/>`. There are a limited number of options for this value, of which the two common ones are `soap:Server` and `soap:Client`. A `soap:Server` fault code could indicate a problem such as the server being unable to connect to a database. In this case, resending the message may well succeed. If `soap:Client` is specified, it often means that the message is incorrectly formatted and will not succeed without some modification.

A more human-readable error message is stored in the `<faultstring/>` element, which contains application-specific error details. If a secondary system, such as a database, is the primary cause of a web service error, information pertaining to this error may be returned in an optional `<faultactor/>` element (not shown in the previous example).

Document-Style SOAP

The document style of SOAP relies on XML schemas to designate the format of the request and response. This style seems to be gaining in popularity and some predict that it will eventually all but replace the RPC style. For a lucid explanation of why people are shying away from RPC with SOAP encoding, see `http://msdn.microsoft.com/library/en-us/dnsoap/html/argsoape.asp`.

A document-style request may not look that different from an RPC-style request. For example, the RPC request example from the previous section could be a valid document-style request by simply removing the `soap:encodingStyle` attribute. The difference is that an RPC request always follows the same style, with the method name in a containing element around its parameters; the document-style request has no such constraints. Here's an example that is completely different from an RPC request:

```
<?xml version="1.0" encoding="utf-8" ?>
<soap:Envelope xmlns:soap="http://schemas.xmlsoap.org/soap/envelope/">
  <soap:Body>
    <w:add xmlns:w="http://www.wrox.com/services/math" op1="4.5" op2="5.4" />
  </soap:Body>
</soap:Envelope>
```

Note that the highlighted line contains the method name (add) and two operands (op1 and op2) in a single element. This construct is not possible using RPC-style requests. The document style has this flexibility because there is an accompanying XML schema. A web service can use this XML schema to validate the structure of the request; the service is then free to use the information in the request appropriately. Responses follow the same basic rules as requests: they can be very similar to RPC style or completely different, again based on an XML schema.

> **Web services created using Visual Studio .NET are, by default, in document style (although this can be changed by applying various attributes to the underlying code).**

At this point, you might be wondering where the XML schema is kept and how it is made available to both the client and the service. The answer to those questions lies in yet another abbreviation: WSDL.

WSDL

Web Services Description Language (WSDL) is another XML-based language that was created to describe the usage of a particular web service, or rather, how a particular service could be called. The resulting specification describes an incredibly dense language, designed to be extremely flexible and allow for as much re-use as possible; it is the sort of document that is manually constructed only by the most ardent enthusiast. Typically, a software tool is used for the initial WSDL file creation and then hand tweaked, as necessary.

The following is a WSDL file describing a sample math service with a single add method (which you will be building later):

```
<?xml version="1.0" encoding="utf-8"?>
<wsdl:definitions
              xmlns:http="http://schemas.xmlsoap.org/wsdl/http/"
              xmlns:soap="http://schemas.xmlsoap.org/wsdl/soap/"
              xmlns:s="http://www.w3.org/2001/XMLSchema"
              xmlns:tns="http://www.wrox.com/services/math"
              xmlns:wsdl="http://schemas.xmlsoap.org/wsdl/"
              targetNamespace="http://www.wrox.com/services/math">
  <wsdl:types>
    <s:schema elementFormDefault="qualified"
              targetNamespace="http://www.wrox.com/services/math">
```

```
      <s:element name="add">
        <s:complexType>
          <s:sequence>
            <s:element minOccurs="1" maxOccurs="1" name="op1" type="s:float" />
            <s:element minOccurs="1" maxOccurs="1" name="op2" type="s:float" />
          </s:sequence>
        </s:complexType>
      </s:element>
      <s:element name="addResponse">
        <s:complexType>
          <s:sequence>
            <s:element minOccurs="1" maxOccurs="1" name="addResult"
                       type="s:float" />
          </s:sequence>
        </s:complexType>
      </s:element>
    </s:schema>
  </wsdl:types>
  <wsdl:message name="addSoapIn">
    <wsdl:part name="parameters" element="tns:add" />
  </wsdl:message>
  <wsdl:message name="addSoapOut">
    <wsdl:part name="parameters" element="tns:addResponse" />
  </wsdl:message>
  <wsdl:portType name="MathSoap">
    <wsdl:operation name="add">
      <wsdl:documentation>
       Returns the sum of two floats as a float
      </wsdl:documentation>
      <wsdl:input message="tns:addSoapIn" />
      <wsdl:output message="tns:addSoapOut" />
    </wsdl:operation>
  </wsdl:portType>
  <wsdl:binding name="MathSoap" type="tns:MathSoap">
    <soap:binding transport="http://schemas.xmlsoap.org/soap/http"
                  style="document" />
    <wsdl:operation name="add">
      <soap:operation soapAction="http://www.wrox.com/services/math/add"
                      style="document" />
      <wsdl:input>
        <soap:body use="literal" />
      </wsdl:input>
      <wsdl:output>
        <soap:body use="literal" />
      </wsdl:output>
    </wsdl:operation>
  </wsdl:binding>
  <wsdl:service name="Math">
    <wsdl:documentation>
      Contains a number of simple arithmetical functions
    </wsdl:documentation>
    <wsdl:port name="MathSoap" binding="tns:MathSoap">
      <soap:address location="http://localhost/Math/Math.asmx" />
    </wsdl:port>
  </wsdl:service>
</wsdl:definitions>
```

Remember that this WSDL is describing only a basic service that adds two numbers; for simplicity, the three other methods you will be implementing have been removed. Although this WSDL file is long and complex, you should understand what its various sections mean.

The document element, `<wsdl:definitions/>`, encompasses the content and allows the declaration of various namespaces. The next element, `<wsdl:types/>`, contains the XML schema used by the service. Inside of this element is `<s:schema/>`, which describes the format of all elements that can appear in the `<soap:Body/>` of either the request or the response.

The first element described in the schema is `<add/>`. Since the `<s:schema/>` element has `elementFormDefault` set to `qualified`, `<add/>` is assumed to be in the namespace designated by the `targetNamespace` attribute, `http://www.wrox.com/services/math`. The `<add/>` element is then declared to contain a sequence of two other elements, `<op1/>` and `<op2/>`. Both of these elements have `minOccurs` and `maxOccurs` set to 1, which means that they must both appear once and once only. They also both have a `type` attribute of `s:float`, which is one of the built-in XML schema types.

> You can find a complete list of XML schema data types at `www.w3.org/TR/xmlschema-0/#CreatDt`. If your service needs more complicated types than these, you can construct complex types by aggregating and restricting these base types.

Next in the schema is another `<s:element/>`, this one describing `<addResponse/>`. This element is defined to have one child element, `<addResult/>`, which contains the result of the operation (also defined as type `s:float`). This is the last entry in the included XML schema.

Back in the main body of the WSDL file is a short section describing two `<wsdl:message/>` elements: `addSoapIn` and `addSoapOut`. Each of these elements has a `<wsdl:part/>` element that specifies the element in the XML schema to use. These both refer to the two elements `add` and `addResponse`, respectively. This section states the format of each message.

The following section, `<wsdl:portType/>`, is used to group the `<wsdl:message>` elements into operations. An *operation* is considered to be a single unit of work and, therefore, comprises of a `<wsdl:input>` and normally a `<wsdl:output>` and an optional `<wsdl:fault>` element. The preceding example has one `<wsdl:portType>` and describes a `<wsdl:operation/>` named add. The message attributes on its `<wsdl:input>` and `<wsdl:output>` children refer back to the `<wsdl:message>` elements previously defined. There is also a `<wsdl:documentation/>` element containing a user-friendly description of the method. (You will learn where this information comes from later in the chapter.)

After the port type is a `<wsdl:binding/>` block. A *binding* pairs an operation with a protocol used to communicate with the service. There are three bindings described in the WSDL specification, SOAP, HTTP GET/POST, and MIME.

This chapter concentrates on the SOAP binding. The HTTP GET/POST binding deals with how URLs are constructed (for GET requests) or how the form data is encoded (for POST requests). The MIME binding allows parts of the message, normally the output, to be expressed in different mime types. This means that one part of the response could be in XML, whereas a second part could be in HTML.

You can read more about these alternative bindings at `www.w3.org/TR/2002/WD-wsdl12-bindings-20020709/`.

First, the name of the binding is set to MathSoap, and the type points to the MathSoap port type defined in the <wsdl:portType> section. Second, the <soap:binding/> element uses the transport attribute to specify that the service operates over HTTP. The <wsdl:operation/> element simply defines the name of the method, add. The <soap:operation/> element contains the soapAction that needs to be incorporated into the header of the HTTP request as well as the style attribute, which specifies that the SOAP message will be a document type rather than an RPC type.

> *The main difference between a document-style message and an RPC-style message is that the document style sends the message as elements within the <soap:body> that can have whatever structure the sender and receiver agree on using the embedded schema as a guide. An RPC-style message, however, has an element named after the method being called. This in turn will have one element for each parameter the method accepts.*

The <soap:operation/> element has two children, <wsdl:input> and <wsdl:output>, which are used to further describe the request and response format. In this case, the <soap:body> specifies a use attribute of literal. In practical terms, this is the only option with document-style services; with RPC-style services the choice extends to *encoded*, in which case the <soap:body> would further specify exactly which encoding type was to be used for the parameter types.

The final part of the document, <wsdl:service/>, deals with how to call the service from a client. It also contains a human-readable description of the service and the <wsdl:port/> element, which references the MathSoap binding in the last document section. Perhaps the most important element in this section is <soap:address/>, which contains the crucial location attribute containing the URL needed to access the service.

```
<wsdl:service name="Math">
  <wsdl:documentation>
    Contains a number of simple arithmetical functions
  </wsdl:documentation>
  <wsdl:port name="MathSoap" binding="tns:MathSoap">
    <soap:address location="http://localhost/Math/Math.asmx" />
  </wsdl:port>
</wsdl:service>
```

Looking at a complete WSDL file may be a bit daunting for new developers, but the good news is that you will probably never have to hand code one yourself. In fact, the example file in this section was created automatically by the .NET web service, which examines the underlying code and generates the necessary XML.

> *XML schemas are a vast topic and a full discussion is outside the scope of this book. If you'd like to learn more about XML schemas, consider picking up Beginning XML, 3rd Edition (Wiley Publishing, ISBN 0-7645-7077-3), or for a web tutorial, visit* www.w3schools.com/schema/default.asp.

REST

Representational State Transfer, often abbreviated as REST, describes a way of using the existing HTTP protocol to transmit data. Although used mostly for web services, REST can be used for any type of HTTP-based request and response systems as well. In regard to web services, REST enables you to call a given URL in a specific format to return data (which will also be in a specific format). This data may contain further information on how to retrieve even more data. For the web service usage, the data will be returned as XML.

For example, suppose Wrox would like to provide a way for others to retrieve a list of all authors. REST-style web services use simple URLs to access data; the Wrox Book service could use this URL to retrieve the list of authors:

```
http://www.wrox.com/services/authors/
```

This service may return an XML representation of the known authors along with information on how to access details about each one, such as:

```xml
<?xml version="1.0" encoding="utf-8" ?>
<authors xmlns:xlink="http://www.w3.org/1999/xlink"
         xmlns="http://www.wrox.com/services/authors-books"
         xlink:href="http://www.wrox.com/services/authors/">
  <author forenames="Michael" surname="Kay"
    xlink:href="http://www.wrox.com/services/authors/kaym"
    id="kaym"/>
  <author forenames="Joe" surname="Fawcett"
    xlink:href="http://www.wrox.com/services/authors/fawcettj"
    id="fawcettj"/>
  <author forenames="Jeremy" surname="McPeak"
    xlink:href="http://www.wrox.com/services/authors/mcpeakj"
    id="mcpeakj"/>
  <author forename="Nicholas" surname="Zakas"
    xlink:href="http://www.wrox.com/services/authors/zakasn"
    id="zakasn"/>
  <!--
    More authors
  -->
</authors>
```

There are a couple of things to note about this XML. First, a default namespace of `http://www.wrox.com/services/authors-books` is declared so that any un-prefixed elements, such as `<authors/>`, are assumed to belong to this namespace. This means that the `<authors/>` element can be differentiated from another element with a similar name but from a different namespace. The namespace URI, `http://www.wrox.com/services/authors-books`, is used simply as a unique string; there is no guarantee that an actual resource is available at that location. The key is that it is a *Uniform Resource Identifier* (URI), which is simply an identifier, not a *Uniform Resource Locator* (URL), which would indicate that a resource is available at a specific location.

Second, note the use of the `href` attribute from the `http://www.w3.org/1999/xlink` namespace. Although not essential, many REST-style services have now standardized on this notation for what, in HTML, would be a standard hyperlink.

XLink is a way of linking documents that goes way beyond the straightforward hyperlinks of HTML. It provides capabilities to specify a two-way dependency so that documents can be accessible from each other as well as indicating how a link should be activated — for example, by hand, automatically, or after a preset time. Its cousin, XPointer, is concerned with specifying sections within a document and arose from the need for a more powerful notation than the simple named links within HTML pages.

Although they have both reached recommendation status at the W3C, they are still not widely used. For more information, visit www.w3.org/XML/Linking.

If used in a web site or web application, the XML returned from the REST service would be transformed, either client-side or server-side, to a more user-friendly format (most likely HTML) — perhaps something like this:

```html
<html>
  <head>
    <title>Wrox Authors</title>
  </head>
  <body>
    <a href="http://www.wrox.com/services/authors/kaym">Michael Kay</a>
    <a href="http://www.wrox.com/services/authors/fawcettj">Joe Fawcett</a>
    <a href="http://www.wrox.com/services/authors/mcpeakj">Jeremy McPeak</a>
    <a href="http://www.wrox.com/services/authors/zakasn">Nicholas Zakas</a>
  </body>
</html>
```

The user could then retrieve individual author data by following one of the links, which may return XML similar to this:

```xml
<?xml version="1.0" encoding="utf-8" ?>
<author xmlns:xlink="http://www.w3.org/1999/xlink"
        xmlns="http://www.wrox.com/services/authors-books"
        xlink:href="http://www.wrox.com/services/authors/fawcettj"
        id="fawcettj" forenames="Joe" surname="Fawcett">
  <books>
    <book
      xlink:href="http://www.wrox.com/services/books/0764570773"
      isbn="0764570773" title="Beginning XML"/>
    <book
      xlink:href="http://www.wrox.com/services/books/0471777781"
      isbn="0471777781" title="Professional Ajax"/>
  </books>
</author>
```

Again, you see that the elements are in the http://www.wrox.com/services/authors-books namespace and the xlink:href attribute is a way to extract further information. An HTML representation of this data may look like this:

```html
<html>
  <head>
    <title>Author Details</title>
  </head>
  <body>
    <p>Details for
    <a href="http://www.wrox.com/services/authors/fawcettj">Joe Fawcett</a></p>
    <p>Books</p>
    <a href="http://www.wrox.com/services/books/0764570773">Beginning XML</a>
    <a href="http://www.wrox.com/services/books/0471777781">Professional Ajax</a>
  </body>
</html>
```

And if, per chance, the user feels like following the link for *Professional Ajax*, he or she may receive the following XML in response:

```xml
<?xml version="1.0" encoding="utf-8" ?>
<book xmlns:xlink="http://www.w3.org/1999/xlink"
      xmlns="http://www.wrox.com/services/authors-books"
      xlink:href="http://www.wrox.com/services/books/0471777781"
      isbn="0471777781">
  <genre>Web Programming</genre>
  <title>Professional AJAX</title>
  <description>How to take advantage of asynchronous JavaScript
   and XML to give your web pages a rich UI.</description>
  <authors>
    <author forenames="Nicholas" surname="Zakas"
      xlink:href="http://www.wrox.com/services/authors/zakasn"
      id="zakasn" />
    <author forenames="Jeremy" surname="McPeak"
      xlink:href="http://www.wrox.com/services/authors/mcpeakj"
      id="mcpeakj" />
    <author forenames="Joe" surname="Fawcett"
      xlink:href="http://www.wrox.com/services/authors/fawcettj"
      id="fawcettj" />
  </authors>
</book>
```

REST-style services are fairly straightforward and follow a repeating pattern. For example, you may get a complete list of authors by using `http://www.wrox.com/services/authors/`, whereas a slight modification, adding an author ID at the end, may retrieve information about a single author, perhaps from `http://www.wrox.com/services/authors/fawcettj`.

The service can be implemented in any number of ways. It could be through static web pages or, more likely, some sort of server-side processing such as ASP, JSP, or PHP, that fetch data from a database and return the appropriately constructed XML. In this case the URL would be mapped by the server into an application-specific way of retrieving the data, possibly by invoking a stored procedure on the database in question.

> You can read more about REST-style services (also called RESTful services) at `www.network world.com/ee/2003/eerest.html`.

The .NET Connection

By most accounts, Microsoft spearheaded the web services movement with the introduction of SOAP. When Microsoft presented SOAP to IBM as a way of transporting data, IBM quickly came on board, helping to develop what later became WSDL. With the combined force of Microsoft and IBM, many more big companies jumped on board, such as Oracle, Sun, and HP. The standards were established and the beginning of the web service era was on the horizon, but there was a catch: there were no tools to facilitate the creation of web services. That's where .NET came in.

Microsoft released the .NET Framework in 2000 with the aim of providing a platform-independent development framework to compete with Java. Since Microsoft started nearly from scratch with the .NET initiative, they built in strong support for XML, as well as the creation and consumption of web services using SOAP and WSDL. Using .NET, there are simple ways to provide a web services wrapper around existing applications as well as exposing most .NET classes using web services.

When developing web services, you can decide how much interaction with SOAP and WSDL is necessary. There are tools to shield developers from the underlying structure, but you can also change fine details if necessary. The 2005 version of the .NET Framework makes even more use of XML and web services.

Design Decisions

Although the .NET Framework makes web service development easier, it is by no means the only way to create them. Just like any other programming task, there are several design and development decisions that must be made. Remember, web services provide a platform-independent way of requesting and receiving data, so the service consumer doesn't need (or in many cases want) information about how it is implemented. Unfortunately, there are some things to be aware of when interoperability is a concern:

❑ **Not all platforms support the same data types.** For example, many services return an ADO.NET dataset. A system without .NET will be unlikely to understand this data form. Similarly, arrays can be problematic because they can be represented in any number of ways.

❑ **Some services are more tolerant of missing or extra headers in the request.** This problem is allied to consumers that do not send all the correct headers, which can create problems, especially when it comes to securing a service.

In an effort to overcome these and other related issues, the Web Services Interoperability Organization was formed. You can find its aims, findings, and conformance recommendations at www.ws-i.org/.

When creating a web service, your first decision is which platform to use. If you choose Windows, you'll almost certainly use IIS as your web server. You can use ASP.NET to create your web services, or ASP for older versions of IIS (though this is more difficult). The examples in this chapter use ASP.NET.

If you are using UNIX or Linux, you will likely be using JSP or PHP, both of which have open source web servers available. Using these, you need to program in Java or PHP, respectively, to create web services.

The Axis project (http://ws.apache.org/axis/) has development tools for both Java and C++.

For PHP there are also plenty of options, including PhpXMLRPC (http://phpxmlrpc.source forge.net/) and Pear SOAP (http://pear.php.net/package/SOAP).

After you've chosen your language, you'll need to decide who will have access to your service. Will your application be the only one calling it, or will your service be accessible publicly? If the latter, you will need to take into account the interoperability issues discussed previously; if the former, you can take advantage of some of the specialized features provided by the client or the server.

With a web service created, the next step is to *consume* it. Any application that calls a web service is considered a consumer. Typically, consuming a web service follows a distinct pattern: create a request, send the request, and act on the response received. The exact method for taking these steps is up to the functionality that is accessible by the consumer.

Creating a Windows Web Service

Now it's time to move away from the specifications and theories to create a simple web service. The web service described in this section uses document-style SOAP requests and responses to implement the Math service described in the WSDL file earlier in this chapter. Note that this process uses free tools available from Microsoft, which involve a little more work than if you were to use, say, Visual Studio .NET. However, the extra work you'll do in this section will aid in your understanding of web services and could pay handsome dividends later in your development career should anything go wrong with an auto-generated service.

System Requirements

To create this service, you will need three minimum requirements:

❏ A Windows machine running IIS 5 or greater. This comes as standard on all XP Professional machines and on all servers from Windows 2000 onwards.

❏ The .NET Framework must be installed on the machine running IIS. You will also need the .NET Software Development Kit (SDK) on the machine you are developing on. For the purposes of this example, it is assumed that you are developing on the machine that is running IIS. (You can download both the .NET Framework and the SDK from `http://msdn.microsoft.com/net framework/downloads/updates/default.aspx`.)

❏ A text editor to write the code. This can simply be Notepad, which is standard on all Windows machines and is more than adequate for the purposes of this example (although for serious development an editor that supports syntax highlighting is preferable).

Configuring IIS

The first task is to create a home for your service. Go to Start⇨Administrative Tools and select Internet Information Services. (Alternatively, enter **%SystemRoot%\System32\inetsrv\iis.msc** in the Start⇨Run box and click the OK button.) Expand the tree on the left to show the Default Web Site node, and then right-click and choose New⇨Virtual Directory, as shown in Figure 6-1. This will bring up the Virtual Directory Creation Wizard, where you choose the name of the web service folder as seen by the client (see Figure 6-2).

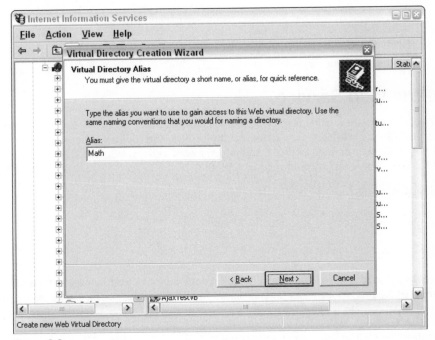

Figure 6-1

Figure 6-2

Name the folder **Math**, and then click Next. On the next screen, browse to the standard IIS directory of
`C:\InetPub\wwwroot`. Create a new folder, also named **Math**, directly below this folder. Accept the
defaults for the remaining screens of the wizard. When this is done, use Windows Explorer to create a
new folder underneath Math named **bin**, which will hold the DLL once the service is built. Your folder
hierarchy should now look like Figure 6-3.

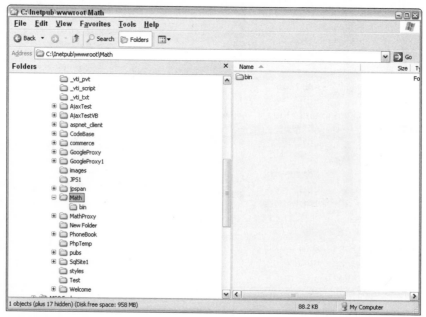

Figure 6-3

Coding the Web Service

The web service you are creating is quite simple. Its name is *Math*, and it implements the four basic
arithmetic operations: addition, subtraction, multiplication, and division. These four operations each
accept two parameters, defined as floats, and return a float as the result. The class itself will be coded in
C#, and the web service will be published in ASP.NET.

Create a new file in your favorite text editor and add the following three lines:

```
using System;
using System.Web;
using System.Web.Services;
```

This code doesn't add any extra functionality, but it does save you from having to type fully qualified
class names. Since you will be using several classes from these namespaces, it saves space to reference
them here.

Next, create a namespace called *Wrox.Services* and a class called *Math* that inherits from `System.Web`
`.Services.WebService`:

```
namespace Wrox.Services
{
   [WebService (Description = "Contains a number of simple arithmetical functions",
              Namespace = "http://www.wrox.com/services/math")]

   public class Math : System.Web.Services.WebService
   {
     //class code here
   }

}
```

The namespace keyword is used to in a similar way as namespaces in XML; it means the full name of the Math class is Wrox.Services.Math. Immediately inside the namespace definition is an attribute called WebService, which marks the class on the following line as a web service. Doing this enables extra functionality for the class, such as generating a WSDL file. You will also notice that a Description parameter is included (and will also appear in the WSDL file).

Then comes the class name, Math, which inherits from the base class of System.Web.Services.WebService. Inheriting from this class means that you don't need to worry about any specific code for writing web services; the base class handles all of this. You can simply focus on writing the methods that will be published as part of the web service.

Defining a method to be used in a web service is as easy as writing a regular method and tagging it with the special WebMethod attribute:

```
[WebMethod(Description = "Returns the sum of two floats as a float")]
public float add(float op1, float op2)
{
   return op1 + op2;
}
```

Once again, the code is very simple. (What could be simpler than an addition operation?) Any method that has a WebMethod attribute preceding it is considered part of the web service. The Description parameter will become part of the generated WSDL file. Although you can write as many methods as you'd like, here is the complete code for this example, including the four arithmetic methods:

```
using System;
using System.Web;
using System.Web.Services;

namespace Wrox.Services
{
   [WebService (Description = "Contains a number of simple arithmetical functions",
              Namespace = "http://www.wrox.com/services/math")]
   public class Math : System.Web.Services.WebService
   {

     [WebMethod(Description = "Returns the sum of two floats as a float")]
     public float add(float op1, float op2)
     {
       return op1 + op2;
```

```
      }

      [WebMethod(Description = "Returns the difference of two floats as a float")]
      public float subtract(float op1, float op2)
      {
        return op1 - op2;
      }

      [WebMethod(Description = "Returns the product of two floats as a float")]
      public float multiply(float op1, float op2)
      {
        return op1 * op2;
      }

      [WebMethod(Description = "Returns the quotient of two floats as a float")]
      public float divide(float op1, float op2)
      {
        return op1 / op2;
      }
    }
  }
```

Save this file in the Math directory and name it `Math.asmx.cs`.

Create another text file and enter the following line:

```
<%@WebService Language="c#" Codebehind="Math.asmx.cs" Class="Wrox.Services.Math" %>
```

This is the ASP.NET file that uses the `Math` class you just created. The `@WebService` directive tells the page to act like a web service. The meaning of the other attributes should be fairly obvious: `Language` specifies the language of the code to use; `Codebehind` specifies the name of the file that the code exists in; and `Class` specifies the fully qualified name of the class to use. Save this file in Math directory as well, with the name `Math.asmx`.

Creating the Assembly

After you have created these two files, you can proceed with the next stage: compiling the source code into an assembly that will be housed in a DLL. To do this, you can use the C# compiler that comes with the .NET SDK. This will be in your Windows directory below the `Microsoft.Net\Framework\` `<version number>` folder (for example, `C:\WINDOWS\Microsoft.NET\Framework\v1.1.4322\`).

The easiest way to compile and debug the code is to create a batch file. Create another text file and enter the following (it should all be on one line despite the formatting of the book):

```
C:\WINDOWS\Microsoft.NET\Framework\v1.1.4322\csc.exe /r:System.dll
/r:System.Web.dll
/r:System.Web.Services.dll /t:library /out:bin\Math.dll  Math.asmx.cs
```

Remember to modify the path to `csc.exe` if necessary and save it to the Math folder as `MakeService.bat`.

> If you are using Notepad, be careful using the Save As dialog box. Make sure that the File Type box is set to All Files, or else enclose the file name in double quotes. Otherwise, Notepad adds a `.txt` extension to your file.

Next, you need to compile the DLL. Open a command prompt from Start⇨Run and type **cmd**. Now navigate to the Math folder by typing **cd \inetpub\wwwroot\Math**. Finally, run the following batch file:

```
C:\inetpub\wwwroot\Math\MakeService.bat
```

If all is well, you should be greeted with the compiler displaying some version and copyright information, and then a blank line. This is good news and indicates that the compilation was successful. (If there were any errors, they will be outputted to the console. Check the lines indicated and correct any syntax or spelling mistakes.)

Assuming the DLL has compiled, you are ready to test the service. One of the joys of .NET web services is that a whole test harness is created automatically for you. Open your web browser and navigate to `http://localhost/Math/math.asmx`. You should soon see a page similar to the one displayed in Figure 6-4.

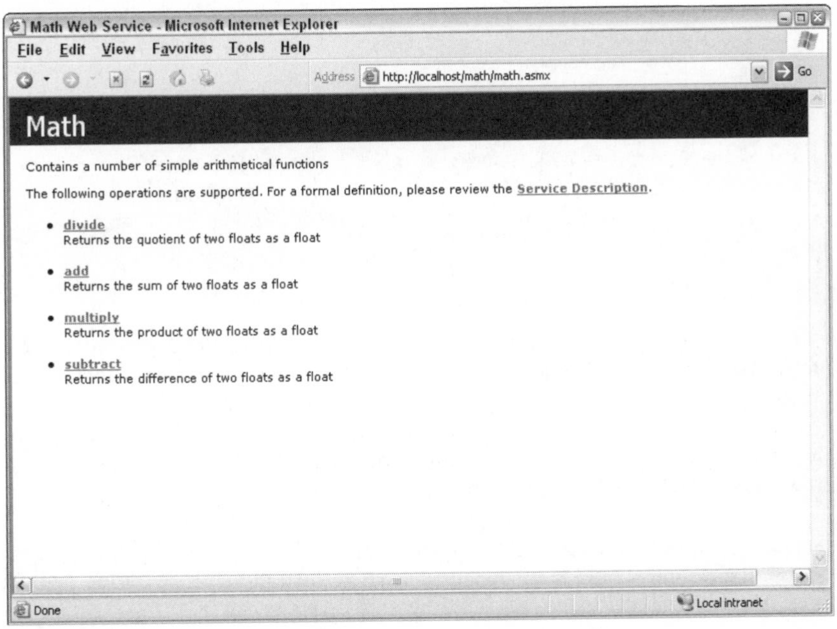

Figure 6-4

You have the choice to try any of the four methods or you can view the generated WSDL file by clicking the Service Description link. This reveals a WSDL file similar to the example earlier in the chapter, but this will have entries for all four methods.

> **Another way of viewing the WSDL file is to add** ?WSDL **to the web service URL, such as** http://localhost/Math/math.asmx?WSDL.

Since you have probably had enough of the add method, try the divide method. Clicking the link from the previous screen should display the page in Figure 6-5.

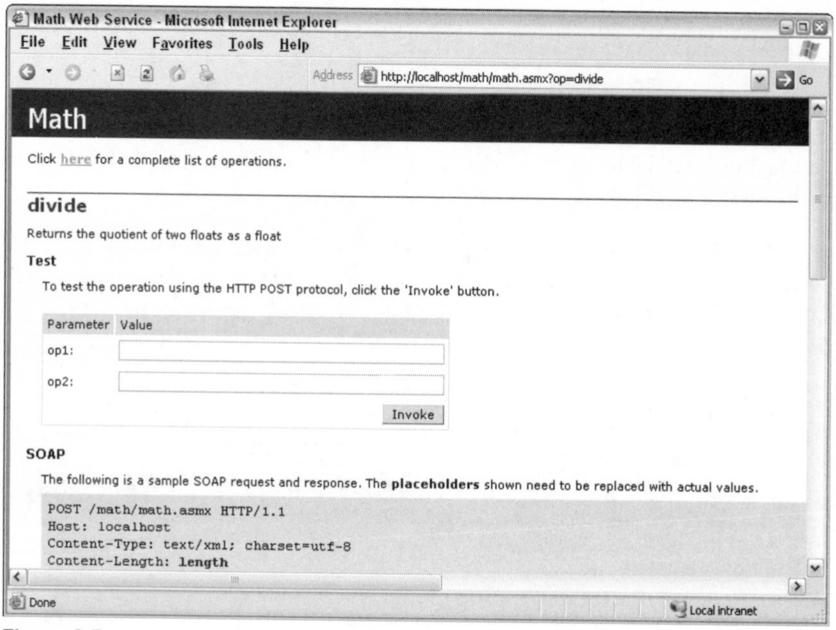

Figure 6-5

Below the divide heading is the description you used with the WebMethod attribute, and below that is a small test form. If you enter two numbers, such as 22 and 7, you'll receive a response such as the one displayed in Figure 6-6.

In a production environment, you can now remove the Math.asmx.cs file, as it is no longer needed. The Math.asmx simply passes on all requests directly to the DLL.

This test harness does not use SOAP for the request and response. Instead, it passes the two operands as a POST request; the details of how to do this are shown at the bottom of the divide page in Figure 6-5. Now that you have a web service defined, it's time to use Ajax to call it.

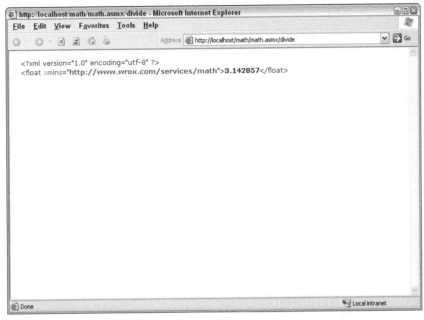

Figure 6-6

Web Services and Ajax

Now that you have a basic understanding of web services, and have created your own, you're probably wondering what this has to do with Ajax. Quite simply, web services are another avenue for Ajax applications to retrieve information. In the last chapter, you learned how to retrieve and use RSS and Atom feeds to display information to the user, which is very similar to using web services. The main difference is that by using web services, you are able to pass information to the server that can be manipulated and sent back; you aren't simply pulling information.

You can use JavaScript to consume a web service from within a web page so long as your users have a modern browser. Internet Explorer 5.0 and higher, as well as the Mozilla family of browsers (including Firefox), all have some functionality that allows web services to be consumed.

Creating the Test Harness

First, you'll need a test harness to test the various approaches to calling web services from the browser. This test harness is fairly simple: there is a list box to select one of the four arithmetic operations to execute, a text box for each of the two operands, and a button to invoke the service. These controls are disabled until the page has fully loaded. Below those controls is another text box to display any valid result as well as two text areas to display the request and response data:

```html
<html>
  <head>
    <title>Web Service Test Harness</title>
    <script type="text/javascript">

        var SERVICE_URL = "http://localhost/Math/Math.asmx";
        var SOAP_ACTION_BASE = "http://www.wrox.com/services/math";

        function setUIEnabled(bEnabled)
        {
            var oButton = document.getElementById("cmdRequest");
            oButton.disabled = !bEnabled;
            var oList = document.getElementById("lstMethods");
            oList.disabled = !bEnabled
        }

        function performOperation()
        {
            var oList = document.getElementById("lstMethods");
            var sMethod = oList.options[oList.selectedIndex].value;
            var sOp1 = document.getElementById("txtOp1").value;
            var sOp2 = document.getElementById("txtOp2").value;

            //Clear the message panes
            document.getElementById("txtRequest").value = "";
            document.getElementById("txtResponse").value = "";
            document.getElementById("txtResult").value = "";
            performSpecificOperation(sMethod, sOp1, sOp2);
        }
    </script>
  </head>
  <body onload="setUIEnabled(true)">
    Operation: <select id="lstMethods" style="width: 200px" disabled="disabled">
      <option value="add" selected="selected">Add</option>
      <option value="subtract">Subtract</option>
      <option value="multiply">Multiply</option>
      <option value="divide">Divide</option>
    </select>
    <br/><br/>
    Operand 1: <input type="text" id="txtOp1" size="10"/><br/>
    Operand 2: <input type="text" id="txtOp2" size="10"/><br/><br/>
    <input type="button" id="cmdRequest"
       value="Perform Operation"
       onclick="performOperation();" disabled="disabled"/>
    <br/><br/>
    Result: <input type="text" size="20" id="txtResult">
    <br/>
    <textarea rows="30" cols="60" id="txtRequest"></textarea>
    <textarea rows="30" cols="60" id="txtResponse"></textarea>
  </body>
</html>
```

The setUIEnabled() function is used to enable and disable the user interface of the test harness. This ensures that only one request is sent at a time. There are also two constants defined, SERVICE_URL and SOAP_ACTION_BASE, that contain the URL for the web service and the SOAP action header required to call it, respectively. The button calls a function named `performOperation()`, which gathers the relevant data and clears the text boxes before calling `performSpecificOperation()`. This method must be defined by the particular test being used to execute the web service call (which will be included using a JavaScript file). Depending on your personal browser preferences, the page resembles Figure 6-7.

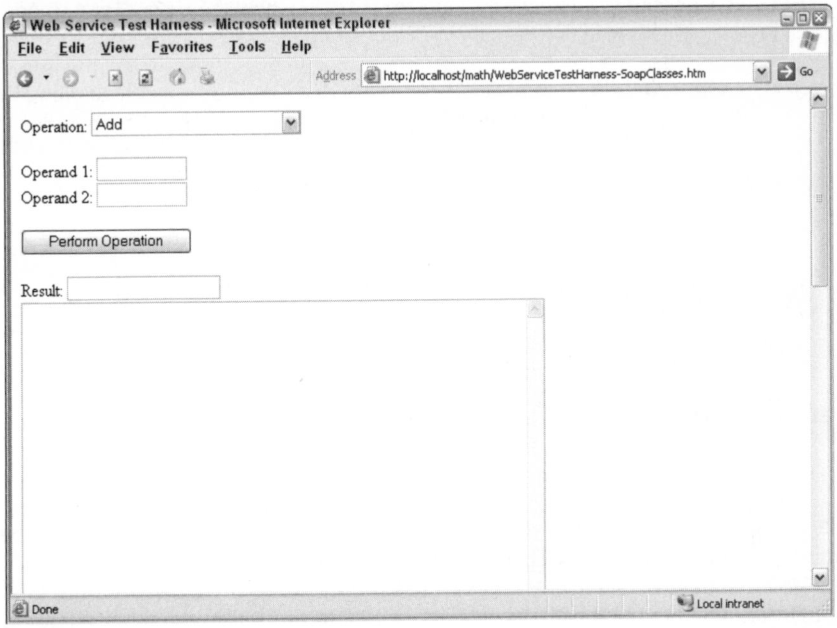

Figure 6-7

The Internet Explorer Approach

In an early effort to get developers excited about web services, Microsoft developed and released a web service behavior for Internet Explorer. *Behaviors* enable you to redefine the functionality, properties, and methods of an existing HTML element or to create an entirely new one. The advantage of behaviors is the encapsulation of functionality into a single file, ending with the `.htc` extension. Although the promise of behaviors never lived up to the hype, the web service behavior is a solid component that can be very useful to web developers. You can download the behavior from `http://msdn.microsoft.com/library/default.asp?url=/workshop/author/webservice/webservice.asp`.

> *This file and the others associated with this chapter are included in the code download for Professional Ajax, at www.wrox.com.*

You can add behaviors to elements in a number of ways. The most straightforward is to use the element's CSS `style` property. To add the web service behavior to a `<div/>`, the code would be:

```
<div id="divServiceHandler" style="behavior: url(webservice.htc);"></div>
```

This assumes that the behavior is in the same folder on the server as the web page.

To show how to use this behavior, create a new version of the test harness and insert the highlighted line directly below the <body/> element, as follows:

```
<body onload="setUIEnabled(true);">
<div id="divServiceHandler" style="behavior: url(webservice.htc);"></div>
Operation: <select id="lstMethods" style="width: 200px" name="lstMethods"
                    disabled="disabled">
```

The next step is to define the performSpecificOperation() method specific to using the web service behavior. This method accepts three arguments: the method name and the two operands. The code is as follows:

```
var iCallId = 0;
function performSpecificOperation(sMethod, sOp1, sOp2)
{
    var oServiceHandler = document.getElementById("divServiceHandler");
    if (!oServiceHandler.Math)
    {
        oServiceHandler.useService(SERVICE_URL + "?WSDL", "Math");
    }
    iCallId = oServiceHandler.Math.callService(handleResponseFromBehavior,
                                        sMethod, sOp1, sOp2);
}
```

A variable, iCallId, is initialized to zero. Although this plays no part in the test, it can be used to keep track of multiple simultaneous calls. Then, a reference to the <div/> element that has the behavior attached is stored in oServiceHandler. Next, a test is done to see if the behavior has already been used by checking to see whether the Math property exists. If it doesn't exist, you must set up the behavior by passing the URL of the WSDL file and a identifying name for the service to useService(). The reason for the identifier is to enable the behavior to use more than one service at a time. The callService() method is then executed, passing in a callback function (handleResponseFromBehavior()), the name of the method, and the two arguments.

When the response is received, the callback function, handleResponseFromBehavior(), will be called:

```
function handleResponseFromBehavior(oResult)
{
    var oResponseOutput = document.getElementById("txtResponse");
    if (oResult.error)
    {
        var sErrorMessage = oResult.errorDetail.code
                            + "\n" + oResult.errorDetail.string;
        alert("An error occurred:\n"
            + sErrorMessage
            + "See message pane for SOAP fault.");
        oResponseOutput.value = oResult.errorDetail.raw.xml;
    }
    else
    {
        var oResultOutput = document.getElementById("txtResult");
        oResultOutput.value = oResult.value;
        oResponseOutput.value = oResult.raw.xml;
    }
}
```

The callback function is passed an `oResult` object containing details about the call. If the `error` property is not zero, the relevant SOAP fault details are displayed; otherwise `oResult.value`, the returned value, is displayed on the page.

You can place the `performSpecificOperation()` and `handleResponseFromBehavior()` functions in an external JavaScript file and include them in the test harness page using the `<script/>` element, as follows:

```
<script type="text/javascript" src="WebServiceExampleBehavior.js"></script>
```

As you can see, using the web service behavior is fairly straightforward. All the work is done by the behavior behind the scenes, and although the `webservice.htc` file is a bit large for a script file (51KB), it can provide some very useful functionality.

If you want to see how the behavior works, feel free to examine the `webservice.htc` *file in a text editor. Be warned, however; it was not meant as a tutorial and contains nearly 2300 lines of JavaScript.*

The Mozilla Approach

Modern Mozilla-based browsers, such as Firefox and Netscape, have some high-level SOAP classes built into their implementation of JavaScript. These browsers seek to wrap the basic strategy of making SOAP calls with easier-to-use classes. As with the previous example, you first must define the `performSpecificOperation()` function:

```
function performSpecificOperation(sMethod, sOp1, sOp2)
{
  var oSoapCall = new SOAPCall();
  oSoapCall.transportURI = SERVICE_URL;
  oSoapCall.actionURI = SOAP_ACTION_BASE + "/" + sMethod;
  var aParams = [];
  var oParam = new SOAPParameter(sOp1, "op1");
  oParam.namespaceURI = SOAP_ACTION_BASE;
  aParams.push(oParam);
  oParam = new SOAPParameter(sOp2, "op2");
  oParam.namespaceURI = SOAP_ACTION_BASE;
  aParams.push(oParam);
  oSoapCall.encode(0, sMethod, SOAP_ACTION_BASE, 0, null, aParams.length, aParams);
  var oSerializer = new XMLSerializer();
  document.getElementById("txtRequest").value =
                    oSerializer.serializeToString(oSoapCall.envelope);
  setUIEnabled(false);


  //more code here}
```

This script takes advantage of a number of built-in classes, the first of which is `SOAPCall`. This class wraps web service functionality in a similar way to the web service behavior for Internet Explorer. After creating an instance of `SOAPCall`, you set two properties: `transportURI`, which points to the web service location, and `actionURI`, which specifies the SOAP action and method name.

Next, two parameters are created using the SOAPParameter constructor, which takes the value and the name of the parameter to create. Each parameter has its namespace URI set to the value of the targetNamespace in the WSDL schema section. In theory this shouldn't be necessary, but the Mozilla SOAP classes seem to be designed with the RPC style in mind and our service uses the document style, so this extra step is needed. Both of these parameters are pushed onto the aParams array. The encode() method prepares all the data for the call. There are seven parameters for this call. The first is the version of SOAP being used, which can be set to zero unless it is important that a specific version is needed. The second parameter is the name of the method to use, and the third is that of the targetNamespace from the schema portion of the WSDL file. The next parameter is the count of how many extra headers are needed in the call (none in this case), followed by an array of these headers (here set to null). The last two parameters contain the number of SOAPParameter objects being sent and the actual parameters, respectively.

Next, you actually need to send the request, which you can do by using the asyncInvoke() method, as follows:

```
function performSpecificOperation(sMethod, sOp1, sOp2)
{
  var oSoapCall = new SOAPCall();
  oSoapCall.transportURI = SERVICE_URL;
  oSoapCall.actionURI = SOAP_ACTION_BASE + "/" + sMethod;
  var aParams = [];
  var oParam = new SOAPParameter(sOp1, "op1");
  oParam.namespaceURI = SOAP_ACTION_BASE;
  aParams.push(oParam);
  oParam = new SOAPParameter(sOp2, "op2");
  oParam.namespaceURI = SOAP_ACTION_BASE;
  aParams.push(oParam);   oSoapCall.encode(0, sMethod, SOAP_ACTION_BASE, 0, null,
                    aParams.length, aParams);
  document.getElementById("txtRequest").value =
                      oSerializer.serializeToString(oSoapCall.envelope);
  setUIEnabled(false);

  oSoapCall.asyncInvoke(
                      function (oResponse, oCall, iError)
                      {
                          var oResult = handleResponse(oResponse, oCall, iError);
                          showSoapResults(oResult);
                      }
                      );
}
```

The asyncInvoke() method accepts only one argument: a callback function (handleResponse()). This function will be passed three arguments by the SOAP call: a SOAPResponse object, a pointer to the original SOAP call (to track multiple instances, if necessary), and an error code. These are all passed to the handleResponse function for processing, when the call returns:

```
function handleResponse(oResponse, oCall, iError)
{
  setUIEnabled(true);
  if (iError != 0)
  {
```

```
        alert("Unrecognized error.");
        return false;
     }
     else
     {
       var oSerializer = new XMLSerializer();
       document.getElementById("txtResponse").value =
                      oSerializer.serializeToString(oResponse.envelope);
       var oFault = oResponse.fault;
       if (oFault != null)
       {
         var sName = oFault.faultCode;
         var sSummary = oFault.faultString;
         alert("An error occurred:\n"  + sSummary
                                + "\n" + sName
                                + "\nSee message pane for SOAP fault");
         return false;
       }
       else
       {
         return oResponse;
       }
     }
   }
```

If the `error` code is not zero, an error has occurred that can't be explained. This happens only rarely; in most cases an error will be returned through the `fault` property of the response object.

Another built-in class is used now, `XMLSerializer`. This takes an XML node and can convert it to a string or a stream. In this case a string is retrieved and displayed in the right-hand text area.

If `oResponse.fault` is not `null`, a SOAP fault occurred, so an error message is built and displayed to the user and no further action taken. Following a successful call, the response object is passed out as the function's return value and processed by the `showSoapResults()` function:

```
   function showSoapResults(oResult)
   {

     if (!oResult) return;
     document.getElementById("txtResult").value =
     oResult.body.firstChild.firstChild.firstChild.data;
   }
```

After checking that `oResult` is valid, the value of the `<methodResult>` element is extracted using the DOM.

There is a method of the `SoapResponse` named `getParameters`, which, in theory, can be used to retrieve the parameters in a more elegant manner. It does not seem to work as advertised with document style calls, however, necessitating the need to examine the structure of the `soap:Body` using more primitive methods.

The Universal Approach

The only way to consume web services on almost all modern browsers is by using XMLHttp. Because Internet Explorer, Firefox, Opera, and Safari all have some basic support for XMLHttp, this is your best bet for cross-browser consistency. Unfortunately, this type of consistency comes at a price — you are responsible for building up the SOAP request by hand and posting it to the server. You are also responsible for parsing the result and watching for errors.

The two protagonists in this scenario are the XmlHttp ActiveX class from Microsoft and the XmlHttpRequest class that comes with the more modern Mozilla-based browsers listed above. They both have similar methods and properties, although in the time-honored fashion of these things Microsoft was first on the scene before standards had been agreed on, so the later released Mozilla version is more W3C compliant. The basic foundation of these classes is to allow an HTTP request to be made to a web address. The target does not have to return XML — virtually any content can be retrieved — and the ability to post data is also included. For SOAP calls, the normal method is to send a POST request with the raw <soap:Envelope> as the payload.

In this example, you'll once again be calling the test harness. This time, however, you'll be using the zXML library to create XMLHttp objects and constructing the complete SOAP call on your own. This library uses a number of techniques to examine which XML classes are supported by the browser. It also wraps these classes and adds extra methods and properties so that they can be used in a virtually identical manner. The generation of the SOAP request string is handled in a function called getRequest():

```
function getRequest(sMethod, sOp1, sOp2)
{
    var sRequest = "<soap:Envelope xmlns:xsi=\""
                + "http://www.w3.org/2001/XMLSchema-instance\" "
                + "xmlns:xsd=\"http://www.w3.org/2001/XMLSchema\" "
                + "xmlns:soap=\"http://schemas.xmlsoap.org/soap/envelope/\">\n"
                + "<soap:Body>\n"
                + "<" + sMethod + " xmlns=\"" + SOAP_ACTION_BASE + "\">\n"
                + "<op1>" + sOp1 + "</op1>\n"
                + "<op2>" + sOp2 + "</op2>\n"
                + "</" + sMethod + ">\n"
                + "</soap:Body>\n"
                + "</soap:Envelope>\n";
    return sRequest;
}
```

The getRequest() function is pretty straightforward; it simply constructs the SOAP string in the appropriate format. (The appropriate format can be seen using the .NET test harness described in the creation of the Math service.) The completed SOAP string is returned by getRequest() and is used by performSpecificOperation() to build the SOAP request:

```
function performSpecificOperation(sMethod, sOp1, sOp2) {
    oXmlHttp = zXmlHttp.createRequest();
    setUIEnabled(false);
    var sRequest = getRequest(sMethod, sOp1, sOp2);
    var sSoapActionHeader = SOAP_ACTION_BASE + "/" + sMethod;
    oXmlHttp.open("POST", SERVICE_URL, true);
    oXmlHttp.onreadystatechange = handleResponse;
    oXmlHttp.setRequestHeader("Content-Type", "text/xml");
```

```
        oXmlHttp.setRequestHeader("SOAPAction", sSoapActionHeader);
        oXmlHttp.send(sRequest);
        document.getElementById("txtRequest").value = sRequest;
    }
```

First, a call is made on the zXmlHttp library to create an XMLHttp request. As stated previously, this will be an instance of an ActiveX class if you are using Internet Explorer or of XmlHttpRequest if you are using a Mozilla-based browser. The open method of the object received attempts to initialize the request. The first parameter states that this request will be a POST request containing data, and then comes the URL of the service, followed by a Boolean parameter specifying whether this request will be asynchronous or whether the code should wait for a response after making the call.

The onreadystatechange property of the request specifies which function will be called when the state of the request alters.

The performSpecificOperation() function then adds two headers to the HTML request. The first specifies the content type to be text/xml, and the second adds the SOAPAction header. This value can be read from the .NET test harness page or can be seen in the WSDL file as the soapAction attribute of the relevant <soap:operation/> element. Once the request is sent, the raw XML is displayed in the left text box. When the processing state of the request changes, the handleResponse() function will be called:

```
function handleResponse()
{
  if (oXmlHttp.readyState == 4)
  {
    setUIEnabled(true);
    var oResponseOutput = document.getElementById("txtResponse");
    var oResultOutput = document.getElementById("txtResult");
    var oXmlResponse = oXmlHttp.responseXML;
    var sHeaders = oXmlHttp.getAllResponseHeaders();
    if (oXmlHttp.status != 200 || !oXmlResponse.xml)
    {
      alert("Error accessing Web service.\n"
            + oXmlHttp.statusText
            + "\nSee response pane for further details.");
      var sResponse = (oXmlResponse.xml ? oXmlResponse.xml : oXmlResponseText);
      oResponseOutput.value = sHeaders + sResponse;
      return;
    }
    oResponseOutput.value = sHeaders + oXmlResponse.xml;
    var sResult =
oXmlResponse.documentElement.firstChild.firstChild.firstChild.firstChild.data;
    oResultOutput.value = sResult;
  }
}
```

The handleResponse() function reacts to any change of state in the request. When the readyState property equals 4, which equates to complete, there will be no more processing and it can be checked to see if there is a valid result.

If the `oXmlHttp.status` does not equal `200` or the `responseXML` property is empty, an error has occurred and a message is displayed to the user. Should the error be a SOAP fault, that information is also displayed in the message pane. If, however, the error wasn't a SOAP fault, the `responseText` is displayed. If the call has succeeded, the raw XML is displayed in the right text box.

Assuming that the XML response is available, there are a number of ways to extract the actual result including XSLT, using the DOM or text parsing; unfortunately, very few of these work across browsers in a consistent manner. The DOM method of gradually stepping through the tree is not very elegant, but it does have the merit of being applicable to whichever variety of XML document is in use.

Cross-Domain Web Services

So far in this chapter you've been calling a service that resides on the same domain as the page accessing it. By doing this, you have avoided the problem of cross-domain scripting (also known as *cross-site scripting*, or XSS). As discussed earlier in this book, this problem is caused by the fact that there are security risks in allowing calls to external web sites. If the web service is on the same domain as the calling page, the browser will permit the SOAP request, but what if you want to use one of the Google or Amazon.com services?

For this you'll need to use a *server-side proxy*, which runs on your web server and makes calls on behalf of the client. The proxy then returns the information it receives back to the client. The setup resembles that of a web proxy server that is commonplace in corporate networks. In that model, all requests are passed to a central server that retrieves the web page and passes it to the requestor.

The Google Web APIs Service

Google provides a number of methods that can be called through its web service, including methods for retrieving cached copies of pages as well as the more obvious results for a given search phrase. The method you will use to demonstrate a server-side proxy is `doSpellingSuggestion`, which takes a phrase and returns what Google believes you meant to type. If your phrase is not misspelled or is so obscure that it cannot hazard a suggestion, an empty string is returned.

> The developers' kit for the Google Web APIs service can be found at `www.google.com/apis/index.html`. The kit contains the service's SOAP and WSDL standards, as well as examples in C#, Visual Basic .NET, and Java.
>
> You will need to register with Google to receive a security key to allow you to access the service. There are also rules about how it can be used both commercially and for development purposes.

Setting Up the Proxy

After you have downloaded the Google documentation and received your key, you need to set up a service on your own server that will accept the calls from your users and pass them to Google. The basic service is built in the same way as the Math service discussed earlier.

To begin, open the IIS admin tool (Start⇨Administrative Tools⇨Internet Information Services). Expand the tree on the left to show the Default Web Site node, and then right-click and choose New⇨Virtual Directory. In the Alias field of the Virtual Directory Creation Wizard, name your new directory **GoogleProxy**, and then click Next. On the next screen, browse to the standard IIS directory of C:\InetPub\wwwroot, and create a new folder, also named **GoogleProxy**. Accept the defaults for the remaining screens of the wizard, and then use Windows Explorer to create a new folder below GoogleProxy named **bin**.

Next, open your text editor and create the following file, all on one line:

```
<%@ WebService Language="c#"
    Codebehind="GoogleProxy.asmx.cs" Class="Wrox.Services.GoogleProxyService" %>
```

Save this as GoogleProxy.asmx in the GoogleProxy directory.

Now create the main file, GoogleProxy.asmx.cs:

```csharp
using System;
using System.Web;
using System.Web.Services;
using GoogleService;

namespace Wrox.Services
{
  [WebService (Description = "Enables calls to the Google API",
               Namespace = "http://www.wrox.com/services/googleProxy")]
  public class GoogleProxyService : System.Web.Services.WebService
  {
    readonly string GoogleKey = "EwVqJPJQFHL4inHoIQMEP9jExTpcf/KG";

    [WebMethod(
     Description = "Returns Google spelling suggestion for a given phrase.")]
    public string doSpellingSuggestion(string Phrase)
    {
      GoogleSearchService s = new GoogleSearchService();
      s.Url = "http://api.google.com/search/beta2";
      string suggestion = "";
      try
      {
        suggestion = s.doSpellingSuggestion(GoogleKey, Phrase);
      }
```

```
        catch(Exception Ex)
        {
          throw Ex;
        }
        if (suggestion == null) suggestion = "No suggestion found.";
        return suggestion;
      }
    }
  }
```

Remember to enter the value of your Google key for the GoogleKey variable, and then save this file to the same location as the others.

The code itself is fairly straightforward; all the real work is done by the GoogleSearchService. The method doSpellingSuggestion creates an instance of the GoogleSearchService class. The URL of the service is then set. This step is not always necessary, but we've found that it often helps to be able to change the URL of services easily. In a production environment the URL would be read from a configuration file, enabling you to move between servers easily.

The doSpellingSuggestion method is now called, passing in the Google key and the Phrase argument. This is another advantage of using a server-side proxy: you can keep sensitive information such as your key away from the client-side environment of the browser.

If an exception is thrown, it will be re-thrown and returned as a SOAP fault. If the returned suggestion is null, a suitable string is returned; otherwise, the suggestion is passed back directly.

You now create the class to interact with Google. Begin by copying the GoogleSearch.wsdl file into the GoogleProxy folder, and then open a command prompt, navigate to GoogleProxy, and run the following (you can ignore warnings about a missing schema):

```
WSDL /namespace:GoogleService /out:GoogleSearchService.cs GoogleSearch.wsdl
```

The WSDL utility reads the GoogleSearch.wsdl file and creates the source code for a class to communicate with the service. The class will reside in the GoogleService namespace, as instructed by the first parameter to WSDL. This source code needs to be turned into a DLL and to do this you need to use the C# compiler as you did before. Enter the following at the command prompt or use the batch file named MakeGoogleServiceDLL.bat from the code download:

> WSDL.exe **seems to be installed in a number of different places, depending on what other Microsoft components are on the machine. On machines with Visual Studio .NET installed, it is likely to be in** C:\Program Files\Microsoft Visual Studio .NET 2003\SDK\v1.1\Bin, **but you may need to search for it on your machine.**

```
C:\WINDOWS\Microsoft.NET\Framework\v1.1.4322\csc.exe /r:System.dll
/r:System.Web.dll /r:System.Web.Services.dll /t:library
/out:bin\GoogleSearchService.dll  GoogleSearchService.cs
```

As before, the /r: parameters are telling the compiler which DLLs are needed to provide support classes to the target DLL of GoogleSearchService.

The last stage is to compile the GoogleProxy class itself:

```
C:\WINDOWS\Microsoft.NET\Framework\v1.1.4322\csc.exe /r:System.dll
/r:System.Web.dll /r:System.Web.Services.dll /r:bin\GoogleSearchService.dll
/t:library /out:bin\GoogleProxy.dll GoogleProxy.asmx.cs
```

Notice that a reference is passed in for the GoogleSearchService.dll just created.

You are now ready to test the service by entering the following URL in your browser:

```
http://localhost/GoogleProxy/GoogleProxy.asmx
```

You should be greeted with the standard screen, as shown in Figure 6-8.

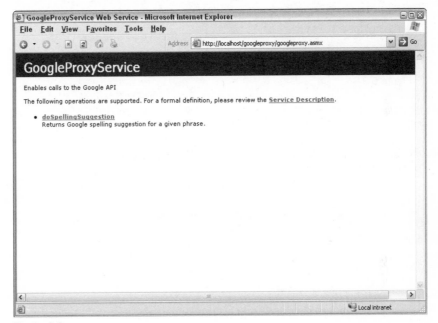

Figure 6-8

Click the doSpellingSuggestion link to try out the method using the built-in test harness, as shown in Figure 6-9.

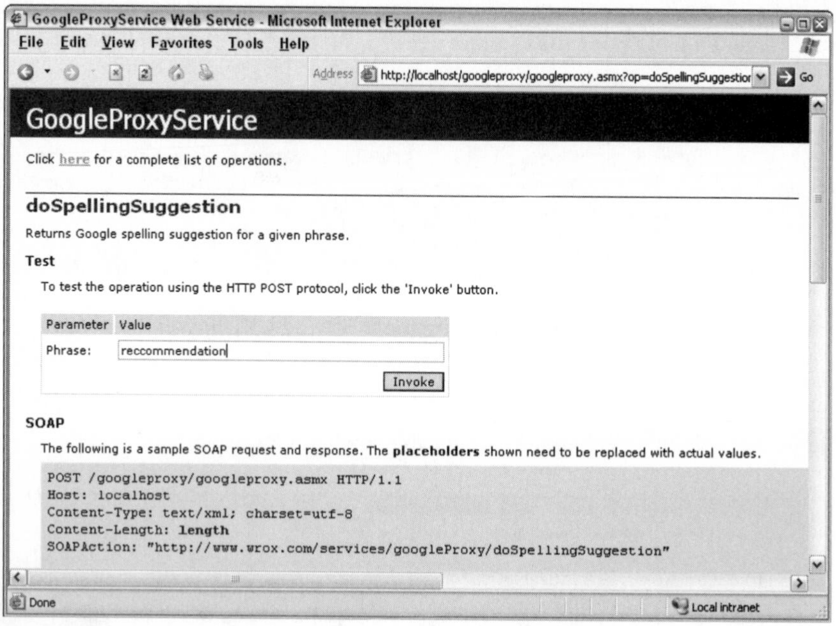

Figure 6-9

When you click the Invoke button, you will see the XML returned, as shown in Figure 6-10.

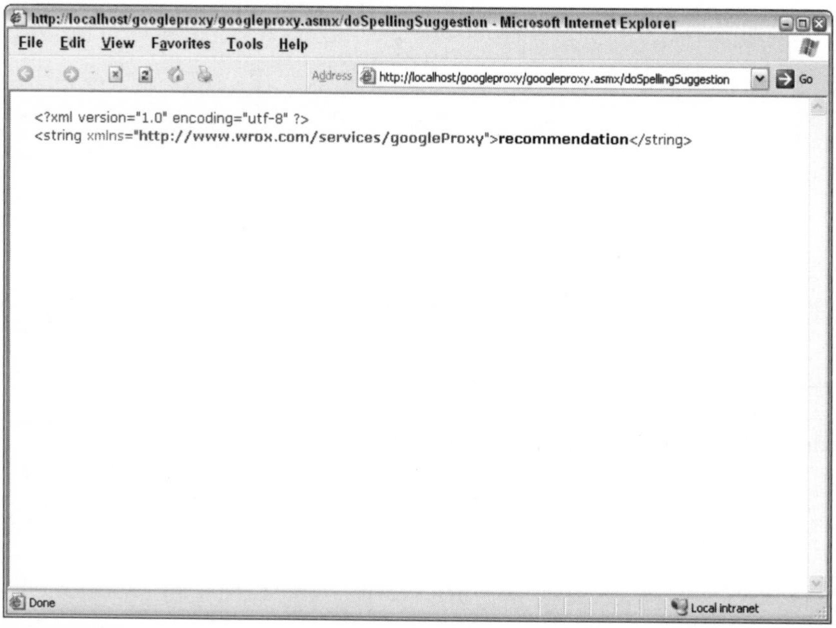

Figure 6-10

Summary

This chapter introduced you to the concept of web services, an architecture allowing the transfer of data from one location on the Internet to another. You learned about the evolution of web services and associated technologies, such as SOAP, WSDL, and REST. The similarities and differences between SOAP and REST services were also discussed.

Next, you learned how to create your own web service using ASP.NET and C#. This involved downloading the .NET SDK and using the built-in web service creation and management tools. You learned how to inspect and test your web service using the generated .NET test harness.

You then moved on to create a test harness client for Internet Explorer, and then one for Mozilla, using different techniques to call the web service. You were introduced to the web service behavior for Internet Explorer and the high-level SOAP classes in Mozilla. The last test harness created is intended to be universal, using XMLHttp to send and receive SOAP messages.

Last, you learned about cross-domain issues with web services and how to avoid them using a server-side proxy.

In this chapter the SOAP specifications were used to pass arguments between the client and the server. Although this is a robust and flexible method, it adds a lot of overhead to the process and means that the client must be able to handle XML and all its attendant complexity. The next chapter shows a simpler and less formal way of passing data between machines called JavaScript Object Notation (JSON).

7

JSON

With the still-rising popularity of web services, XML has practically become the de facto standard for data transmission. However, XML is not without its detractors. For example, some consider it to be overly verbose for data transmission purposes, necessitating many more bytes of information to be sent across the Internet to accomplish what could have been done in a much smaller form. To take this into consideration, new forms of XML compression and even entire new XML formats, such as Binary XML, have been developed. All these solutions work on extending or adding on to XML, making backwards compatibility an issue. Douglas Crockford, a long-time software engineer, proposed a new data format built on JavaScript called *JavaScript Object Notation* (JSON).

Up until this point, you've used either plain text or XML to transmit data back and forth to the server. This chapter introduces the use of JSON in Ajax communication as an alternative to these more traditional data formats.

What Is JSON?

JSON is a very lightweight data format based on a subset of the JavaScript syntax, namely array and object literals. Because it uses JavaScript syntax, JSON definitions can be included within JavaScript files and accessed without the extra parsing that comes along with XML-based languages. But before you can use JSON, it's important to understand the specific JavaScript syntax for array and object literals.

Array Literals

For those unfamiliar with JavaScript literal notation, array literals are specified by using square brackets ([and]) to enclose a comma-delimited list of JavaScript values (meaning a string, number, Boolean, or null value), such as:

```
var aNames = ["Benjamin", "Michael", "Scott"];
```

You can then access the values in the array by using the array name and bracket notation:

```
alert(aNames[0]);    //outputs "Benjamin"
alert(aNames[1]);    //outputs "Michael"
alert(aNames[2]);    //outputs "Scott"
```

Note that the first position in the array is 0, and the value in that position is "Benjamin".

Because arrays in JavaScript are not typed, they can be used to store any number of different data types:

```
var aValues = ["string", 24, true, null];
```

This array contains a string, followed by a number, followed by a Boolean, followed by a null value. This is completely legal and perfectly fine JavaScript.

If you were to define an array without using literal notation, you would have to use the Array constructor, such as:

```
var aValues = new Array("string", 24, true, null);
```

> It's important to note that either way is acceptable when writing JavaScript, but only array literals are valid in JSON.

Object Literals

Object literals are used to store information in name-value pairs, ultimately creating an object. An object literal is defined by two curly braces ({ and }). Inside of these can be placed any number of name-value pairs, defined with a string, a colon, and the value. Each name-value pair must be followed with a comma, except for the last one (making this more like defining an associative array in Perl). For example:

```
var oCar = {
    "color" : "red",
    "doors" : 4,
    "paidFor" : true
};
```

This code creates an object with three properties named color, doors, and paidFor, each containing different values. You can access these properties by using the object name and dot notation, such as:

```
alert(oCar.color);    //outputs "red"
alert(oCar.doors);    //outputs "4"
alert(oCar.paidFor);  //outputs "true"
```

You can also use bracket notation and pass in the name of the property as a string value (like the way it was defined using object literal notation):

```
alert(oCar["color"]);    //outputs "red"
alert(oCar["doors"]);    //outputs "4"
alert(oCar["paidFor"]);  //outputs "true"
```

The same object could be created using the JavaScript `Object` constructor, like this:

```
var oCar = new Object();
oCar.color = "red";
oCar.doors = 4;
oCar.paidFor = true;
```

As you can see, the object literal notation requires much less code than using the `Object` constructor.

> **Once again, although either approach is valid in JavaScript, only object literal notation is valid in JSON.**

Mixing Literals

It's possible to mix object and array literals, creating an array of objects or an object containing an array. Suppose you wanted to create an array of car objects similar to the one created in the last section. You could do so as follows:

```
var aCars = [
    {
        "color" : "red",
        "doors" : 2,
        "paidFor" : true
    },
    {
        "color" : "blue",
        "doors" : 4,
        "paidFor" : true
    },
    {
        "color" : "white",
        "doors" : 2,
        "paidFor" : false
    }
];
```

This code defines an array, `aCars`, which has three objects in it. The three objects each have properties named `color`, `doors`, and `paidFor`. (Each object represents a car, of course.) You can access any of the information in the array by using a combination of bracket and dot notation. For example, to get the number of doors on the second car in the array, the following line will do the trick:

```
alert(aCars[1].doors);    //outputs "4"
```

In this example, you are first getting the value in the second position of the array (position 1) and then getting the property named `doors`.

You can also define the array to be inside of object literals, such as:

```
var oCarInfo = {
    "availableColors" : [ "red", "white", "blue" ],
    "availableDoors" : [ 2, 4 ]
};
```

This code defines an object called oCarInfo that has two properties, availableColors and availableDoors. Both of these properties are arrays, containing strings and numbers, respectively. To access a value here, you just reverse the order of the bracket and dot notation. So, to get to the second available color, you can do this:

```
alert(oCarInfo.availableColors[1]);
```

In this example, you are first returning the property named availableColors, and then getting the value in the second position (position 1). But what does all this have to do with JSON?

JSON Syntax

JSON syntax is really nothing more than the mixture of object and array literals to store data. The only difference from the examples in the last section is that JSON doesn't have variables. Remember, JSON represents only data; it has no concept of variables, assignments, or equality. Therefore, the JSON code for the last example is simply:

```
{
    "availableColors" : [ "red", "white", "blue" ],
    "availableDoors" : [ 2, 4 ]
}
```

Note that the variable oCarInfo has been removed, as has the semicolon following the closing curly brace. If this were transmitted via HTTP to a browser, it would be fairly quick because of the small number of characters. Suppose this data was retrieved by using XMLHTTP (or some other form of client-server communication) and stored in a variable named sJSON. You now have a string of information, not an object and certainly not an object with two arrays. To transform it into an object, you can simply use the JavaScript eval() function, like so:

```
var oCarInfo = eval("(" + sJSON + ")");
```

This example surrounds the JSON text with parentheses and then passes that string into the eval() function, which acts like a JavaScript interpreter. The result of this operation is a JavaScript object identical to the oCarInfo object defined in the last section. You can access information in this object in the exact same way:

```
alert(oCarInfo.availableColors[0]);    //outputs "red"
alert(oCarInfo.availableDoors[1]);     //ouputs "4"
```

> It's very important to include the extra parentheses around any JSON string before passing it into eval(). Remember, curly braces also represent statements in JavaScript (such as used with the if statement). The only way the interpreter knows that the curly braces represent an object and not a statement is to look for an equals sign before it or to look for parentheses around it (which indicates that the code is an expression to be evaluated instead of a statement to be run).

You can see the obvious benefits of using JSON as a data format for JavaScript communication: it takes the evaluation of the data out of your hands and, therefore, grants you faster access to the information contained within.

JSON Encoding/Decoding

As part of his resource on JSON, Crockford has created a utility that can be used to decode and encode between JSON and JavaScript objects. The source for this tool can be downloaded at `www.crockford.com/JSON/json.js`.

You may be asking yourself, "Didn't I just learn to decode JSON using the `eval()` function?" The answer is yes, but there is an inherent flaw in using `eval()`: it will evaluate any JavaScript code passed into it, not just JSON. This could be a huge security risk when dealing with enterprise web applications. To deal with this issue, you can use the `JSON.parse()` method (defined in the aforementioned file), which will parse and convert only JSON code into JavaScript. For example:

```
var oObject = JSON.parse(sJSON);
```

Also provided with the utility is a way to convert JavaScript objects into a JSON string for transmission. (There is no such built-in way to do this in JavaScript.) All you need to do is pass an object into the `JSON.stringify()` method. Consider the following example:

```
var oCar = new Object();
oCar.doors = 4;
oCar.color = "blue";
oCar.year = 1995;
oCar.drivers = new Array("Penny", "Dan", "Kris");

document.write(JSON.stringify(oCar));
```

This code outputs the following JSON string:

```
{"doors":4,"color":"blue","year":1995,"drivers":["Penny","Dan","Kris"]}
```

With this, you're now ready to transmit the information to whatever destination makes sense for you.

JSON versus XML

As mentioned previously, one of the advantages of JSON over XML is that it's more compact. XML is considered by some to be overly verbose for its purpose. But what does this mean exactly? Consider the following XML data:

```
<classinfo>
    <students>
        <student>
            <name>Michael Smith</name>
            <average>99.5</average>
            <age>17</age>
            <graduating>true</graduating>
        </student>
        <student>
            <name>Steve Johnson</name>
            <average>34.87</average>
            <age>17</age>
            <graduating>false</graduating>
```

```
        </student>
        <student>
            <name>Rebecca Young</name>
            <average>89.6</average>
            <age>18</age>
            <graduating>true</graduating>
        </student>
    </students>
</classinfo>
```

This example contains information about three students in a class. Right away, there is some XML information that isn't entirely necessary: the `<classinfo>` and `<students/>` elements. These elements help to define the overall structure and meaning of the information, but the actual information you're interested in is the students and their information. Plus, for each piece of information about the students, the name of the information is repeated twice, although the actual data is repeated only once (for example, `"name"` appears both in `<name>` and `</name>`. Consider the same information formatted as JSON:

```
{ "classinfo" :
    {
        "students" : [
            {
                "name" : "Michael Smith",
                "average" : 99.5,
                "age" : 17,
                "graduating" : true
            },
            {
                "name" : "Steve Johnson",
                "average" : 34.87,
                "age" : 17,
                "graduating" : false
            },
            {
                "name" : "Rebecca Young",
                "average" : 89.6,
                "age" : 18,
                "graduating" : true
            }
        ]
    }
}
```

As you can see, a lot of the superfluous information isn't present. Since closing tags aren't necessary to match opening tags, it greatly reduces the number of bytes needed to transmit the same information. Not including spaces, the JSON data is 224 bytes, whereas the comparable XML data is 365 bytes, saving more than 100 bytes. (This is why Crockford, JSON's creator, calls it the "fat free alternative to XML.")

The disadvantage to JSON-formatted data as compared to XML is that it's less readable to the layperson. Because XML is verbose, it's fairly easy to understand what data is being represented. JSON, with its shorthand notation, can be difficult to decipher using the naked eye. Of course, an argument can be made that data exchange formats should never be viewed with the naked eye. If you're using tools to create and parse the data being passed back and forth, then there is really no reason to have the data be human readable. But this begs the question: Are there any JSON tools available? The answer is yes.

Server-Side JSON Tools

As you know by now, Ajax has to do with the interaction between the client and the server, so JSON would be of no use for this purpose unless there were server-side tools to aid in the encoding and decoding. As luck would have it, there are quite a few JSON utilities for server-side languages. Although it is beyond the scope of this book to discuss every one of these tools, it is useful to take a look at one and then develop a solution using it.

JSON-PHP

JSON-PHP is a PHP utility to ease the encoding and decoding of JSON information. This utility, written by Michal Migurski, is available for free at http://mike.teczno.com/json.html. All you need to begin using JSON in PHP is to include the JSON.php file in your page and make use of the JSON object.

Creating new instance of the JSON object is quite simple:

```php
<?php
    require_once("JSON.php");
    $oJSON = new JSON();
?>
```

The first line includes the JSON.php file that contains the JSON object definition. The second line simply instantiates the object and stores it in the variable $oJSON. Now you're ready to start encoding and decoding JSON in your PHP page.

To encode a PHP object into a JSON string, use the encode() method, which accepts a single argument: an object to encode, which can be an array or a full-fledged object. It doesn't matter how the object or array was created, whether using a class definition or not; all objects can be encoded using this method. Consider the following class definition:

```php
<?php
    class Person {

        var $age;
        var $hairColor;
        var $name;
        var $siblingNames;

        function Person($name, $age, $hairColor) {
            $this->name = $name;
            $this->age = $age;
            $this->hairColor = $hairColor;
            $this->siblingNames = array();
        }
    }
?>
```

This PHP code defines a class called `Person` that stores some personal information. You would use this class as follows:

```php
<?php
    $oPerson = new Person("Mike", 26, "brown");
    $oPerson->siblingNames[0] = "Matt";
    $oPerson->siblingNames[1] = "Tammy";
?>
```

To encode the `$oPerson` object, you simply pass it into the `encode()` method, like this:

```php
<?php
    $sJSONText = $oJSON->encode($oPerson);
?>
```

This creates a JSON string of:

```
{"age":26,"hairColor":"brown","name":"Mike","siblingNames":["Matt","Tammy"]}
```

The `$oPerson` object is now ready to be transferred to JavaScript or any other language that can support JSON-encoded information.

But what if you already have a JSON string? That's where the `decode()` method is used.

Suppose you have the JSON string displayed previously and want to create a PHP object from it. Just pass the string into the `decode()` method:

```php
<?php
    $oPerson = $oJSON->decode($sJSONText);
?>
```

Now the `$oPerson` variable can be used just like the one in the previous example, as if it were created using the `Person` class:

```php
<?php
    print("<h3>Person Information</h3>");
    print("<p>Name: ".$oPerson->name."<br />");
    print("Age: ".$oPerson->age."<br />");
    print("Hair Color: ".$oPerson->hairColor."<br />");
    print("Sibling Names:</p><ul>");

    for ($i=0; $i < count($oPerson->siblingNames); $i++) {
        print("<li>".$oPerson->siblingNames[$i]."</li>");
    }

    print("</ul>");
?>
```

This code prints out the information contained in the `$oPerson` object, proving that the object has been constructed appropriately. JSON-PHP will be used in several projects throughout this book because it is quite simply the easiest way to deal with JSON in a server-side language.

Other Tools

You can find a number of JSON tools for server-side languages, so no matter what your preference is, you can use the power of JSON:

- ❑ **C#/.NET:** The C# JSON library, written by Douglas Crockford, is available at `www.crockford.com/JSON/cs/`.

- ❑ **ColdFusion:** The CFJSON library, written by Jehiah Czebotar, is available at `http://jehiah.com/projects/cfjson/`.

- ❑ **Java:** The JSON in Java utilities, written by Douglas Crockford, are available at `www.crockford.com/JSON/java/`. Can be used in JSP.

- ❑ **Perl:** The JSON library, written by Makamaka Hannyaharamitu, is available at `http://search.cpan.org/dist/JSON/`.

- ❑ **PHP:** In addition to JSON-PHP, there is also php-json, a C extension for PHP written by Omar Kilani and available at `www.aurore.net/projects/php-json/`. You must be comfortable with compiling PHP with extensions.

- ❑ **Python:** The json-py library, written by Patrick D. Logan, is available at `https://sourceforge.net/projects/json-py/`.

Douglas Crockford also maintains a fairly comprehensive list of JSON utilities at `www.crockford.com/JSON/index.html`. Check there before searching for JSON utilities for any other language.

Creating an Autosuggest Text Box

The best way to learn about any new programming concept is to put it into a practical example. Google Suggest (located at `www.google.com/webhp?complete=1`) is a very simple Ajax application that many programmers have spent time dissecting, analyzing, and re-creating. If you haven't yet taken a look at the live application, please do so now; it will greatly aid in your understanding of the following example.

Functionality such as this, suggesting to the user values to type in, has been around in desktop applications for some time now. Google Suggest brought the idea to the Web and generated a lot of excitement while doing it. As mentioned earlier in the book, Google Suggest really was one of the early Ajax applications that got developers excited about the concept. It seems fitting to attempt to emulate the behavior of Google Suggest to help others understand Ajax.

The example built in this section aids in the selection of states or provinces in a personal information form. For sites that deal with international customers, it is often vital to include the state or province along with the country. However, it's not optimal to load every state and province in the entire world into a drop-down box for the user to select from. It's much easier to let the user start typing, and then retrieve only those results that would make the most sense. Autosuggest functionality is perfect for this use case.

Functionality Overview

Before building anything, it's always helpful to understand exactly what you're building. Anyone can say they are going to emulate the functionality of Google Suggest, but what does that mean? The example you will build in this section has the following functionality:

❑ **Typeahead:** As the user is typing, the rest of the text box fills in with the best suggestion at the time. As the user continues to type, the text box automatically adjusts its suggestion. The suggested text always appears selected (highlighted). This should work no matter how fast the user types.

❑ **Suggestions list:** Also as the user is typing, a drop-down list of other suggestions is displayed. These suggestions are generated automatically while the user types so that there is no discernible delay.

❑ **Keyboard controls:** When the suggestions are displayed, the user is able to scroll up and down the list by using the up and down arrows on the keyboard and select a suggestion. Pressing Enter places the value into the text box and hides the suggestion list. The Esc key can also be used to hide the suggestions.

❑ **Hide suggestions:** The drop-down suggestion list is smart enough to hide itself whenever the text box is not used or when the browser window is hidden.

You probably didn't realize that Google Suggest was doing so much. This is the key with Ajax: you don't think about what's going on because it works in an intuitive way.

The HTML

The first step in any client-side component is to build the HTML that will be used. For the autosuggest text box, this includes the text box itself as well as the drop-down list of suggestions. You're probably familiar with the HTML text box:

```
<input type="text" name="txtAutosuggest" value="" />
```

In most cases, this line would be enough to use a text box. The problem is that some browsers (notably Internet Explorer on Windows and Mozilla Firefox on all operating systems) provide autocomplete functionality that drops down a list of suggestions based on values you've entered before. Since this would compete directly with the suggestions you'll be providing, this has to be turned off. To do so, set the autocomplete attribute to off:

```
<input type="text" name="txtAutosuggest" value="" autocomplete="off" />
```

Now you can be assured that there will be no interference from the autocomplete browser behavior. The only other user interface component to design is the drop-down list of suggestions.

The suggestion drop-down list is nothing more than an absolutely positioned <div/> element that is positioned below the text box so as to give the illusion of being a drop-down list (see Figure 7-1).

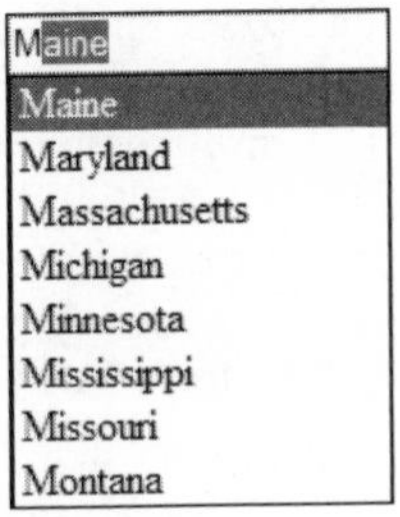

Figure 7-1

Inside of this <div/> element are several other <div/> elements, one for each suggestion. By changing the style of these elements, it's possible to achieve the look of highlighting a given suggestion. The HTML to create the list displayed in Figure 7-1 is as follows:

```
<div class="suggestions">
    <div class="current">Maine</div>
    <div>Maryland</div>
    <div>Massachusetts</div>
    <div>Michigan</div>
    <div>Minnesota</div>
    <div>Mississippi</div>
    <div>Missouri</div>
    <div>Montana</div>
</div>
```

This HTML won't be coded directly into the main HTML file; instead, it will be created dynamically by JavaScript code. However, you need to know the general format of the HTML in order to create it appropriately.

Of course, some CSS is needed to make the drop-down list function properly. The outermost <div/> has a class of suggestions, which is defined as:

```
div.suggestions {
    -moz-box-sizing: border-box;
    box-sizing: border-box;
    background-color: white;
    border: 1px solid black;
    position: absolute;
}
```

The first two lines of this CSS class are for browsers that support two forms of box sizing: content box and border box (for more information, read www.quirksmode.org/css/box.html). In quirks mode, Internet Explorer defaults to border box; in standards mode, Internet Explorer defaults to content box. Most other DOM-compliant browsers (Mozilla, Opera, and Safari) default to content box, meaning that there is a difference in how the <div/> element will be rendered among browsers. To provide for this, the first two lines of the CSS class set rendering to border box. The first line, -moz-box-sizing, is

201

Mozilla-specific and used for older Mozilla browsers; the second line is for browsers that support the official CSS3 `box-sizing` property. Assuming that you use quirks mode in your page, this class will work just fine. (If you use standards mode, simply remove these first two lines.)

The remaining styles simply add a border and specify that the `<div/>` element be absolutely positioned.

Next, a little bit of formatting is needed for the drop-down list items:

```
div.suggestions div {
    cursor: default;
    padding: 0px 3px;
}
```

The first line specifies the default cursor (the arrow) to be displayed when the mouse is over an item in the drop-down list. Without this, the cursor would display as the caret, which is the normal cursor for text boxes and web pages in general. The user needs to believe that the drop-down item is not a part of the regular page flow, but an attachment to the text box, and changing the cursor helps. The second line simply applies some padding to the item (which you can modify as you wish).

Last, some CSS is needed to format the currently selected item in the drop-down list. When an item is selected, the background will be changed to blue and the text color will be changed to white. This provides a basic highlight that is typically used in drop-down menus:

```
div.suggestions div.current {
    background-color: #3366cc;
    color: white;
}
```

All these styles are to be contained in an external CSS file named `autosuggest.css`.

The Database Table

In order to easily query the states and provinces that match a particular text snippet, it is necessary to use a database table. There are a few open source database products that can be paired nicely with PHP, but the most common one is MySQL (available at www.mysql.org). Many web hosting companies that offer PHP hosting also offer one or more MySQL databases as well, so for this example, MySQL will be the database used.

> **Although this example is intended to be used with MySQL, it should be able to run on other databases with little or no modification.**

The database table can be very simple for this example, although you may need more information to make it practical for your needs. To get this to work, you really need only a single column to store the state and province names. However, it's always best to define a primary key, so this table will include a second column containing an auto-incremented ID number for each state or province. The following SQL statement creates a table named `StatesAndProvinces` with two columns, `Id` and `Name`:

```
CREATE TABLE StatesAndProvinces (
    Id INT NOT NULL AUTO_INCREMENT,
    Name VARCHAR(255) NOT NULL,
    PRIMARY KEY (Id)
) COMMENT = 'States and Provinces';
```

Of course, the time-consuming part is to fill in state and province names from various countries around the world. The code download for this example, available at www.wrox.com, includes a SQL file that will populate the table with all U.S. states as well as one that will insert all Canadian provinces and territories.

Setting up this information in a database table enables you to quickly get a list of suggestions for text the user has typed in. If the user has typed the letter M, for example, you can run the following query to get the first five suggestions:

```
SELECT *
FROM StatesAndProvinces
WHERE Name LIKE 'M%'
ORDER BY Name ASC
LIMIT 0, 5
```

This statement returns a maximum of five suggestions, in alphabetical order, for all names starting with M. Later, this will be used in the PHP code that returns the suggestions.

The Architecture

In Chapter 1, you saw the basic architecture of an Ajax solution involving the user interface and Ajax engine on the client. The autosuggest architecture follows this general format, where the user interface is the autosuggest control and the Ajax engine is a suggestion provider (see Figure 7-2).

Autosuggest Control Architecture

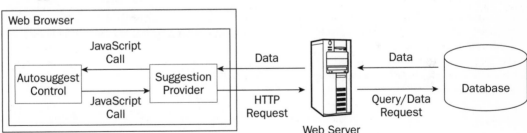

Figure 7-2

In this architecture, the autosuggest control has no idea where the suggestions are coming from; they could be coming from the client or the server. All the autosuggest control knows is how to call the suggestion provider to get suggestions for the text contained within the text box. The suggestion provider handles all the server communication and notifies the autosuggest control when the suggestions are available. To accomplish this, both the autosuggest control and the suggestion provider need to implement specific interfaces so that each knows what method to call on the other.

The Classes

Two classes are necessary to represent the two client-side components of the autosuggest functionality, appropriately called `AutoSuggestControl` and `SuggestionProvider`. The `AutoSuggestControl` is assigned a `SuggestionProvider` when it is created so that all requests go through it. The `SuggestionProvider` has only one method, `requestSuggestions()`, which is called by the `AutoSuggestControl` whenever suggestions are needed. This method takes two arguments: the `AutoSuggestControl` itself and a Boolean value indicating whether the control should type ahead when the suggestions are returned.

When the suggestions have been retrieved, the `SuggestionProvider` calls the `autosuggest()` method of the `AutoSuggestControl`, passing in the array of suggestions as well as the typeahead flag that was passed into it. This allows for a delay between the request for suggestions and the response, making it possible to use asynchronous requests. This approach sounds more complicated than it is; Figure 7-3 represents the interaction between these two objects in a clearer manner.

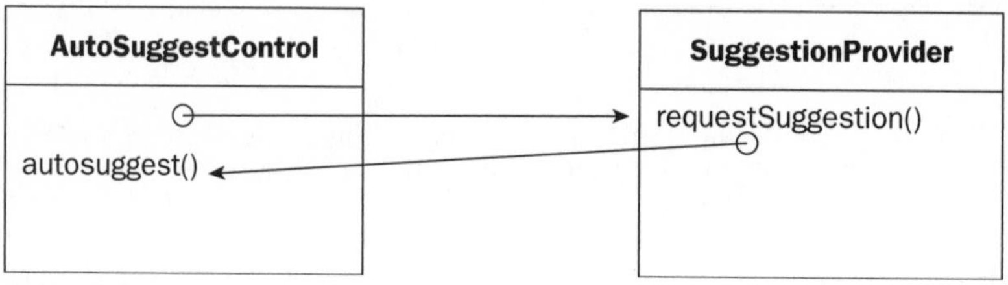

Figure 7-3

With the architecture designed, it's time to start coding.

The AutoSuggest Control

The `AutoSuggestControl` class is the wrapper for all autosuggest functionality. To work properly, the control needs to know which text box to work on and the suggestion provider to use. This makes for a relatively simple constructor:

```
function AutoSuggestControl(oTextbox, oProvider) {
    this.provider = oProvider;
    this.textbox = oTextbox;
}
```

It's upon this simple base that the complex functionality of an autosuggest text box will be built.

Since the `AutoSuggestControl` class is quite complicated, it's much simpler to break up its explanation into specific types of functionality. The following sections build on each other, and the complete code can be downloaded from www.wrox.com.

Implementing Typeahead

To implement the first feature, typeahead, it's helpful to understand exactly how it works. Typeahead text boxes look at what the user has typed and then makes a suggestion, highlighting only the part that was added automatically. For example, if you were to type *Ma* into a text box, the suggestion may be *Maine*, but only *ine* would be highlighted. Doing this allows the user to continue typing without interruption because any new characters simply replace the highlighted section.

Originally, the only type of highlighting possible using JavaScript was to highlight all the text in the text box using the `select()` method, as follows:

```
var oTextbox = document.getElementById("txtState");
oTextbox.select();
```

This code gets a reference to a text box with the ID of `txtState` and then selects all the text contained within it. Although this functionality is fine for many everyday uses, it's not very helpful for implementing typeahead. Thankfully, both Internet Explorer and Firefox have ways of selecting parts of the text instead of the entire item (for other browsers, this feature is not available). But as usual, the two biggest combatants in the browser world do things in two completely different ways.

The Internet Explorer solution is to use a text range. Not to be confused with DOM ranges, an Internet Explorer text range is an invisible selection of text on the page, beginning on a single character and ending on a single character. When a text range is filled out, you can highlight just the text contained within it, which is perfect for typeahead. To create a text range for a specific text box, you use the `createTextRange()` method that Internet Explorer provides on every text box.

Once you have a text range, its methods enable you to select certain parts of the text. Although there are many text range methods, the only ones of interest for this example are `moveStart()` and `moveEnd()`, both of which accept two arguments: a unit and a number. The unit can be `character`, `word`, `sentence`, or `textedit`, whereas the number indicates the number of units to move from the start or end of the text (this should be a positive number for `moveStart()` and a negative for `moveEnd()`). When the endpoints of the text range are set, you can call its `select()` method to highlight just those characters. For example, to select just the first three characters in a text box, you could do this:

```
var oRange = oTextbox.createTextRange();
oRange.moveStart("character", 0);
oRange.moveEnd("character", 3 - oTextbox.value.length);
oRange.select();
oTextbox.focus();
```

Note that to get the appropriate value for `moveEnd()`, it's necessary to subtract the length of the text in the text box from the number of characters to select (3). The last step is to set the focus to the text box so that the selection is visible. (Text can be selected only when the text box has focus.) The process is a bit involved in Internet Explorer, but pretty easy to script. Firefox, on the other hand, is very straightforward.

Text boxes in Firefox have a non-standard method called `setSelectionRange()`, which accepts two arguments: the index of the character to start with and the index of character after the last character to select. So, to select the first three characters in a text box using Mozilla, you need only two lines of code:

```
oTextbox.setSelectionRange(0,3);
oTextbox.focus();
```

The first method you'll need in the `AutoSuggestControl` class is a method to select a range of characters in a browser-specific way. This method, called `selectRange()`, handles all the dirty work for you:

```
AutoSuggestControl.prototype.selectRange = function (iStart, iEnd) {
    if (this.textbox.createTextRange) {
        var oRange = this.textbox.createTextRange();
        oRange.moveStart("character", iStart);
        oRange.moveEnd("character", iEnd- this.textbox.value.length);
        oRange.select();
    } else if (this.textbox.setSelectionRange) {
        this.textbox.setSelectionRange(iStart, iEnd);
    }

    this.textbox.focus();
};
```

This method uses feature detection, the process of detecting certain browser features, to determine how to select the characters. It tests for the existence of the `createTextRange()` method to determine whether the Internet Explorer text ranges should be used, and tests for the `setSelectionRange()` method to determine whether the Firefox method should be used. The arguments are the first character to select and the number of characters to select. These values are then passed to the browser-specific methods of text selection.

The typeAhead() Method

Now that you can select specific parts of the text box, it's time to implement the typeahead functionality. To do this, a `typeAhead()` method is defined that accepts a single argument: the suggestion to display in the textbox. The suggestion being passed in is assumed to be appropriate (and assumed to have at least one character). This method then does three things:

1. It gets the length of the text already in the text box.

2. It places the suggestion into the text box.

3. It selects only the portion of the text that the user didn't type using the information from step 1.

Additionally, since typeahead can be supported only in Internet Explorer and Firefox, you should check to make sure one of those browsers is being used. If the browser doesn't support text selection, then none of the steps should be executed so as not to interrupt the user's typing. Once again, testing for the `createTextRange()` and `setSelectionRange()` methods of the text box is the way to go:

```
AutoSuggestControl.prototype.typeAhead = function (sSuggestion) {
    if (this.textbox.createTextRange || this.textbox.setSelectionRange) {
        var iLen = this.textbox.value.length;
        this.textbox.value = sSuggestion;
        this.selectRange(iLen, sSuggestion.length);
    }
};
```

With this method complete, you now need another method to call it and pass in the suggestion. This is where the `autosuggest()` method comes in.

The autosuggest() Method

Perhaps the most important method in the control is `autosuggest()`. This single method is responsible for receiving an array of suggestions for the text box and then deciding what to do with them. Eventually, this method will be used to implement the full autosuggest functionality (including drop-down suggestions), but for now, it's used to implement typeahead only.

Because `autosuggest()` will be passed an array of suggestions, you have your pick as to which one to use for the typeahead value. It's recommended to always use the first value in the array to keep it simple. The problem is that there may not always be suggestions for a value, in which case an empty array will be passed. You shouldn't call `typeAhead()` if there are no suggestions, so it's important to check the length of the array first:

```
AutoSuggestControl.prototype.autosuggest = function (aSuggestions) {
    if (aSuggestions.length > 0) {
        this.typeAhead(aSuggestions[0]);
    }
};
```

But where do the suggestions come from? It's actually the job of the suggestion provider to call this method and pass in the suggestions. Implementation of this feature is discussed later in the chapter.

Handling Key Events

Of course the autosuggest functionality has to be tied into the text box using events. There are three events that deal with keys: `keydown`, `keypress`, and `keyup`. The `keydown` event fires whenever the user presses a key on the keyboard but before any changes occur to the text box. This obviously won't help with autosuggest because you need to know the full text of the text box; using this event would mean being one keystroke behind. For the same reason, the `keypress` event can't be used. It is similar to `keydown`, but fires only when a character key is pressed. The `keyup` event, however, fires after changes have been made to the text box, which is exactly when autosuggest should begin working.

Setting up an event handler for the text box involves two steps: defining a function and assigning it as an event handler. The function is actually a method of the autosuggest control, called `handleKeyUp()`. This method expects the `event` object to be passed in as an argument (how to accomplish this is discussed later) so that it can tell whether the key being pressed should enact the autosuggest functionality. Since `keyup` fires for all keys, not just character keys, you'll receive events when someone uses a cursor key, the Tab key, and any other key on the keyboard. To avoid interfering with how a text box works, suggestions should be made only when a character key is pressed. This is where the event object's `keyCode` property enters the picture.

The `keyCode` property is supported by most modern browsers (including Internet Explorer on Windows and Macintosh, Firefox, Opera, and Safari) and returns a numeric code representing the key that was pressed. Using this property, it's possible to set up behaviors for specific keys. Since the autosuggest functionality should happen only when character keys are pressed, you need to check this property for an appropriate value before proceeding. Believe it or not, the easiest way to do this is actually to detect the keys that you want to ignore. This approach is more efficient because there are more character keys than non-character keys. The following table displays the key codes for all keys that should be ignored:

Key	Code	Key	Code
Backspace	8	Print Screen	44
Tab	9	Delete	46
Enter	13	F1	112
Shift	16	F2	113
Ctrl	17	F3	114
Alt	18	F4	115
Pause/Break	19	F5	116
Caps Lock	20	F6	117
Esc	27	F7	118
Page Up	33	F8	119
Page Down	34	F9	120
End	35	F10	121
Home	36	F11	122
Left Arrow	37	F12	123
Up Arrow	38		
Right Arrow	39		
Down Arrow	40		

You may notice a pattern among the key codes. It looks like all keys with a code less than or equal to 46 should be ignored and all keys with codes between 112 and 123 should be ignored. This is generally true, but there is an exception. The space bar has a key code of 32, so you actually need to check to see if the code is less than 32, between 33 and 46, or between 112 and 123. If it's not in any one of these groups, then you know it's a character key.

Here's what the handleKeyUp() method looks like:

```
AutoSuggestControl.prototype.handleKeyUp = function (oEvent) {
    var iKeyCode = oEvent.keyCode;

    if (iKeyCode < 32 || (iKeyCode >= 33 && iKeyCode <= 46)
            || (iKeyCode >= 112 && iKeyCode <= 123)) {

        //ignore
    } else {
        this.provider.requestSuggestions(this);
    }
};
```

When a user presses a character key, the autosuggest functionality begins by calling the suggestion provider's `requestSuggestions()` method and passing a pointer to the autosuggest control as an argument. Remember, it's the suggestion provider that will call the `autosuggest()` method defined earlier. The `requestSuggestions()` method begins the process of retrieving suggestions for usage.

With this method defined, it must be assigned as the event handler for the text box. It's best to create a separate method to handle initializations for the control such as this (there will be more in the future). The `init()` method serves this purpose:

```
AutoSuggestControl.prototype.init = function () {
    var oThis = this;
    this.textbox.onkeyup = function (oEvent) {
        if (!oEvent) {
            oEvent = window.event;
        }
        oThis.handleKeyUp(oEvent);
    };
};
```

The `init()` method starts by creating a pointer to the `this` object so that it may be used later. An anonymous function is defined for the text box's onkeyup event handler. Inside of this function, the `handleKeyUp()` method is called using the `oThis` pointer. (Using `this` here would refer to the text box instead of the autosuggest control.)

Since this method requires the event object to be passed in, it's necessary to check for both DOM and Internet Explorer event objects. The DOM event object is passed in as an argument to the event handler, whereas the Internet Explorer event object is a property of `window`. Instead of doing a browser detect, you can check to see if the `oEvent` object is passed into the event handler. If not, then assign `window.event` into the `oEvent` variable. The `oEvent` variable can then be passed directly into the `handleKeyUp()` event handler.

The `init()` method should be called from within the `AutoSuggestControl` constructor:

```
function AutoSuggestControl(oTextbox, oProvider) {
    this.provider = oProvider;
    this.textbox = oTextbox;
    this.init();
}
```

That's all it takes to implement the typeahead functionality of the autosuggest control. At this point, you are displaying a single suggestion to the user as they type. The goal is, of course, to provide multiple suggestions using a drop-down list.

Showing Multiple Suggestions

Earlier in the chapter you took a look at the HTML and CSS used for the drop-down list of suggestions. Now the task is to create the HTML programmatically and apply the CSS to create the actual functionality; this is a multistep process. First, a property is needed to store the `<div/>` element because various methods of the `AutoSuggestControl` need access to it. This property is called `layer` and is initially set to `null`:

```
function AutoSuggestControl(oTextbox, oProvider) {
    this.layer = null;
    this.provider = oProvider;
    this.textbox = oTextbox;
    this.init();
}
```

The drop-down list will be created after you define a few simple methods to help control its behavior. The simplest method is hideSuggestions(), which hides the drop-down list after it has been shown:

```
AutoSuggestControl.prototype.hideSuggestions = function () {
    this.layer.style.visibility = "hidden";
};
```

Next, a method is needed for highlighting the current suggestion in the drop-down list. The highlightSuggestion() method accepts a single argument, which is the <div/> element containing the current suggestion. The purpose of this method is to set the <div/> element's class attribute to current on the current suggestion and clear the class attribute on all others in the list. Doing so provides a highlighting effect on the drop-down list similar to the regular form controls. The algorithm is quite simple: iterate through the child nodes of the layer. If the child node is equal to the node that was passed in, set the class to current; otherwise, clear the class attribute by setting it to an empty string:

```
AutoSuggestControl.prototype.highlightSuggestion = function (oSuggestionNode) {

    for (var i=0; i < this.layer.childNodes.length; i++) {
        var oNode = this.layer.childNodes[i];
        if (oNode == oSuggestionNode) {
            oNode.className = "current"
        } else if (oNode.className == "current") {
            oNode.className = "";
        }
    }
};
```

With these two methods defined, it's time to create the drop-down list <div/>. The createDropDown() method creates the outermost <div/> element and defines the event handlers for the drop-down list. To create the <div/> element, use the createElement() method and then assign the various styling properties:

```
AutoSuggestControl.prototype.createDropDown = function () {

    this.layer = document.createElement("div");
    this.layer.className = "suggestions";
    this.layer.style.visibility = "hidden";
    this.layer.style.width = this.textbox.offsetWidth;
    document.body.appendChild(this.layer);

    //more code to come
};
```

This code first creates the `<div/>` element and assigns it to the `layer` property. From there, the `className` (equivalent to the `class` attribute) is set to `suggestions`, as is needed for the CSS to work properly. The next line hides the layer, since it should be invisible initially. Then, the width of the layer is set equal to the width of the text box by using the text box's `offsetWidth` property (this is optional depending on your individual needs). The very last line adds the layer to the document. With the layer created, it's time to assign the event handlers to control it.

At this point, the only concern is making sure that the drop-down list is functional if the user uses the mouse. That is, when the drop-down list is visible, moving the mouse over a suggestion should high-light it. Likewise, when a suggestion is clicked on, it should be placed in the text box and the drop-down list should be hidden. To make this happen, you need to assign three event handlers: `onmouseover`, `onmousedown`, and `onmouseup`.

The `onmouseover` event handler is used simply to highlight the current suggestion; `onmousedown` is used to select the given suggestion (place the suggestion in the text box and hide the drop-down list); and `onmouseup` is used to set the focus back to the text box after a selection has been made. Because all these events are fired by the drop-down list itself, it's best just to use a single function for all of them, as follows:

```
AutoSuggestControl.prototype.createDropDown = function () {

    this.layer = document.createElement("div");
    this.layer.className = "suggestions";
    this.layer.style.visibility = "hidden";
    this.layer.style.width = this.textbox.offsetWidth;
    document.body.appendChild(this.layer);

    var oThis = this;

    this.layer.onmousedown = this.layer.onmouseup =
    this.layer.onmouseover = function (oEvent) {
        oEvent = oEvent || window.event;
        oTarget = oEvent.target || oEvent.srcElement;

        if (oEvent.type == "mousedown") {
            oThis.textbox.value = oTarget.firstChild.nodeValue;
            oThis.hideSuggestions();
        } else if (oEvent.type == "mouseover") {
            oThis.highlightSuggestion(oTarget);
        } else {
            oThis.textbox.focus();
        }
    };

};
```

The first part of this section is the assignment of `oThis` equal to the `this` object. This is necessary so that a reference to the `AutoSuggestControl` object is accessible from within the event handler. Next, a compound assignment occurs, assigning the same function as an event handler for `onmousedown`, `onmouseup`, and `onmouseover`. Inside of the function, the first two lines are used to account for the different event models (DOM and IE), using a logical OR (||) to assign the values for `oEvent` and `oTarget`. (The target will always be a `<div/>` element containing a suggestion.)

If the event being handled is mousedown, then set the value of the text box equal to the text inside of the event target. The text inside of the <div/> element is contained in a text node, which is the first child node. The actual text string is contained in the text node's nodeValue property. After the suggestion is placed into the text box, the drop-down list is hidden.

When the event being handled is mouseover, the event target is passed into the highlightSuggestion() method to provide the hover effect; when the event is mouseup, the focus is set back to the text box (this fires immediately after mousedown).

Positioning the Drop-Down List

To get the full effect of the drop-down list, it's imperative that it appears directly below the text box. If the text box were absolutely positioned, this wouldn't be much of an issue. In actual practice, text boxes are rarely absolutely positioned and more often are placed inline, which presents a problem in aligning the drop-down list. To calculate the position where the drop-down list should appear, you can use the text box's offsetLeft, offsetTop, and offsetParent properties.

The offsetLeft and offsetTop properties tell you how many pixels away from the left and top of the offsetParent an element is placed. The offsetParent is usually, but not always, the parent node of the element, so to get the left position of the text box, you need to add up the offsetLeft properties of the text box and all of its ancestor elements (stopping at <body/>), as seen below:

```
AutoSuggestControl.prototype.getLeft = function () {

    var oNode = this.textbox;
    var iLeft = 0;

    while(oNode.tagName != "BODY") {
        iLeft += oNode.offsetLeft;
        oNode = oNode.offsetParent;
    }

    return iLeft;
};
```

The getLeft() method begins by pointing oNode at the text box and defining iLeft with an initial value of 0. The while loop will continue to add oNode.offsetLeft to iLeft as it traverses up the DOM structure to the <body/> element.

The same algorithm can be used to get the top of the text box:

```
AutoSuggestControl.prototype.getTop = function () {

    var oNode = this.textbox;
    var iTop = 0;

    while(oNode.tagName != "BODY") {
        iTop += oNode.offsetTop;
        oNode = oNode.offsetParent;
    }

    return iTop;
};
```

These two methods will be used to place the drop-down list in the correct location.

Adding and Displaying Suggestions

The next step in the process is to create a method that adds the suggestions into the drop-down list and then displays it. The showSuggestions() method accepts an array of suggestions as an argument and then builds up the necessary DOM elements to display them. From there, the method positions the drop-down list underneath the text box and displays it to the user:

```
AutoSuggestControl.prototype.showSuggestions = function (aSuggestions) {

    var oDiv = null;
    this.layer.innerHTML = "";

    for (var i=0; i < aSuggestions.length; i++) {
        oDiv = document.createElement("div");
        oDiv.appendChild(document.createTextNode(aSuggestions[i]));
        this.layer.appendChild(oDiv);
    }

    this.layer.style.left = this.getLeft() + "px";
    this.layer.style.top = (this.getTop()+this.textbox.offsetHeight) + "px";
    this.layer.style.visibility = "visible";
};
```

The first line simply defines the variable oDiv for later use. The second line clears the contents of the drop-down list by setting the innerHTML property to an empty string. Then, the for loop creates a <div/> element and a text node for each suggestion before adding it to the drop-down list layer.

The next section of code starts by setting the left position of the layer using the getLeft() method. To set the top position, you need to add the value from getTop() to the height of the text box (retrieved by using the offsetHeight property). Without doing this, the drop-down list would appear directly over the text box. (Remember, getTop() retrieves the top of the text box, not the top of the drop-down list layer.) Last, the layer's visibility property is set to visible to show it.

Updating the Functionality

In order to show the drop-down list of suggestions, you'll need to make several changes to the functionality defined previously.

The first update is the addition of a second argument to the autosuggest() method, which indicates whether the typeahead functionality should be used (the reason why will be explained shortly). Naturally, the typeAhead() method should be called only if this argument is true. If there's at least one suggestion, typeahead should be used and the drop-down list of suggestions should be displayed by calling showSuggestions(); if there's no suggestions, the drop-down list should be hidden by calling hideSuggestions():

```
AutoSuggestControl.prototype.autosuggest = function (aSuggestions, bTypeAhead) {
    if (aSuggestions.length > 0) {
        if (bTypeAhead) {
            this.typeAhead(aSuggestions[0]);
```

```
        }
        this.showSuggestions(aSuggestions);
    } else {
        this.hideSuggestions();
    }
};
```

It's also necessary to update the `handleKeyUp()` method for a couple of different reasons. The first reason is to add the `bTypeAhead` argument to the `requestSuggestions()` call. When called from here, this argument will always be `true`:

```
AutoSuggestControl.prototype.handleKeyUp = function (oEvent) {

    var iKeyCode = oEvent.keyCode;

    if (iKeyCode < 32 || (iKeyCode >= 33 && iKeyCode <= 46)
        || (iKeyCode >= 112 && iKeyCode <= 123)) {
        //ignore
    } else {
        this.provider.requestSuggestions(this, true);
    }
};
```

Remember, the `requestSuggestions()` method is defined on the suggestion provider, which is described later in this chapter.

This functionality now works exactly as it did previously, but there are a couple of other keys that require special attention: Backspace and Delete. When either of these keys is pressed, you don't want to activate the typeahead functionality because it will disrupt the process of removing characters from the text box. However, there's no reason not to show the drop-down list of suggestions. For the Backspace (key code of 8) and Delete (key code of 46) keys, you can call `requestSuggestions()`, but this time, pass in `false` to indicate that typeahead should not occur:

```
AutoSuggestControl.prototype.handleKeyUp = function (oEvent) {

    var iKeyCode = oEvent.keyCode;

    if (iKeyCode == 8 || iKeyCode == 46) {
        this.provider.requestSuggestions(this, false);
    } else if (iKeyCode < 32 || (iKeyCode >= 33 && iKeyCode <= 46)
            || (iKeyCode >= 112 && iKeyCode <= 123)) {
        //ignore
    } else {
        this.provider.requestSuggestions(this, true);
    }
};
```

Now when the user is removing characters, suggestions will still be displayed and the user can click one of them to select the value for the text box. This is acceptable, but to really be usable the autosuggest control needs to respond to keyboard controls.

Adding Keyboard Support

The desired keyboard functionality revolves around four keys: the up arrow, the down arrow, Esc, and Enter (or Return). When the drop-down suggestion list is displayed, the user should be able to press the down arrow to highlight the first suggestion, then press it again to move to the second, and so on. The up arrow should then be used to move back up the list of suggestions. As each suggestion is highlighted, the value must be placed in the text box. If the user presses Esc, the suggestions should be hidden and the suggestion should be removed from the text box. When the Enter key is pressed, the suggestions should also be hidden, but the last suggestion should remain highlighted in the text box.

In order for the user to use the up and down arrow keys, you'll need to keep track of the currently selected item in the suggestions list. To do this, you must add two properties to the `AutoSuggestControl` definition, as follows:

```
function AutoSuggestControl(oTextbox, oProvider) {
    this.cur = -1;
    this.layer = null;
    this.provider = oProvider;
    this.textbox = oTextbox;
    this.userText = oTextbox.value;
    this.init();
}
```

The `cur` property stores the index of the current suggestion in the suggestions array. By default, this value is set to -1 because there are no suggestions initially. When the arrow keys are pressed, `cur` will change to point to the current suggestion. The second added property, `userText`, holds the current value of the text box and changes to reflect what the user actually typed.

As `cur` changes, the highlighted suggestion changes as well. To encapsulate this functionality, a method called `goToSuggestion()` is used. This method accepts only one argument, a number whose sign indicates which direction to move in. For instance, any number greater than 0 moves the selection to the next suggestion; any number less than or equal to 0 moves the selection to the previous suggestion. Here's the code:

```
AutoSuggestControl.prototype.goToSuggestion = function (iDiff) {
    var cSuggestionNodes = this.layer.childNodes;

    if (cSuggestionNodes.length > 0) {
        var oNode = null;

        if (iDiff > 0) {
            if (this.cur < cSuggestionNodes.length-1) {
                oNode = cSuggestionNodes[++this.cur];
            }
        } else {
            if (this.cur > 0) {
                oNode = cSuggestionNodes[--this.cur];
            }
        }

        if (oNode) {
            this.highlightSuggestion(oNode);
            this.textbox.value = oNode.firstChild.nodeValue;
        }
    }
};
```

This method begins by obtaining the collection of child nodes in the drop-down layer. Since only `<div/>` elements containing suggestions are child nodes of the layer, the number of child nodes accurately matches the number of suggestions. This number can be used to determine if there are any suggestions (in which case it will be greater than zero). If there are no suggestions, the method need not do anything.

When there are suggestions, a variable named oNode is created to store a reference to the suggestion node to highlight, and the method checks to see which direction to go in. If iDiff is greater than 0, it tries to go to the next suggestion. In doing so, the method first checks to ensure that cur isn't greater than the number of suggestions minus 1 (because the index of the last element in a collection with n elements is $n-1$). Assuming there is a next suggestion, cur is prefix incremented (meaning it assumes its new value before the line it's on executes) to retrieve the node for the next suggestion.

If iDiff is less than or equal to zero, then that means the previous suggestion needs to be highlighted. In that case, you must first check to ensure cur is greater than 0 (if cur isn't at least 1, then there isn't a previous suggestion to go to). Passing that test, cur is then prefix decremented to get a reference to the correct suggestion node.

The last step in the method is to ensure that oNode isn't null. If it's not, then the node is passed to highlightSuggestion() and the suggestion text is placed into the text box; if it is null, then no action is taken.

Another part of keeping track of the selected suggestion is to be sure cur is reset at the correct point; otherwise, you can get some very odd behavior. The correct place to reset cur to –1 is in the autosuggest() method, just before the drop-down list is displayed:

```
AutoSuggestControl.prototype.autosuggest = function (aSuggestions, bTypeAhead){

    this.cur = -1;

    if (aSuggestions.length > 0) {
        if (bTypeAhead) {
            this.typeAhead(aSuggestions[0]);
        }

        this.showSuggestions(aSuggestions);
    } else {
        this.hideSuggestions();
    }
};
```

Along the same lines, it's important to set userText to the correct value. This should be done in the handleKeyUp() method:

```
AutoSuggestControl.prototype.handleKeyUp = function (oEvent) {

    var iKeyCode = oEvent.keyCode;
    this.userText = this.textbox.value;

    if (iKeyCode == 8 || iKeyCode == 46) {
        this.provider.requestSuggestions(this, false);

    } else if (iKeyCode < 32 || (iKeyCode >= 33 && iKeyCode <= 46)
```

```
                   || (iKeyCode >= 112 && iKeyCode <= 123)) {
          //ignore
      } else {
          this.provider.requestSuggestions(this, true);
      }
  };
```

This small addition saves what the user typed before asking for suggestions. This will be very useful when dealing with the Esc key. With these two methods updates, all that's left is to make sure that `goToSuggestion()` gets called at the right time.

To handle the up arrow, down arrow, Esc, and Enter keys, a `handleKeyDown()` method is necessary. Similar to `handleKeyUp()`, this method also requires the `event` object to be passed in. And once again, you'll need to rely on the key code to tell which key was pressed. The key codes for the up arrow, down arrow, Esc, and Enter keys are 38, 40, 27, and 13, respectively. The `handleKeyDown()` method is defined as follows:

```
AutoSuggestControl.prototype.handleKeyDown = function (oEvent) {
    switch(oEvent.keyCode) {
        case 38: //up arrow
            this.goToSuggestion(-1);
            break;
        case 40: //down arrow
            this.goToSuggestion(1);
            break;
        case 27: //esc
            this.textbox.value = this.userText;
            this.selectRange(this.userText.length, 0);
            /* falls through */
        case 13: //enter
            this.hideSuggestions();
            oEvent.returnValue = false;
            if (oEvent.preventDefault) {
                oEvent.preventDefault();
            }
            break;
    }
};
```

When the up arrow is pressed (key code 38), the `goToSuggestion()` method is called with an argument of –1, indicating that the previous selection should be selected. Likewise, when the down arrow is pressed (key code 40), `goToSuggestion()` is called with 1 as an argument to highlight the next suggestion. If Esc is pressed (key code 27), there are a couple of things to do.

First, you need to set the text box value back to the original text that the user typed. Second, you need to set the selection of the text box to be after what the user typed so that he or she can continue typing. This is done by setting the selection range to the length of the text with a selection length of zero. Then, this case falls through to the Enter key's case (key code 13), which hides the suggestions list. This way, the code contains only one call to `hideSuggestions()` instead of two. Remember, when the user presses the up or down arrows, the suggestion is automatically placed into the text box. This means that when the Enter key is pressed, you need only hide the drop-down list of suggestions.

For both Esc and Enter, you also must block the default behavior for the key press. This is important to prevent unintended behavior, such as the Enter key submitting the form when the user really just wanted to select the current suggestion. The default behavior is blocked first by setting `event.returnValue` equal to `false` (for IE) and then calling `preventDefault()` (if it's available, for Firefox).

Updating init()

Now that all this new functionality has been added, it must be initialized. Previously, the `init()` method was used to set up the `onkeyup` event handler; now it must be extended to also set up the `onkeydown` and `onblur` event handlers, as well as to create the drop-down suggestion list. The `onkeydown` event handler is set up in a similar manner as `onkeyup`:

```
AutoSuggestControl.prototype.init = function () {

    var oThis = this;

    this.textbox.onkeyup = function (oEvent) {
        if (!oEvent) {
            oEvent = window.event;
        }

        oThis.handleKeyUp(oEvent);
    };

    this.textbox.onkeydown = function (oEvent) {

        if (!oEvent) {
            oEvent = window.event;
        }

        oThis.handleKeyDown(oEvent);
    };

    //more code to come
};
```

As you can see, the same algorithm is used with the `onkeydown` event handler: first, determine the location of the event object, and then pass it into the `handleKeyDown()` method.

Up to this point, the only way the drop-down list is hidden is when the user presses the Enter key. But what if the user clicks elsewhere on the screen or uses the Tab key to switch to a new form field? To prepare for this event, you must set up an `onblur` event handler, which hides the suggestions whenever the text box loses focus:

```
AutoSuggestControl.prototype.init = function () {

    var oThis = this;

    this.textbox.onkeyup = function (oEvent) {
        if (!oEvent) {
            oEvent = window.event;
```

```
        }

        oThis.handleKeyUp(oEvent);
    };

    this.textbox.onkeydown = function (oEvent) {

        if (!oEvent) {
            oEvent = window.event;
        }

        oThis.handleKeyDown(oEvent);
    };

    this.textbox.onblur = function () {
        oThis.hideSuggestions();
    };

    this.createDropDown();
};
```

You'll also notice that the `createDropDown()` method is called to create the initial drop-down list structure. This completes the keyboard support for the autosuggest control, but there is one more thing to take into account.

Fast-Type Support

Because the `handleKeyUp()` method requests suggestions whenever a key is pressed, you may be wondering if it can keep up when someone is typing quickly. The answer is no. You may be surprised to know that it is possible to type too fast for the event handling to keep up. In this case, you get suggestions that are too late (including letters you never typed) and a very choppy user experience (with long pauses as you type). So, how can you make sure that fast typists aren't left out of this functionality?

Quite simply, you should wait a short amount of time before requesting suggestions from the server. This can be done using the `setTimeout()` method, which delays the calling of a function for a set time interval. The new functionality works like this: a timeout ID is saved in the `AutoSuggestControl` object. If another key is pressed before the timeout has been activated, the existing timeout is cleared and a new one is put in its place. So basically, when a user presses a key, the control waits a certain amount of time before requesting suggestions. If another key is pressed before the request is made, the control cancels the original request (by clearing the timeout) and asks for a new request to be made after the same amount of time. In this way, you can be sure that the request for suggestions goes out only while the user has paused typing.

To implement this functionality, the first thing you need is a property to hold the timeout ID. You can add the `timeoutId` property directly to the `AutoSuggestControl` class, as follows:

```
function AutoSuggestControl(oTextbox, oProvider) {
    this.cur = -1;
    this.layer = null;
    this.provider = oProvider;
    this.textbox = oTextbox;
    this.timeoutId = null;
    this.userText = oTextbox.value;
    this.init();
}
```

219

Next, update the `handleKeyUp()` method to make use of this new property:

```
AutoSuggestControl.prototype.handleKeyUp = function (oEvent /*:Event*/) {

    var iKeyCode = oEvent.keyCode;
    var oThis = this;

    this.userText = this.textbox.value;

    clearTimeout(this.timeoutId);

    if (iKeyCode == 8 || iKeyCode == 46) {

        this.timeoutId = setTimeout( function () {
            oThis.provider.requestSuggestions(oThis, false);
        }, 250);

    } else if (iKeyCode < 32 || (iKeyCode >= 33 && iKeyCode < 46)
            || (iKeyCode >= 112 && iKeyCode <= 123)) {
        //ignore
    } else {
        this.timeoutId = setTimeout( function () {
            oThis.provider.requestSuggestions(oThis, true);
        }, 250);
    }
};
```

The first new line in this method stores a reference to the `this` object, which is important when using the `setTimeout()` method. The second new line of code clears any timeout that may have already been started; this cancels and suggestion request that may have been initiated. The other two sections of new code change the call to the `requestSuggestions()` to occur after 250 milliseconds (which is plenty of time for this purpose). Each call is wrapped in an anonymous function that is passed into `setTimeout()`. The result of `setTimeout()`, the timeout ID is stored in the new property for later usage. All in all, this ensures that no requests will be made unless the user has stopped typing for at least 250 milliseconds.

This completes the code for the `AutoSuggestControl` class. All of the functionality has been implemented, and all that's left is to create a suggestion provider to call.

The Suggestion Provider

The `SuggestionProvider` class is relatively simple compared to the `AutoSuggestControl` since it has only one purpose: to request suggestions from the server and forward them to the control. To do so, `SuggestionProvider` needs an instance of `XmlHttp`. Instead of using a new object for each request, the same object will be used over and over, to avoid the overhead of creating and destroying objects in rapid succession. This single instance is created using the zXML library's `zXmlHttp` factory and stored in a property called `http`:

```
function SuggestionProvider() {
    this.http = zXmlHttp.createRequest();
}
```

The lone method of the suggestion provider is `requestSuggestions()`, which you may remember from the architecture discussion. This method accepts two arguments: the `AutoSuggestControl` to work on and a flag indicating whether typeahead should be used. The complete code is as follows:

```
SuggestionProvider.prototype.requestSuggestions = function (oAutoSuggestControl,
                                                            bTypeAhead) {

    var oHttp = this.http;

    //cancel any active requests
    if (oHttp.readyState != 0) {
        oHttp.abort();
    }

    //define the data
    var oData = {
        requesting: "StatesAndProvinces",
        text: oAutoSuggestControl.userText,
        limit: 5
    };

    //open connection to server
    oHttp.open("post", "suggestions.php", true);
    oHttp.onreadystatechange = function () {
        if (oHttp.readyState == 4) {
            //evaluate the returned text JavaScript (an array)
            var aSuggestions = JSON.parse(oHttp.responseText);

            //provide suggestions to the control
            oAutoSuggestControl.autosuggest(aSuggestions, bTypeAhead);
        }
    };

    //send the request
    oHttp.send(JSON.stringify(oData));

};
```

The first line inside the method sets `oHttp` equal to the stored `XmlHttp` object. This is done simply for convenience and keeping the code clean. Next, you check to make sure that there isn't already a request waiting for a response. If the `XmlHttp` object is ready to be used cleanly, its `readyState` will be 0; otherwise, you must cancel the existing request (by calling `abort()`) before making another request.

Because the data being sent to the server is to be JSON-encoded, you first need to create an object (`oData`) to hold the information. There are three pieces of information being sent: the table to get the data out of, the current value in the text box, and the maximum number of suggestions to retrieve (5). The maximum number of suggestions is important because it prevents long database queries from being executed repeatedly.

Next, a request is opened to `suggestions.php`, the server-side component of the control. This request is asynchronous (last argument of `open()` is set to `true`), so it's necessary to provide an `onreadystate-change` event handler. The event handler first checks to ensure that the `readyState` is 4, and then parses the returned text as a JSON array of values. This array, along with the original typeahead flag, is then passed back to the `AutoSuggestControl` via the `autosuggest()` method.

The last step in this method is, of course, to send the request. Note that since the request is doing a POST, the data has to be passed into the send() method. The oData object is first encoded into JSON before being sent.

With that, the SuggestionProvider class is complete. The only thing left to do is to write the suggestions.php file that uses the data that is sent.

The Server-Side Component

In many ways, the server-side component for the autosuggest control is the most straightforward: it's just a single thread being executed from top to bottom, with no functions or methods to be concerned about. Note that because this is a PHP page, all the code discussed in this section must be contained within a PHP code block (<?php . . . ?>).

The first part of the page is to set the content type to text/plain, indicating that this is a plain text file and shouldn't be handled as anything else. You can optionally specify a character set, but make sure that it is Unicode-compatible, such as UTF-8, since all Unicode characters are valid in JavaScript. Here's the line that accomplishes assigning the content type:

```
header("Content-Type: text/plain; charset=UTF-8");
```

Next, include the JSON-PHP library and create a new instance of the JSON object:

```
require_once("JSON.php");
$oJSON = new JSON();
```

Normally when data is sent to a PHP page, you can use $_GET, $_POST, or $_REQUEST to retrieve it. In this case, however, the data isn't being sent in traditional name/value pairs; instead, it's being sent as a JSON string, and there is no built-in support for this specific type of data. Instead, you need to get the body of the request and decode it manually. The body of any request is available in PHP through $HTTP_RAW_POST_DATA, which contains the original, encoded content that was sent. Because the JSON string wasn't URL encoded, however, you can just pass this directly into the decode() method to reconstitute the oData object:

```
$oData = $oJSON->decode($HTTP_RAW_POST_DATA);
```

You'll also need an array to store the suggestions in:

```
$aSuggestions = array();
```

If there are no suggestions, no values will be added to the array and an empty array ([]) will be returned to the client.

Before tapping the database for suggestions, make sure that there is actually text in the text box. Suggestions are requested when the user hits Delete or Backspace, so there's a possibility that the text box could be empty. You should check for this first by seeing if the length of the text is greater than 0; if so, you can continue on to query the database.

The query string itself is built up from the data submitting from the client. The name of the table, the LIKE statement, and the number of results to return are all incorporated into the SQL query. The following code creates a connection to the database, executes the query, and then adds the results of the query to the $aSuggestions array:

```
if (strlen($oData->text) > 0) {

    //create the SQL query string
    $sQuery = "Select Name from ".$oData->requesting." where Name like '".
            $oData->text."%' order by Name ASC limit 0,".$oData->limit;

    //make the database connection
    $oLink = mysql_connect($sDBServer,$sDBUsername,$sDBPassword);
    @mysql_select_db($sDBName) or die("Unable to open database");

    if($oResult = mysql_query($sQuery)) {
        while ($aValues = mysql_fetch_array($oResult,MYSQL_ASSOC)) {
            array_push($aSuggestions, $aValues['Name']);
        }
    }

    mysql_free_result($oResult);
    mysql_close($oLink);
}
```

This code should be fairly familiar to you as it is the same basic algorithm used throughout the book to access a MySQL database using PHP. (You must fill in the appropriate values for $sDBServer, $sDBUsername, and $sDBPassword to reflect your database settings.) The only unique part is that the results are being stored in an array, which facilitates the conversion into a JSON string to be sent back to the client.

The actual encoding is the very last step of the page. In one step, you can encode the array and output it to the page:

```
echo($oJSON->encode($aSuggestions));
```

Now it's up to the client to parse the JSON code correctly.

The Client-Side Component

So far, you've built the HTML, CSS, JavaScript, and PHP to be used by the autosuggest control. The only thing left to do is to assemble it all into a page that you can use. The most important thing to remember is the inclusion of all necessary JavaScript files. In this case, you need to include json.js, zxml.js, and autosuggest.js. Also important is the inclusion of the style sheet file, autosuggest.css.

It's also necessary to instantiate the AutoSuggestControl after the page has completely loaded, using the onload event handler. The complete code for the example page is:

```html
<html>
    <head>
        <title>Autosuggest Example</title>
        <script type="text/javascript" src="json.js"></script>
        <script type="text/javascript" src="zxml.js"></script>
        <script type="text/javascript" src="autosuggest.js"></script>
        <link rel="stylesheet" type="text/css" href="autosuggest.css" />
        <script type="text/javascript">
            window.onload = function () {
                var oTextbox = new
AutoSuggestControl(document.getElementById("txtState"), new SuggestionProvider());
            }
        </script>
    </head>
    <body>
        <form method="post" action="your_action.php">
            <table border="0">
                <tr>
                    <td>Name:</td>
                    <td><input type="text" name="txtName" id="txtName" /></td>
                </tr>
                <tr>
                    <td>Address 1:</td>
                    <td><input type="text" name="txtAddress1"
                            id="txtAddress1" /></td>
                </tr>
                <tr>
                    <td>Address 2:</td>
                    <td><input type="text" name="txtAddress2"
                            id="txtAddress2" /></td>
                </tr>
                <tr>
                    <td>City:</td>
                    <td><input type="text" name="txtCity" id="txtCity" /></td>
                </tr>
                <tr>
                    <td>State/Province:</td>
                    <td><input type="text" name="txtState" id="txtState"
                            autocomplete="off" /></td>
                </tr>
                <tr>
                    <td>Zip Code:</td>
                    <td><input type="text" name="txtZip" id="txtZip" /></td>
                </tr>
                <tr>
                    <td>Country:</td>
                    <td><input type="text" name="txtCountry"
                            id="txtCountry" /></td>
                </tr>
            </table>
            <input type="submit" value="Save Information" />
        </form>
    </body>
</html>
```

Note that once the necessary files are included, you need to place only one line of JavaScript in the `window.onload` event handler to set up the functionality:

```
var oTextbox = new AutoSuggestControl(document.getElementById("txtState"),
                                new SuggestionProvider());
```

This line creates a new `AutoSuggestControl` object, passing a reference to the text box with the id of `txtState` and a new `SuggestionProvider()` class. It's important that this line be executed in the `onload` event handler because `document.getElementById()` isn't 100 percent accurate until the entire page has been loaded.

The example itself is done in a way in which this control may be used: filling in personal information. This could be a page where customers can update their information or it could be a shipping form. Whichever way you choose to use this functionality, it is sure to improve the usability of your form. An autosuggest control, although not as flashy as some Ajax solutions, really is a good example of how Ajax can be used in a non-interfering way.

Summary

In this chapter, you learned all about JavaScript Object Notation (JSON) as an alternative data transmission format to XML. You learned that JSON has several advantages over XML for data transmission needs, including a smaller amount of code to represent the same data and a logical object-and-array structure that most programming languages can understand and use.

You also learned that while JavaScript can understand and interpret JSON natively, there are several server-side libraries that provide the same functionality. You learned about a JavaScript utility for parsing and encoding JSON data, as well as the JSON-PHP library that can be used to do the same for PHP.

The chapter went on to describe how to make an Ajax-assisted autosuggest control that enables you to display suggestions based on what the user has typed. This control works similar to the way that Google Suggest does and takes into account user interaction with the mouse and keyboard as well as providing for fast typists. This control helped to illustrate the power of simple Ajax solutions.

The next chapter will expand on what you've learned here to create reusable Ajax widgets for your web site. These widgets can use a variety of data transmission formats, including JSON.

8

Web Site Widgets

Both on the desktop and on the Web, widgets have become a highly sought-after commodity. A *widget* is a mini, self-containing application that performs a specific purpose. Programs like Konfabulator (www.konfabulator.com) offered users a platform to run widgets on their computers. Ranging from newsreaders to eBay feedback monitors, these widgets provide useful information to people that want them. They are applications that require little to no setup and perform only their allotted function.

On the Web, most widgets were primarily limited to static DHTML widgets, designed to emulate operating system controls such as menus, structure trees, and toolbars. While these widgets provided a means to emulate traditional applications, they didn't offer much more than that.

Thanks to the capabilities of XMLHttp, web widgets are beginning to change to incorporate data manipulation and retrieval with DHTML, creating rich web widgets that normally are found only on the desktop.

In this chapter, you will create four web widgets using PHP, ASP.NET, DHTML, and Ajax: a news ticker, a weather widget, a web search widget, and a site search widget. The following sections will walk you through the creation of these widgets and how to apply them to your web page.

Creating a News Ticker Widget

Popular on both television news networks and web sites, the news ticker displays current events in a scrolling format. Unlike the static nature of television, the Web enables users to interact with these tickers. If something catches their eyes, they can click the news item and it takes them to their desired information.

The widget built in this section, a news ticker, provides this functionality (see Figure 8-1). Like any other Ajax-enabled application, it comes in two parts: a server application and a client application.

For this project, you will use PHP to perform the server's function: to behave as a proxy to retrieve requested feeds for the client. The client application consists of the usual suspects: DHTML and JavaScript.

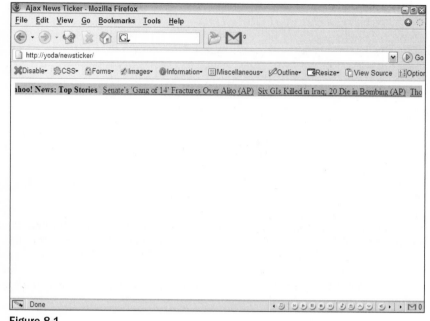

Figure 8-1

The Server-Side Component

The server application, written in PHP as already stated, is extremely simple. To request information from the server, the URL should contain a `url` variable in the query string:

```
newsticker.php?url=http://rss.news.yahoo.com/rss/topstories
```

Because the server's only job is to retrieve remote information, the server application code is only a few lines:

```php
<?php
header("Content-Type: text/xml");
header("Cache-Control: no-cache");

if ( isset( $_GET["url"] ) ) {
    $remoteUrl = $_GET["url"];

    $xml = file_get_contents($remoteUrl);

    echo $xml;
}

?>
```

The first two lines set the `Content-Type` and `Cache-Control` headers, respectively. As mentioned in Chapter 5, it is important to set the MIME content type to `text/xml`; otherwise, Mozilla Firefox doesn't recognize the data as XML. It also is important to set the `Cache-Control` header to `no-cache` because Internet Explorer caches all data retrieved via XMLHttp unless explicitly told not to.

In the next line of code, the query string is checked for the `url` query item. To do this, use the `isset()` function, which returns a Boolean value based on whether a variable, function, or object exists. The value of `url` is assigned to the `$remoteUrl` variable and passed to `file_get_contents()`. This function opens a file (local or remote), reads the file, and returns its contents as a string. Last, the file's contents, stored in the `$xml` variable, are written to the page.

With the proxy completed, a client needs to be authored to take advantage of the proxy's service.

The Client-Side Component

Before delving into the code, the client's functionality should be discussed. The client:

1. Builds the HTML to display the news feeds.

2. Requests data from the server application. When the server responds with the requested data, the client parses the data with XParser.

3. Places the parsed data into the HTML.

4. Uses DHTML to animate the ticker.

5. Polls for updated data every 1.5 minutes.

In addition, a few user interface criteria must be met:

❑ The data in the ticker, news article titles, should be links that take the user to the specified news article.

❑ The ticker should stop scrolling when the user's mouse enters the ticker and resume scrolling when the user mouses out.

The client-side code consists of two classes: the NewsTicker class, which builds the ticker in HTML format, animates the ticker with a scrolling animation, and provides the ability to add news feeds into the ticker, and the NewsTickerFeed class, which requests the feed, parses it, places it in the HTML, and polls for new data.

The NewsTicker Class

The NewsTicker class is the main class of the client-side code. The constructor accepts one argument: the HTMLElement to append the news ticker:

```
function NewsTicker(oAppendTo) {
    var oThis = this;
    this.timer = null;
    this.feeds = [];
```

These first few lines of code initialize the properties of the NewsTicker class. First, a pointer to the object is created by assigning the variable oThis. The timer property, initially set to null, will control the scrolling animation (setTimeout() returns a unique timer identifier). The feeds property is an array of NewsTickerFeeds objects.

229

The next two properties create the primary elements of this widget:

```
this.tickerContainer = document.createElement("div");
this.ticker = document.createElement("nobr");

this.tickerContainer.className = "newsTickerContainer";
this.ticker.className = "newsTicker";
```

These properties, `tickerContainer` and `ticker`, reference newly created `<div/>` and `<nobr/>` elements, respectively. The `tickerContainer` element does what its name implies: it contains all elements of the widget, whereas the `ticker` element scrolls the news feeds contained in it. The `<nobr/>` tag is chosen because it does not allow any breaks in the text; otherwise, text would pop into view instead of scrolling as a result of word wrapping. The HTML code output by this constructor is:

```
<div class="newsTickerContainer">
    <nobr class="newsTicker"></nobr>
</div>
```

As a part of the user interface, remember that the scrolling animation stops when users move their mouse over the news ticker. To facilitate this functionality, assign event handlers for the `onmouseover` and `onmouseout` events of `tickerContainer`:

```
this.tickerContainer.onmouseover = function () {
    clearTimeout(oThis.timer);
};

this.tickerContainer.onmouseout = function () {
    oThis.tick();
};
```

In the `onmouseover` event handler, `clearTimeout()` clears the `timer` property, which stops the animation. Notice the use of the `oThis` pointer, since the scope changes inside the event handler. The `onmouseout` event handler causes the animation to begin again by calling the `tick()` method, which performs the animation.

The next step is to append the ticker element to `tickerContainer`, and to append the widget's HTML to its parent `HTMLElement`:

```
this.tickerContainer.appendChild(this.ticker);

var oToAppend = (oAppendTo) ?oAppendTo:document.body;
oToAppend.appendChild(this.tickerContainer);
```

The first line of this code appends `ticker` to `tickerContainer`, which results in the HTML seen earlier in this section. The next line offers a convenience for developers. If `oAppendTo` exists, the constructor's argument, then the widget is appended to the value of `oAppendTo`. If it doesn't, however, the HTML is appended to `document.body`. This gives the argument a default value, so if you want to append the widget directly to the document, you do not have to pass an argument.

The final lines of the constructor initialize the ticker:

```
this.ticker.style.left = this.tickerContainer.offsetWidth + "px";
this.tick();
```

The first line of code positions the ticker at the farthest right edge of `tickerContainer`. (The animation scrolls from right to left.)

> Internet Explorer and Firefox have different modes in which they render markup differently according to the doctype specified in the HTML page. Under what is known as standards mode, you must add + "px" to any line of code that positions an element, or the browser will not position the element.

Finally, calling the `tick()` method starts the animation, and the final constructor code looks like this:

```
function NewsTicker(oAppendTo) {
    var oThis = this;
    this.timer = null;
    this.feeds = [];
    this.tickerContainer = document.createElement("div");
    this.ticker = document.createElement("nobr");

    this.tickerContainer.className = "newsTickerContainer";
    this.ticker.className = "newsTicker";

    this.tickerContainer.onmouseover = function () {
        clearTimeout(oThis.timer);
    };

    this.tickerContainer.onmouseout = function () {
        oThis.tick();
    };

    this.tickerContainer.appendChild(this.ticker);

    var oToAppend = (oAppendTo)?oAppendTo:document.body;
    oToAppend.appendChild(this.tickerContainer);

    this.ticker.style.left = this.tickerContainer.offsetWidth + "px";
    this.tick();
}
```

Doing the Animation

The basic logic of any animation is to move an element by a set amount of pixels and repeat this operation until the element reaches a specific location on the page. The scrolling animation used in this widget is probably the simplest type of animation you can perform: a linear, right-to-left movement until the ticker's right edge reaches the container's left edge. This last part is the limit of the animation and can be expressed by `-this.ticker.offsetWidth`. When the ticker reaches this position in the page, the animation begins again.

The `tick()` method begins by gathering this information:

```
NewsTicker.prototype.tick = function () {
    var iTickerLength = -this.ticker.offsetWidth;
    var oThis = this;
```

The `iTickerWidth` variable contains the ending point of the animation: the negative `offsetWidth` of the ticker. Once again, a pointer to the `NewsTicker` object is assigned to `oThis`.

To perform animations, a timeout is set at a low interval of time to repeat a function that moves the desired element. In the case of this animation, it is a function inside the `tick()` method:

```
var doSetTimeout = function() {
    oThis.tick();
};
```

You could use external variables, functions, or methods to aid in the animation, but that approach isn't very object oriented. Keeping the animation logic inside the `tick()` method makes the widget easier to deploy and maintain.

The first step in the animation is to decide whether the ticker contains any data, as there's no use in scrolling an empty `<nobr/>` element:

```
if (this.ticker.innerHTML) {

}
```

This code checks the element's `innerHTML` property; any HTML present in the ticker means data exists and the animation should begin:

```
if (this.ticker.innerHTML) {
    if (this.ticker.offsetLeft > iTickerLength) {
        var iNewLeft = this.ticker.offsetLeft - 1;
        this.ticker.style.left = iNewLeft + "px";
    }
}
```

This new code moves the ticker. The first new line checks the location of the ticker (`offsetLeft`) in relation to the animation's boundary (`iTickerLength`). If the location is greater than the limit, the animation continues. The next line gets the new left position of the ticker: one pixel to the left. The last line of this code block sets the left position to reflect the value contained in `iNewLeft`. This, however, is only one part of the animation. The ticker continues to move until it reaches the boundary; therefore, you must reset the ticker to its original location:

```
NewsTicker.prototype.tick = function () {
    var iTickerLength = this.ticker.offsetWidth;
    var oThis = this;

    var doSetTimeout = function() {
        oThis.tick();
```

```
        };

        if (this.ticker.innerHTML) {
            if (this.ticker.offsetLeft > -iTickerLength) {
                var iNewLeft = this.ticker.offsetLeft - 1;
                this.ticker.style.left = iNewLeft + "px";
            } else {
                this.ticker.style.left = this.tickerContainer.offsetWidth + "px";
            }
        }
        this.timer = setTimeout(doSetTimeout,1);
    };
```

The first block of new code does this. At the end of the animation, the ticker is once again placed at the right edge of the container. The last new line sets a timeout for the doSetTimeout() function contained within tick(). This causes tick() to run every millisecond, so the animation is ongoing until it is stopped by clearing the timeout (when the user mouses over the container).

Adding Feeds

One final method of the NewsTicker class is the add() method, which adds a feed to the ticker and populates the feeds array:

```
NewsTicker.prototype.add = function (sUrl) {
    var feedsLength = this.feeds.length;

    this.feeds[feedsLength] = new NewsTickerFeed(this, sUrl);
};
```

This method accepts one argument: the URL to the remote feed. A NewsTickerFeed object is then created as an element of the feeds array. This array isn't used in any of the class's code, other than initializing and populating the array. It exists merely for convenience for developers that may want to access the different feeds in the ticker.

The NewsTickerFeed Class

A news ticker isn't so handy without content to display. The NewsTickerFeed class pulls the required feeds, parses them with XParser, and assembles and adds the HTML to the ticker. The class's constructor accepts two arguments: The first argument is a reference to its parent NewsTicker object; this allows access to the NewsTicker object's properties and methods when needed. The second argument is the URL of the feed you want to obtain.

```
function NewsTickerFeed(oParent, sUrl) {
    this.parent = oParent;
    this.url = sUrl;
    this.container = null;

    this.poll();
}
```

Compared to the `NewsTicker` class's constructor, the `NewsTickerFeed` class's constructor is relatively simple. This class has three properties: `parent`, a reference to the parent `NewsTicker` object; `url`, the URL of the feed; and `container`, a `<span/>` element that contains the feed's information.

Polling for New Information

The `poll()` method, called before the constructor exits, makes the request to the server application. It also automatically checks for updates every minute and a half:

```
NewsTickerFeed.prototype.poll = function () {
    var oThis = this;

    var oReq = zXmlHttp.createRequest();
    oReq.onreadystatechange = function () {
        if (oReq.readyState == 4) {
            if (oReq.status == 200) {
                oThis.populateTicker(oReq.responseText);
            }
        }
    };

    var sFullUrl = encodeURI("newsticker.php?url=" + this.url);

    oReq.open("GET", sFullUrl, true);
    oReq.send(null);
}
```

This code creates the XMLHttp object. First, you'll notice the ever-popular technique of assigning a pointer to the `NewsTickerFeed` object to `oThis`. The next code block creates an XMLHttp object with the zXml library and defines the `onreadystatechange` event handler. On a successful request, the `responseText` property is sent to the `populateTicker()` method.

Before making the actual request, it is important to encode the URL. This ensures any characters such as white space, ampersands, quote marks, and so on are converted to their corresponding escape sequence for proper transmission.

One final addition to `poll()` is the automatic updating. To facilitate this, use a similar approach to the `tick()` method of the `NewsTicker` class:

```
NewsTickerFeed.prototype.poll = function () {
    var oThis = this;

    var oReq = zXmlHttp.createRequest();
    oReq.onreadystatechange = function () {
        if (oReq.readyState == 4) {
            if (oReq.status == 200) {
                oThis.populateTicker(oReq.responseText);
            }
        }
    };

    var sFullUrl = encodeURI("newsticker.php?url=" + this.url);

    oReq.open("GET", sFullUrl, true);
```

```
        oReq.send(null);

    var doSetTimeout = function () {
        oThis.poll();
    };

    setTimeout(doSetTimeout, 90000);
}
```

This new code creates another function called `doSetTimeout()` to pass to the `setTimeout()` method. Because this version of `doSetTimeout()` exists only in the scope of the `poll()` method, it will not interfere with the previous function of the same name in `tick()`. The `poll()` method is now set to run every 1.5 minutes and will update the feed.

Adding Content

The final method of the `NewsTickerFeed` class is `populateTicker()`, mentioned earlier because it's called in `poll()`. This method accepts the XMLHttp `responseText` property as its argument and parses it with `XParser`:

```
NewsTickerFeed.prototype.populateTicker = function (sXml) {
    var oParser = new XParser(sXml, true);
}
```

By passing the second argument with the value of `true`, `XParser` treats the first argument as serialized XML and will not make its own XMLHttp request. With the XML now parsed, you can start to create the HTML:

```
NewsTickerFeed.prototype.populateTicker = function (sXml) {
    var oParser = new XParser(sXml, true);

    var spanLinkContainer = document.createElement("span");

    var aFeedTitle = document.createElement("a");
    aFeedTitle.className = "newsTicker-feedTitle";
    aFeedTitle.href = oParser.link.value;
    aFeedTitle.target = "_new";
    aFeedTitle.innerHTML = oParser.title.value;

    spanLinkContainer.appendChild(aFeedTitle);
}
```

The first step is to create an element to encapsulate all the links. This element serves a purpose of convenience: when the feed is updated, it is easier to remove one element with several children than it is to remove several elements one at a time. Also, don't confuse this container with the `container` property. The latter contains `spanLinkContainer`.

To separate the different feeds in the ticker, the feed's title is used. This too is a link; so if the user clicks on the link, a new window pops up taking them to the feed's web site. This link is given a CSS class of `newsTicker-feedTitle` and is appended to `spanLinkContainer`.

Next, create the link items by iterating through the `items` array of the `XParser` object:

```
NewsTickerFeed.prototype.populateTicker = function (sXml) {
    var oParser = new XParser(sXml, true);

    var spanLinkContainer = document.createElement("span");

    var aFeedTitle = document.createElement("a");
    aFeedTitle.className = "newsTicker-feedTitle";
    aFeedTitle.href = oParser.link.value;
    aFeedTitle.target = "_new";
    aFeedTitle.innerHTML = oParser.title.value;

    spanLinkContainer.appendChild(aFeedTitle);

    for (var i = 0; i < oParser.items.length; i++) {
        var item = oParser.items[i];

        var aFeedLink = document.createElement("a");
        aFeedLink.href = item.link.value;
        aFeedLink.target = "_new";
        aFeedLink.className = "newsTicker-feedItem";
        aFeedLink.innerHTML = item.title.value;

        spanLinkContainer.appendChild(aFeedLink);
    }
}
```

Each link opens a new window when clicked and has a CSS class of `newsTicker-feedItem`. When the link is completed, it is appended to `spanLinkContainer`, which you now add to the ticker:

```
NewsTickerFeed.prototype.populateTicker = function (sXml) {
    var oParser = new XParser(sXml, true);

    var spanLinkContainer = document.createElement("span");

    var aFeedTitle = document.createElement("a");
    aFeedTitle.className = "newsTicker-feedTitle";
    aFeedTitle.href = oParser.link.value;
    aFeedTitle.target = "_new";
    aFeedTitle.innerHTML = oParser.title.value;

    spanLinkContainer.appendChild(aFeedTitle);

    for (var i = 0; i < oParser.items.length; i++) {
        var item = oParser.items[i];

        var aFeedLink = document.createElement("a");
        aFeedLink.href = item.link.value;
        aFeedLink.target = "_new";
        aFeedLink.className = "newsTicker-feedItem";
```

```
            aFeedLink.innerHTML = item.title.value;

            spanLinkContainer.appendChild(aFeedLink);
    }
    if (!this.container) {
        this.container = document.createElement("span");
        this.container.className = "newsTicker-feedContainer";
        this.parent.ticker.appendChild(this.container);
    } else {
        this.container.removeChild(this.container.firstChild);
    }

    this.container.appendChild(spanLinkContainer);
}
```

When a NewsTickerFeed class is first created, remember the container property is declared but given a null value. This is done for a couple of reasons. First, remember that the ticker's animation does not begin until it contains HTML. To keep the animation from running prematurely, the element referenced by container should not be added until the feed's data is retrieved, parsed, and assembled into HTML. This makes appending the container to the ticker occur in populateTicker().

Second, because this operation takes place in populateTicker(), it is important to not add the same container to the ticker over and over again, or else the ticker will exhibit strange behavior (not to mention the browser could crash). Therefore, when the previous code executes, it checks if container has been initialized. If not, the <span/> element is created and appended to the ticker; otherwise, the link container is removed from container, and the newly created link container is added to the widget.

Of course, displaying the data is meaningless if you don't spice it up to your own liking.

Styling the News

Before looking at the CSS, it is important to know the HTML structure:

```
<div class="newsTickerContainer">
    <nobr class="newsTicker">
        <span class="newsTicker-feedContainer">
            <span>
                <a />
                <a />
            </span>
        </span>
        <span class="newsTicker-feedContainer">
            <span>
                <a />
                <a />
            </span>
        </span>
    </nobr>
</div>
```

The outermost `<div/>` element is important for two reasons. First, it encapsulates every part of the widget. Second, it is the viewing box for the news items. Because it contains every element in the widget, it must be an extremely wide box, but you don't want to all the data seen until it enters the visible area. Therefore, you must set the CSS `overflow` property:

```
.newsTickerContainer {
    overflow: hidden;
    position: relative;
    background-color: silver;
    height: 20px;
    width: 100%;
    padding-top: 2px;
}
```

Setting the `overflow` property to `hidden` hides any contained content not currently visible. Also, set the `position` property to `relative` to ensure that the ticker moves in relation to `newsTickerContainer` and not the document's body. Any other CSS property is up to you to set. In the example code, the height, width, padding, and background color are assigned.

The next element, the ticker, contains all the feeds added to the widget. This `<nobr/>` element is absolutely positioned so that it can be moved through JavaScript:

```
.newsTicker {
    position: absolute;
    height: 25px;
}
```

The only required property is `position`, or else the ticker may not scroll. Any other CSS property can be placed to give it the look and feel you desire.

The last two elements exposing CSS classes are the links: `newsTicker-feedTitle` and `newsTicker-feedItem`. The first is the link to the news site. Although none of the following properties are required, they set the feed's title apart from the remaining links:

```
.newsTicker-feedTitle {
    margin: 0px 6px 0px 6px;
    font-weight: bold;
    color: black;
    text-decoration: none;
}
```

There are six pixels of space on the left and right sides, giving distance from the feed items. The text is bold, black, and has no underline, thus causing more separation in likeness between this link and the others.

The only formatting the feed items have are four pixels of space on each side, giving the links a defined look while still maintaining what the user expects (links!).

```
.newsTicker-feedItem {
    padding: 4px;
}
```

The beauty of CSS is its ability to change the look and feel of any page or widget, regardless of markup (in most circumstances). Play around with it to come up with your own look to make it fit within your web page.

Implementing the News Ticker Widget

Because the back-end code is PHP, setting up this widget is as simple as uploading files and referencing them in your HTML. (PHP is required, of course). To add the JavaScript and CSS into your page, simply add the `<script/>` and `<link/>` tags:

```
<!DOCTYPE html PUBLIC "-//W3C//DTD XHTML 1.1//EN"
            "http://www.w3.org/TR/xhtml11/DTD/xhtml11.dtd">

<html xmlns="http://www.w3.org/1999/xhtml" >
<head>
    <title>Ajax News Ticker</title>
    <link rel="stylesheet" type="text/css" href="css/newsticker.css" />
    <script type="text/javascript" src="js/zxml.js"></script>
    <script type="text/javascript" src="js/xparser.js"></script>
    <script type="text/javascript" src="js/newsticker.js"></script>
</head>
<body>


</body>
</html>
```

You'll also need to instantiate a new instance of `NewsTicker`. Remember, `NewsTicker` adds itself to an `HTMLElement`, so it's best to create the object when the page loads with the `onload` event:

```
<!DOCTYPE html PUBLIC "-//W3C//DTD XHTML 1.1//EN"
            "http://www.w3.org/TR/xhtml11/DTD/xhtml11.dtd">

<html xmlns="http://www.w3.org/1999/xhtml" >
<head>
    <title>Ajax News Ticker</title>
    <link rel="stylesheet" type="text/css" href="css/newsticker.css" />
    <script type="text/javascript" src="js/zxml.js"></script>
    <script type="text/javascript" src="js/xparser.js"></script>
    <script type="text/javascript" src="js/newsticker.js"></script>
    <script type="text/javascript">
    function init() {
        var newsTicker = new NewsTicker();
        newsTicker.add("http://rss.news.yahoo.com/rss/topstories");
    }

    onload = init;
    </script>
</head>
<body>


</body>
</html>
```

Because this widget uses XParser to parse the news feeds, any RSS 2.0 and Atom feed can be used with this widget. (The preceding example pulls the Yahoo! Top Stories feed). Cast away those boring blog rolls; make them scroll!

Creating a Weather Widget

Weather information is popular to display both on the desktop and on the Web. Many applications and widgets are solely devoted to retrieving and displaying this information. Naturally, Ajax is well suited for this type of widget.

The Weather.com SDK

The first step in creating this widget is locating a source of weather information. Probably the most popular is the Weather.com XML weather service. It is this information that you will use to create this weather widget.

The use of the Weather.com XML service hinges upon following their guidelines. To use their XML feeds you must first register for a license. To register, go to http://registration.weather.com/registration/xmloap/step1/. After your registration, Weather.com will send you an e-mail with a link to the XML feed SDK and provide you with your license key and partner ID.

For web-based applications, like this widget, you must limit how often you retrieve information from the service. As specified in the SDK documentation, the refresh rate for the Current Conditions information is 30 minutes; therefore, the server application must cache the retrieved weather information and only refresh the information every 30 minutes. There are two ways to accomplish this:

1. Create a smart thread that runs independently of the web application and pulls the feed every 30 minutes. The application then solely uses the cached feed and never worries about the time span between information pulls.

2. With every page request, the application can keep track of the last time the feed was retrieved, and allow refreshing of the data only after 30 minutes have passed.

Both architectures will serve this widget's purpose. In fact, the smart thread solution is ideal. Communication between the server and the remote host are the same in both situations; however, the smart thread requires only one file system operation every half hour (writing the cached feed). Unfortunately, ASP.NET applications time out after 20 minutes of inactivity, which can result in old cached data. It is possible to change this behavior; however, it requires access to the machine.config file, and not everyone has access to that configuration file in their environment. Therefore, this widget will use the second solution.

The Server-Side Component

You can use any .NET-enabled language to write the back-end code; however, the examples in this chapter use the C# language. At the heart of the server application lie two classes created within the

`Wrox.ProfessionalAjax.Weather` namespace. You can compile these classes into a class library (a .dll file) or use them natively within the application. The choice is ultimately yours; however, this exercise incorporates the classes directly into the application, so no reference to an external library is needed.

The WeatherSettings Class

The `WeatherSettings` class contains all the information required to pull weather information from Weather.com. Only three pieces of information are required to retrieve this data: your license key, your partner ID, and the location ID. These settings are located in an external XML document called `config.xml` whose structure looks like this:

```
<weather>
    <ids>
        <license>[LICENSEKEY]</license>
        <partner>[PARTNERID]</partner>
        <location>[LOCATION CODE]</location>
    </ids>
</weather>
```

This is a simple XML document, as you can see. The `<ids/>` element contains the information required to retrieve weather information. The `<license/>`, `<partner/>`, and `<location/>` elements contain the license key, partner ID, and location ID, respectively.

Note that you need to replace the bracketed items with your own information.

The `WeatherSettings` class extracts this information and assigns it to private variables. The class's constructor takes one argument: the path to the application.

```
public Settings(string path)
{
    XmlDocument xml = new XmlDocument();
    xml.Load(path + "/config.xml");

    _partnerId = xml.SelectSingleNode("/weather/ids/partner").InnerText;
    _licenseKey = xml.SelectSingleNode("/weather/ids/license").InnerText;
    _location = xml.SelectSingleNode("/weather/ids/location").InnerText;
}
```

All data processing of the `WeatherSettings` class takes place here in the constructor. First, the `config.xml` file is loaded into an `XmlDocument` object. This enables you to traverse the DOM tree and extract the needed information. If you use the `SelectSingleNode()` method, the individual elements contained in the `<id/>` element are retrieved and their value obtained with the `InnerText` property. This information is assigned to the private string fields _partnerId, _licenseKey, and _location.

To access these private fields, accessors (which you learned about in Chapter 5) are used to retrieve the value of the corresponding private field:

```
public string PartnerId
{
    get
    {
        return _partnerId;
```

```
        }
    }

    public string LicenseKey
    {
        get
        {
            return _licenseKey;
        }
    }

    public string LocationId
    {
        get
        {
            return _location;
        }
    }
```

The public fields `ParnerId`, `LicenseKey`, and `LocationId` return the values of `_partnerId`, `_licenseKey`, and `_location`, respectively. These accessors provide read-only access to the private fields.

The WeatherInfo Class

The `WeatherInfo` class provides methods to retrieve the information from the Weather.com XML service. Like the `WeatherSettings` class, the `WeatherInfo` constructor accepts one argument that contains the path to the application:

```
    public WeatherInfo(string path)
    {
        _path = path;
        _cachedFile = String.Format("{0}/weather_cache.xml",_path);
        _settings = new Settings(path);
    }
```

This class has three private fields, two of which are the strings `_path` and `_cachedFile`. The former is assigned the path argument, and the latter contains the path to the cached weather feed. The third private field, `_settings`, is a `WeatherSettings` object.

Getting Weather Data from the Web

Aside from the aforementioned private members, the `WeatherInfo` class also contains several private methods. One such method, called `_getWebWeather()`, gets the weather feed from the remote host and returns a string containing the feed's contents:

```
    private string _getWebWeather()
    {
        string xmlStr = String.Empty;
        return xmlStr;
    }
```

According to the SDK, the URL to retrieve the weather feed looks like the following:

```
http://xoap.weather.com/weather/local/[locID]?cc=*&prod=xoap&par=[partID]&key=[lic]
```

The information contained in brackets is the location ID, partner ID, and license key. Using the `String.Format()` method, you can format the URL to contain your own settings information:

```
string baseUrl =
    "http://xoap.weather.com/weather/local/{0}?cc=*&prod=xoap&par={1}&key={2}";

string url = String.Format(baseUrl, _settings.LocationId, _settings.PartnerId,
    _settings.LicenseKey);
```

This is primarily where the `_settings` object is used. The resulting string returned from `String.Format()` is complete with the required information that the Weather.com guidelines dictate.

The next operation in `_getWebWeather()` makes a request to the remote host and retrieves the weather feed:

```
using (WebClient client = new WebClient())
{
    //Read the results
    try
    {
        using (StreamReader reader = new StreamReader(client.OpenRead(url)))
        {
            xmlStr = reader.ReadToEnd();
        }
    }
    catch (WebException exception)
    {
        xmlStr = _writeErrorDoc(exception);
    }
}
```

At the beginning of this code, a `WebClient` object is created. If you'll remember from Chapter 5, you used an `HttpWebRequest` object to retrieve data from the remote host. You could do the same for this widget, but as you can see from the previous code, `WebClient` uses a much simpler interface.

To read the remote server's response, use the `OpenRead()` method. This method returns a `Stream` object that you can read with a `StreamReader` class. The `StreamReader` class's `ReadToEnd()` method reads the stream and returns it as a string to `xmlStr`. If for some reason this operation fails (most likely as a result of not finding the remote host), an error document is created by the `_writeErrorDoc()` and used in place of the weather feed.

At this point in the method, you have some XML data to use: the weather feed or the error document. The next few processes in the method perform an XSL transformation on the XML data. Transforming the data at the server is advantageous for several reasons. For one, it greatly simplifies the client-side code. The data sent to the client is already in HTML, so it is easily added to the page. A server-side transformation also makes the client work less. The data is complete when it reaches the client; no other data manipulation, other than placing in the page, is required.

XSL transformations in .NET closely resemble the transformations provided by MSXML covered in Chapter 4. The first step in a transformation is to create the objects involved:

```
XslTransform xslt = new XslTransform();
XmlDocument xml = new XmlDocument();
using (StringWriter stringWriter = new StringWriter()) {
```

Transformations in .NET include an XslTransform object, an XmlDocument object, and a StringWriter object, which contains the resulting transformed data. The next step in the transformation process is to load the XML data into the XmlDocument object and the XSL document into the XslTransform object:

```
xml.LoadXml(xmlStr);
xslt.Load(_path + "/weather.xslt");
```

The LoadXml() method of the XmlDocument class resembles the loadXML() method in the MSXML library. It accepts a string argument representing the XML data. The XSL document is loaded into the XslTransform object via the Load() method. This method takes one argument: a string containing the path to the XSL document.

The final step is to perform the transformation and retrieve the resulting data from the StringWriter:

```
xslt.Transform(xml, null, stringWriter, null);
xmlStr = stringWriter.ToString();
```

The Transform() method has several overloads. Overloaded methods are methods of the same name that perform the same function, but which accept different arguments. This particular overload accepts the XML document in the first position, an argument list (or parameter list) to pass to the XSLT processor in the second position, the StringWriter to serve as output in the third position, and an XmlResolver to handle any XML namespaces in the last position. Once the transformation is complete, you can use the ToString() method to obtain the transformed data from the StringWriter.

The final step in _getWebWeather() is to cache the data. This is done with a StreamWriter, which writes the data in UTF-8 encoding:

```
using (StreamWriter writer = new StreamWriter(_cachedFile))
{
    writer.Write(xmlStr);
}
```

The StreamWriter class constructor accepts a string argument containing the path to the file to write to. The StreamWriter writes the contents of xmlStr to the file and is promptly closed and disposed of when the using block exits.

In order for the application to update the contents of weather_cache.xml, *ASP.NET must have the proper modify permissions for the file.*

The completed code of _getWebWeather() is as follows:

```csharp
private string _getWebWeather()
{
    //Just to keep things clean, an unformatted URL:
    string baseUrl =
        "http://xoap.weather.com/weather/local/{0}?cc=*&prod=xoap&par={1}&key={2}";

    //Now format the url with the needed information
    string url = String.Format(baseUrl, _settings.LocationId, _settings.PartnerId,
            _settings.LicenseKey);

    //String that the weather feed will be written to
    string xmlStr = String.Empty;

    //Use a web client. It's less coding than an HttpWebRequest.
    using (WebClient client = new WebClient())
    {
        //Read the results
        try
        {
            using (StreamReader reader = new StreamReader(client.OpenRead(url)))
            {
                xmlStr = reader.ReadToEnd();
            }
        }
        catch (WebException exception)
        {
            xmlStr = _writeErrorDoc(exception);
        }
    }

    XslTransform xslt = new XslTransform();
    XmlDocument xml = new XmlDocument();

    using (StringWriter sringWriter = new StringWriter())
    {
        xml.LoadXml(xmlStr);
        xslt.Load(_path + "/weather.xslt");
        xslt.Transform(xml,null,sringWriter,null);
        xmlStr = sringWriter.ToString();
    }

    //Write the cached file
    using (StreamWriter writer = new StreamWriter(_cachedFile))
    {
        writer.Write(xmlStr);
    }

    //Finally, return the feed data.
    return xmlStr;
}
```

Reading Cached Weather Data

Another private method of the `WeatherInfo` class is the `_getCachedWeather()` method. As its name suggests, its function is to retrieve the data from the cached feed. Like the previously discussed method, `_getCachedWeather()` also returns a string:

```
private string _getCachedWeather()
{
    string str = String.Empty;

    //Open and read the cached weather feed.
    using (StreamReader reader = new StreamReader(_cachedFile))
    {
        str = reader.ReadToEnd();
    }

    //Return the contents
    return str;
}
```

First, the variable `str` is created and initialized as an empty string; this variable will contain the contents of the cached file when it is read. Next, a `StreamReader` object is created and opens the cached weather feed, the contents of which are read via the `ReadToEnd()` method and stored in `str`. Finally, `_getCachedWeather()` exits and returns the `str` value.

The `_getWebWeather()` and `_getCachedWeather()` methods are the primary workhorses of the application. However, as you've probably already noted, they're private members. In other words, there is no way to access them externally when you create an instance of this class. A public method, `GetWeather()`, provides makeshift access to these private methods.

Deciding Which Version to Use

The `GetWeather()` method is a public method that returns a string retrieved from either `_getCachedWeather()` or `_getWebWeather()`. This method determines whether to pull the feed from the Web or from the cache. This decision is based on the time that the cached file was last modified.

The .NET Framework provides a structure called `DateTime`, which is used extensively throughout the Framework. When a date or time is needed, chances are a `DateTime` instance is available. Such is the case with getting dates and times associated with a file. To retrieve the "Date Modified" file system property of the cached file, write a public accessor called `LastModified` as follows:

```
public DateTime LastModified
{
    get
    {
        if ((File.Exists(_cachedFile)))
        {
            return File.GetLastWriteTime(_cachedFile);
        }
        else
        {
            return new DateTime(1,1,1);
        }
    }
}
```

This code snippet gets the date and time of when the cached file was last written to. First, you must check the existence of the cached file, or else an error is thrown when you try to retrieve the `DateTime` information. If it exists, the `GetLastWriteTime()` method retrieves the date and time of when it was last written to. If the file does not exist, a `DateTime` instance is created using the earliest possible values by passing the value of 1 for the year, month, and day. This ensures that the application will always pull a new feed if the cached file does not exist.

The `GetWeather()` method uses this information to decide whether to pull a newer feed:

```
DateTime timeLimit = LastModified.AddMinutes(30);
```

Using the `AddMinutes()` method, 30 minutes is added to the time `LastModified` returns. This new `DateTime` instance, `timeLimit`, will be compared to the current time by using the `CompareTo()` method:

```
if (DateTime.Now.CompareTo(timeLimit) > -1)
{
    return _getWebWeather();
}
else
{
    return _getCachedWeather();
}
```

The `CompareTo()` method returns an integer value. If the current time (specified by `DateTime.Now`) is greater than `timeLimit`, the returned integer is greater than zero. If the two times are equal, the method returns zero. If the current time is less than `timeLimit`, then `-1` is returned. In this code, the retrieval of a newer feed occurs only when at least 30 minutes have passed; otherwise, the cached version is retrieved.

Writing the Error Document

One final method of the `WeatherInfo` class need mentioning: `_writeErrorDoc()`. As stated before, this method writes a simple error document in XML to be used in the event the remote host cannot be contacted. It accepts one argument, a `WebException` instance:

```
private string _writeErrorDoc(WebException exception)
{
    XmlDocument xml = new XmlDocument();
    xml.LoadXml("<errorDoc />");

    XmlElement alertElement = xml.CreateElement("alert");
    alertElement.InnerText = "An Error Occurred!";

    XmlElement messageElement = xml.CreateElement("message");
    messageElement.InnerText = exception.Message;

    xml.DocumentElement.AppendChild(alertElement);
    xml.DocumentElement.AppendChild(messageElement);

    return xml.OuterXml;
}
```

In the first two lines of code, an XmlDocument object is created and loaded with a simple XML document (only the root element). The error document contains only two elements: <alert/> and <message/>. The DOM methods in .NET resemble the DOM methods in Internet Explorer and Firefox. The first element, <alert/>, is created with the CreateElement() method. Using the InnerText property, it receives its text node. The same procedure is used to create the <message/> element. This element will house the message from the WebException object.

When all elements are created and populated with their needed data, they are appended to the document via the AppendChild() method, and the serialized XML data, output by the OuterXml property, is returned.

To finish off the class, two accessors grant access to the _settings and _cachedFile private members:

```
public Settings Settings
{
    get
    {
        return _settings;
    }
}

public string CachedFile
{
    get
    {
        return _cachedFile;
    }
}
```

This will ensure that you can access this data outside of the class, as necessary.

Using the WeatherInfo Class

The majority of the work is completed with the server-side application. All that remains is to put the WeatherInfo class to work. The ASP.NET file weather.aspx serves as the proxy between the client and the Weather.com XML service. It is in this page that you will use the WeatherInfo class.

The first step in implementing this class is to create an instance of it:

```
WeatherInfo weather = new WeatherInfo(Server.MapPath(String.Empty));
string weatherData = weather.GetWeather();
```

In this code, an instance of the WeatherInfo class is created by passing the path to the application to the constructor with Server.MapPath(Sring.Empty). With this new instance, you can use the GetWeather() method and retrieve the weather information, which is stored in weatherData.

The next step is to set the needed headers:

```
Response.ContentType = "text/xml";
Response.CacheControl = "no-cache";
Response.AddHeader("Weather-Modified",
                weather.LastModified.ToFileTime().ToString());
```

The first two lines should look familiar. They set the MIME content type to `text/xml` and tell the browser not to cache the feed. The third line, however, shows a custom HTTP header called `Weather-Modified`. This header provides the client-side code a means to check if a new version of weather data is available.

The value assigned to this header consists of a long integer (returned by the `ToFileTime()` method) representing the time returned by the `LastModified` property. Because this value is based on the `Modified` attribute of the file system (remember the `LastModified` property of the `WeatherInfo` class returns that value), it will remain the same until the file is updated. This makes it ideal for checking for new updates on the client-side.

Finally, output the weather data, as follows:

```
Response.Write(weatherData);
```

You now need a client to consume the information.

The Client-Side Component

The client code for this widget is surprisingly simple thanks to all the work the server application performs. All that remains for the client is to retrieve the data. The `AjaxWeatherWidget` class does just that:

```
function AjaxWeatherWidget(oElement) {
    this.element = (oElement)?oElement:document.body;
    this.lastModified = null;

    this.getWeather();
}
```

The `AjaxWeatherWidget` constructor accepts one argument: the `HTMLElement` to append the data, which is assigned to the `element` property. In the event that no argument is supplied, `element` becomes `document.body`. As in the News Ticker widget example, this class also automatically checks for updates, which is why the `lastModified` property exists. The constructor calls `getWeather()`, a method that retrieves the weather data from the server, before it exits.

Getting Data from the Server

The `getWeather()` method contacts the server application and retrieves the weather information with XMLHttp. It also polls the server every minute for updated information:

```
AjaxWeatherWidget.prototype.getWeather = function () {
    var oThis = this;

    var doTimeout = function () {
        oThis.getWeather();
    };
```

The method starts by creating a pointer to the object by assigning oThis. This pointer is then used inside the nested function doTimeout(), which calls the getWeather() method. The doTimeout() function is used to make continuous updates.

Next, an XMLHttp object makes a request to the server:

```
AjaxWeatherWidget.prototype.getWeather = function () {
    var oThis = this;

    var doTimeout = function () {
        oThis.getWeather();
    };

    var oReq = zXmlHttp.createRequest();
    oReq.onreadystatechange = function () {
        if (oReq.readyState == 4) {
            if (oReq.status == 200) {
                var lastModified = oReq.getResponseHeader("Weather-Modified");

                if (lastModified != oThis.lastModified) {
                    oThis.lastModified = lastModified;
                    oThis.element.innerHTML = oReq.responseText;
                }
            }
        }
    };

    oReq.open("GET", "weather.aspx", true);
    oReq.send(null);
```

When the request is successful, the first item retrieved from the server's response is the Weather-Modified header with the getResponseHeader() method. To see if the requested data is newer than the preexisting data, compare the value of the Weather-Modified header to that of the lastModifed property of the AjaxWeatherWidget object. If they match, the data is the same; if not, then updated data exists and is appended to the chosen HTMLElement via the innerHTML property.

Finally, set a timeout for the doTimeout() function, which executes every minute:

```
setTimeout(doTimeout, 60000);
```

Customizing the Weather Widget

Out of the box, this widget fits nicely into a sidebar, providing visitors with the weather information you dictate. The look of the widget relies upon custom images as well as the weather images provided in the SDK (see Figure 8-2).

Figure 8-2

Giving the widget the look and feel in the example files relies heavily upon CSS positioning; nearly every element is absolutely positioned, so the HTML structure isn't extremely important. All you need is valid (X)HTML:

```
<div id="weatherContainer">
    <div id="weatherIcon"><img src="img/weather/32.png" /></div>
    <div id="weatherTemp">70</div>
    <div id="weatherLocation">Dallas, TX (75226)</div>
    <div id="weatherWind">Wind:
        <div>13 MPH S</div>
    </div>
    <div id="weatherTime">Last Update:
        <span>7:45 PM</span>
    </div>
</div>
```

This XHTML is a result of an XSL transformation. When going over each piece of information in this section, the XPath expression to the location of the information in the XML feed is given.

To achieve this look, it is important to note that the containing `<div/>` element, `weatherContainer`, does not have a default (inherit) position; otherwise, the contained, absolutely positioned elements will position themselves based on the document and not `weatherContainer`:

```css
#weatherContainer {
    position: relative;
    background: url('../img/background.gif');
    width: 220px;
    height: 149px;
}
```

A relative position doesn't interfere with the page flow unless you provide top and left coordinates. The background of this `<div/>` element is a custom-made GIF file the same size as the `<div/>`: 220 pixels wide and 149 pixels high.

The SDK includes Weather.com's own images to provide a visual display of the current weather conditions. These image files are PNG images and are named `xx.png`, where `xx` is a number. This number, found in the XML feed, resides at `weather/cc/icon` (cc stands for current conditions). To accomplish the look of the example, give this element an absolute position, which enables you to place it anywhere in its container and removes it from the document flow.

```css
#weatherIcon {
    position: absolute;
    top: -25px;
    left: -25px;
}
```

This code places the image 25 pixels to the left and top from the top-left corner of the container. Because the images provided by Weather.com are PNGs, additional coding is required for Internet Explorer because the browser ignores the transparency information.

Microsoft exposes a DirectX filter called `AlphaImageLoader`, which makes PNGs correctly display transparency. However, the use of this filter is limiting, as it must be applied with CSS. To solve this issue, you can download the PNG Behavior at WebFX (http://webfx.eae.net/dhtml/pngbehavior/pngbehavior.html). It is an excellent tool, and is perfect in this situation. To use it, simply add the following rule to your CSS:

```css
#weatherIcon img {
    width: 128px;
    height: 128px;
    behavior: url("css/pngbehavior.htc");
}
```

In Internet Explorer, this rule applies the PNG Behavior to every `<img/>` element in the widget, but it only applies the `AlphaImageLoader` filter for PNG files. All other `<img/>` tags with `.gif`, `.jpg`, or any other extension are left alone. The filter property is Internet Explorer–specific; therefore, all other browsers ignore the property and its value.

> **You must set the** `height` **and** `width` **properties when using** `AlphaImageLoader`.

The next item in the widget is the temperature, contained in a `<div/>` element with an `id` of `weatherTemp` and located in the XML at `weather/cc/temp`. The styling of this information is as follows:

```css
#weatherTemp {
    position: absolute;
    color: white;
    font: bold 48px Tahoma;
    right: 12px;
    top: 5px;
}
```

Positioning this element as absolute enables you to place it anywhere in the container you want. In this situation, its location resides in the top-right corner. The text contained in this element is colored white and is 48 pixels tall.

Below the temperature is the weather location information. From the XML feed, this information is located in `weather/loc/dnam`. This text is colored white, and uses a smaller font:

```css
#weatherLocation {
    font: 12px Tahoma;
    color: white;
    position: absolute;
    right: 12px;
    top: 60px;
}
```

Once again, this element is absolutely positioned. The right edge is 12 pixels from the right edge of `weatherContainer` and is 60 pixels from its top. The font is 12 pixels tall and in the Tahoma typeface.

The wind is another important piece of information to display. In the XML document, the information is located in `weather/cc/wind`:

```css
#weatherWind {
    position: absolute;
    font: bold 12px Tahoma;
    color: white;
    left: 85px;
    top: 85px;
}

#weatherWind div {
    font-weight: normal;
}
```

If you'll remember from the HTML structure discussed earlier in this section, `weatherWind` contains another `<div/>` element. This inner `<div/>` contains the actual wind information, whereas its parent merely serves as a label and positions the information. Unlike the previous elements, `weatherWind` is positioned using the `left` property, instead of `right`, to position the element horizontally, and the element is positioned 85 pixels from the top. The label text is bolded, whereas the wind information is not.

The final piece of information this widget displays is the time it was last updated. This information also exists in the XML data. Its location: `weather/loc/tm`. Like the wind information previously discussed, the HTML structure for the time information consists of a parent element (`weatherTime`) and a child element (`<span/>`). The outer element positions the information and serves as a label; the inner element contains the actual time information:

```css
#weatherTime {
    position: absolute;
    font: bold 12px Tahoma;
    color: white;
    left: 85px;
    bottom: 5px;
}

#weatherTime span {
    font-weight: normal;
}
```

The premise behind the time is the same as the wind, except with a `<span/>` the data is displayed inline instead of on a new line.

Because this widget depends on the XSL stylesheet, total customization essentially rests in your hands; you have the ability to completely change the markup, structure, and style of the data. In this section, the path to the information was given for each element. These few elements are by no means a full list of the available elements in the XML feed. The SDK does not cover these elements; however, this information resides within the Weather.com DTD, located at www.weather.com/documentation/xml/weather.dtd.

Implementing the Weather Widget

Because the back-end code consists mainly of a C# class, your options of implementation are twofold:

1. You can add the class to an already existing ASP.NET-enabled web site. Doing so would require a recompilation of your code. If you take this route, you will need to modify the `weather.aspx` page to fit your namespace.

2. You can use the code contained in the downloadable examples as its own free-standing mini application. You can follow the steps outlined at the end of Chapter 5 on how to do this.

The choice is ultimately yours, but the remainder of the section assumes you chose the latter option. To implement the `AjaxWeatherWidget` class, you should reference the proper CSS and JavaScript files in your HTML:

```html
<!DOCTYPE html PUBLIC "-//W3C//DTD XHTML 1.1//EN"
        "http://www.w3.org/TR/xhtml11/DTD/xhtml11.dtd">

<html xmlns="http://www.w3.org/1999/xhtml" >
<head>
    <title>Ajax Weather</title>
    <link rel="stylesheet" type="text/css" href="css/weatherwidget.css"/>
    <script type="text/javascript" src="js/zxml.js"></script>
    <script type="text/javascript" src="js/weatherwidget.js"></script>
```

```
    </head>
    <body>
    </body>
    </html>
```

The Weather widget's only outside dependency is the zXml library, which you also should reference in your HTML.

All that remains is to create an `AjaxWeatherWidget` object and append it to an HTML element:

```
<!DOCTYPE html PUBLIC "-//W3C//DTD XHTML 1.1//EN"
        "http://www.w3.org/TR/xhtml11/DTD/xhtml11.dtd">

<html xmlns="http://www.w3.org/1999/xhtml" >
<head>
    <title>Ajax Weather</title>
    <link rel="stylesheet" type="text/css" href="css/weatherwidget.css"/>
    <script type="text/javascript" src="js/zxml.js"></script>
    <script type="text/javascript" src="js/weatherwidget.js"></script>
    <script type="text/javascript">
    function init() {
        var divMyWeather = document.getElementById("myWeather");
        var oWeather = new AjaxWeatherWidget(divMyWeather);
    }

    onload = init;
    </script>
</head>
<body>
    <div id="myWeather"></div>
</body>
</html>
```

This new code adds another `<script/>` element containing a function called `init()`. Inside this function, retrieve a reference to the `<div/>` element with `myWeather` as its ID. This `<div/>` element will serve as the weather widget container. Also, it is important to run `init()` during the `onload` event, as the browser will not find the `myWeather` `<div/>` element and will not append the widget to it.

Creating a Web Search Widget

The most widely used function of the Web is searching. It's not even an option; if you want to find any information, the search engines of the Web are the places you have to go to.

With the ever-expanding technology of the Web, conventional search engines are opening the doors to more unconventional means to get you to the content you desire. The first to jump onto the scene was Yahoo! with their Y!Q service (`http://yq.search.yahoo.com/publisher/index.html`). This new service enables you to search from any web page, provided the page's author includes it in their web page. It is a service to provide related search results to the content at hand, giving readers more information at their fingertips without leaving your page.

The Yahoo! Y!Q service is a great idea, but it hasn't surfaced without criticism. The main argument? It requires the use of Yahoo!'s JavaScript and you have to add a `<form/>` element, meeting the Yahoo! requirements, to perform the search. For many web site authors, it takes too much effort to provide the service. And after all the work, the search results are presented in the Yahoo! style, breaking the look and feel of your web site.

Thankfully, Yahoo! isn't the only search engine breaking into this "provide search results from your web site" service. MSN Search (`http://search.msn.com`) provides a similar service, except it enables the web developer to control the look, feel, and implementation. This ability comes from MSN Search providing RSS versions of its search results, making it possible to subscribe to a particular search or add the results to your page using Ajax methods.

> Google has yet to throw its hat into this new spin on "search from your site" technique, although, at the time of this writing, Google released Google BlogSearch Beta (`http://blogsearch.google.com`), which provides results returned in either RSS or Atom formats.

The Server-Side Component

Perform a search with MSN Search, and you'll see an orange XML image at the bottom of the results page. Clicking this image takes you to a new page, giving you the URL to subscribe to the search:

```
http://search.msn.com/results.aspx?q=[SEARCHTERM]&format=rss
```

With this knowledge, you can write the server-side code to retrieve the remote feed. For the widget, you will use PHP to retrieve the search feed. The URL to request information from the server application looks like this:

```
websearch.php?search=[SEARCHTERM]
```

There's only one variable in the query string: `search`. Therefore, the application should look for this query item. The code for the server-side application closely resembles that of the NewsTicker widget.

```php
<?php
header("Content-Type: text/xml");
header("Cache-Control: no-cache");

if ( isset($_GET["search"]) ) {

    $searchTerm = urlencode( stripslashes($_GET["search"]) );

    $url = "http://search.msn.com/results.aspx?q=$searchTerm&format=rss";

    $xml = file_get_contents($url);

    echo $xml;
}
?>
```

As you know by now, the first two lines set the required headers so that the browser will handle the data correctly. The next line of code uses the `isset()` function to determine whether the search key is present in the query string.

The search term should go through a variety of functions in order to send a proper request to the remote host. First, it is passed to the `stripslashes()` function. If magic quotes are enabled in the PHP configuration (which is the default), any quote that reaches the PHP engine is automatically escaped with a slash: `\"search query\"`. The `stripslashes()` function removes these escape sequence, leaving only `"search query"`. After the slashes' removal, it then goes to the `urlencode()` function, which properly encodes characters to be used in a query string. Spaces, quotes, ampersands, and so on are all encoded.

> If the search term does not go through these processes, the MSN server will return a code `400: Bad Request`.

When the search term is ready for transmission, it is included into the URL and stored in the `$url` variable. Finally, the `file_get_contents()` function opens the remote file, reads the contents, and returns it as a string to the `$xml` variable, which is printed to the page using the `echo` command.

The Client-Side Component

The client-side code departs from the classes created earlier in this chapter. Instead of creating a class and using instances of that class, this widget consists of a static object called `msnWebSearch`:

```
var msnWebSearch = {};
```

Here, you see the use of object literal notation creating the `msnWebSearch` object. You will use this object in the `onclick` event of an `HTMLElement` in order to perform a search:

```
<a href="#" onclick='msnWebSearch.search(event,"Professional Ajax"); return
false;'>
    Professional Ajax
</a>
```

This object exposes several methods to get the search results and to draw and position the HTML to contain the data. The first method to cover is `drawResultBox()`, which draws the HTML. The HTML this method draws looks like this:

```
<div class="ajaxWebSearchBox">
    <div class="ajaxWebSearchHeading">MSN Search Results
        <a class="ajaxWebSearchCloseLink" href="#">X</a>
    </div>

    <div class="ajaxWebSearchResults">
        <a class="ajaxWebSearchLink" target="_new" />
        <a class="ajaxWebSearchLink" target="_new" />
    </div>
</div>
```

The result box is divided into two parts: a heading and a results pane (see Figure 8-3). The heading tells the user that this new box contains results from an MSN search. It also contains an X, which will close the box. The results pane contains block-style links, which opens a new window when clicked.

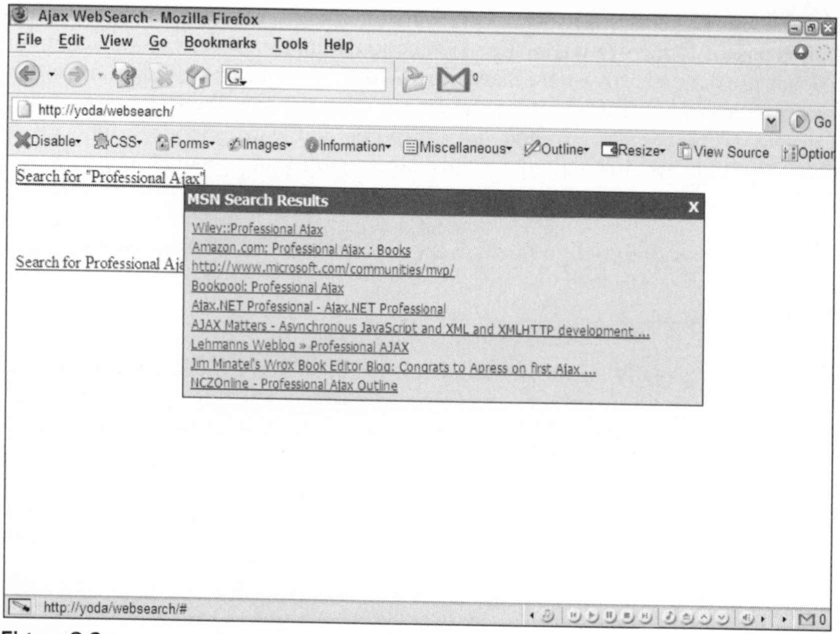

Figure 8-3

Drawing the Results User Interface

The code to generate this HTML is rather lengthy because the elements are generated using DOM methods. The drawResultBox() method accepts one argument, an event object:

```
msnWebSearch.drawResultBox = function (e) {
    var divSearchBox= document.createElement("div");
    var divHeading = document.createElement("div");
    var divResultsPane = document.createElement("div");
    var aCloseLink = document.createElement("a");
```

These first lines create the HTML elements via the createElement() method. After the elements have been created, you can begin to assign their properties. The first two elements to finalize are aCloseLink and divHeading:

```
aCloseLink.href = "#";
aCloseLink.className = "ajaxWebSearchCloseLink";
aCloseLink.onclick = this.close;
aCloseLink.appendChild(document.createTextNode("X"));

divHeading.className = "ajaxWebSearchHeading";
divHeading.appendChild(document.createTextNode("MSN Search Results"));
divHeading.appendChild(aCloseLink);
```

The first four lines complete the link that closes the result box. A method, `close()`, becomes the handler for the link's `onclick` event. The next group of lines populate the heading `<div/>` with text and the closing link.

When this result box is drawn into the page, a response from the server application has not been received yet. To show the user that something is happening (other than a box popping out of nowhere), it would be nice for the user to see a message stating that data is loading (see Figure 8-4). To do this, create another element and append it to the `divResultsPane` element:

```
var divLoading = document.createElement("div");
divLoading.appendChild(document.createTextNode("Loading Search Feed"));

divResultsPane.className = "ajaxWebSearchResults";
divResultsPane.appendChild(divLoading);
```

This code creates the loading message and appends it to `divResultsPane`, while also assigning the class name to `divResultsPane`.

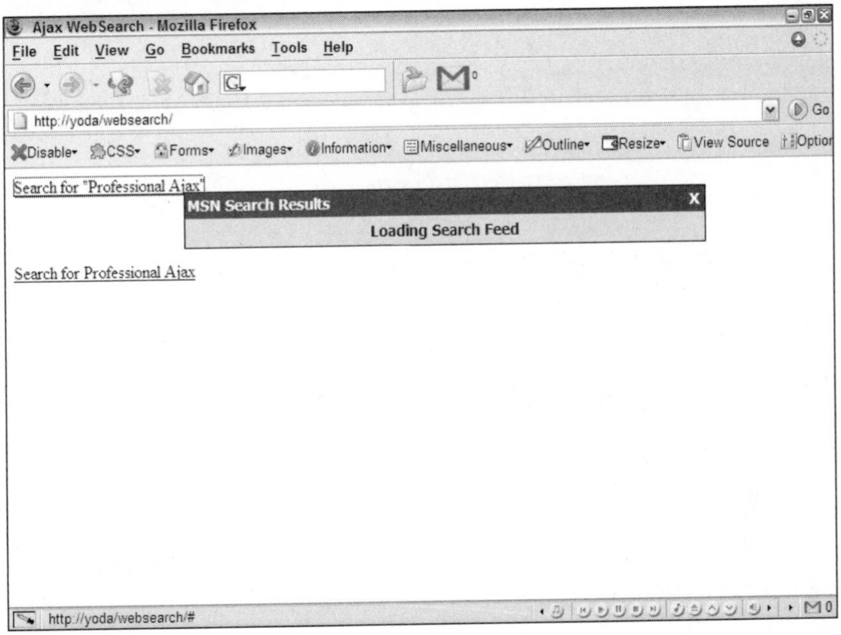

Figure 8-4

With these elements completed, all that remains is to add them to the `divSearchBox` element:

```
divSearchBox.className = "ajaxWebSearchBox";
divSearchBox.appendChild(divHeading);
divSearchBox.appendChild(divResultsPane);

document.body.appendChild(divSearchBox);
```

This code appends the `divHeading` and `divResultsPane` elements to the search box, and appends the search box to the page.

The final step in `drawResultBox()` is to position the newly drawn box and return `divSearchBox` to its caller:

```
msnWebSearch.drawResultBox = function (e) {
    var divSearchBox= document.createElement("div");
    var divHeading = document.createElement("div");
    var divResultsPane = document.createElement("div");
    var aCloseLink = document.createElement("a");

    aCloseLink.href = "#";
    aCloseLink.className = "ajaxWebSearchCloseLink";
    aCloseLink.onclick = this.close;
    aCloseLink.appendChild(document.createTextNode("X"));

    divHeading.className = "ajaxWebSearchHeading";
    divHeading.appendChild(document.createTextNode("MSN Search Results"));
    divHeading.appendChild(aCloseLink);

    var divLoading = document.createElement("div");
    divLoading.appendChild(document.createTextNode("Loading Search Feed"));

    divResultsPane.className = "ajaxWebSearchResults";
    divResultsPane.appendChild(divLoading);

    divSearchBox.className = "ajaxWebSearchBox";
    divSearchBox.appendChild(divHeading);
    divSearchBox.appendChild(divResultsPane);

    document.body.appendChild(divSearchBox);

    this.position(e, divSearchBox);

    return divSearchBox;
};
```

The way the `msnWebSearch` object is set up, `divSearchBox` must be returned to its caller for other operations. The `position()` method, as you may have guessed, positions the search box. It accepts two arguments: the `event` object passed to `drawResultBox()` and the `divSearchBox` element:

```
msnWebSearch.position = function (e, divSearchBox) {
    var x = e.clientX + document.documentElement.scrollLeft;
    var y = e.clientY + document.documentElement.scrollTop;

    divSearchBox.style.left = x + "px";
    divSearchBox.style.top = y + "px";
};
```

The first two lines get the left and top positions to place the search results box. Two pieces of information are required to perform this operation. First is the x and y coordinates of the mouse. This information is stored in the `clientX` and `clientY` properties.

These coordinates, however, are insufficient to properly position the results box because the `clientX` and `clientY` properties return the mouse position in relation to the client area in the browser window, not the actual coordinates in the page. To account for this, use the `scrollLeft` and `scrollTop` properties of the document element. With the final coordinates calculated, you can finally position the box where the user clicked the mouse.

Displaying the Results

The `populateResults()` method populates the result pane with the search results. It accepts two arguments: the element to contain the results and an `XParser` object:

```
msnWebSearch.populateResults = function (divResultsPane,oParser) {
    var oFragment = document.createDocumentFragment();

    divResultsPane.removeChild(divResultsPane.firstChild);
```

This method generates `<a/>` elements programmatically with DOM methods, so these elements will be appended to a document fragment created in the first line. The next line removes the loading `<div/>` element appended in `drawResultBox()`.

The next step is to create the links:

```
for (var i = 0; i < oParser.items.length; i++) {
    var oItem = oParser.items[i];

    var aResultLink = document.createElement("a");
    aResultLink.href = oItem.link.value;
    aResultLink.className = "ajaxWebSearchLink";
    aResultLink.target = "_new";
    aResultLink.appendChild(document.createTextNode(oItem.title.value));

    oFragment.appendChild(aResultLink);
}
```

This code cycles through the items of the feed and generates links from the data and appends the `<a/>` element to the document fragment.

When the loop exits, the document fragment is appended to `divResultsPane` to display the search results:

```
divResultsPane.appendChild(oFragment);
```

Closing the Results Box

To close the search results box, the `msnWebSearch` object provides the `close()` method. If you'll remember from the `drawResultsBox()` method, the `close()` method handles the `onclick` event of the link responsible for closing the box:

```
msnWebSearch.close = function () {
    var divSearchBox = this.parentNode.parentNode;
    document.body.removeChild(divSearchBox);

    return false;
};
```

The search box isn't really closed; in fact, it is removed from the document. To do this, retrieve the divSearchBox element. The first line does this by retrieving the parent node of this element's parent. Because close() handles the onclick event, this references the link. The next line removes the divSearchBox element from the document. The last line, return false, forces the browser not to follow the default behavior of a link (going to the location noted in the href attribute).

Building the Search Interface

The last method of the msnWebSearch object is search(), which provides the interface to perform a search. You can call search() with the onclick event of an element. It accepts two methods, an event object and the search term:

```
msnWebSearch.search = function (e,sSearchTerm) {
    var divSearchBox = this.drawResultBox(e);
    var url = encodeURI("websearch.php?search=" + sSearchTerm);

    var oParser = new XParser(url);
    oParser.onload = function () {
        msnWebSearch.populateResults(divSearchBox.childNodes[1],oParser);
    };
};
```

The first line calls the drawResultBox() method and passes the event, e, to it. The next line encodes the URL for proper transmission. This URL is passed to the XParser constructor to create a new parser. The parser's onload event handler calls the populateResult() method when the search feed is finished loading to populate the search box with results.

Of course, one of the reasons for building this widget is to make it fit the look of your own site.

Customizing the Web Search Widget

Thanks to CSS, you can easily customize the widget for your existing site and any redesign you may have later down the road.

The first CSS class discussed is ajaxWebSearchBox, the class for the search box. Because the box is positioned, it must have a position of absolute:

```
.ajaxWebSearchBox
{
    position: absolute;
    background-color: #0d1e4a;
    width: 500px;
    padding: 1px;
}
```

The absolute position is the only requirement. All other properties are optional according to your tastes. In this example, the box has a darkish-blue background, a width of 500 pixels, and 1 pixel of padding on all four sides. This padding will give the box a 1-pixel border around the box's contents.

The next class is `ajaxWebSearchHeading`, which contains the box's heading text and the closing link. To position the closing link in the top-right corner, it is absolutely positioned. Because of this, it requires `ajaxWebSearchHeading` to have a `position` of `relative`:

```
.ajaxWebSearchHeading
{
    position: relative;
    background-color: #1162cc;
    font: bold 14px tahoma;
    height: 21px;
    color: white;
    padding: 3px 0px 0px 2px;
}
```

Once again, the only required property is the `position` property. The remaining properties help to give the element a heading look. The background color is a lighter blue with white, bold text 14 pixels high and in the Tahoma font. The element's height is 21 pixels and is padded on the top and left edges.

As stated previously, the closing link's position is absolute:

```
a.ajaxWebSearchCloseLink
{
    position: absolute;
    right: 5px;
    top: 3px;
    text-decoration: none;
    color: white;
}

a:hover.ajaxWebSearchCloseLink
{
    color: red;
}
```

The element is positioned 5 pixels from the right and 3 pixels from the top, placing the element in the top-right corner. This link does not have any text-decoration and is colored white. When the user hovers over the link, the text color turns red.

Notice that no `visited` or `active` pseudo classes are used. This is because the window always ignores the `href` attribute of this link (it has `return false` in its event handler). Therefore, the link is never truly active or visited.

Next, the `ajaxWebSearchResults` class styles the results pane:

```
.ajaxWebSearchResults
{
    background-color: #d3e5fa;
    padding: 5px;
}
```

There are no required CSS properties for this element. The existing properties are merely to define the results pane and make it relatively easy to read. The background color is a light blue, and 5 pixels of padding surround the edges. You can also style the loading message:

```
.ajaxWebSearchResults div
{
    text-align: center;
    font: bold 14px tahoma;
    color: #0a246a;
}
```

This element does not have a class name, but you can still style it by using the `parent child` notation shown in the preceding example. This example places the text in the center of the `<div/>` element and gives it a bold, blue font 14 pixels high.

The last elements you need to style are the result links. These have a class name of `ajaxWebSearchLink`:

```
a.ajaxWebSearchLink
{
    font: 12px tahoma;
    padding: 2px;
    display: block;
    color: #0a246a;
}

a:hover.ajaxWebSearchLink
{
    color: white;
    background-color: #316ac5;
}

a:visited.ajaxWebSearchLink
{
    color: purple;
}
```

The only required property is the `display` property, which is set to `block`. This gives every link its own line. The padding, two pixels worth, gives a bit of separation between the links, making them easier to read. The font-face is Tahoma and is 12 pixels high. Their color is a dark blue, giving a nice contrast to the light blue background of `ajaxWebSearchResults`.

When the user hovers over these links, the background color is set to blue, whereas the text color changes to white.

The `visited` pseudo class is set, in the last rule in the previous code. This is to provide users with user interface cues they are already used to. By having the `visited` pseudo class set to display a color of purple, users know they've already visited that link, which can save them time by not visiting a page they may not want to.

As stated earlier in this section, this widget differs greatly from the past widgets you've created in this chapter; so, let's take a look at how to implement it.

Implementing the Web Search Widget

Implementing this widget is simple. First, you must upload the `websearch.php` file to your web server (of course, PHP must be installed, too). Next, you need an HTML document to reference all the components. The `msnWebSearch` object relies on the `XParser` class, which in turn depends on the zXml library. You must reference these files:

```
<!DOCTYPE html PUBLIC "-//W3C//DTD XHTML 1.0 Transitional//EN"
        "http://www.w3.org/TR/xhtml1/DTD/xhtml1-transitional.dtd">
<html xml:lang="en" lang="en"  xmlns="http://www.w3.org/1999/xhtml">
<head>
    <meta http-equiv="Content-Type" content="text/html; charset=utf-8" />
    <title>Ajax WebSearch</title>
    <link rel="stylesheet" type="text/css" href="css/websearch.css" />
    <script type="text/javascript" src="js/zxml.js"></script>
    <script type="text/javascript" src="js/xparser.js"></script>
    <script type="text/javascript" src="js/websearch.js"></script>
</head>

<body>

</body>
</html>
```

To perform a search, set the `msnWebSearch.search()` method as the element's `onclick` handler:

```
<!DOCTYPE html PUBLIC "-//W3C//DTD XHTML 1.0 Transitional//EN"
        "http://www.w3.org/TR/xhtml1/DTD/xhtml1-transitional.dtd">
<html xml:lang="en" lang="en"  xmlns="http://www.w3.org/1999/xhtml">
<head>
    <meta http-equiv="Content-Type" content="text/html; charset=utf-8" />
    <title>Ajax WebSearch</title>
    <link rel="stylesheet" type="text/css" href="css/websearch.css" />
    <script type="text/javascript" src="js/zxml.js"></script>
    <script type="text/javascript" src="js/xparser.js"></script>
    <script type="text/javascript" src="js/websearch.js"></script>
</head>

<body>
```

```
    <a href="#" onclick='msnWebSearch.search(event,"\"Professional Ajax\"");
        return false;'>Search for "Professional Ajax"</a>

    <br /><br /><br /><br />

    <a href="#" onclick='msnWebSearch.search(event,"Professional Ajax");
        return false;'>Search for Professional Ajax</a>
```

```
</body>
</html>
```

The first new link performs a search for the exact phrase Professional Ajax, whereas the second searches for all the words. Also note the `return false` in the `onclick` event. Once again, this forces the browser to ignore the `href` attribute and is required. Clicking these links will draw the search box at the mouse's cursor, and you'll have the search results just pixels away.

Creating a Site Search Widget

Search functionality is an integral part of any web site; it enables your viewers to find the data they desire quickly and easily. However, conventional search mechanisms suffer from the same problems as the rest of the Web: they require a page refresh and possibly losing data when the search is performed.

Within the past year, many Ajax solutions have cropped up with one standing out above the rest: LiveSearch. LiveSearch (http://blog.bitflux.ch/wiki/LiveSearch), developed by the people at BitFlux (www.bitflux.ch), is a search-as-you-type solution to emulate the Apple Spotlight feature in OSX Tiger.

LiveSearch presents a new take on web site searches, but it also has its critics. For one, it offers a different approach to achieving the desired results. The average user is used to entering his or her search criteria and pressing a Search button. LiveSearch, on the other hand, uses the `onkeypress` DOM event and returns the results as you type. This method may be more efficient in terms of getting your results, but it is unexpected by the user, which can cause confusion.

This next widget is an Ajax solution for searching a site that uses a SQL database as a data store. It will feature a user interface that users are already accustomed to: a search box, a submit button, and a `<div/>` element that displays the search results (see Figure 8-5).

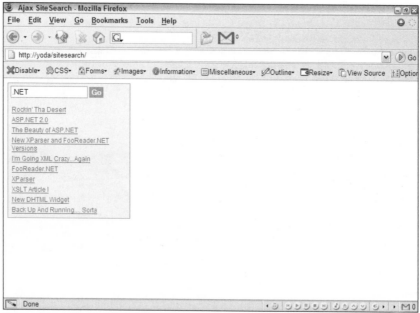

Figure 8-5

The Server-Side Component

You will use the .NET Framework and C# language to interface with an MSSQL database to perform the search query. The returned results will be in JSON, thanks to the JSON C# library mentioned in Chapter 7 (www.crockford.com/JSON/cs/). The code in the following sections will use a SQL query to search a database containing the posts on a web log (blog).

The Database Information

The database table for this specific blog is relatively simple. It contains four columns: id, title, date, and posting. The following SQL statement creates this table, called BlogPosts:

```
CREATE TABLE BlogPosts (
    id int IDENTITY (1, 1) NOT NULL,
    date datetime NOT NULL,
    title text NOT NULL,
    posting text NOT NULL
)
```

When this query runs, it creates the table, but it is empty. The code download for this example, located at www.wrox.com, contains a SQL file that will add records to the table.

There are primarily two pieces of desired information needed for the search results: id (used in the URL to the blog post) and title. With this knowledge, you can create the search query:

```
SELECT TOP 10
id, title
FROM BlogPosts
WHERE posting LIKE '%SEARCHSTRING%' OR
title LIKE '%SEARCHSTRING%'
ORDER BY date DESC
```

This query selects the id and title columns from the BlogPosts table where the contents of posting and title contain an instance of the search string. The results returned are ordered by descending date, and only ten records are returned.

Before delving into the code, however, the returned data structure needs discussing.

The Returned Data Structure

The only two pieces of information retrieved are the blog post ID and its title, and a result of a search could contain more than one blog post. At this point, you need a result set of objects that each contains title and id properties:

```
[
    {
        title : "Title 1",
        id    : "1"
    },

    {
        title : "Title 2",
        id    : "2"
```

```
    },
    {
        title : "Title 3",
        id    : "3"
    }
]
```

This code illustrates what the data returned from the server looks like. The structure is an array containing several objects, each with `title` and `id` properties. With the result set mapped out, you can now approach the `SiteSearch` class.

The SiteSearch Class

This widget uses a simple class called `SiteSearch` to connect to the database, perform the search query, and return the results as a JSON string. This class has one private field `_conString`, the connection string to the MSSQL database, and accepts a string argument containing the connection string:

```
private string _conString;

public SiteSearch(string connectionString)
{
    _conString = connectionString;
}
```

As you can see, the constructor is extremely simple. The only operation performed is assigning `_conString` the value of the `connectionString` argument. As you've probably already guessed, the class's sole method, `Search()`, is the meat and potatoes of the class.

The `Search()` method accepts one argument: the search string. This search string is used in a `String.Format()` method to format the search query:

```
public string Search (string searchString)
{
    string query = String.Format("SELECT TOP 10 id, title FROM BlogPosts
        WHERE posting LIKE '%{0}%' OR title LIKE '%{0}%' ORDER BY date DESC",
        searchString);
```

The variable `query` now holds the completed query string used later in the method.

The JSON C# library provides the ability to build JSON strings dynamically. Two classes are used to create these strings: `JSONArray` and `JSONObject`. As you might have guessed, `JSONArray` creates an array, whereas `JSONObject` creates an object. Referring back to the returned data structure, remember the client code expects an array of objects. Therefore, the next step is to instantiate a `JSONArray` object:

```
Nii.JSON.JSONArray jsa = new Nii.JSON.JSONArray();
```

For the moment, this is all the JSON code used, and you won't see it again until further in the database operation.

Next, create a database connection and a `SqlCommand`:

```
using (SqlConnection conn = new SqlConnection(_conString))
{
    SqlCommand command = new SqlCommand(query, conn);
    conn.Open();
```

This code creates the database connection using the connection string stored in `_conString`. A new `SqlCommand` is then created using the search query and database connection. This essentially prepares the query to run against the database, which the next few lines illustrate:

```
using (SqlDataReader reader = command.ExecuteReader())
{


}
```

This code creates a `SqlDataReader` returned by the `ExecuteReader()` method. This data reader provides the ability to read the result from the executed database query. Before any data is retrieved from the data reader, you should first check if the result contains any rows. You can do this using the `HasRows` property:

```
using (SqlDataReader dataReader = command.ExecuteReader())
{
    try {
        if (reader.HasRows)
        {
            int i = 0;
            while (reader.Read())
            {

            }
        }
    }
    catch {}
}
```

This code uses the `HasRows` property to determine if the data reader contains any rows. If so, the processing of the contained data can begin.

The `while` loop is used to read the result set through the `Read()` method of the `SqlDataReader` class. The `Read()` method returns a Boolean value; when the end of the result set is reached, `Read()` returns `false` and the loop exits. Inside the loop, you create a `JSONObject` object and populate it with its properties and their values with the `put()` method. The `put()` method of the `JSONObject` class accepts two arguments: a string containing the property name and that property's value. To access the database column's value, pass the column name as the index to `dataReader`:

```
using (SqlDataReader dataReader = command.ExecuteReader())
{
    try {
        if (reader.HasRows)
        {
```

```
                    int i = 0;
                    while (reader.Read())
                    {
                            JSONObject jso = new JSONObject();
                            jso.put("title",reader["title"]);
                            jso.put("id",reader["id"]);

                            jsa.put(i++,jso);
                    }
            }
        catch {}
    }
```

When the JSONObject is populated, you add it to the JSONArray object created earlier. The JSONArray class exposes a put() method as well, but the arguments are a bit different. The first is the index of the existing element of the array, while the second is the JSONObject object.

When the loop exits, the JSONArray is completed and ready for returning. But what if the query returned no results? The client-side code handles this functionality. In the event that no rows are found from the query, an empty array is returned. The client-side code will check the length of the result set, and perform the necessary operation.

At this point, the JSON string construction is complete. To retrieve the string representation of the JSONArray, use the ToString() method:

```
    return jsa.ToString();
```

This last line of the Search() method returns the JSON string that can be written into the page.

Building the Search Page

With the working class completed, all that remains on the server-side is the search page. This page will accept an argument in the query string called search, which contains the search term. An example query string could look like the following:

```
    http://yoursite.com/search.aspx?search=ajax
```

To provide this functionality, check for the existence of this parameter by using the Response.QueryString collection:

```
    Response.CacheControl = "no-cache";
    Response.ContentType = "text/plain; charset=UTF-8";

    if (Request.QueryString["search"] != null)
    {

    }
```

The first two lines should be familiar to you by now. The first line sets the `CacheControl` header to `no-cache` so that the browser will not cache the data, while the second sets the MIME `ContentType` to `text/plain` with UTF-8 encoding.

As you learned in Chapter 7, plain text with Unicode encoding is the desired content-type for JSON strings.

After the headers are set, the existence of the `search` parameter in the query string is checked. Inside the `if` code block, a `SiteSearch` object is instantiated:

```
if (Request.QueryString["search"] != null)
{
    string searchTerm = Request.QueryString["search"];
    string conStr = "uid=sa;pwd=pass;data source=localhost;initial
        catalog=BlogPosts";

    SiteSearch siteSearch = new SiteSearch(con);
}
```

The first new line creates the `searchTerm` variable, a string storing the value of the `search` parameter in the query string, followed by the database connection string.

Connecting to an MSSQL database in C# is quite different from connecting to a MySQL database with PHP, demonstrated in Chapter 7. In PHP, the user name, password, and database host name were passed to the `mysql_connect()` function. In C# (and other .NET languages, for that matter), this information is contained in what is called a *connection string*. As seen in the previous example, this connection string contains name/value pairs separated by semicolons. The names in the preceding sample mean the following:

❑ **uid:** The user name for the particular database. In the previous example, `sa` is a built-in user meaning Super-Admin.

❑ **pwd:** The password to connect to the database.

❑ **data source:** The host name or IP address of the database server.

❑ **initial catalog:** The database name your queries are run against.

Of course, the information in the connection string should reflect the login information of your own MSSQL database; therefore, feel free to change the information wherever needed. Changing this information requires you to recompile the web application; however, a widget should be ready to use out of the box (or ZIP file), so a different approach is desirable.

The `web.config` file of an ASP.NET application contains configuration settings available for accessing within the application. This file's purpose is twofold:

1. It provides a central location for all application settings.

2. It provides a secure means of storing settings that contain sensitive data (such as database information), as the web server will not serve `.config` files.

Inside the `web.config file`, you'll notice that it is nothing more than an XML file with the document root being `<configuration/>`. To add your own custom settings, add an element called `<appSettings/>` as the first child of `<configuration/>`:

```
<configuration>
    <appSettings>


    </appSettings>
```

To add a setting, use the `<add/>` element, which has `key` and `value` attributes:

```
<appSettings>
    <add key="connectionStr" value="uid=sa;pwd=pass;data source=localhost;
            initial catalog=BlogPosts"/>
</appSettings>
```

With the connection string now a part of the application settings, the `if` block can be changed to the following:

```
if (Request.QueryString["search"] != null)
{
    string searchTerm = Request.QueryString["search"];
    string conStr = ConfigurationSettings.AppSettings["connectionStr"];

    SiteSearch siteSearch = new SiteSearch(conStr);
}
```

This code is slightly different from the code earlier. Instead of hard coding the database information, the information is pulled from the application settings with the `ConfigurationSettings.AppSettings` collection. Pass the value from the `key` attribute in the `web.config` file to the `AppSettings` collection, and the value is retrieved.

> The `ConfigurationSettings` **object is from the** `System.Configuration` **namespace, so you need to add** `System.Configuration` **to the** using **statements at the beginning of the class file.**

With the `SiteSearch` object instantiated, the final steps inside the `if` block is to perform the search and output the results to the page:

```
if (Request.QueryString["search"] != null)
{
    string searchTerm = Request.QueryString["search"];
    string conStr = ConfigurationSettings.AppSettings["connectionStr"];

    SiteSearch siteSearch = new SiteSearch(conStr);

    string json = siteSearch.Search(searchTerm);
    Response.Write(json);
}
```

The new lines in this code call the `Search()` method to perform the search. The resulting JSON string is returned and stored in the `json` variable, which is then written to the page via the `Response.Write()` method.

You could add an `else` block to handle the case when the search parameter in the query string does not exist; however, the client-side code will handle form validation making it unnecessary to do so.

With the `.aspx` file complete, the final code looks like this:

```
Response.CacheControl = "no-cache";
Response.ContentType = "text/plain; charset=UTF-8";

if (Request.QueryString["search"] != null)
{
    string searchTerm = Request.QueryString["search"];
    string conStr = ConfigurationSettings.AppSettings["connectionStr"];

    SiteSearch siteSearch = new SiteSearch(conStr);

    string json = siteSearch.Search(searchTerm);
    Response.Write(json);
}
```

The Client-Side Component

Client functionality is overly important, especially for a widget such as this. Before using the search capabilities of your site, the user already made the assumption of how it works. Therefore, it is important to follow a couple of guidelines:

❑ **The user will enter text to search and press either Enter or the Submit button.** The search-as-you-type feature of LiveSearch is revolutionary, but it goes against what the user is already accustomed to. Near instantaneous results without a page refresh is enough new functionality.

❑ **The user expects to be told when no results are found.** If you'll remember from the `SiteSearch` class, an empty JSON array is returned when no results are found; therefore, this responsibility is passed to the client code.

These guidelines may seem like a no-brainer, but it is important to consider the user's experience. What's hip and cool isn't necessarily always the right thing to do.

The User Interface

The first step in any client-side component is to build the user interface with HTML. For this widget, you will use four elements contained within a `<div/>` element:

```
<div class="ajaxSiteSearchContainer">
    <form class="ajaxSiteSearchForm">
        <input class="ajaxSiteSearchTextBox" />
        <input type="submit" value="Go" class="ajaxSiteSearchButton" />
    </form>
    <div class="ajaxSiteSearchResultPane">
        <a class="ajaxSiteSearchLink" href="http://yoursite.com">Result Text</a>
    </div>
</div>
```

Every element contains a `class` attribute. This ensures that the widget is easily customizable with CSS, and you can tailor it to fit in almost every web site.

Of course, you will not add this HTML directly into the HTML code of your web site; JavaScript dynamically creates the HTML and appends it to the desired HTML element.

The AjaxSiteSearch Class

The `AjaxSiteSearch` class encapsulates everything needed to display the user interface, make requests to the server, and display the server's response, aside from the CSS information and other dependencies. The class's constructor accepts one argument, an HTML element to append the search user interface:

```
function AjaxSiteSearch(oElement) {

}
```

The first step is to write the HTML elements that make up the user interface. This is done, naturally, with DOM methods:

```
var oThis = this;
this.result = null;

this.widgetContainer = document.createElement("div");
this.form = document.createElement("form");
this.textBox = document.createElement("input");
this.submitButton = document.createElement("input");
this.resultPane = document.createElement("div");

this.widgetContainer.className = "ajaxSiteSearchContainer";
this.form.className = "ajaxSiteSearchForm";
this.textBox.className = "ajaxSiteSearchTextBox";
this.submitButton.className = "ajaxSiteSearchButton";
this.resultPane.className = "ajaxSiteSearchResultPane";

this.submitButton.type = "submit";
this.submitButton.value = "Go";
```

The first line of this code creates the `oThis` variable, a pointer to the object. This comes in handy later in the constructor. The following lines create the needed HTML elements and assign their class names, and the Submit button's `type` and `value` attributes are set to `submit` and `Go`, respectively.

When the user clicks the Submit button or presses the Enter key when the form has focus, the form's `onsubmit` event fires. The following event handler will start the search process:

```
this.form.onsubmit = function () {
    oThis.clearResults();

    return false;
};
```

This is where the object pointer's use is required. Inside the `onsubmit` event handler, the scope changes; so, `this` references the `<form/>` element instead of the `AjaxSiteSearch` object. Because the event handler makes calls to the `AjaxSiteSearch` object, an external variable referencing the object is required, and that is what `oThis` does.

The first line of the `onsubmit` event handler calls the object's `clearResults()` method. This method, covered later, removes any links in the results list from a prior search. This ensures that only the results from the current search request are displayed. In the last line, the value of `false` is returned. This overrides the form's default behavior, which is to submit the form.

Also during the `onsubmit` event, the form is validated. If the text box does not contain any text, the user is notified that no text is entered:

```
this.form.onsubmit = function () {
    oThis.clearResults();

    if (oThis.textBox.value != "") {
        oThis.search();
    } else {
        alert("Please enter a search term");
    }

    return false;
};
```

If text is entered, however, the object's `search()` method is called. This method, also covered shortly, is responsible for retrieving the search term and making the XMLHttp request to the server.

With the elements created and the `onsubmit` event handler written, all that remains in the constructor is appending the elements to the document:

```
this.form.appendChild(this.textBox);
this.form.appendChild(this.submitButton);
this.widgetContainer.appendChild(this.form);
this.widgetContainer.appendChild(this.resultPane);

var oToAppend = (oElement)?oElement:document.body;
oToAppend.appendChild(this.widgetContainer);
```

Because this widget appends itself to the given HTML element, it is a good idea to create an `AjaxSiteSearch` object during the page's `onload` event. Otherwise, the desired destination element could not exist, thus throwing an error.

Clearing the Results

The `clearResults()` method is a simple method to remove all child nodes in the results `<div/>` element:

```
AjaxSiteSearch.prototype.clearResults = function () {
    while (this.resultPane.hasChildNodes()) {
        this.resultPane.removeChild(this.resultPane.firstChild);
    }
};
```

This method utilizes the `hasChildNodes()` method, a method exposed by a node in the DOM. As long as the results `<div/>` contains children, the first child is removed. It is a simple method, but it gets the job done.

Making the XMLHttp Request

As stated before, the `search()` method makes the request to the server to perform the search:

```
AjaxSiteSearch.prototype.search = function () {
    var oThis = this;
    var sUrl = encodeURI("search.aspx?search=" + this.textBox.value);

    var oReq = zXmlHttp.createRequest();
    oReq.onreadystatechange = function () {
        if (oReq.readyState == 4) {
            if (oReq.status == 200) {
                oThis.handleResponse(oReq.responseText);
            }
        }
    };

    oReq.open("GET", sUrl, true);
    oReq.send();
};
```

The familiar first line creates a pointer to the object used inside of the XMLHttp object's `onreadystatechange` event handler. The second line encodes the search URL and search term with the `encodeURI()` function. Doing this replaces certain characters with their appropriate escape sequence (for example: white space is turned into %20).

The remainder of the code performs the XMLHttp request. On a successful request, the `responseText` is passed to the `handleResponse()` method.

Processing the Information

The `handleResponse()` method takes the server's response (the JSON string), decodes it, and displays the results as links in the results `<div/>` element. This method accepts one argument, a JSON string:

```
AjaxSiteSearch.prototype.handleResponse = function (sJson) {
    this.result = JSON.parse(sJson);
};
```

This code takes the `sJson` argument and passes it to the `JSON.parse()` method to convert the string into JavaScript.

Now that the information can be used programmatically, the code begins to go through a decision-making process. Remember, the result from the server is an array of objects; therefore, you can use the `length` property to determine if the search returned any results:

```
AjaxSiteSearch.prototype.handleResponse = function (sJson) {
    this.result = JSON.parse(sJson);

    if (this.result.length > 0) {
        //Results go here
    } else {
        alert("Your search returned no results.");
    }
};
```

Naturally, if any results are present, you want to display that information. If not, the user is notified through an alert box that no results were found from their search.

Displaying the results is as simple as creating <a/> elements:

```
AjaxSiteSearch.prototype.handleResponse = function (sJson) {
    this.result = JSON.parse(sJson);

    if (this.result.length > 0) {
        var oFragment = document.createDocumentFragment();
        for (var i = 0; i < this.result.length; i++) {
            var linkResult = document.createElement("a");
            linkResult.href = "http://yoursite.com/?postid=" + this.result[i].id;
            linkResult.innerHTML = this.result[i].title;
            linkResult.className = "ajaxSiteSearchLink";

            oFragment.appendChild(linkResult);
        }

        this.resultPane.appendChild(oFragment);
    } else {
        alert("Your search returned no results.");
    }
};
```

The first new line of code creates a document fragment to append the <a/> elements to. The next block of code, a for loop, generates the links. Notice the assignment of the href property of the link. In order for this to work on your site, you must change the href value to reflect your own web site.

When the link creation is complete, it is added to the document fragment, which is appended to the results <div/> element. These links remain visible until a new search is performed, which will clear the results pane and populate it with new results.

Customizing the Site Search Widget

To make the Site Search widget conform to your page's look and feel, it was designed to be fully customizable. Every element in the widget has a corresponding CSS classification, making customization a snap.

The outermost <div/> element, the widget's container, has the CSS class ajaxSiteSearchContainer. You can give your search widget its overall look with this element; you can also set a global style, since all elements will inherit many of its style properties:

```
div.ajaxSiteSearchContainer
{
    background-color: #fdfed4;
    border: 1px solid #7F9DB9;
    font: 12px arial;
    padding: 5px;
    width: 225px;
}
```

The first two lines set the background color of the element and its border, respectively. These two properties give the visual idea that everything within the border and background color belongs to the widget. This can be helpful to the user, especially when text seems to appear from the nether. The next line sets the font-size and -family for the widget. This setting is inherited by the results <div/> element and the links it contains. The 5-pixel padding is mainly for visual purposes; otherwise, everything could look scrunched together. Last, the width is applied to the widget. This confines the widget into a specified space, and text will wrap accordingly.

The <form/> element also possesses the ability for styling. The given class name for this element is ajaxSiteSearchForm:

```
form.ajaxSiteSearchForm {}
```

This example does not apply any style to the element, but the ability exists to do so. By applying padding or a border (or any other style for that matter), you can give the visual impression of separating the form from the results.

The <form/> contains two child elements, the text box and the Submit button, both of which are <input/> elements:

```
input.ajaxSiteSearchTextBox
{
    border: 1px solid #7F9DB9;
    padding: 2px;
}

input.ajaxSiteSearchButton
{
    background-color: #7F9DB9;
    border: 0px;
    color: white;
    font-weight: bold;
    margin-left: 3px;
    padding: 1px;
}
```

The text box's CSS (class ajaxSiteSearchTextBox) gives the box a solid, colored border 1 pixel in width and pads the contents by 2 pixels. The button, whose class name is ajaxSiteSearchButton, has a background color and no border but is padded on all sides by one pixel. The text inside the button is white and bold. It is scooted 3 pixels to the right by setting its left margin to 3 pixels.

The results <div/> in this example does not have any styling. Instead, it inherits the font-size and -family from its parent:

```
div.ajaxSiteSearchResultPane {}
```

The final elements in this widget are the links:

```css
a.ajaxSiteSearchLink
{
    color: #316ac5;
    display: block;
    padding: 2px;
}

a:hover.ajaxSiteSearchLink
{
    color: #9b1a1a;
}
```

In the example CSS, only two states are styled: a normal link and a link when the mouse hovers over it. In the former (default) state, the links are treated as block-level elements, meaning that each link starts on its own line. They have a bluish color and contain two pixels of padding. When the user mouses over a link, the hover state is activated. The only style change made is the color, which turns the text color from bluish to reddish.

These style properties are for example only; the real fun with widgets is making them your own and fitting them into your own page. Feel free to bend these elements to your will.

Implementing the Site Search Widget

Much like the weather widget, your options of implementation are twofold:

1. You can add the class to an already existing ASP.NET-enabled web site. Doing so would require a recompilation of your code. Doing so, however, would require you to recompile your code and modify the search.aspx page to fit your namespace.

2. You can use the code contained in the downloadable examples as its own free-standing mini application. You can follow the steps outlined at the end of Chapter 5 on how to do this.

Just like the weather widget, the choice of implementation is yours; however, the remainder of the code assumes you chose the latter option. On the client page, you need to reference all files needed to use this widget. The AjaxSiteSearch class depends on the zXml and JSON libraries to function properly:

```html
<!DOCTYPE html PUBLIC "-//W3C//DTD XHTML 1.1//EN"
        "http://www.w3.org/TR/xhtml11/DTD/xhtml11.dtd">
<html xmlns="http://www.w3.org/1999/xhtml" >
<head>
    <title>Ajax SiteSearch</title>
    <link rel="stylesheet" type="text/css" href="css/ajaxsitesearch.css" />
    <script type="text/javascript" src="js/json.js"></script>
    <script type="text/javascript" src="js/zxml.js"></script>
    <script type="text/javascript" src="js/ajaxsitesearch.js"></script>
</head>
<body>

</body>
</html>
```

To instantiate an `AjaxSiteSearch` object, use the `new` keyword:

```
<!DOCTYPE html PUBLIC "-//W3C//DTD XHTML 1.1//EN"
        "http://www.w3.org/TR/xhtml11/DTD/xhtml11.dtd">
<html xmlns="http://www.w3.org/1999/xhtml" >
<head>
    <title>Ajax SiteSearch</title>
    <link rel="stylesheet" type="text/css" href="css/ajaxsitesearch.css" />
    <script type="text/javascript" src="js/json.js"></script>
    <script type="text/javascript" src="js/zxml.js"></script>
    <script type="text/javascript" src="js/ajaxsitesearch.js"></script>
    <script type="text/javascript">
    function init() {
        var oSiteSearch = new AjaxSiteSearch();
    }

    onload = init;
    </script>
</head>
<body>

</body>
</html>
```

When creating the `AjaxSiteSearch` object, pass the desired element you want the widget to be appended to. If no `HTMLElement` is passed to the constructor, it is appended to the `document.body`. Creating an object automatically generates the required HTML elements, so there is nothing left to do to implement the widget.

Summary

In this chapter, you took the skills you have learned thus far and applied them to building your own web-based widgets. This chapter showed you many practical widgets that Ajax makes possible.

First, you learned how to build a news ticker widget with PHP, DHTML, and Ajax to display news feeds in a scrolling format and auto-update itself. You also learned how to build a widget to consume the Weather.com XML service, transform the XML, and display the data to the user.

The chapter went on to describe how to create two widgets revolving around searches. The first widget displayed results from the MSN search service, which can output search results in RSS. Through PHP, this widget retrieved the search result feed and a static JavaScript object displayed the results to the user. The second search widget searched a blog's database using MSSQL. Using the C# JSON library, you learned how to build JSON strings and output them to the client.

AjaxMail

One of the most popular Ajax applications is Gmail, a web-based e-mail system that incorporates a lot of Ajax techniques to create a seamless user experience. Gmail loads a single page and then makes changes to reflect user actions, eliminating almost entirely the "click-and-wait" experience of most web applications. There is a lot of back-and-forth with the server to retrieve information that the user never knows is occurring because of the system's design. Because Gmail is an excellent example of how to build an Ajax-based web application, this chapter focuses on developing a similar application called AjaxMail.

In this chapter, you will use techniques learned throughout the book to bring AjaxMail to life. Both hidden frames and the XMLHttp object will be used for communicating with the server, and you will be reminded when and how to use each technique. Remember, the whole point of using Ajax is to improve the user's experience; this chapter gives you the opportunity to see firsthand how to create an application with the user in mind.

Requirements

Before building a web application, it's always good to define the requirements and build to them. You may never have considered the requirements for an e-mail application before. You probably use an e-mail application like Outlook, Thunderbird, or Eudora on a daily basis and have never really stopped to think about all the things it must do to provide a good user experience. For simplicity, AjaxMail will support a subset of what these applications do (although it is easy enough to extend the functionality on your own).

The requirements for AjaxMail are:

❑   Support for POP3 to receive mail and SMTP to send mail

❑   Ability to read a list of e-mail messages from the server

❑   Visual indication if a message contains an attachment

❑ Ability to read an individual e-mail with support for plain text messages only

❑ Notification when new mail messages arrive

❑ Ability to send, forward, and reply to messages

To implement these requirements, a variety of Ajax patterns and communication techniques will be used. There is extensive use of XMLHttp, requiring the use of the zXml library, as well as some hidden iframes. In building this application, you will learn how to incorporate and integrate the various techniques you have learned in this book.

Architecture

AjaxMail is built using PHP for the server-side language and MySQL for the database. A database is necessary to keep track of information relating to specific messages, such as what folder they are in and whether they have been read. Both of these can be accomplished by setting specific flags for a message in the database.

There are two folders in AjaxMail: Inbox and Trash. When a message is deleted from the Inbox, it is moved to the Trash. The message is permanently deleted when the Trash is emptied; otherwise, the message remains in the Trash. (It is also possible to restore a message from the Trash and place it back in the Inbox.) Even though this chapter uses only these two folders, you may use as many folders as you wish.

Each time a request is made to the server, AjaxMail checks to see if there are any new messages in the specified POP3 e-mail account. If there are, the messages are downloaded and saved into the MySQL database. The messages are then read out of the database and sent back to the client.

Resources Used

AjaxMail uses several open source software libraries to achieve its functionality:

❑ **zXml Library:** The cross-browser XML JavaScript library used throughout this book. Available at www.nczonline.net/downloads/.

❑ **Douglas Crockford's JSON JavaScript Library:** The JavaScript JSON parser. Available at www.json.org.

❑ **PHPMailer:** A PHP SMTP e-mail sending solution. Available at http://phpmailer.sourceforge.net/.

❑ **JSON-PHP:** The PHP JSON library. Available at http://mike.teczno.com/json.html.

❑ **POP3Lib:** A PHP POP3 mail interface written by one of your authors, Jeremy McPeak. Available at www.wdonline.com/php/pop3lib.zip.

Note that all these resources are included in the book's example code downloads, available at www.wrox.com.

The Database Tables

Because AjaxMail will need e-mails to be stored in the database, several tables must be created. If you have sufficient rights to create a new database on the MySQL server, you should create a database named *AjaxMail*. (You may also use any other database that is already set up.) There are three tables to add: `AjaxMailFolders`, `AjaxMailMessages`, and `AjaxMailAttachments`.

The first table, `AjaxMailFolders`, defines the various folders available in AjaxMail:

```
CREATE TABLE AjaxMailFolders (
  FolderId int(11) NOT NULL auto_increment,
  Name text NOT NULL,
  PRIMARY KEY  (FolderId)
);

INSERT INTO AjaxMailFolders VALUES (1, 'Inbox');
INSERT INTO AjaxMailFolders VALUES (2, 'Trash');
```

Each folder in AjaxMail is assigned a `FolderId` (an autoincrementing primary key) and a name. For the purposes of this chapter, there are only two folders: Inbox and Trash. You can feel free to add more to suit your own needs.

The `AjaxMailMessages` table holds each e-mail's information. It consists of 11 columns: a unique identification number (autoincremented so you don't need to worry about it), the different fields of an e-mail (To, From, Subject, and so on), what folder it exists in (Inbox, Trash, and so on), and whether the user has read the e-mail. You can create the table using the following SQL statement:

```
CREATE TABLE AjaxMailMessages (
    MessageId int(11) NOT NULL auto_increment,
    `To` text NOT NULL,
    CC text NOT NULL,
    BCC text NOT NULL,
    `From` text NOT NULL,
    Subject text NOT NULL,
    Date bigint(20) default NULL,
    Message text NOT NULL,
    HasAttachments tinyint(1) NOT NULL default '0',
    Unread tinyint(1) NOT NULL default '1',
    FolderId int(11) NOT NULL default '0',
    PRIMARY KEY  (MessageId)
);
```

The `MessageId` field is an autoincrementing field and provides the e-mail with a unique ID number in the database; it is also the table's primary key. The To, CC, BCC, From, Subject, Date, and Message fields are parts of an e-mail message. (To and From must be enclosed in backtick symbols because they are keywords in SQL.) The `HasAttachments` and `Unread` fields are `tinyint`, which means they can have values of 0 or 1 (false or true). Finally, the `FolderId` field contains the ID number of the folder in which the message is stored. This enables you to select messages that exist only in the Inbox or Trash folders.

If an e-mail contains any attachments, they are stored in the AjaxMailAttachments table:

```
CREATE TABLE AjaxMailAttachments (
  AttachmentId int(11) NOT NULL auto_increment,
  MessageId int(11) NOT NULL default '0',
  Filename text NOT NULL,
  ContentType text NOT NULL,
  Size int(11) NOT NULL default '0',
  Data longtext NOT NULL,
  PRIMARY KEY  (AttachmentId)
)
```

Like the AjaxMailMessages table, the AjaxMailAttachments table contains an autoincrementing field. This filed is called AttachmentId and provides each attachment with a unique ID number. The next field, MessageId, houses the message ID of the e-mail to which it was attached (this number matches the MessageId field in AjaxMailMessages). Next, the Filename and ContentType columns store the attachment's reported file name and content-type (both are necessary to enable the user to download the attachment later). Last, the Size and Data fields store the attachment's size (in bytes) and the binary/text data of the file, respectively.

The Configuration File

Much like any application, AjaxMail relies on a configuration file, called config.inc.php, to provide information required to function properly. As this information is required in many different areas of the application, it's best to store it as constants. In PHP, constants give you the advantage of being available in every scope of the application, meaning that you don't need to define them using the global keyword as you do with other global variables.

To create a constant in PHP, use the define() method, passing in the name of the constant (as a string) and its value. For example:

```
define("MY_CONSTANT", "my value");
```

The first group of constants relates directly to your MySQL database:

```
define("DB_USER", "root");
define("DB_PASSWORD", "password");
define("DB_SERVER", "localhost");
define("DB_NAME", "AjaxMail");
```

These constants are used when connecting to the database and must be replaced to reflect your database settings. Next, some constants are needed to provide information about your POP3 server:

```
define("POP3_USER", "test@domain.com");
define("POP3_PASSWORD", "password");
define("POP3_SERVER", "mail.domain.com");
```

Once again, these constants must be replaced with the information specific to your POP3 server. As you may have guessed, you also must supply some information about the SMTP server:

```
define("SMTP_DO_AUTHORIZATION", true);
define("SMTP_USER", "test@domain.com");
define("SMTP_PASSWORD", "password");
define("SMTP_SERVER", "mail.domain.com");

define("EMAIL_FROM_ADDRESS", "test@domain.com");
define("EMAIL_FROM_NAME", "Joe Somebody");
```

The first four lines set constant variables relating to user authentication for your SMTP server. The first variable sets whether or not your SMTP server requires user authentication to send e-mail. If set to true, the SMTP_USER and SMTP_PASSWORD must be set. (false means no authentication is required to send mail through the SMTP server.)

The second group of SMTP settings defines the user settings. You should set EMAIL_FROM_ADDRESS to contain your e-mail address, and set EMAIL_FROM_NAME to contain your name. When you send an e-mail, your recipient will see these values as the sender.

The final setting is the MESSAGES_PER_PAGE constant, which defines how many e-mail messages should be displayed per page:

```
define("MESSAGES_PER_PAGE", 10);
```

These constants are used throughout the application: when retrieving e-mail, connecting to the database, sending mail, and even when displaying the information.

The AjaxMailbox Class

The code contained in the file called AjaxMail.inc.php serves as the workhorse of the server-side application. This file houses the AjaxMailbox class, which is the primary interface by which all the mail is handled. A few helper classes, mainly used for JSON encoding, also exist in this file.

The AjaxMailbox class, which you will build in this section, begins with an empty class declaration:

```
class AjaxMailbox {

    //more code here
}
```

Database Operations

It's the responsibility of AjaxMailbox to handle all the interaction with the database. To facilitate this communication, several methods relate just to the database.

The first method is `connect()`, which, as you may expect, initiates a connection to the database:

```
class AjaxMailbox {

    function connect() {
        $conn = mysql_connect(DB_SERVER, DB_USER, DB_PASSWORD)
            or die("Could not connect : " . mysql_error());
        mysql_select_db(DB_NAME);
        return $conn;
    }

    //more code here
}
```

Using the database constants defined in `config.inc.php`, this method creates a database connection and stores it in the variable `$conn`. Then, the specific database is selected and `$conn` is returned. Of course, you also need to be able to disconnect from the database:

```
class AjaxMailbox {

    function connect() {
        $conn = mysql_connect(DB_SERVER, DB_USER, DB_PASSWORD)
            or die("Could not connect : " . mysql_error());
        mysql_select_db(DB_NAME);
        return $conn;
    }

    function disconnect($conn) {
        mysql_close($conn);
    }

    //more code here
}
```

The `disconnect()` method accepts a connection object (the same one returned from `connect()`) and uses `mysql_close()` to close that connection.

During development of a database application, you may sometimes end up with bad data in your database tables. At such times, it's best just to clear all the data from the tables and start fresh. As a means of database maintenance, `AjaxMailbox` has a method, `clearAll()`, that does just this:

```
class AjaxMailbox {

    //connect and disconnect methods

    function clearAll() {
        $conn = $this->connect();

        $query = "truncate table AjaxMailMessages";
        mysql_query($query, $conn);

        $query = "truncate table AjaxMailAttachments";
```

```
        mysql_query($query,$conn);

        $this->disconnect($conn);
    }

    //more code here

}
```

This method begins by calling `connect()` to create a database connection. Then, two SQL statements are executed, using the `TRUNCATE` command to clear out both `AjaxMailMessages` and `AjaxMailAttachments`. The `TRUNCATE` command is used for two reasons. First, it is generally faster than deleting every row in a table, and second, it clears the `AUTO_INCREMENT` handler, so any fields that automatically increment will start back at 1. The last step is to disconnect from the database by calling `disconnect()`.

Retrieving E-mail

Retrieving e-mail from a POP3 server is not an easy task, and it is beyond the scope of this book to walk you through the lengthy process. Instead, AjaxMail uses POP3Lib to interface with the POP3 server. This library contains numerous classes that aid in this type of communication. These classes are used in the `checkMail()` method, which is responsible for downloading messages from the POP3 server and inserting them into the database.

The method begins by creating a new instance of the `Pop3` class, which is the POP3Lib main class for communicating with a POP3 server. Its constructor accepts four arguments, three of which are required. The first argument is the POP3 server name, the second is the user name, the third is the password for that user name, and the fourth (optional) argument is the port at which to connect to the POP3 server (default is 110). To create a connection to the POP3 server, use the `login()` method. This method returns a Boolean value indicating the success (`true`) or failure (`false`) of the login attempt:

```
class AjaxMailbox {

    //database methods

    function checkMail() {
        $pop = new Pop3(POP3_SERVER, POP3_USER, POP3_PASSWORD);

        if ($pop->login()) {
            //Email downloading/database manipulation code here.
        }

    }

    //more code here

}
```

The `checkMail()` method begins by creating a `Pop3` object using the constant information defined in `config.inc.php`. Then, the `login()` method is called to try connecting to the server.

With a successful login, the `Pop3` object retrieves the number of messages found on the server and assigns this value to the `mailCount` property. Additionally, the `messages` array is initialized and populated with the header information of all e-mails residing on the server (the header information includes to, from, subject, date, and attachment information). Each item in the messages array at this point is a `Pop3Header` object.

To retrieve the entire e-mail, which includes the headers, message, and attachments, you must call the `getEmails()` method. This method completely repopulates the `messages` array with `Pop3Message` objects that contain all the e-mail information. A `Pop3Message` object has the following properties and methods:

Property/Method	Description
from	The sender's e-mail address.
to	The recipient's e-mail address. This property also contains all recipients if the e-mail was sent with multiple addresses in the To field.
subject	The subject of the e-mail.
cc	The recipient information held in the CC field.
bcc	If you receive an e-mail as a blind carbon copy, your e-mail address is in this property.
date	The date of the e-mail in RFC 2822 format.
unixTimeStamp	The date in a Unix timestamp (number of seconds since midnight on January 1, 1970).
hasAttachments	A Boolean value indicating whether the e-mail contains one or more attachments.
attachments	An array of attachments sent with the e-mail.
getTextMessage()	Retrieves the plain text body of an e-mail.
getHTMLMessage()	Retrieves the HTML body of an e-mail (if any).

These properties and methods are used to extract information about an e-mail and insert it into the database.

After a successful login, the first thing to do is to check for any e-mails on the server. You can do so by using the `mailCount` property. If `mailCount` is greater than zero, `getEmails()` is called to retrieve all the e-mail information and a database connection is made, anticipating the insertion of new e-mails:

```
class AjaxMailbox {

    //database methods

    function checkMail() {
```

```
        $pop = new Pop3(POP3_SERVER, POP3_USER, POP3_PASSWORD);

        if ($pop->login()) {

            if ($pop->mailCount > 0) {

                $conn = $this->connect();
                $pop->getEmails();

                //more code here

                $this->disconnect($conn);
            }

            $pop->logoff();
        }
    }

    //more code here

}
```

In this code snippet, the `disconnect()` and `logoff()` methods are called in their appropriate locations. The `logoff()` method, as you may have guessed, closes the connection to the POP3 server.

With all the e-mail information now retrieved, you can begin inserting data into the database by iterating over the e-mails in the `messages` array:

```
class AjaxMailbox {

    //database methods

    function checkMail() {
        $pop = new Pop3(POP3_SERVER, POP3_USER, POP3_PASSWORD);

        if ($pop->login()) {

            if ($pop->mailCount > 0) {

                $conn = $this->connect();
                $pop->getEmails();

                foreach ($pop->messages as $message) {
                    $query = "insert into AjaxMailMessages(`To`,CC,BCC,`From`,";
                    $query .=
                        "Subject,`Date`,Message,HasAttachments,FolderId,Unread)";
                    $query .= " values('%s','%s','%s','%s','%s',%s,'%s',"
                            .$message->hasAttachments.",1,1)";
                    $query = sprintf($query,
                                (addslashes($message->to)),
                                (addslashes($message->cc)),
                                (addslashes($message->bcc)),
```

```
                                    (addslashes($message->from)),
                                    (addslashes($message->subject)),
                                    $message->unixTimeStamp,
                                    (addslashes($message->getTextMessage())))
                        );

                $result = mysql_query($query, $conn);

                //more code here

            }
            $this->disconnect($conn);
        }

        $pop->logoff();
    }
}

//more code here

}
```

A foreach loop is used to iterate over the messages array. For each message, a SQL INSERT statement is created and then executed. Since the SQL statement is so long, sprintf() is used to insert the information into the right location. Note that each value, (aside from unixTimeStamp) must be encoded using addslashes() so that the string will be proper SQL syntax. The statement is executing using mysql_query(). The only remaining part is to deal with attachments.

You can determine if a message has attachments by using the hasAttachments property of a message. If there are attachments, you first must retrieve the ID of the most recently added e-mail message. (Remember, attachments are tied to the e-mail from which they were attached.) After the ID is determined, SQL INSERT statements are created for each attachment:

```
class AjaxMailbox {

    //database methods

    function checkMail() {
        $pop = new Pop3(POP3_SERVER, POP3_USER, POP3_PASSWORD);

        if ($pop->login()) {

            if ($pop->mailCount > 0) {

                $conn = $this->connect();
                $pop->getEmails();

                foreach ($pop->messages as $message) {
                    $query = "insert into AjaxMailMessages(`To`,CC,BCC,`From`,";
                    $query .=
                        "Subject,`Date`,Message,HasAttachments,FolderId,Unread)";
                    $query .= " values('%s','%s','%s','%s','%s',%s,'%s',"
```

```
                              .$message->hasAttachments.",1,1)";
                $query = sprintf($query,
                                (addslashes($message->to)),
                                (addslashes($message->cc)),
                                (addslashes($message->bcc)),
                                (addslashes($message->from)),
                                (addslashes($message->subject)),
                                $message->unixTimeStamp,
                                (addslashes($message->getTextMessage()))
                        );

                $result = mysql_query($query, $conn);

                if ($message->hasAttachments) {

                    $messageId = mysql_insert_id($conn);

                    foreach ($message->attachments as $attachment) {
                        $query = "insert into AjaxMailAttachments(MessageId,";
                        $query .= "Filename, ContentType, Size, Data)";
                        $query .= "values($messageId, '%s', '%s', '%s', '%s')";
                        $query = sprintf($query,
                                        addslashes($attachment->fileName),
                                        $attachment->contentType,
                                        strlen($attachment->data),
                                        addslashes($attachment->data));
                        mysql_query($query, $conn);
                    }
                }

            }
            $this->disconnect($conn);
        }

        $pop->logoff();
    }
}

//more code here

}
```

The most recently inserted ID can be retrieved using `mysql_insert_id()`. Then, the attachments are iterated over using a `foreach` loop. Each item in the attachments array is a `Pop3Attachment` object. This class represents attachment data for a particular e-mail and contains three properties: `contentType`, which contains the attachment's MIME content-type, `fileName`, which represents the file name of the attachment, and `data`, which contains the actual attachment file data. Depending on the content-type of the attachment, `data` can be either binary or plain text information.

Once again, the `sprintf()` function is used to format the query string. Notice the use of `strlen()` on the attachment data; this retrieves the size of the data in bytes for easy retrieval later on. After the string has been formatted, the query is run against the database to insert the data into `AjaxMailAttachments`. This concludes the `checkMail()` method.

This method is never called directly; instead, it is called whenever a request to the server is made. In essence, checkMail() is piggy-backed onto other requests so that the user is always viewing the most recent data.

Getting the E-mail List

Probably the most common operation of the application is to retrieve a list of e-mails to display to the user. The method responsible for this operation, getFolderPage(), accepts two arguments: the ID number of the folder and the page number to retrieve:

```
class AjaxMailbox {

    //database methods

    //check mail method

    function getFolderPage($folder, $page) {
        $this->checkMail();

        //more code here
    }

}
```

When called, getFolderPage() first calls checkMail() to ensure that the most recent data is available in the database. If there are any new messages, they will be inserted into the database so that any queries run thereafter will be up-to-date.

The next step is to build a JSON string to send back to the client. To aid in this, a generic class called JSONObject is defined:

```
class JSONObject {
}
```

A JSONObject instance is used merely to hold data until it is time to be serialized into the JSON format. For getFolderPage(), this object contains information about the folder. The JSON data contains many useful bits of information: the total number of messages (messageCount), the current page (page), the total number of pages (pageCount), the folder number (folder), the first message returned (firstMessage), the total number of unread messages (unreadCount), and finally an array of messages in the page (messages). The data structure looks like this:

```
{
    "messageCount":0,
    "page":1,
    "pageCount":1,
    "folder":1,
    "firstMessage":0,
    "unreadCount": 0,
    "messages":[]
}
```

The JSONObject is created and initialized with several properties relating to information in the database:

```
class AjaxMailbox {

    //database methods

    //check mail method

    function getFolderPage($folder, $page) {
        $this->checkMail();

        $conn = $this->connect();

        $query = "select count(MessageId) as count from AjaxMailMessages";
        $query .= " where FolderId=$folder";

        $result = mysql_query($query, $conn);
        $row = mysql_fetch_assoc($result);

        $info = new JSONObject();
        $info->messageCount = (int) $row["count"];
        $info->page = $page;
        $info->pageCount = (int) ceil($info->messageCount/MESSAGES_PER_PAGE);
        $info->folder = $folder;

        $firstMessageNum = ($page-1) * MESSAGES_PER_PAGE;
        $info->firstMessage = $firstMessageNum+1;
        $info->messages = array();

        $info->unreadCount = $this->getUnreadCount($conn);

        //more code here
    }

}
```

Using the SQL count() function, you can easily retrieve the total number of messages in a given folder. A JSONObject is created and stored in $info, and its messageCount property is set to the value retrieved from the database. Next, the page number is assigned to the page property (this is the same value that was passed into the method). The pageCount property determines how many total pages exist for the current folder. This is done by dividing the messageCount by the MESSAGES_PER_PAGE constant and applying the mathematical ceiling function (essentially, round up to the nearest whole number). Then, the folder ID is assigned to the folder property.

Next, the index of the first message to display on the page is calculated and stored in $firstMessageNum. This number is important because it keeps the database from retrieving too much information. The $info object is assigned a property of firstMessage that is equal to $firstMessageNum plus one. This is done because this value will be displayed to the user, and you never want to show message number zero; the first message should always be message number one. A property called messages is created and initialized to an empty array; this will contain message objects later.

The last step in this section of code is to create a property named unreadCount and assign it the number of unread messages in the database. To do so, use the getUnreadCount() method, defined as follows:

```
class AjaxMailbox {

    //other methods

    function getUnreadCount($conn) {
        $query = "select count(MessageId) as UnreadCount from AjaxMailMessages";
        $query .= " where FolderId=1 and Unread=1";
        $result = mysql_query($query, $conn);
        $row = mysql_fetch_assoc($result);
        return intval($row["UnreadCount"]);
    }

    //other methods

}
```

After getting this information, it's time to retrieve specific e-mail messages. To do so, execute a query on all messages in a given folder, ordered by the date. This is where the first message number comes into play; by adding a LIMIT statement to the end of the query, you can ensure the exact messages are contained in the result set. By specifying the first message number and then the total number of messages, the LIMIT statement retrieves just those messages:

```
class AjaxMailbox {

    //database methods

    //check mail method

    function getFolderPage($folder, $page) {
        $this->checkMail();

        $conn = $this->connect();

        $query = "select count(MessageId) as count from AjaxMailMessages";
        $query .= " where FolderId=$folder";

        $result = mysql_query($query, $conn);
        $row = mysql_fetch_assoc($result);

        $info = new JSONObject();
        $info->messageCount = (int) $row["count"];
        $info->page = $page;
        $info->pageCount = (int) ceil($info->messageCount/MESSAGES_PER_PAGE);
        $info->folder = $folder;

        $firstMessageNum = ($page-1) * MESSAGES_PER_PAGE;
        $info->firstMessage = $firstMessageNum+1;
```

```
        $info->messages = array();

        $info->unreadCount = $this->getUnreadCount($conn);

        $query = "select * from AjaxMailMessages where FolderId=$folder";
        $query .= " order by date desc limit $firstMessageNum, ";
        $query .= MESSAGES_PER_PAGE;

        $result = mysql_query($query, $conn);


        //more code here
    }


}
```

The complete SQL statement selects all messages where the value in `FolderId` matches `$folder` and orders the returned rows by date in descending order. It also starts the selection from the value in `$firstMessageNum`, and retrieves only the amount specified by `MESSAGES_PER_PAGE`.

At this point, there are two possible scenarios: either the database returned results or it didn't. In the application, it is important to know when either situation takes place. Thankfully, it is easy to discern when a query is not successful. The `mysql_query()` function returns `false` on an unsuccessful query; therefore, you can check to see if a query failed by checking the `$result` variable. If there is an error, it can be returned in a property of the `$info` object. Otherwise, you'll need to iterate through the rows that were returned, creating a new `JSONObject` for each message and adding it to the `messages` array:

```
class AjaxMailbox {

    //database methods

    //check mail method

    function getFolderPage($folder, $page) {
        $this->checkMail();

        $conn = $this->connect();

        $query = "select count(MessageId) as count from AjaxMailMessages";
        $query .= " where FolderId=$folder";

        $result = mysql_query($query, $conn);
        $row = mysql_fetch_assoc($result);

        $info = new JSONObject();
        $info->messageCount = (int) $row["count"];
        $info->page = $page;
        $info->pageCount = (int) ceil($info->messageCount/MESSAGES_PER_PAGE);
        $info->folder = $folder;

        $firstMessageNum = ($page-1) * MESSAGES_PER_PAGE;
        $info->firstMessage = $firstMessageNum+1;
```

```
$info->messages = array();

$info->unreadCount = $this->getUnreadCount($conn);

$query = "select * from AjaxMailMessages where FolderId=$folder";
$query .= " order by date desc limit $firstMessageNum, ";
$query .= MESSAGES_PER_PAGE;

$result = mysql_query($query, $conn);
if (!$result) {
    $info->error = mysql_error($conn);
} else {
    while ($row = mysql_fetch_assoc($result)) {
        $message = new JSONObject();
        $message->id = $row['MessageId'];
        $message->from = $row['From'];
        $message->subject = $row['Subject'];
        $message->date = date("M j Y", intval($row["Date"]));
        $message->hasAttachments = ($row['HasAttachments'] == 1);
        $message->unread = ($row['Unread'] == 1);
        $info->messages[] = $message;
    }
}

$this->disconnect($conn);
return $info;
}

}
```

In this code, the $result variable is checked. If the query failed, an error property is added to the $info object and assigned the error message retrieved from mysql_error(). Client-side code can then check this property to determine if an error occurred. If the query executed successfully, a new instance of JSONObject is created to contain the message information; this is stored in $message. This object is populated with all the information from the $row object, paying particular attention to format the message date so that it displays the month, day, and year only. (This eliminates the need for JavaScript to format the date.) Also, since the HasAttachments and Unread fields are bits, they are compared to the number 1 so that the corresponding properties on $message are filled with Boolean values instead of integers. The last line inside of the while loop adds the $message object to the end of the messages array.

After that is completed, you can safely disconnect from the database (using disconnect()) and return the $info object. It is up to the process using getFolderPage() to JSON-encode the object to be sent to the client.

Getting a Specific Message

Retrieving a specific message involves two helper classes, AjaxMailMessage and AjaxMailAttachmentHeader, and a method of the AjaxMailbox class called getMessage(). The two helper classes are used purely to store information that will later be JSON-encoded and sent to the client.

The first helper class, `AjaxMailMessage`, represents a single e-mail message:

```
class AjaxMailMessage {

    var $to;
    var $from;
    var $cc;
    var $bcc;
    var $subject;
    var $message;
    var $date;
    var $attachments;
    var $unread;
    var $hasAttachments;
    var $id;

    function AjaxMailMessage() {
        $this->attachments = array();
    }
}
```

The properties of this class resemble those of the field names in the database; the sole exception is the `attachments` property, which is an array of attachments associated with this e-mail. The JSON structure of the `AjaxMailMessage` class looks like this:

```
{
    to : "to",
    from : "from",
    cc : "cc",
    bcc : "bcc",
    subject : "subject",
    message : "message",
    date : "date",
    attachments : [],
    unread : false,
    hasAttachments : true,
    id : 1
}
```

The attachments array actually contains instances of `AjaxMailAttachmentHeader`, which provide general information about an attachment without containing the actual binary or text data:

```
class AjaxMailAttachmentHeader {
    var $id;
    var $filename;
    var $size;

    function AjaxMailAttachmentHeader($id, $filename, $size) {
        $this->id = $id;
        $this->filename = $filename;
        $this->size = "" . (round($size/1024*100)/100)." KB";
    }
}
```

The constructor for this class accepts three arguments: the attachment ID (the value of the `AttachmentId` column of the `AjaxMailAttachments` table), the file name, and the size of the attachment in bytes. The size is converted into a string (indicated by the number of kilobytes in the file) by dividing the size by 1024 and then rounding to the nearest hundredth of a kilobyte (so you can get a string such as "0.55 KB"). When JSON-encoded, the `AjaxMailAttachmentHeader` object is added to the previous JSON structure, as follows:

```
{
    "to" : "to",
    "from" : "from",
    "cc" : "cc",
    "bcc" : "bcc",
    "subject" : "subject",
    "message" : "message",
    "date" : "date",
    "attachments" :
    [
        {
            "id" : 1,
            "filename" : "filename",
            "size" : "1KB"
        }
    ],
    "unread" : false,
    "hasAttachments" : true,
    "id" : 1
}
```

The `getMessage()` method utilizes these two classes when assembling the data for transmission to the client. This method takes one argument, the message ID number that corresponds to the `MessageId` column in the `AjaxMailMessages` table:

```
class AjaxMailbox {

    //other methods

    function getMessage($messageId) {
        $conn = $this->connect();

        //get the information
        $query = "select MessageId, `To`, `From`, CC, BCC, Subject, Date, ";
        $query .= "Message, HasAttachments, Unread from AjaxMailMessages where";
        $query .= " MessageId=$messageId";
        $result = mysql_query($query, $conn);
        $row = mysql_fetch_assoc($result);

        //more code here

    }

    //other methods
}
```

This method begins by making a connection to the database using the `connect()` method. Then, a query to retrieve the various parts of the e-mail is created (stored in `$query`) and executed, with the results ending up in the `$row` object.

The next step is to create an `AjaxMailMessage` object and populate it with all the data from the database:

```
class AjaxMailbox {

    //other methods

    function getMessage($messageId) {
        $conn = $this->connect();

        //get the information
        $query = "select MessageId, `To`, `From`, CC, BCC, Subject, Date, ";
        $query .= "Message, HasAttachments, Unread from AjaxMailMessages where";
        $query .= " MessageId=$messageId";
        $result = mysql_query($query, $conn);
        $row = mysql_fetch_assoc($result);

        $message = new AjaxMailMessage();
        $message->id = $row["MessageId"];
        $message->to = $row["To"];
        $message->cc = $row["CC"];
        $message->bcc = $row["BCC"];
        $message->unread = ($row["Unread"]==1);
        $message->from = $row["From"];
        $message->subject = $row["Subject"];
        $message->date = date("M j, Y h:i A", intval($row["Date"]));
        $message->hasAttachments = ($row["HasAttachments"]==1);
        $message->unreadCount = $this->getUnreadCount($conn);
        $message->message = $row["Message"];

        //more code here
    }

    //other methods
}
```

As with `getFolderPage()`, the database fields represented as bits are compared to 1 to get a Boolean value. The date is also formatted into a longer string, one that contains both the date and time (formatted as in "Oct 28, 2005 05:17 AM"). You'll also notice that the `unreadCount` property is added to the message. Although this doesn't pertain to the message itself, it helps to keep the user interface updated with the most recent number of unread mails in the database.

The last part of this method is to return information about the attachments (if any).

```
class AjaxMailbox {

    //other methods

    function getMessage($messageId) {
```

```
        $conn = $this->connect();

        //get the information
        $query = "select MessageId, `To`, `From`, CC, BCC, Subject, Date, ";
        $query .= "Message, HasAttachments, Unread from AjaxMailMessages where";
        $query .= " MessageId=$messageId";
        $result = mysql_query($query, $conn);
        $row = mysql_fetch_assoc($result);

        $message = new AjaxMailMessage();
        $message->id = $row["MessageId"];
        $message->to = $row["To"];
        $message->cc = $row["CC"];
        $message->bcc = $row["BCC"];
        $message->unread = ($row["Unread"]==1);
        $message->from = $row["From"];
        $message->subject = $row["Subject"];
        $message->date = date("M j, Y h:i A", intval($row["Date"]));
        $message->hasAttachments = ($row["HasAttachments"]==1);
        $message->unreadCount = $this->getUnreadCount($conn);
        $message->message = $row["Message"];

        if ($message->hasAttachments) {
            $query = "select AttachmentId,Filename,Size from AjaxMailAttachments";
            $query .= " where MessageId=$messageId";

            $result = mysql_query($query, $conn);

            while ($row = mysql_fetch_assoc($result)) {
                $message->attachments[] = new AjaxMailAttachmentHeader(
                                              $row["AttachmentId"],
                                              $row["Filename"],
                                              (int) $row["Size"]);

            }
        }

        $this->disconnect($conn);
        return $message;
    }

    //other methods
}
```

In this section of code, you begin by verifying whether there are any attachments on the e-mail. If an attachment exists, a query is run to return all the attachments in the database. Note that the actual contents of the attachment aren't returned, just the attachment ID, file name, and size. Using a `while` loop to iterate over the results, a new `AjaxMailAttachmentHeader` is created for each attachment and added to the `$message` object's `attachments` array. After that, you need only disconnect from the database and return the `$message` object. Once again, it is up to the process using this method to JSON-encode the returned object.

Sending an E-mail

AjaxMail relies on the PHPMailer library (http://phpmailer.sourceforge.net) to send e-mails. This full-featured library enables you to send mail either through an SMTP server or the sendmail application (www.sendmail.org). As discussed earlier, AjaxMail uses SMTP exclusively.

The method used to send mail is called sendMail(). This method accepts four arguments, with only the first three being required. These arguments are $to (the string containing the e-mail addresses to send to), $subject (the subject of the e-mail), $message (the body of the e-mail), and $cc (which can optionally specify who to send a carbon copy to).

The first step in this method is to create an instance of the PHPMailer class and assign the To and CC fields. You can add these by using the AddAddress() and AddCC() methods of the PHPMailer object, respectively. Each of these accepts two arguments: the e-mail address and the real name of the person. This presents a problem in that the $to and $cc arguments can contain multiple e-mail addresses separated by semicolons or commas, and may consist of *name <e-mail>* pairs. For example, an e-mail sent to two recipients without carbon copying could look like this:

```
Joe Somebody <joe@somebody.com>; Jim Somebody <jim@somebody.com>
```

You must take this into account when sending mail using PHPMailer:

```php
class AjaxMailbox {

    //other methods here

    function sendMail($to, $subject, $message, $cc="") {
        $mailer = new PHPMailer();

        $tos = preg_split ("/;|,/", $to);
        foreach ($tos as $to) {
            preg_match("/(.*?)<?(.*?)>?/i", $to, $matches);

            $mailer->AddAddress($matches[2],str_replace('"','',$matches[1]));
        }

        if ($cc != "") {
            $ccs = preg_split ("/;|,/", $cc);

            foreach ($ccs as $cc) {
                preg_match("/(.*?)<?(.*?)>?/i", $cc, $matches);

                $mailer->AddCC($matches[2],str_replace('"','',$matches[1]));
            }
        }

        //more code here
    }

    //other methods here
}
```

The first line in the method creates an instance of PHPMailer. In the next line, the $to string is split by both semicolons and commas with the preg_split() function, which returns an array of e-mail addresses. Then, iterating through the $tos array, the code checks for a match to *real name <email>* with the preg_match() function. The regular expression used in the preg_match() function returns an array with three matches. The first is the entire string, the second is the real name if it exists, and the third is the e-mail address. You can then add the addresses by using AddAddress() and passing in the second and third matches. Since the real name may be enclosed in quotes, str_replace() is used to strip out any quotes that may be in the real name part of the string. This same process is repeated for the $cc string, where the AddCC() method is used.

You will always have three elements in the $matches array, even if no name is in the string.

Next, you need to assign the pertinent SMTP information to the $mailer object, along with the subject and message body. Then, you can send the e-mail:

```
class AjaxMailbox {

    //other methods here

    function sendMail($to, $subject, $message, $cc="") {
        $mailer = new PHPMailer();

        $tos = preg_split ("/;|,/", $to);
        foreach ($tos as $to) {
            preg_match("/(.*?)<?(.*?)>?/i", $to, $matches);

            $mailer->AddAddress($matches[2],str_replace('"','',$matches[1]));
        }

        if ($cc != "") {
            $ccs = preg_split ("/;|,/", $cc);

            foreach ($ccs as $cc) {
                preg_match("/(.*?)<?(.*?)>?/i", $cc, $matches);

                $mailer->AddCC($matches[2],str_replace('"','',$matches[1]));
            }
        }

        $mailer->Subject = $subject;
        $mailer->Body = $message;
        $mailer->From = EMAIL_FROM_ADDRESS;
        $mailer->FromName = EMAIL_FROM_NAME;
        $mailer->SMTPAuth = SMTP_DO_AUTHORIZATION;
        $mailer->Username = SMTP_USER;
        $mailer->Password = SMTP_PASSWORD;
        $mailer->Host = SMTP_SERVER;
        $mailer->Mailer = "smtp";

        $mailer->Send();
        $mailer->SmtpClose();

        //more code here
```

```
    }

    //other methods here
}
```

For the first two properties, `Subject` and `Body`, simply use the values that were passed into the method. You set their values equal to those passed to the method. Next, the `From` and `FromName` properties are set to the constant values from `config.inc.php`; the first represents the sender's e-mail address, and the second contains the sender's real name (which many e-mail clients simply display as the sender).

The properties following those are the SMTP authorization settings. Some SMTP servers require authentication to send e-mail messages and some don't. If `SMTPAuth` is `false`, PHPMailer attempts to send e-mails without sending the `Username` and `Password`. If `true`, the class sends those values to the server in an attempt to authorize the sending of the e-mail.

The final two properties before sending an e-mail are the SMTP server and the method of which to send. The `Host` property is assigned to `SMTP_SERVER` and the `Mailer` property is set to `"smtp"`, indicating the type of mailer being used (as opposed to "sendmail").

After setting those properties, you can invoke the `Send()` method to actually send the e-mail and then call `SmtpClose()` to close the SMTP connection. But the method isn't quite done yet. The client still needs to know if the e-mail message was sent successfully. To do that, you'll need to create a response object containing information about the transmission:

```
class AjaxMailbox {

    //other methods here

    function sendMail($to, $subject, $message, $cc="") {
        $mailer = new PHPMailer();

        $tos = preg_split ("/;|,/", $to);
        foreach ($tos as $to) {
            preg_match("/(.*?)<?(.*?)>?/i", $to, $matches);

            $mailer->AddAddress($matches[2],str_replace('"','',$matches[1]));
        }

        if ($cc != "") {
            $ccs = preg_split ("/;|,/", $cc);

            foreach ($ccs as $cc) {
                preg_match("/(.*?)<?(.*?)>?/i", $cc, $matches);

                $mailer->AddCC($matches[2],str_replace('"','',$matches[1]));
            }
        }

        $mailer->Subject = $subject;
        $mailer->Body = $message;
        $mailer->From = EMAIL_FROM_ADDRESS;
        $mailer->FromName = EMAIL_FROM_NAME;
```

```
            $mailer->SMTPAuth = SMTP_DO_AUTHORIZATION;
            $mailer->Username = SMTP_USER;
            $mailer->Password = SMTP_PASSWORD;
            $mailer->Host = SMTP_SERVER;
            $mailer->Mailer = "smtp";

            $mailer->Send();
            $mailer->SmtpClose();

            $response = new JSONObject();

            if ($mailer->IsError()) {
                $response->error = true;
                $response->message = $mailer->ErrorInfo;
            } else {
                $response->error = false;
                $response->message = "Your message has been sent.";
            }

            return $response;
        }

        //other methods here
    }
```

A `JSONObject` is instantiated to carry the information back to the client. PHPMailer provides a method called `IsError()`, which returns a Boolean value indicating the success or failure of the sending process. If it returns `true`, that means the e-mail was not sent successfully, so the `$response` object has its `error` property set to `true` and the error message is extracted from the `ErrorInfo` property of `$mailer`. Otherwise, the `error` property is set to `false` and a simple confirmation message is sent. The last step is to return the `$response` object.

Getting Attachment Data

When attachments are stored in the database, you need a way to get them back out. The `getAttachment()` method provides all the information necessary to enable a user to download an attachment. This method takes one argument, the attachment ID, and returns an `AjaxMailAttachment` object. The `AjaxMailAttachment` class is another helper that encapsulates all the information about an attachment:

```
class AjaxMailAttachment {
    var $contentType;
    var $filename;
    var $size;
    var $data;

    function AjaxMailAttachment($contentType, $filename, $size, $data) {
        $this->contentType = $contentType;
        $this->filename = $filename;
        $this->size = $size;
        $this->data = $data;
    }
}
```

The `getAttachment()` method itself is fairly straightforward:

```
class AjaxMailbox {

    //other methods here

    function getAttachment($attachmentId) {
        $conn = $this->connect();

        $query = "select * from AjaxMailAttachments where ";
        $query .= " AttachmentId=$attachmentId";
        $result = mysql_query($query, $conn);
        $row = mysql_fetch_assoc($result);

        $this->disconnect($conn);

        return new AjaxMailAttachment(
            $row["ContentType"],
            $row["Filename"],
            $row["Size"],
            $row["Data"]
        );
    }

    //other methods here
}
```

This code connects to the database with the `connect()` method and performs the database query. This particular query selects all fields from `AjaxMailAttachments` where `AttachmentId` is equal to the method's argument. After running the query, the database connection is closed and an `AjaxMailAttachment` object is returned containing all the information about the attachment.

Handling the Trash

Four methods in the `AjaxMailbox` class deal with moving messages to and from the Trash. The first method, `deleteMessage()`, doesn't actually delete the e-mail message; instead, it updates the `FolderId` column in the database to have a value of 2, meaning that the message now resides in the Trash. This method accepts one argument, the identification number of the message:

```
class AjaxMailbox {

    //other methods here

    function deleteMessage($messageId) {
        $conn = $this->connect();

        $query = "update AjaxMailMessages set FolderId=2 where ";
        $query .= " MessageId=$messageId";
        mysql_query($query,$conn);

        $this->disconnect($conn);
    }

    //other methods here
}
```

This method simply connects to the database, runs the SQL statement to change the `FolderId`, and then disconnects from the database. Of course, you can also restore a message from the Trash once it has been moved there. To do so, simply set the `FolderId` back to 1; this is the job of the `restoreMessage()` method.

The `restoreMessage()` method also accepts one argument, the message ID, and follows the same basic algorithm:

```
class AjaxMailbox {

    //other methods here

    function restoreMessage($messageId) {
        $conn = $this->connect();

        $query = "update AjaxMailMessages set FolderId=1 where ";
        $query .= " MessageId=$messageId";
        mysql_query($query,$conn);

        $this->disconnect($conn);
    }

    //other methods here
}
```

This method mirrors `deleteMethod()`, with the only difference being the value of `FolderId` to be set.

From time to time, there will be a lot of e-mail messages in the Trash. There may come a time when the user decides that he or she no longer needs them and the Trash should be emptied. The `emptyTrash()` method deletes every message with a `FolderId` value of 2 as well as any attachments those messages may have had.

The `emptyTrash()` method relies on two queries to delete the message and attachment information in the database. The first query deletes the attachments of messages in the Trash, and the second query deletes the messages themselves:

```
class AjaxMailbox {

    //other methods here

    function emptyTrash() {
        $conn = $this->connect();

        $query = "delete from AjaxMailAttachments where MessageId in ";
        $query .= " (select MessageId from AjaxMailMessages where FolderId=2)";

        mysql_query($query, $conn);

        $query = "delete from AjaxMailMessages where FolderId=2";
        mysql_query($query,$conn);

        $this->disconnect($conn);
    }

    //other methods here
}
```

The first query uses a feature called sub-querying to select MessageIds of messages that are in the Trash. Sub-queries are a feature in MySQL 4 and above (if you use MySQL 3.x, you need to upgrade before using this code). The second query is very straightforward, simply deleting all messages with a FolderId of 2. The last step, of course, is to disconnect from the database.

Marking Messages as Read

Nearly every e-mail client marks messages as unread when they first arrive. This feature enables users to keep track of the messages they previously read and easily tell which messages are new. The methods responsible for this feature in AjaxMail resemble those of deleting and restoring messages because they simply accept a message ID as an argument and then update a single column in the database.

The first method, markMessageAsRead(), marks the message as read after the user opens it:

```
class AjaxMailbox {

    //other methods here

    function markMessageAsRead($messageId) {
        $conn = $this->connect();

        $query = "update AjaxMailMessages set Unread=0 where MessageId=$messageId";
        mysql_query($query,$conn);

        $this->disconnect($conn);
    }

    //other methods here
}
```

This code runs an UPDATE statement that sets the message's Unread column to 0, specifying the message as read.

Similarly, the method to mark a message as unread performs almost the exact same query:

```
class AjaxMailbox {

    //other methods here

    function markMessageAsUnread($messageId) {
        $conn = $this->connect();

        $query = "update AjaxMailMessages set Unread=1 where MessageId=$messageId";
        mysql_query($query,$conn);

        $this->disconnect($conn);
    }

    //other methods here
}
```

The only difference between the markMessageAsUnread() method and the markMessageAsRead() method is the value the Unread column is assigned when you run the query.

Performing Actions

AjaxMail, like many other PHP applications, relies on an action-based architecture to perform certain operations. In other words, the application queries a separate PHP file that handles certain actions and executes code according to the action. There are several files that perform action requests from the client in different ways.

AjaxMailAction.php

The `AjaxMailAction.php.` file is one of the files used by the client to perform various actions. Your first step in writing this file is to include all the required files. Because this file uses the `AjaxMailbox` class, you need to include quite a few files, including the `config.inc.php` file, the four files in POP3Lib, `AjaxMail.inc.php`, and `JSON.php` for JSON encoding:

```php
require_once("inc/config.inc.php");
require_once("inc/pop3lib/pop3.class.php");
require_once("inc/pop3lib/pop3message.class.php");
require_once("inc/pop3lib/pop3header.class.php");
require_once("inc/pop3lib/pop3attachment.class.php");
require_once("inc/AjaxMail.inc.php");
require_once("inc/JSON.php");
```

You also need to set several headers:

```php
header("Content-Type: text/plain");
header("Cache-Control: No-Cache");
header("Pragma: No-Cache");
```

The first header sets the `Content-Type` to `text/plain`, a requirement because this page returns a JSON-encoded string as opposed to HTML or XML. Because this file will be used repeatedly, you must include the `No-Cache` headers described in Chapter 3 to avoid incorrect data.

When using `AjaxMailAction.php`, at least three pieces of information are sent: the action to perform, the current folder ID, and the page number. An optional fourth piece of information, a message ID, can be sent as well. So, the query string for this file may look something like this:

```
AjaxMailAction.php?action=myAction&page=1&folder=1&id=123
```

Because the message ID is used only in certain circumstances, you don't have to retrieve it until needed. In the meantime, you can retrieve the three other arguments as follows:

```php
$folder = $_GET["folder"];
$page = (int) $_GET["page"];
$action = $_GET["action"];
```

This code retrieves the values of the variables in the query string. The page number is cast to an integer value for compatibility with methods in `AjaxMailbox`. Next, create an instance of `AjaxMailbox` and `JSON`, as well as a variable named `$output`, which will be filled with a JSON string:

```
$mailbox = new AjaxMailbox();

$oJSON = new JSON();

$output = "";
```

The next step is to perform the desired action. Using a `switch` statement on the `$action` enables you to easily determine what should be done. There are two actions that need the message ID argument, `delete` and `restore`:

```
switch($action) {
    case "delete":
        $mailbox->deleteMessage($_GET["id"]);
        break;
    case "restore":
        $mailbox->restoreMessage($_GET["id"]);
        break;
    case "empty":
        $mailbox->emptyTrash();
        break;
    case "getfolder":
        //no extra processing needed
        break;
}
```

This code performs a specific operation based on the `$action` string. In the case of `delete`, the `deleteMessage()` method is called and the message ID parameter is passed in. For `restore`, the `restoreMessage()` method is called with the message ID. If `empty` is the action, the `emptyTrash()` method is called. Otherwise, if the action is `getfolder`, no additional operation is required. This is because `AjaxMailAction.php` always returns JSON-encoded folder information regardless of the action that is performed:

```
$info = $mailbox->getFolderPage($folder, $page);
$output = $oJSON->encode($info);
echo $output;
```

Here, the `getFolderPage()` method is used to retrieve a list of e-mails to return to the client. Remember, `getFolderPage()` checks for new messages before returning a list, so you will have the most recent information. The result of `getFolderPage()` is encoded using `$oJSON->encode()` and then output to the client using the `echo` operator.

AjaxMailNavigate.php

AjaxMail uses both XMLHttp and a hidden iframe to make requests back to the server. The `AjaxMailNavigate.php` file is used inside the hidden iframe and, as such, must contain valid HTML and JavaScript code. This file expects the same query string as `AjaxMailAction.php` because it uses the same information.

The first part of this file is the PHP code that performs the requested action:

```php
<?php
    require_once("inc/config.inc.php");
    require_once("inc/pop3lib/pop3.class.php");
    require_once("inc/pop3lib/pop3message.class.php");
    require_once("inc/pop3lib/pop3header.class.php");
    require_once("inc/pop3lib/pop3attachment.class.php");
    require_once("inc/AjaxMail.inc.php");
    require_once("inc/JSON.php");

    header("Cache-control: No-Cache");
    header("Pragma: No-Cache");

    $folder = $_GET["folder"];
    $page = (int) $_GET["page"];
    $id = "";
    if (isset($_GET["id"])) {
        $id = (int) $_GET["id"];
    }
    $action = $_GET["action"];

    $mailbox = new AjaxMailbox();
    $oJSON = new JSON();

    $output = "";

    switch($action) {
        case "getfolder":
            $info = $mailbox->getFolderPage($folder, $page);
            $output = $oJSON->encode($info);
            break;
        case "getmessage":
            $message = $mailbox->getMessage($id);
            if ($message->unread) {
                $mailbox->markMessageAsRead($id);
            }
            $output = $oJSON->encode($message);
            break;
        default:
            $output = "null";
    }
?>
```

This file requires the same include files as `AjaxMailAction.php`, although it needs only the no cache headers because the content being returned is HTML (not `plain/text`). Next, the information is pulled out of the query string and stored in variables. New instances of `AjaxMailbox` and `JSON` are created in anticipation of performing an action.

As with `AjaxMailAction.php`, the `$action` variable is placed into a `switch` statement to determine what to do. The `getfolder` action calls `getFolderPage()` to retrieve the information for the given page in the given folder. The result is JSON-encoded and stored in the `$output` variable.

If the action is `getmessage`, the `getMessage()` method is called. If the message hasn't been read, it is marked as read. The message is then JSON-encoded and assigned to the `$output` variable. If the `$action` is something else, `$output` is assigned a value of `null`.

The next part of the page is the HTML content:

```
<!DOCTYPE html PUBLIC "-//W3C//DTD XHTML 1.0 Transitional//EN"
    "http://www.w3.org/TR/xhtml1/DTD/xhtml1-transitional.dtd">
<html xmlns="http://www.w3.org/1999/xhtml" xml:lang="en" lang="en">
    <head>
        <title>Ajax Mail Navigate</title>
    </head>
    <body>
        <script language="JavaScript" type="text/javascript">
        //<![CDATA[

            window.onload = function () {
                var oInfo = <?php echo $output ?>;
<?php
    switch($action) {
        case "getfolder":
            echo "parent.oMailbox.displayFolder(oInfo);";
            break;
        case "getmessage":
            echo "parent.oMailbox.displayMessage(oInfo);";
            break;
        case "compose":
            echo "parent.oMailbox.displayCompose();";
            break;
        case "reply":
            echo "parent.oMailbox.displayReply();";
            break;
        case "replyall":
            echo "parent.oMailbox.displayReplyAll();";
            break;
        case "forward":
            echo "parent.oMailbox.displayForward();";
            break;
    }
?>
            };

        //]]>
        </script>
    </body>
</html>
```

In this part of the page, the `$output` variable is output to the page into the JavaScript variable `oInfo`. Because `$output` is either `null` or a JSON-encoded string, it is valid JavaScript. The variable is assigned in the `window.onload` event handler. Then, based on the `$action`, a different JavaScript method is output to the page and called.

AjaxMailSend.php

To handle the sending of e-mail from the client, the AjaxMailSend.php file is used. Its sole purpose is to gather the information from the server and then send the e-mail. It needs to include config.inc.php, JSON.php, and AjaxMail.inc.php, as with the other files. However, it doesn't need to include the POP3Lib files because there will be no interaction with the POP3 server. Instead, the PHPMailer files class.phpmailer.php and class.smtp.php must be included:

```php
<?php
    require_once("inc/config.inc.php");
    require_once("inc/phpmailer/class.phpmailer.php");
    require_once("inc/phpmailer/class.smtp.php");
    require_once("inc/JSON.php");
    require_once("inc/AjaxMail.inc.php");

    header("Content-Type: text/plain");
    header("Cache-control: No-Cache");
    header("Pragma: No-Cache");

    $to = $_POST["txtTo"];
    $cc = $_POST["txtCC"];
    $subject = $_POST["txtSubject"];
    $message = $_POST["txtMessage"];

    $mailbox = new AjaxMailbox();

    $oJSON = new JSON();

    $response = $mailbox->sendMail($to, $subject, $message, $cc);
    $output = $oJSON->encode($response);
    echo $output;
?>
```

You'll note that the same headers are set for this page as they are for AjaxMailAction.php because it will also return a JSON-encoded string. The next section gathers the information from the submitted form. Then, new instances of AjaxMailbox and JSON are created. The information from the form is passed into the sendMail() method, and the response is JSON-encoded and then output using echo.

AjaxMailAttachment.php

The last file, AjaxMailAttachment.php, facilitates the downloading of a specific attachment. This file accepts a single query string parameter: the ID of the attachment to download. To do this, you need to once again include all the POP3Lib files, config.inc.php, and AjaxMail.inc.php:

```php
<?php
    require_once("inc/config.inc.php");
    require_once("inc/pop3lib/pop3.class.php");
    require_once("inc/pop3lib/pop3message.class.php");
    require_once("inc/pop3lib/pop3header.class.php");
    require_once("inc/pop3lib/pop3attachment.class.php");
    require_once("inc/AjaxMail.inc.php");

    $id = $_GET["id"];
```

```
    $mailbox = new AjaxMailbox();
    $attachment = $mailbox->getAttachment($id);

    header("Content-Type: $attachment->contentType");
    header("Content-Disposition: attachment; filename=$attachment->filename");

    echo $attachment->data;
?>
```

After including the required files, the attachment ID is retrieved and stored in $id. A new AjaxMailbox object is created and getAttachment() is called to retrieve the specific attachment information. Next, the content-type header is set to the content-type of the attachment (retrieved from $attachment->contentType) and the content-disposition header is set to attachment, passing in the file name of the attachment. This second header does two things. First, it forces the browser to show a dialog box asking if you want to open the file or save it; second, it suggests the file name to use when downloading the file. The last part of the file outputs the attachment data to the page, effectively mimicking a direct file download.

The User Interface

The key to any successful (and useful) web application is the design of the user interface. Because AjaxMail is meant to demonstrate the use of Ajax techniques, the user interface is quite simple and bare-bones. There are three different views of the user interface:

❑   **Folder view:** Displays a folder of messages (either Inbox or Trash).

❑   **Read view:** Displays a received message.

❑   **Compose view:** Displays a form so that you can send e-mails.

All the views are designed to be very simple, and all are loaded when the main page, index.php, is initially loaded.

The basic layout of index.php is as follows:

```
<!DOCTYPE html PUBLIC "-//W3C//DTD XHTML 1.0 Transitional//EN"
    "http://www.w3.org/TR/xhtml1/DTD/xhtml1-transitional.dtd">
<html xmlns="http://www.w3.org/1999/xhtml" xml:lang="en" lang="en">
    <head>
        <title>Ajax Mail</title>
        <link rel="stylesheet" type="text/css" href="styles/AjaxMail.css" />
        <script type="text/javascript" src="scripts/zxml.js"></script>
        <script type="text/javascript" src="scripts/json.js"></script>
        <script type="text/javascript" src="scripts/AjaxMail.js"></script>
    </head>
    <body>
        <ul id="ulMainMenu">
            <li id="liCompose">
                <span class="link" id="spnCompose">Compose Mail</span></li>
            <li><span class="link" id="spnInbox">Inbox
```

```
                <span id="spnUnreadMail"></span></span></li>
          <li><span class="link" id="spnTrash">Trash</span>
              (<span class="link" id="spnEmpty">Empty</span>)</li>
      </ul>
      <div id="divNotice"></div>
      <div id="divFolder">
          <!-- folder view -->
      </div>
      <div id="divReadMail" style="display: none">
          <!-- read mail view -->
      </div>

      <div id="divComposeMail" style="display: none">
          <!-- compose mail view -->
      </div>
      <iframe id="iLoader" src="about:blank"></iframe>
   </body>
</html>
```

The page requires a style sheet, `AjaxMail.css`, along with three JavaScript files, the zXml library file (`zxml.js`), the JSON library (`json.js`), and the JavaScript file containing all the AjaxMail functionality (`AjaxMail.js`). Within the body is an unordered list containing three links, one each for Compose Mail, the Inbox, and the Trash. The Trash link also has a link for Empty next to it, which can be used to purge any messages in the Trash. Because each of these links is to call a JavaScript function, there is no need to use a regular `<a/>` tag. Instead, each link is implemented as a `<span/>` with a CSS class of `link`, which formats the text to look like a regular link. The first link, Compose Mail, is made bold to call it out from the others. The complete CSS for the main menu (contained in `AjaxMail.css`) is as follows:

```css
span.link {
    text-decoration: underline;
    color: blue;
    cursor: pointer;
    cursor: hand;
}

#ulMainMenu {
    position: absolute;
    left: 0px;
    top: 0px;
    margin: 0px;
    padding: 10px;
}

#ulMainMenu li {
    display: block;
    padding: 2px 0px 2px 0px;
    margin: 0px;
    font-size: 80%;
}

#ulMainMenu #liCompose {
    font-weight: bold;
    padding: 2px 0px 8px 0px;
}
```

Next in the index.php page is a <div/> element called divNotice. This element is used to display notifications to the user, which is critical in an Ajax application. Because the page itself doesn't reload or change to another page, there is no indication if a particular operation was successful. This area is used to relay such information.

AjaxMail needs two different types of notifications: one for general information and one for error information. General information includes such things as notifying the user when an e-mail is sent or deleted; error information is important when one of these actions is supposed to occur but doesn't. A general information notification appears as a yellow box with a small "i" icon to the left, whereas an error notification appears as a red box with an exclamation point icon to the left (see Figure 9-1).

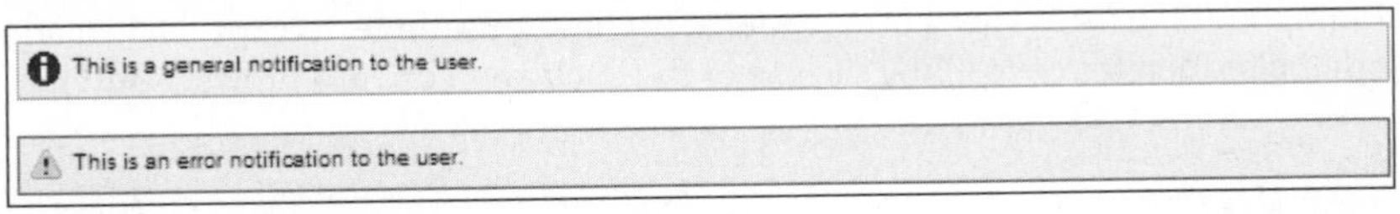

Figure 9-1

The divNotice element is dynamically assigned text as well as an appropriate CSS class, info or error, to create the desired appearance. The styles are defined as follows:

```css
#divNotice {
    -moz-box-sizing: border-box;
    box-sizing: border-box;
    padding: 4px;
    background-repeat: no-repeat;
    background-position: 4px 4px;
    padding-left: 24px;
    font-size: 60%;
    font-family: Arial,Helvetica,Sans-Serif;
    visibility: hidden;
    height: 16px;
    position: absolute;
    top: 5px;
    left: 150px;
    width: 600px;
}

div.info {
    background-color: #F7FFCD;
    background-image: url(../images/icon_info.gif);
    border: 1px solid #A5A54A;
}

div.error {
    background-color: #FFE6E6;
    background-image: url(../images/icon_alert.gif);
    border: 1px solid red;
}
```

By using the background-image property to assign the appropriate icon, you are able to completely control the appearance of the notification area by using styles instead of worrying about changing an

`<img/>` element when the style is changed. The `background-position` property states where the image should appear and setting the `background-repeat` property to `no-repeat` ensures that only one copy of the image will be visible.

After the notification element comes a `<div/>` for each of the three AjaxMail views. The `<div/>` element for the folder view, `divFolder`, is first in the page and is always visible by default. The other two `<div/>` elements, `divReadMail` and `divComposeMail`, each have their display property set to `none` so that they are not visible when the page is first loaded. The contents of each `<div/>` element will be discussed later.

The last part of the page is an `<iframe/>` called `iLoader`. This hidden frame is used to navigate back and forth throughout the three views of AjaxMail. Anytime a user interface switch is made, the request goes through the hidden frame to allow the use of the Back and Forward browser buttons.

The Folder View

The folder view is the first thing the user sees after the application is loaded. It consists of the title of the folder (either Inbox or Trash), a pagination control that displays which messages are being displayed and the total number of messages, and a list of e-mail messages (see Figure 9-2). Taking a cue from Gmail, AjaxMail doesn't use table headers for the list of messages because people are accustomed to seeing e-mail listed by the person who sent it, subject, and date.

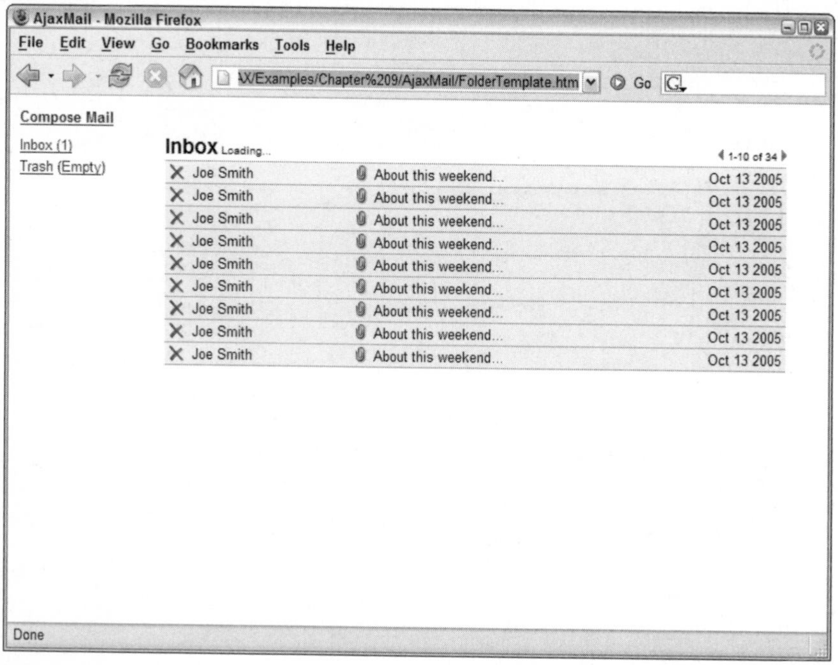

Figure 9-2

You may notice that the traditional check box next to each e-mail is missing. That's because there is only one thing you can do with an e-mail in AjaxMail: delete it. Instead of a check box, there is a red X next to each e-mail that can be clicked to delete it (move it to the Trash). When you switch to the Trash folder, the icons change to a green arrow that, when clicked, moves the e-mail back into the Inbox (see Figure 9-3).

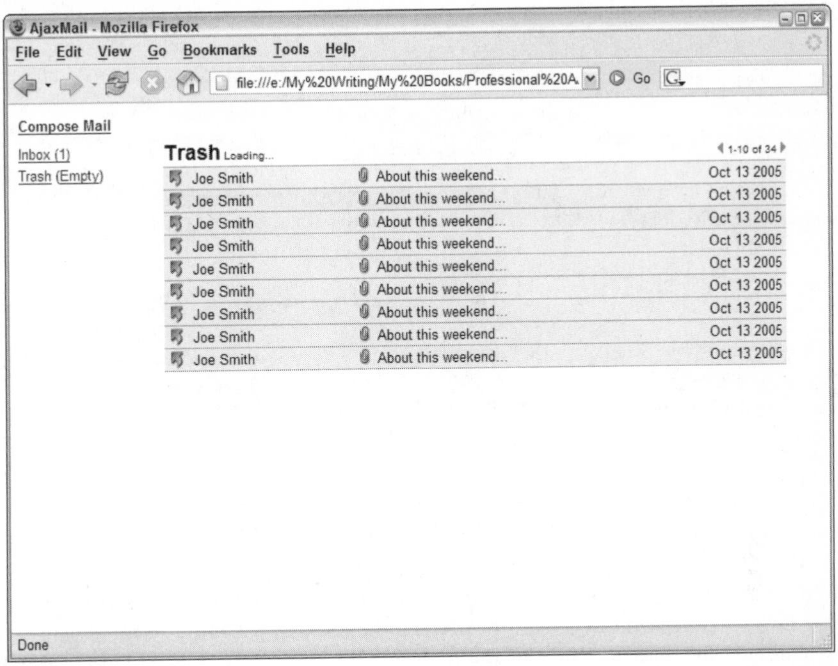

Figure 9-3

Aside from this difference, the folder view is the same regardless of which folder is displayed. Additionally, each e-mail has an optional attachment indicator that appears next to the subject if the e-mail contains an attachment. This icon is displayed only when an attachment is detected on the e-mail; otherwise, it is hidden.

There's also a small "loading" message next to the name of the folder. This is used to indicate when there is an open request to the server and disappears when the request is complete. While a request is processing, no other actions can be taken to prevent overriding of requests.

The HTML for the folder view is fairly simple because a large amount of the display is created by JavaScript depending on data received from the server:

```
<div id="divFolder">
    <div id="divFolderHeader" class="header">
        <h1 id="hFolderTitle">Inbox</h1>
        <div id="divFolderStatus" class="status">Loading...</div>
        <div id="divItemCount">
            <img src="images/btn_prev.gif" alt="Previous Page"
                title="Previous Page" id="imgPrev" />
            <span id="spnItems"></span>
```

```
                    <img src="images/btn_next.gif" alt="Next Page"
                        title="Next Page" id="imgNext" />
            </div>
        </div>
        <table border="0" cellpadding="0" cellspacing="0" id="tblMain">
            <thead>
                <tr id="trTemplate">
                    <td><img src="images/icon_delete.gif" /></td>
                    <td class="from"></td>
                    <td class="attachment">
                        <img src="images/icon_attachment.gif" title="Attachment"
/></td>
                    <td class="subject"></td>
                    <td class="date" nowrap="nowrap"></td>
                </tr>
                <tr id="trNoMessages">
                    <td colspan="5">There are no messages in this folder.</td>
                </tr>
            </thead>
            <tbody>
                <tr style="visibility: hidden">
                    <td colspan="5"></td>
                </tr>
            </tbody>
        </table>
    </div>
</div>
```

The first thing to notice about this code is that nearly every element has an `id` attribute assigned. Any element that must be accessed via JavaScript needs to have an `id` attribute so that it can be accessed using the `document.getElementById()` method directly. For example, `hFolderTitle` contains the name of the folder, which is assigned by JavaScript after the folder data is retrieved. Because this will happen frequently, the JavaScript needs a reference to this element. Likewise, the `divFolderStatus` element that contains the loading message needs an `id` attribute so that it can be shown and hidden when appropriate. The `spnItems` element will be filled in with information about which messages are being displayed. The trickiest part of the HTML is the table to display the messages.

Within the table is a `<thead/>` element that contains two rows: one called `trTemplate` and one called `trNoMessages`. These rows are used as templates by JavaScript to create rows on-the-fly. Since rows with these formats will be needed frequently, it is faster and more effective to create the HTML and hide it from the user then to duplicate it and fill in the necessary information. You'll see how this is done later in the chapter. For now, just know that neither of these rows is directly visible by the user.

The `<tbody/>` element contains a single hidden row. This is done to set the initial browser measurements for the table. Without this, each table row would be displayed incorrectly initially because the browser had no standards from which to base its measurements. Providing this hidden row gives the browser enough information to make sure that any further rows are displayed properly.

Read View

The read view is quite simply designed to display an e-mail message so that the user can read it (see Figure 9-4). It consists of a subject line followed by spaces for the sender's e-mail address, the recipient's e-mail address, and the message date. There are also additional spaces for displaying both CC and BCC information if necessary.

Figure 9-4

Under the message header information are links for Reply, Reply All, Forward, and View Attachments. The last link appears only if there are attachments on the message. Each of the first three links switches you to the compose view with some pre-filled information allowing you to easily send an e-mail.

Below the links is the message body. Because AjaxMail supports only plain-text messages, it's easy to format the text using CSS. If there are any attachments, they are listed below the main message text. You can click the name of an attachment to download it.

The read view HTML is also very simple for the same reason, because most of the information is added later on by JavaScript.

```
<div id="divReadMail" style="display: none">
    <div class="header">
        <h1 id="hSubject"></h1>
    </div>
     <div class="message-headers">
        <div id="divMessageFrom"></div>
        <div id="divMessageDate"></div>
```

```
        </div>
        <div id="divMessageTo"></div>
        <div id="divMessageCC"></div>
        <div id="divMessageBCC"></div>
        <ul class="message-actions">
            <li><span class="link" id="spnReply">Reply</span></li>
            <li><span class="link" id="spnReplyAll">Reply All</span></li>
            <li><span class="link" id="spnForward">Forward</span></li>
            <li id="liAttachments"><a href="#attachments">View Attachments</a></li>
        </ul>
        <div id="divMessageBody"></div>
        <a name="attachments" id="aAttachments">Attachments</a>
        <div id="divMessageAttachments">
            <ul id="ulAttachments">
            </ul>
        </div>
    </div>
</div>
```

As with the folder view, nearly every element for the read view has an id attribute. The hSubject element is used to display the subject of the message, whereas the divMessageBody element is used to display the message text. The divMessageFrom, divMessageDate, divMessageTo, divMessageCC, and divMessageBCC elements are used to display each type of header information for the message. Immediately following those elements are the message actions, Reply, Reply All, Forward, and View Attachments. Note that only the View Attachments link uses an <a/> element. This is to take advantage of HTML anchors to move the screen's view down the page to the attachments list. All the other links are implemented using <span/> elements with the link CSS class. The attachments are listed in the ulAttachments element. If there are no attachments, the entire divMessageAttachments element is hidden.

Compose View

The compose view does a lot of work in the user interface for AjaxMail. It is used not only to create new e-mail messages, but also for replying to and forwarding e-mails. To keep things simple for this book, the compose view supports only the To and CC fields (no BCC) and does not enable you to send attachments.

This view consists of a text box for the To, CC, and subject fields, and the message of the e-mail (see Figure 9-5). There are also two links, Send and Cancel. Send begins the process of sending the e-mail, and Cancel places the user back into the previous view (either folder view or read view).

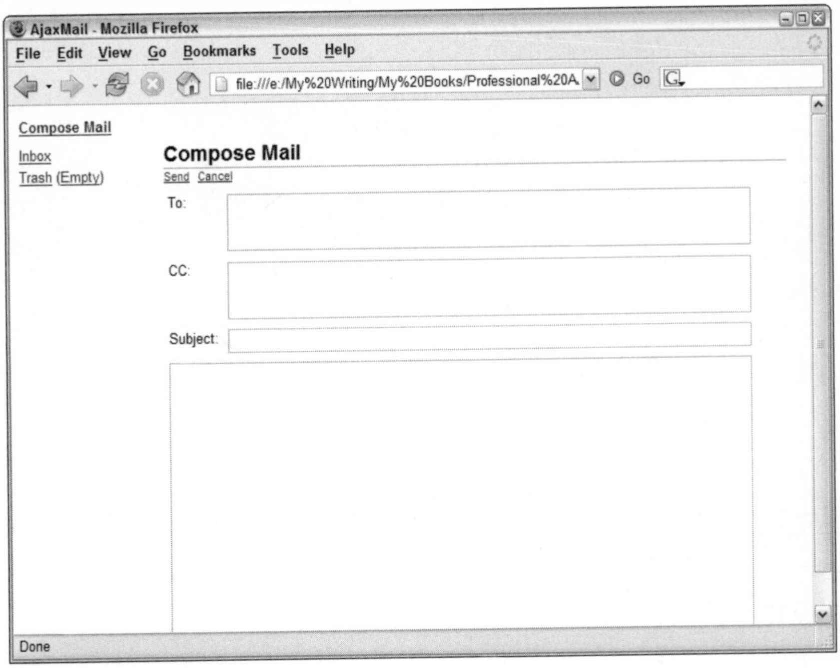

Figure 9-5

The HTML for this view consists mostly of a form with text fields:

```html
<div id="divComposeMail" style="display: none">
    <div class="header">
        <h1 id="hComposeHeader">Compose Mail</h1>
    </div>
    <div id="divComposeMailForm">
        <ul id="ulComposeActions" class="message-actions">
            <li><span class="link" id="spnSend">Send</span></li>
            <li><span class="link" id="spnCancel">Cancel</span></li>
        </ul>
    <div id="divComposeBody">
        <form method="post" name="frmSendMail">
            <table border="0" cellpadding="0" cellspacing="0">
                <tr>
                    <td class="field-label-container">
                        <label for="txtTo" class="field-label">To:</label></td>
                    <td class="field-container">
                        <textarea rows="2" cols="30" id="txtTo" name="txtTo"
                                  class="form-field"></textarea></td>
                </tr>
                <tr>
                    <td class="field-label-container">
                        <label for="txtCC" class="field-label">CC:</label></td>
                    <td class="field-container">
                        <textarea rows="2" cols="30" id="txtCC" name="txtCC"
```

```
                                    class="form-field"></textarea></td>
                </tr>
                <tr>
                    <td class="field-label-container">
                        <label for="txtSubject"
                                class="field-label">Subject:</label></td>
                    <td class="field-container">
                        <input type="text" id="txtSubject" name="txtSubject"
                                class="form-field" /></td>
                </tr>
                <tr>
                    <td class="message-container" colspan="2">
                        <textarea id="txtMessage" name="txtMessage" rows="15"
                                cols="30" class="form-field"></textarea></td>
                </tr>
            </table>
        </form>
    </div>
    </div>
    <div id="divComposeMailStatus" style="display: none">
        <h2>Sending...</h2>
        <img src="images/sendmail.gif" />
    </div>
</div>
```

There are two main parts of this view: divComposeBody, which contains the form, and divComposeMailStatus, which displays a notification that a message is being sent. When Send is clicked, divComposeMailStatus is shown with the Sending . . . message as well as an animated image to indicate that the message is in the process of being sent. If an error occurs during the process, an alert will be displayed to the user and the form will once again be made visible. If, on the other hand, the message goes through without any problems, the user is returned to the previous view (as if he or she clicked Cancel) and a notification is displayed stating that the message was sent successfully.

Layout

To ensure the user interface has a consistent feel, each view must be laid out so that one can easily slide into the place of the others when necessary. To accomplish this, each view is positioned absolutely in the same location:

```
#divFolder,
#divReadMail,
#divComposeMail {
    position: absolute;
    top: 35px;
    left: 150px;
    width: 600px;
    -moz-box-sizing: border-box;
    box-sizing: border-box;
}
```

The last two CSS properties, `-moz-box-sizing` and `box-sizing`, are used to ensure that the measurements are the same across all browsers. By default, Internet Explorer renders everything using the border box calculations, whereas others don't. These two lines (the first for Mozilla, the second for others) ensure that the size remains consistent regardless of the browser. The rest of the style information places each view in the same location on the screen and makes each view have the same width (although the height is allowed to grow and shrink, as necessary).

Next, the iframe must be hidden so that it doesn't disrupt the page flow. Because the iframe's `id` attribute is set, you can refer to it directly:

```css
#iLoader {
    display: none;
}
```

Also remember that the `<thead/>` element needs to be hidden so that it won't display the template rows in the folder view:

```css
thead {
    display: none;
}
```

Tying It All Together

Now that you know all about the architecture, database, user interface, and server-side components, it's time to glue it all together using JavaScript. To begin, you need to define some constants. The first constants are simply locations of various resources that need to be used by AjaxMail:

```javascript
var sAjaxMailURL = "AjaxMailAction.php";
var sAjaxMailNavigateURL = "AjaxMailNavigate.php";
var sAjaxMailAttachmentURL = "AjaxMailAttachment.php";
var sAjaxMailSendURL = "AjaxMailSend.php";

var sImagesDir = "images/";
var sRestoreIcon = sImagesDir + "icon_restore.gif";
var sDeleteIcon = sImagesDir + "icon_delete.gif";
var sInfoIcon = sImagesDir + "icon_info.gif";
var sErrorIcon = sImagesDir + "icon_alert.gif";
var aPreloadImages = [sRestoreIcon, sDeleteIcon, sInfoIcon, sErrorIcon];
```

The first parts of this code simply define the URLs used to make requests back to the server. These will be used later to integrate the Ajax interface. The second part of this code identifies images that are necessary for the user interface and then places them into an array called `aPreloadImages`. These images are preloaded so that the user interface responds quickly:

```javascript
for (var i=0; i < aPreloadImages.length; i++) {
    var oImg = new Image();
    oImg.src = aPreloadImages[i];
}
```

This code uses an `Image` object, which is essentially an invisible `<img/>` element. Because not all of these images are necessary when the application is first loaded, most won't be loaded until used for the first time. This could result in a delay that may be confusing to users. Preloading the images prevents this issue from occurring.

Next, there are some messages and strings that need to be displayed to the user. It helps to define these early in the code so that it's easy to change the messages in the future, if necessary:

```
var sEmptyTrashConfirm =
           "You are about to permanently delete everything in the Trash. Continue?";
var sEmptyTrashNotice = "The Trash has been emptied.";
var sDeleteMailNotice = "The message has been moved to the Trash.";
var sRestoreMailNotice = "The message has been moved to your Inbox.";
var sRestore = "Restore";
var sDelete = "Move to the Trash";
var sTo = "To ";
var sCC = "CC ";
var sBCC = "BCC ";
var sFrom = "From ";
```

When one of the notices is displayed, you really want to show it only for a short amount of time so that it doesn't become distracting to the user or blend in with the rest of the screen. The variable `iShowNoticeTime` indicates the duration (in number of milliseconds) for a notice to appear on the screen. By default, this is 5 seconds (5000 milliseconds):

```
var iShowNoticeTime = 5000;
```

The last bit of code to be defined ahead of time is a couple of constants and an array:

```
var INBOX = 1;
var TRASH = 2;
var aFolders = ["","Inbox", "Trash"];
```

In this code, the first two variables are constants defining the numeric identifiers for the Inbox and Trash folders. These coincide with the values they have in the database. The array of strings contains the names for each of the folders so these don't have to be returned from the database all the time. The first string in the array is empty since it will never be used. (There is no folder with a numeric ID of zero.)

> In an actual implementation, you may choose to have these variables generated by some server-side process that reads the values out of the database and outputs appropriate JavaScript code. For simplicity in this example, these values are defined right in the JavaScript file.

Helper Functions

Before diving into the main part of the code, there are some helper functions that are necessary. *Helper functions* are functions that aren't necessarily specific to a particular application but perform some process that is necessary. AjaxMail has a handful of helper functions.

The first helper function is one that you have seen before. The `getRequestBody()` function was introduced in Chapter 2 to serialize the data in an HTML form so that it can be passed into an XMLHttp request. This function is necessary once again for AjaxMail. To refresh your memory, here's what the function looks like:

```
function getRequestBody(oForm) {
    var aParams = new Array();

    for (var i=0 ; i < oForm.elements.length; i++) {
        var sParam = encodeURIComponent(oForm.elements[i].name);
        sParam += "=";
        sParam += encodeURIComponent(oForm.elements[i].value);
        aParams.push(sParam);
    }

    return aParams.join("&");
}
```

This code is exactly the same as it was in Chapter 2 and will be used to send e-mail messages.

One problem with e-mail addresses is that they can be specified in any number of formats. For example:

❑   myname@somewhere.com

❑   My Real Name <myname@somewhere.com>

❑   "My Real Name" <myname@somewhere.com>

If you use e-mail frequently, you'll probably recognize these formats as they are used in most major e-mail applications. When displaying an e-mail's sender in the folder view, AjaxMail displays the real name only. If no real name is present, the e-mail address is shown. To handle this, a helper function called `cleanupEmail()` is used:

```
var reNameAndEmail = /(.*?)<(.*?)>/i;

function cleanupEmail(sText) {
    if (reNameAndEmail.test(sText)) {
        return RegExp.$1.replace(/"/g, "");
    } else {
        return sText;
    }
}
```

The most important part of the function is actually the regular expression `reNameAndEmail`, which matches a string containing both a real name and an e-mail address regardless of the use of quotation marks. Inside the function, the text is tested against this regular expression. If `test()` returns `true`, that means the e-mail address contains both pieces of information and you should extract the real name (which is stored in `RegExp.$1`). However, this name may have quotation marks in it, so the next step is to replace all the quotation marks with an empty string using the `replace()` method. If, on the other hand, the regular expression doesn't match the text that was passed in, this means that it contains just an e-mail address, so it is returned without any changes.

The last helper function is called `htmlEncode()`, and it simply replaces greater-than (>), less-than (<), ampersand (&), and quote (" ") characters with their appropriate HTML entities. This ensures that no dangerous HTML will be created when reading text from an e-mail:

```
function htmlEncode(sText) {
    if (sText) {
        return sText.replace(/&/g, "&amp;").replace(/</g, "&lt;").replace(/>/g,
                                    "&gt;").replace(/"/g, "&quot;")
    } else {
        return "";
    }
}
```

This function also checks to make sure text is passed in. If `sText` is `null`, the function returns an empty string; otherwise, the replacements are done using the `replace()` method.

The Mailbox

The main part of the AjaxMail application is the mailbox. This is a single JavaScript object containing all the properties and methods necessary to run the user interface. Because there should be only one instance of this object, it is defined using object literal notation:

```
var oMailbox = {

    info: new Object(),
    processing: false,
    message: new Object(),
    nextNotice: null,

    //more code here
}
```

The mailbox object is stored in a variable named `oMailbox` and has four properties. The first property, `info`, is an object that will contain the folder information for the folder view. This object will be returned from the server but is initialized here to a generic object to avoid possible errors. Next is the `processing` property, which is simply a Boolean flag indicating whether the application is processing a request. When set to `true`, no other processes can be initiated. The third property is `message`, which will contain an object describing the message being read in the read view. Once again, this property is initialized to an empty object in order to avoid possible errors. The last property, `nextNotice`, is used by several callback functions to determine which notice should be displayed once a particular process has completed.

Before you can begin interacting with the user interface, it helps to store references to the elements you'll be using the most. You can do this by using `document.getElementById()` repeatedly, but that would require a lot of lines of code for all the elements used in AjaxMail. Instead, it's faster and more efficient to iterate over all the elements in a page and add a reference to each one that has an `id` attribute. This is part of the job of the `init()` method:

```
init: function () {
    var colAllElements = document.getElementsByTagName("*");
    if (colAllElements.length == 0) {
        colAllElements = document.all;
```

```
        }

    for (var i=0; i < colAllElements.length; i++) {
        if (colAllElements[i].id.length > 0) {
            this[colAllElements[i].id] = colAllElements[i];
        }
    }

    //more code here
},
```

This method first calls `document.getElementsByTagName()` and passes in an asterisk. In DOM-compliant browsers, this should return a collection of all the elements in the document. However, the Internet Explorer implementation doesn't support this usage, so you'll also need to be prepared for this. If the returned collection has no elements (`length` is not greater than zero), this means that Internet Explorer is in use. To work around this limitation, you can use the `document.all` collection (supported in Internet Explorer only) in place of the collection returned from `getElementsByTagName()`. Once `colAllElements` contains a usable collection, you can then iterate over the collection using a `for` loop. If the element has an `id` property (the `length` of the `id` property is greater than zero), a reference is saved on the mailbox object. So `divFolderStatus` is saved to the mailbox object as a property named `divFolderStatus` and can be accessed using `this.divFolderStatus` inside of a method or `oMailbox.divFolderStatus` outside of a method.

Data Loading Methods

The mailbox object uses two types of data: folder information and message information. Folder information is returned as a JSON string from the server and then parsed into an object containing information about the given folder. A typical folder information object looks like this:

```
{
    "messageCount":2,
    "page":1,
    "pageCount":1,
    "folder":1,
    "firstMessage":1,
    "unreadCount": 1,
    "messages":[
        {
            "id":"64",
            "from":"Joe Smith <joe@smith.com>",
            "subject":"Re: How about this weekend?",
            "date":"Oct 29 2005",
            "hasAttachments":false,
            "unread":true
        },
        {
            "id":"63",
            "from":"Joe Smith <joe@smith.com>",
            "subject":"How about this weekend?",
            "date":"Oct 29 2005",
            "hasAttachments":false,
            "unread":false
        }
    ]
}
```

This object is stored in the `info` property of the mailbox so that it can be used by all methods. To assign the data, the `loadInfo()` method is used. Because you may have an object or a JSON string to assign, this method needs to check the type of the argument that is passed in:

```
loadInfo: function (vInfo) {
    if (typeof vInfo == "string") {
        this.info = JSON.parse(vInfo);
    } else {
        this.info = vInfo;
    }
},
```

If `vInfo` is a string, it is parsed into an object using `JSON.parse()`; otherwise, it's an object, so it can be directly assigned to the `info` property. This object is used whenever a folder page is rendered, but there is also some data needed to display an individual e-mail.

The JSON object representing a single e-mail message is in the following format:

```
{
    "id":"63",
    "to":"you@somewhere.com",
    "from":"Joe Smith <joe@smith.com>",
    "cc":"",
    "subject":"How about this weekend?",
    "bcc":"",
    "date":"Oct 29, 2005 05:15 AM",
    "hasAttachments":false,
    "unread":true,
    "message":"I was thinking this weekend would be good? How about you?<br />Joe",
    "attachments":[],
    "unreadCount":8
}
```

When a message is viewed in AjaxMail, this information is assigned to the `message` property so that it is accessible from all methods. The `loadMessage()` method accepts either an object or a JSON string containing this message information and assigns it to the message property:

```
loadMessage: function (vMessage) {
    if (typeof vMessage == "string") {
        this.message = JSON.parse(vMessage);
    } else {
        this.message = vMessage;
    }
},
```

As you can see, this is essentially the same as `loadInfo()`; it just deals with different data. These two methods are critical because they are the primary means of passing data from the server to the client.

User Notification Methods

You will remember the `processing` property from the mailbox object description earlier. To set the value of this property, a special method called `setProcessing()` is used. The sole argument for this method is a Boolean value, set to `true` when the mailbox is processing or `false` when it is not. This method also shows the `divFolderStatus` element whenever the mailbox is processing:

```
setProcessing: function (bProcessing) {
    this.processing = bProcessing;
    this.divFolderStatus.style.display = bProcessing ? "block" : "none";
},
```

If the `bProcessing` argument is true, the `divFolderStatus` element has its `display` property set to `block`, ensuring that it is visible; otherwise, the property is set to `none`, hiding it from view. This method is used throughout the mailbox object to prevent multiple simultaneous requests from occurring.

Another method used throughout is `showNotice()`, which displays a notice to the user regarding the state of a request:

```
showNotice: function (sType, sMessage) {
    var divNotice = this.divNotice;
    divNotice.className = sType;
    divNotice.innerHTML = sMessage;
    divNotice.style.visibility = "visible";
    setTimeout(function () {
        divNotice.style.visibility = "hidden";
    }, iShowNoticeTime);
},
```

This method accepts two arguments: the type of message (either `info` or `error`) and the message to be displayed. The type of message also is the CSS class that will be assigned to `divNotice`, giving it the appropriate format. The message is assigned to the element via the `innerHTML` property, which means you can include HTML code in the message if necessary. After that, the element is made visible to the user by setting the `visibility` property to `visible`. Since the message should be displayed only for a specific amount of time, the `setTimeout()` function is used to determine when the `visibility` property should be set back to `hidden`. The interval is the global variable `iShowNoticeTime` that was defined earlier. Any notice displayed using this method will be shown immediately and then disappear after the designated amount of time.

Communication Methods

There are two different ways that AjaxMail communicates with the server: through XMLHttp and through a hidden iframe. To provide for this, several methods are used to encapsulate most of the communication functionality so that other functions can use them directly.

All XMLHttp GET requests are made through the `request()` method. This method takes three arguments: the action to perform, a callback function to notify when the request is complete, and an optional e-mail message ID. Every request going through this method goes to `AjaxMailAction.php`, passing in the action (the first argument) on the query string. Here's the complete method:

```
request: function (sAction, fnCallback, sId) {
    if (this.processing) return;
    try {
        this.setProcessing(true);
        var oXmlHttp = zXmlHttp.createRequest();
```

```
            var sURL = sAjaxMailURL + "?folder=" +this.info.folder + "&page="
                      + this.info.page + "&action=" + sAction;
        if (sId) {
            sURL += "&id=" + sId;
        }

        oXmlHttp.open("get", sURL, true);
        oXmlHttp.onreadystatechange = function (){
            try {
                if (oXmlHttp.readyState == 4) {
                    if (oXmlHttp.status == 200) {
                        fnCallback(oXmlHttp.responseText);
                    } else {
                        throw new Error("An error occurred while attempting to
contact the server. The action (" + sAction + ") did not complete.");
                    }
                }
            } catch (oException) {
                oMailbox.showNotice("error", oException.message);
            }
        };
        oXmlHttp.send(null);
    } catch (oException) {
        this.showNotice("error", oException.message);
    }
},
```

Note that the very first line checks to see if the mailbox is processing another request. If it is, the function returns without executing the next request. Otherwise, the standard `try...catch` arrangement involving an XMLHttp object is executed. Before anything is done, `setProcessing()` is called to indicate that a request has begun. The URL is constructed by adding the current folder ID and page to the query string, followed by the action to perform. If a message ID is specified (`sID`), that is also added to the query string so that the action can be completed. Next, the XMLHttp object is initialized and the `onreadystatechange` event handler is assigned. Inside the event handler, the callback function (`fnCallback`) is called when the request succeeds, passing in the response text. If an error occurs during this process, a custom error is thrown. When the `catch` statement intervenes, the `showNotice()` method is used to display details about the message.

The method to send an e-mail is very similar, but uses a POST request instead:

```
sendMail: function () {
    if (this.processing) return;
    this.divComposeMailForm.style.display  = "none";
    this.divComposeMailStatus.style.display = "block";

    try {
        this.setProcessing(true);
        var oXmlHttp = zXmlHttp.createRequest();
        var sData = getRequestBody(document.forms["frmSendMail"]);

        oXmlHttp.open("post", sAjaxMailSendURL, true);
        oXmlHttp.setRequestHeader("Content-Type",
```

```
                                           "application/x-www-form-urlencoded");

            oXmlHttp.onreadystatechange = function (){
                try {
                    if (oXmlHttp.readyState == 4) {
                        if (oXmlHttp.status == 200) {
                            sendConfirmation(oXmlHttp.responseText);
                        } else {
                            throw new Error("An error occurred while attempting to
contact the server. The mail was not sent.");
                        }
                    }
                } catch (oException) {
                    oMailbox.showNotice("error", oException.message);
                }
            };
            oXmlHttp.send(sData);
        } catch (oException) {
            this.showNotice("error", oException.message);
        }
    },
```

As with the `request()` method, the `sendMail()` method begins by checking to see if the mailbox is processing a request. If there are no other requests active, some user interface changes are made. First, the compose mail form is hidden from view by setting its `display` property to `none`. Then, the status area is shown by setting its `display` property to `block`. This effectively shows that the mail is being sent as an animated GIF plays.

Next, the `setProcessing()` method is called to indicate a request has begun and a data string is created by calling `getRequestBody()` on the mail form. After initializing the `oXmlHttp` object, the appropriate request header is set. The `onreadystatechange` event handler is the standard setup, and the response text is passed into the `sendConfirmation()` function (described in the upcoming Callback Functions section).

The last communication method is `navigate()`, which is used whenever the user interface change should be recorded in the browser history (allowing the user to click Back and Forward to navigate through the user interface changes). This method uses the hidden iframe to make requests to the server and receive responses back:

```
navigate: function (sAction, sId) {
    if (this.processing) return;
    try {
        this.setProcessing(true);
        var sURL = sAjaxMailNavigateURL + "?folder=" +this.info.folder
                              + "&page=" + this.info.page + "&action=" + sAction;
        if (sId) {
            sURL += "&id=" + sId;
        }
        this.iLoader.src = sURL;
    } catch (oException) {
        this.showNotice("error", oException.message);
    }
},
```

This method accepts only two arguments: an action to perform and an optional message ID (similar to `request()`). As with the other communication methods, this one begins by checking to see if the mailbox is processing another request and exits the method if that is the case. Otherwise, a standard `try...catch` block surrounds the rest of the code to catch any errors that may occur. Then, the `processing` flag is set to `true` to indicate a new request has begun. The URL is constructed in the same manner as in `request()`, adding the message ID only if it has been supplied. Last, the URL is assigned to the iframe via the `src` property. Now it is up to the page returned in the iframe to notify the mailbox that processing has been completed.

Rendering Methods

The most complex methods of the mailbox object are those relating to the rendering of data onto the screen. There are two methods: `renderFolder()`, which displays a mailbox folder, and `renderMessage()`, which displays a single e-mail message. Both of these use a small method called `updateUnreadCount()` that is responsible for updating the number of unread messages next to the Inbox link:

```
updateUnreadCount: function (iCount) {
    this.spnUnreadMail.innerHTML = iCount > 0 ? " (" + iCount + ")" : "";
}
```

This method expects the number of unread messages to be passed in as an argument. If that number is greater than 0, the `spnUnreadMail` element is updated to display that number; otherwise, the element is assigned an empty string. With this method defined, it's time to take a look at the two more complicated methods.

The `renderFolder()` method uses the `info` property to display the appropriate e-mail messages in the folder view. To begin, this method clears the folder view of all message information so that it can easily build up and insert new information:

```
renderFolder: function () {;
    var tblMain = this.tblMain;

    while (tblMain.tBodies[0].hasChildNodes()) {
        tblMain.tBodies[0].removeChild(tblMain.tBodies[0].firstChild);
    }

    //more code here
},
```

This first part of the method stores a reference to `tblMain` in a local variable and then proceeds to remove all the child nodes from the `<tbody/>` element (referenced as `tblMain.tBodies[0]`). With all of the rows removed, it's now okay to start adding rows.

The next part of the method creates the DOM representation for the messages. Note that for simplicity, only the additions to the method are shown:

```
renderFolder: function () {;

    //remove all existing rows

    var oFragment = document.createDocumentFragment();

    if (this.info.messages.length) {
        for (var i=0; i < this.info.messages.length; i++) {
            var oMessage = this.info.messages[i];
            var oNewTR = this.trTemplate.cloneNode(true);
            oNewTR.id = "tr" + oMessage.id;
            oNewTR.onclick = readMail;

            if (oMessage.unread) {
                oNewTR.className = "new";
            }

            var colCells = oNewTR.getElementsByTagName("td");
            var imgAction = colCells[0].childNodes[0];
            imgAction.id = oMessage.id;
            if (this.info.folder == TRASH) {
                imgAction.onclick = restoreMail;
                imgAction.src = sRestoreIcon;
                imgAction.title = sRestore;
            } else {
                imgAction.onclick = deleteMail;
                imgAction.src = sDeleteIcon;
                imgAction.title = sDelete;
            }

            colCells[1].appendChild(
                document.createTextNode(cleanupEmail(oMessage.from)));
            colCells[2].firstChild.style.visibility = oMessage.hasAttachments ?
                "visible" : "hidden";
            colCells[3].appendChild(
                document.createTextNode(htmlEncode(oMessage.subject)));
            colCells[4].appendChild(document.createTextNode(oMessage.date));
            oFragment.appendChild(oNewTR);
        }
    } else {
        var oNewTR = this.trNoMessages.cloneNode(true);
        oFragment.appendChild(oNewTR);
    }

    tblMain.tBodies[0].appendChild(oFragment);

    //more code here
},
```

In this section of the code, the first step is to create a document fragment upon which the DOM will be built. Next, the number of messages is checked. If there is at least one message, the view must be built accordingly; otherwise, a clone of trNoMessages is created and added to the fragment in place of any other rows. When there are messages, however, the process is a bit more involved.

For each message, the process begins by storing the message in a local variable, oMessage. This is retrieved from the info property in the messages array. Next, a clone of the template row trTemplate is created and stored in oNewTR (passing in true to cloneNode() ensures that all nodes are cloned, not just the <tr/> element itself). Next, the ID of the row is assigned by prepending tr to the message's ID. Then, the onclick event handler is assigned to be readMail(), which is defined later in the "Event Handlers" section. If the message hasn't been read yet, oMessage.unread will be true, so the row will be assigned a CSS class of new. The next step is to assign data into each of the table cells.

To make references to the cells easier, the getElementsByTagName() method is used to extract a collection of just the table cells (colCells). The action icon, either to delete or restore the message, is in the first cell. The actual <img/> element is stored in imgAction for easy reference. Then, the image is assigned an ID equal to the message ID. To determine what the image should do when clicked, the current folder is checked by using info.folder. If the current folder is the Trash, then the image is set up to restore the e-mail by setting the onclick, src, and title properties to restore-specific values; otherwise, the icon is set up to delete e-mail by setting the same properties to delete-specific values. Both restoreMail() and deleteMail() are global functions used as event handlers. These are discussed in the "Event Handlers" section.

The second cell in each row should display who the e-mail is from, so oMessage.from is passed to the helper function cleanupEmail(), which was defined earlier in the chapter. The result of this function call is passed into document.createTextNode() to create the text for the cell, which is added using appendChild().

For the third cell in the row, you need to decide if the attachments icon should be displayed or not. If oMessage.hasAttachments is true, then the visibility of the icon is set to visible; otherwise. it's set to hidden. This is done using a compound assignment statement instead of an if statement for simplicity.

The fourth table cell contains the e-mail subject, which is passed into htmlEncode() to ensure that all characters are displayed correctly. This text is then used to create a text node that is added to the cell in the same way as the first cell. The fifth cell simply displays the message date after it is added to it as a text node. Then, the entire row is added to the document fragment before the loop begins again.

Regardless of the number of messages, the fragment is passed into the appendChild() method of the table body to add the rows to the folder view. However, the user interface isn't complete yet; there is still other information that must be updated.

Specifically, the folder title must be displayed, the unread message count must be updated, and the pagination control must be initialized:

```
renderFolder:function () {

    //delete all existing rows

    //create rows for messages

    if (this.hFolderTitle.innerHTML != aFolders[this.info.folder]) {
        this.hFolderTitle.innerHTML = aFolders[this.info.folder];
```

```
    }

    this.updateUnreadCount(this.info.unreadCount);

    this.spnItems.style.visibility = this.info.messages.length ?
        "visible" : "hidden";
    this.spnItems.innerHTML = this.info.firstMessage + "-"
        + (this.info.firstMessage + this.info.messages.length - 1) + " of "
        + this.info.messageCount;

    if (this.info.pageCount > 1) {
        this.imgNext.style.visibility = this.info.page < this.info.pageCount ?
            "visible" : "hidden";
        this.imgPrev.style.visibility = this.info.page > 1 ? "visible" : "hidden";
    } else {
        this.imgNext.style.visibility = "hidden";
        this.imgPrev.style.visibility = "hidden";
    }

    this.divFolder.style.display = "block";
    this.divReadMail.style.display = "none";
    this.divComposeMail.style.display = "none";
},
```

The first step in this section of code is to set the contents of the `hFolderTitle` element to the name of the folder, but only if it's different from the one currently being displayed. To do so, use the `innerHTML` element to both get and set the value (if necessary). Next, the number of unread messages is passed into `updateUnreadCount()` to update the number of unread messages next to the Inbox link.

If there is at least one message, `spnItems` must be displayed. This is the element that displays the currently viewed message count, such as "1-10 of 21." If there is at least one message, its `visibility` property is set to `visible`; otherwise, it is set to `hidden`. Then, the contents of the element are created by using various properties of the `info` object. The `firstMessage` property returns the number of the first message returned in this page. You can then calculate the number of the last message returned by adding the number of messages to `firstMessage` and then subtracting one. The total number of messages is returned in the `messageCount` property.

When there is more than one page of messages to be displayed, the `imgNext` and `imgPrev` images should be shown, but not always at the same time. If you are on the first page, for instance, `imgPrev` should not be shown; likewise for `imgNext` on the last page. By using the `page` property to get the current page, you can determine whether the image should be visible and display the appropriate value for the `visibility` property. Of course, if there is only one page, neither image needs to be displayed.

The very last step is to show the `divFolder` element and hide both `divReadMail` and `divComposeMail` from sight. This initializes the application to the folder view. When the user clicks a message in the list, it brings up the read view, which is rendered by the `renderMessage()` method.

Just as the `renderFolder()` method used the `info` property to determine what to render, the `renderMessage()` method uses the `message` property for the same reason. All the information necessary to display a single e-mail is contained within the `message` property. To begin, you assign the contents of each element in the read view using values from `message`:

```
renderMessage: function () {
    this.hSubject.innerHTML = htmlEncode(this.message.subject);
    this.divMessageFrom.innerHTML = sFrom + " " + htmlEncode(this.message.from);
    this.divMessageTo.innerHTML = sTo + " " + htmlEncode(this.message.to);
    this.divMessageCC.innerHTML = this.message.cc.length ?
        sCC + " " + htmlEncode(this.message.cc) : "";
    this.divMessageBCC.innerHTML = this.message.bcc.length ?
        sBCC + " " + htmlEncode(this.message.bcc) : "";
    this.divMessageDate.innerHTML = this.message.date;
    this.divMessageBody.innerHTML = this.message.message;

    //more code here

    this.updateUnreadCount(this.message.unreadCount);
    this.divFolder.style.display = "none";
    this.divReadMail.style.display = "block";
    this.divComposeMail.style.display = "none";
},
```

Each of the elements responsible for displaying the various parts of the e-mail are assigned data from the message object. Of course, most of these values use `htmlEncode()` to ensure that the data is displayed correctly. For the CC and BCC fields, their values are assigned only if they contain data to begin with. If not, the `divMessageCC` and `divMessageBCC` fields are assigned empty strings, which effectively hides them from view.

Then the unread message count is updated. This is being updated here as well because there's no reason to waste a round trip to the server and not get such a small piece of information. The last step in the process is to hide `divFolder` and `divComposeMail` while showing `divReadMail`. However, there is some code missing from this method. The previous code doesn't take into account attachments.

Dealing with attachments essentially means outputting a list of all the attachments for a message and linking them so that each can be downloaded with a simple click. The `ulAttachments` element, which is part of the code in `index.php`, should be shown only when there is at least one attachment. Here's how to build this section of the view:

```
renderMessage: function () {
    this.hSubject.innerHTML = htmlEncode(this.message.subject);
    this.divMessageFrom.innerHTML = sFrom + " " + htmlEncode(this.message.from);
    this.divMessageTo.innerHTML = sTo + " " + htmlEncode(this.message.to);
    this.divMessageCC.innerHTML = this.message.cc.length ?
        sCC + " " + htmlEncode(this.message.cc) : "";
    this.divMessageBCC.innerHTML = this.message.bcc.length ?
        sBCC + " " + htmlEncode(this.message.bcc) : "";
    this.divMessageDate.innerHTML = this.message.date;
    this.divMessageBody.innerHTML = htmlEncode(this.message.message);

    if (this.message.hasAttachments) {
        this.ulAttachments.style.display = "";

        var oFragment = document.createDocumentFragment();

        for (var i=0; i < this.message.attachments.length; i++) {
            var oLI = document.createElement("li");
```

```
            oLI.className = "attachment";
            oLI.innerHTML = "<a href=\"" + sAjaxMailAttachmentURL + "?id="
                + this.message.attachments[i].id + "\" target=\"_blank\">"
                + this.message.attachments[i].filename + "</a> ("
                + this.message.attachments[i].size + ")";
            oFragment.appendChild(oLI);
        }

        this.ulAttachments.appendChild(oFragment);
        this.liAttachments.style.display = "";
    } else {
        this.ulAttachments.style.display = "none";
        this.liAttachments.style.display = "none";
        this.ulAttachments.innerHTML = "";
    }

    this.updateUnreadCount(this.message.unreadCount);
    this.divFolder.style.display = "none";
    this.divReadMail.style.display = "block";
    this.divComposeMail.style.display = "none";
},
```

Naturally, the first step in rendering attachment information is to check if there are any attachments using the `hasAttachments` property. If there are attachments, the `ulAttachments` element is displayed and the attachments are iterated over, creating a new `<li/>` element for each one and assigning additional information using the `innerHTML` property. Each of these new elements is added to a document fragment for efficiency. When all attachments have had their DOM representation created, the fragment is appended to `ulAttachments`. Then, the `liAttachments` element is displayed by setting its `display` property to an empty string. This element contains the View Attachments link in the message header.

If there are no attachments to the message, `ulAttachments` and `liAttachments` are hidden from view by setting their `display` properties to `none`. Additionally, `ulAttachments` is cleared of all its data by setting `innerHTML` to an empty string. This prevents attachments from showing up on e-mails that they weren't attached to.

Action Methods

With all the Ajax request methods and callback functions in place, you now have all the tools necessary to create the functionality of an e-mail application. For each action, it's important to have a clear idea of how the user interface should respond and what the user would expect.

To begin, consider the task of deleting an e-mail message. When the user clicks on the red X next to a message, the message should be deleted (moved to the Trash). The Back and Forward button are of no use here, because you'd never want to take the user back to a point where the e-mail is still in the list. That means the `request()` method should be used. Next, should this action cause a user interface change? Yes, the message should disappear from the list. Therefore, you need to use the `request()` method with the `loadAndRender()` callback function:

```
deleteMessage: function (sId) {
    this.nextNotice = sDeleteMailNotice;
    this.request("delete", loadAndRender, sId);
},
```

Because you want to delete a specific message, the message ID must be passed into the method. To prepare for the action, the nextNotice property is set to the delete mail notice string. Then, request() is called, passing in the delete string, the loadAndRender() callback function, and the message ID. When the request is completed, the notice is displayed and the user can continue interacting with the application knowing that the message has been moved to the Trash. To restore the message from the Trash, you can use the same methodology.

When the user is viewing the messages in the Trash, a click on the green arrow restores the message (moves it to the Inbox). This is essentially the same as the delete operation; it simply changes where the message is stored. Not surprisingly, the method is very similar:

```
restoreMessage: function (sId) {
    this.nextNotice = sRestoreMailNotice;
    this.request("restore", loadAndRender, sId);
},
```

Once again, this function assigns a notice to be displayed when the request completes and uses request() to restore the message represented by the message ID (sID).

The Trash also has a special action: empty. When the Trash is emptied, all the messages in it are permanently deleted and cannot be recovered. This action is interesting in that it behaves differently depending on what the user is looking at. If the Inbox is being viewed, it's still possible to click the Empty link. In this case, you don't want to change the user interface, aside from letting the user know that the Trash has been emptied. If, on the other hand, the user is viewing the message in the Trash, the user interface should refresh to show that the Trash is empty. Therefore, the emptyTrash() method is a little more involved:

```
emptyTrash: function () {
    if (confirm(sEmptyTrashConfirm)) {
        this.nextNotice = sEmptyTrashNotice;
        if (this.info.folder == TRASH) {
            this.request("empty", loadAndRender);
        } else {
            this.request("empty", execute);
        }
    }
},
```

In this method, the first step is to confirm that the user actually wants to empty the Trash. Using the JavaScript confirm() function with sEmptyTrashConfirm presents a dialog box to the user with two options: OK or Cancel. If the user clicks OK, confirm() returns true and the Trash should be emptied. So, the nextNotice property is assigned as with the previous methods. Next, the currently displayed folder is checked. If it's the Trash, request() is called with the loadAndRender() callback function to update the display; if it's not Trash, request() is called with execute() so that the user interface isn't updated.

Thus far, the methods in this section have dealt with performing an action on e-mail messages. The getMessages() method actually is responsible for retrieving the folder information from the server. It accepts the folder ID and the page number to retrieve as arguments and then uses the navigate() method to retrieve the desired information:

```
getMessages: function (iFolder, iPage) {
    this.info.folder = iFolder;
    this.info.page = iPage;
    this.navigate("getfolder");
},
```

To retrieve the correct message, the folder and page properties of the info object must be set to the appropriate values. Then, when navigate() is called, the URL will contain the correct folder and page information. This method is then used in both nextPage() and prevPage() to move through the different pages of messages in a given folder:

```
nextPage: function () {
    this.getMessages(this.info.folder, this.info.page+1);
},

prevPage: function () {
    this.getMessages(this.info.folder, this.info.page-1);
},
```

Both methods pass in the current folder to getMessages(), but the page argument is different. For nextPage(), the current page number is incremented by one, whereas prevPage() decrements it by one.

There may be times when a user just wants to refresh the information about a folder instead of switching folders. For instance, to check for new mail the user can click the Inbox link while the Inbox is already being displayed. In this case, you don't want to add anything to the browser history because you certainly will never want to go back to an older view of the folder, so you should use request() instead of navigate():

```
refreshFolder: function (iFolder) {
    this.info.folder = iFolder;
    this.info.page = 1;
    this.request("getfolder", loadAndRender);
},
```

This method is very similar to getMessages() in that the folder ID needs to be passed in and assigned to the info.folder property. The page is set to 1 because any refresh needs to begin with the first page. And because the action requires the user interface to change, the loadAndRender() callback function is passed in when calling request().

Navigation Methods

Keeping the navigation straight in an Ajax application can be tricky, but thanks to the navigate() method defined earlier, things are much more straight forward. Whenever you need to move from one view of AjaxMail to another, you can simply pass a string to the navigate() method and wait for the action to be completed. To that end, there are four methods that either directly or indirectly make use of the navigate() method to perform their function:

```
cancelReply: function () {
    history.go(-1);
},

compose: function () {
```

```
        this.navigate("compose");
    },

    forward: function () {
        this.navigate("forward");
    },

    readMessage: function (sId) {
        this.navigate("getmessage", sId);
    },

    reply: function (blnAll) {
        this.navigate("reply" + (blnAll ? "all" : ""));
    },
```

The first method, `cancelReply()`, uses the browser's internal history to do its job. When users click Compose Mail, Forward, Reply, or Reply All, the `navigate()` method is called to put them into compose view. To undo this and move back to the previous view, the `history` object can be used because the move was recorded in the hidden iframe. Using the `go()` method with a –1 value moves the browser back to the previous view.

All the other methods in this section simply pass a string value to `navigate()`, indicating the action that should be taken next. The `readMessage()` method also accepts the ID of the message to retrieve, and the `reply()` method accepts a single Boolean argument that indicates whether the action should be `reply` or `replyall`; when set to `true`, it is the latter.

You'll remember from earlier that `AjaxMailNavigate.php` calls different JavaScript mailbox methods depending on what action has taken place. Each of these methods begins with the word "display," and each has a specific view to initialize.

The `displayFolder()` method does exactly what it says: it displays a folder of e-mail messages. It accepts a folder info object as its only argument and then renders the folder before setting the `processing` flag back to `false`:

```
displayFolder: function (oInfo) {
    this.loadInfo(oInfo);
    this.renderFolder();
    this.setProcessing(false);
},
```

A similar method is `displayMessage()`, which accepts a message information object, loads it, renders the message, and then sets the `processing` flag to `false`:

```
displayMessage: function (oMessage) {
    this.loadMessage(oMessage);
    this.renderMessage();
    this.setProcessing(false);
},
```

These two methods take care of the Folder view and Read view, respectively. The Compose view is a little bit different because there are so many ways it can be used. It can be used to create a new e-mail, in which case all fields are blank, or it could be used to send a reply, reply all, or forward, in which case different information needs to be pre-filled in the form. To facilitate the different requirements of these user actions, a single method is used:

```
displayComposeMailForm: function (sTo, sCC, sSubject, sMessage) {
    this.txtTo.value = sTo;
    this.txtCC.value = sCC;
    this.txtSubject.value = sSubject;
    this.txtMessage.value = sMessage;
    this.divReadMail.style.display = "none";
    this.divComposeMail.style.display = "block";
    this.divFolder.style.display = "none";
    this.setProcessing(false);
},
```

The `displayComposeMailForm()` method accepts all the various information that could be assigned to the compose view and places it into the correct fields. Then, `divReadMail` and `divFolder` are hidden while `divComposeMail` is shown. Last, the `processing` flag is set to `true`. The `displayComposeMailForm()` method is not called by `AjaxMailNavigate.php`, but is instead called by several more specific methods, each catering to a specific action:

```
displayCompose: function () {
    this.displayComposeMailForm("", "", "", "");
},

displayForward: function () {
    this.displayComposeMailForm("", "",
                "Fwd: " + this.message.subject,
                "---------- Forwarded message ----------\n"
                    + this.message.message);
},

displayReply: function () {
    var sTo = this.message.from;
    var sCC = "";

    this.displayComposeMailForm(sTo, sCC, "Re: " + this.message.subject,
        "\n\n\n\n\n" + this.message.from + "said: \n" + this.message.message);

},

displayReplyAll: function () {
    var sTo = this.message.from + "," + this.message.to;
    var sCC = this.message.cc;

    this.displayComposeMailForm(sTo, sCC, "Re: " + this.message.subject,
        "\n\n\n\n\n" + this.message.from + "said: \n" + this.message.message);

},
```

The displayCompose() method, which simply displays a blank compose view, passes in an empty string to displayComposeMailForm(). The displayForward() method prepends "Fwd:" to the front of the message subject and "-----Forwarded Message------" to the front of the message from the e-mail that's currently being viewed. Both displayReply() and displayReplyAll() prepend "Re:" in front of the message subject and then include a short string before the current e-mail's body text. The only difference between these two methods is what the pre-filled values of the To and CC fields are. For displayReply(), the To field is simply filled with whoever sent the message initially; for displayReplyAll(), the To field also includes everyone else the e-mail was sent to and the CC field contains the same CC recipients as the original message.

Initialization Methods

The last section of methods in the mailbox object initializes the properties and data. Earlier you saw the beginnings of the init() method; the next part involves assigning event handlers to various user interface elements:

```
init: function () {
    var colAllElements = document.getElementsByTagName("*");
    if (!colAllElements.length) {
        colAllElements = document.all;
    }

    for (var i=0; i < colAllElements.length; i++) {
        if (colAllElements[i].id.length > 0) {
            this[colAllElements[i].id] = colAllElements[i];
        }
    }

    this.imgPrev.onclick = function () {
        oMailbox.prevPage();
    };
    this.imgNext.onclick = function () {
        oMailbox.nextPage();
    };
    this.spnCompose.onclick = function () {
        oMailbox.compose();
    };
    this.spnEmpty.onclick = function () {
        oMailbox.emptyTrash();
    };
    this.spnReply.onclick = function () {
        oMailbox.reply(false);
    };
    this.spnReplyAll.onclick = function () {
        oMailbox.reply(true);
    };
    this.spnForward.onclick = function () {
        oMailbox.forward();
    };
    this.spnCancel.onclick = function () {
        oMailbox.cancelReply();
    };
    this.spnSend.onclick = function () {
```

```
        oMailbox.sendMail();
    };

    //more code here
},
```

All the event handlers assigned here simply call a mailbox method that was defined earlier in this chapter. You also need to assign the event handlers for the Inbox and Trash links:

```
this.spnInbox.onclick = function () {
    if (oMailbox.info.folder == INBOX) {
        oMailbox.refreshFolder(INBOX);
    } else {
        oMailbox.switchFolder(INBOX);
    }
};

this.spnTrash.onclick = function () {
    if (oMailbox.info.folder == TRASH) {
        oMailbox.refreshFolder(TRASH);
    } else {
        oMailbox.switchFolder(TRASH);
    }
};
```

These lines occur where the "more code here" comment is in the previous listing, but are pulled out here for easier explanation. Each of these two links can perform one of two operations: either switching to the folder view or refreshing it. To determine which of these actions to take, each event handler first checks to see what the currently displayed folder is. For the Inbox link, if the current folder is already Inbox, then it calls refreshFolder(); otherwise it calls switchFolder(). The same holds true for the Trash link, except that it checks to see if Trash is the folder already being displayed.

The init() method is actually called by another method called load(), defined as:

```
load: function () {
    this.init();
    this.getMessages(INBOX, 1);
},
```

This method first initializes the user interface by calling init(), and then makes the initial request for the first page of the Inbox folder using getMessages(). When index.php is loaded, this method must be called (as described later).

Callback Functions

To make use of the request() and sendMail() methods of the mailbox object, several callback functions are necessary. These are functions that take over processing once data has been returned from the server. Each of these functions is standalone; that is, they are not methods of the mailbox object.

When the e-mail messages are first downloaded from the server, the data must be loaded into the info property and then rendered:

```
function loadAndRender(sInfo) {

    oMailbox.loadInfo(sInfo);
    oMailbox.renderFolder();

    if (oMailbox.nextNotice) {
        oMailbox.showNotice("info", oMailbox.nextNotice);
        oMailbox.nextNotice = null;
    }
    oMailbox.setProcessing(false);
}
```

The loadAndRender() function expects a JSON string to be passed in as an argument. That data is loaded using the loadInfo() method. Once that happens, the renderFolder() method is called to begin displaying the new information. After that, the function checks to see if there is a notice that needs to be displayed (stored in nextNotice). If so, that notice is displayed and nextNotice is set back to null. The very last step is to set the processing flag to false, indicating that the mailbox is free to make other requests.

The simpler case is when a command has to be executed on the server without returning any information. When the request has completed, you simply want to display any notification that may be waiting and then reset the processing flag back to false. To do so, use the execute() callback function:

```
function execute(sInfo) {
    if (oMailbox.nextNotice) {
        oMailbox.showNotice("info", oMailbox.nextNotice);
        oMailbox.nextNotice = null;
    }
    oMailbox.setProcessing(false);
}
```

Using this callback function instead of loadAndRender() prevents the user interface from updating when the request completes. The action taken is done purely behind the scenes and is indicated only by the notice (if any) that is displayed. As with loadAndRender(), the last step is to set processing back to false.

The last callback function, sendConfirmation(), is used only when sending mail. It expects a simple JSON object to be returned with two properties: error and message. If error is true, an error has occurred and the message property contains an error message to display to the user; otherwise, the mail was sent successfully and message contains a confirmation message to be displayed using showNotice():

```
function sendConfirmation(sData) {
    var oResponse = JSON.parse(sData);
    if (oResponse.error) {
        alert("An error occurred:\n" + oResponse.message);
    } else {
        oMailbox.showNotice("info", oResponse.message);
        oMailbox.divComposeMail.style.display = "none";
```

```
            oMailbox.divReadMail.style.display = "none";
            oMailbox.divFolder.style.display = "block";
    }
    oMailbox.divComposeMailForm.style.display   = "block";
    oMailbox.divComposeMailStatus.style.display = "none";
    oMailbox.setProcessing(false);
}
```

This function also resets some of the user interface. If the message was sent successfully, it sends the user back to folder view by hiding `divComposeMail` and `divReadMail` and then showing `divFolder`. Regardless of the success, `divComposeMailForm` has its `display` property set back to `block`, whereas `divComposeMailStatus` has its `display` property set to `none`, effectively resetting the compose view.

Event Handlers

The "Action Methods" section described methods of the mailbox object that are used to perform specific actions. To facilitate the assigning of event handlers that use these methods, a handful of small functions are used:

```
function deleteMail() {
    oMailbox.deleteMessage(this.id);
}

function restoreMail() {
    oMailbox.restoreMessage(this.id);
}

function readMail() {
    oMailbox.readMessage(this.id.substring(2));
}
```

Each of these functions simply calls a method of `oMailbox` and passes in some identifier. Because these functions are used as event handlers, the `this` object points to the element upon which the event handler has been assigned. (You could also use `event.srcElement` in Internet Explorer or `event.target` in DOM-compliant browsers.) For `deleteMail()` and `restoreMail()`, the ID of the element is equivalent to a message ID, so it can be passed directly into the `deleteMessage()` and `restoreMessage()` methods, respectively. The `readMail()` function is applied to a table row whose ID is in the format "trID", so the first two character must be stripped off using the `substring()` method before being passed into `readMessage()`.

> By defining these functions globally, you avoid using closures to assign event handlers. Closures are a manner in which it's possible to define a function that makes use of variables defined outside of it. They also happen to be the main cause of memory leaks in many web browsers. Whenever possible, it is preferable to create standalone functions to use as event handlers.

The Last Step

The last step in making AjaxMail functional is to call `oMailbox.load()` when the page has been loaded. To accomplish this, use the window's `onload` event handler:

```
window.onload = function () {
    oMailbox.load();
};
```

Now, when the page has finished loading, the Ajax initialization begins and the application is ready to use.

To test AjaxMail, navigate to `www.yourdomainname.com/AjaxMail/`. This loads the initial view and you are ready to go.

Summary

In this chapter, you learned how to create a full-fledged Ajax application called AjaxMail. You began by designing the server-side architecture. Using PHP and MySQL, you designed a back-end system designed to download messages from a POP3 server and store them in a database. You created several database tables to handle the various data associated with an e-mail application. POP3Lib was used for POP3 communication and PHPMailer was used for SMTP communication.

You then designed a dynamic user interface that doesn't require any page reloads. Communication is accomplished by using a combination of XMLHttp and a hidden iframe. The XMHttp requests performed actions such as deleting specific e-mail message, whereas the hidden iframe was used to allow the Back and Forward buttons to function as usual.

10

Ajax Frameworks

In this chapter, you will see three frameworks that all have a common goal: to make the task of developing Ajax-enabled web sites easier and quicker. They all try to abstract the details concerning the underlying communications between the server and the client, leaving the developer free to concentrate on the more interesting aspects, such as implementing the classes that actually take care of the business logic peculiar to an application.

The frameworks chosen each use a different server-side processing technique: PHP, Java, and ASP.NET, respectively. They all fall into the category of frameworks known as Remote Invocation. This means that the framework is responsible only for providing client-side JavaScript that handles the creating of the `XmlHttpRequest`, converting parameters to a suitable format, and returning values to the page, usually through a callback function. This is in contrast to HTML/JS Generation frameworks, which only require the user to handcraft any customization code but allow less control over the request and response handling.

This chapter focuses on the following three frameworks, among the many available:

❑ **JPSpan:** JPSpan integrates with PHP, a robust and open source server-side language.

❑ **DWR:** DWR allows calls to Java classes on the server.

❑ **Ajax.NET:** Ajax.NET enables communication with server-side classes built with any .NET language.

The examples for each framework follow a common pattern: each demonstrates how to create a business object and call its methods asynchronously from an HTML client.

> *The term business object is given to a class that reflects a real-world entity and has the methods and properties necessary to support working with it from within an application. An example would be a Video class used in a video store's booking system. The Video class might have properties such as* title *and* dailyRentalCost, *and methods such as* isOverdue().

The business object in our examples will represent a customer, a common class in many applications. In a real-life scenario, the Customer class could contain many properties, such as the customer's name, address, and how long he or she had been a client, as well as methods such as getOutstandingOrders().

To make the examples more manageable and allow them to focus on the use of the frameworks, the Customer class used in the examples is much simpler. It has only one method, getAddressFromEmail(), which returns the customer's address given his or her e-mail address as a parameter.

In a well-built application, the business classes, representing real-world entities, are separate from the data classes, which deal with persisting the details to a permanent storage facility, such as a relational database. To keep the examples straightforward, the Customer *class itself will handle retrieving information from the database.*

JPSpan

JPSpan is an Ajax framework built with the intention of integrating client-side JavaScript with server-side code written in PHP. PHP has been around since the mid nineties and has grown from simple beginnings to a full-fledged object-oriented language that can run on both Windows and UNIX/Linux platforms. The main advantages of using PHP over other platforms, such as Java or .NET, are that it is smaller, much simpler to install, and more lightweight, needing only a fraction of the memory of the Java runtime or the .NET CLR.

How It Works

JPSpan works by analyzing a PHP class using reflection. It then emits a number of JavaScript methods that accept the same arguments as the methods of the class on the server. When one of these methods is called, it uses a cross-browser library to instantiate the appropriate XmlHttpRequest for the platform it is running on and posts the data to the server. The response is then read and passed to a function on the client for further use within the page.

Reflection in this case means examining a class to find out its properties and methods. It is a commonly available technique in object-oriented languages and is often used as a way of writing generic code that can work with a large number of classes.

Installing JPSpan

The first thing you need is a web server that supports PHP, version 5. This can be the ubiquitous Apache web server for UNIX/Linux machines or IIS for Windows (although others also support PHP, these are the most common). When installing with IIS there is a choice of running the PHP processor as an out of process server using CGI or in process using ISAPI. The first method is recommended for reliability, the second for performance. For the purposes of this chapter, the ISAPI installation was chosen.

You can find the PHP installation, along with a list of compatible web servers, at http://uk.php.net. *There is a comprehensive set of instructions with a list of Frequently Asked Questions detailing how to resolve some common difficulties and problems.*

The actual JPSpan installation can be found at `http://sourceforge.net/projects/jpspan`. Aside from the documentation and some examples, it consists of a number of PHP pages alongside several JavaScript files. The entry point, `JPSpan.php`, sits in a folder named `JPSpan`, which is best placed directly under the root of your web server (for IIS this is typically `C:\InetPub\wwwroot` and for Apache it is `/usr/local/apache/htdocs`). There is a subfolder, also called `JPSpan`, that contains additional PHP and JavaScript files.

Creating the Server-Side Page

There are two stages involved in developing the server-side page: implementing the business classes that will do the actual processing and hooking them into the framework so that they become accessible from the client.

The first stage is to create a standard server-side skeleton page that can be used as a starting point for most JPSpan projects. This consists of the basic plumbing needed to inform JPSpan of the business class as well as other options such as what to do in the event of an error.

The second stage is the coding of the business class or classes to be used, which requires a knowledge of PHP and the syntax used to declare classes. The syntax is very similar to C++ and Java, so any knowledge of those two languages will help.

After the business class has been tested outside of the JPSpan framework, it can be incorporated into the skeleton page ready for use by the client.

The Standard Page Code

The basic structure of a server-side processing page looks something like the following example:

```php
<?php

//Business class to be included here
class Customer
{
   //Customer class implementation to be included here
}


// Including this sets up the JPSPAN constant
require_once '../JPSpan/JPSpan.php';

// Load the PostOffice server
require_once JPSPAN . 'Server/PostOffice.php';

// Create the PostOffice server
$PostOffice = & new JPSpan_Server_PostOffice();

// Register the Customer class with it...
$PostOffice->addHandler(new Customer());

// This allows the JavaScript to be seen by
// just adding ?client to the end of the
```

```
// server's URL

if (isset($_SERVER['QUERY_STRING']) && strcasecmp($_SERVER['QUERY_STRING'],
'client') == 0)
{

  // Compress the output Javascript feature (e.g. strip whitespace)
  // turn this off it has performance problems
  define('JPSPAN_INCLUDE_COMPRESS', false);

  // Display the Javascript client
  $PostOffice->displayClient();

}
else
{
  // This is where the real serving happens...
  // Include error handler
  // PHP errors, warnings and notices serialized to JS
  require_once JPSPAN . 'ErrorHandler.php';

  // Start serving requests...
  $PostOffice->serve();
}

?>
```

Following the opening PHP tag is the place where the code for the actual class will be included. This can be actually in the page or can be held in a separate file and accessed through one of the PHP include mechanisms.

```
<?php
//Business class to be included here
class Customer
{
  //Customer class implementation to be included here
}
```

For minor applications and simple examples, you will often see the code written directly into the page. For a more maintainable approach, as well as to enable you to re-use classes directly and through inheritance, it is better to have them in separate files.

Next comes a critical line:

```
require_once '../JPSpan/JPSpan.php';
```

The require_once directive instructs the PHP processor to make the code within the specified file available to the rest of the page. If the code has already been included, the instruction is ignored. The path shown above assumes that this page resides in a directory at the same level as the JPSpan install. If this is not the case, it will need to be modified. The code in JPSpan.php actually does very little; it simply makes sure that a variable named JPSPAN is initialized and points to the subfolder, also named JPSpan, which contains the main PHP classes and necessary JavaScript files.

The next stage uses the JPSPAN variable along with another require_once directive to make the classes in PostOffice.php available:

```
require_once '../JPSpan/JPSpan.php';
```

```
// Load the PostOffice server
require_once JPSPAN . 'Server/PostOffice.php';
```

A new instance of JPSpan_Server_PostOffice is then created:

```
$PostOffice = & new JPSpan_Server_PostOffice();
```

PostOffice.php contains the class JPSpan_Server_PostOffice, which is used by all JPSpan applications, is responsible for creating the client-side JavaScript methods whose signatures mimic those of Customer. Instead of these methods running locally, however, the arguments are passed to the server using an XmlHttpRequest and any results obtained are returned through the HTTP response.

Next, the Customer class is passed to the JPSpan_Server_PostOffice via the addHandler method:

```
$PostOffice->addHandler(new Customer());
```

The JPSpan_Server_PostOffice uses reflection to examine our business class and create the necessary JavaScript stubs.

The final lines of the page enable the code to serve two purposes: it can provide the client with the necessary JavaScript needed to instigate calls on our server-side class, and the page can also handle the calls themselves. This is done by examining the actual URL used to request the page.

```
if (isset($_SERVER['QUERY_STRING']) &&
        strcasecmp($_SERVER['QUERY_STRING'], 'client') == 0)
{
```

The isset() function is used to check whether a variable refers to anything and returns true or false. Strcasecmp() performs a case-insensitive comparison of two strings, returning 0 if the two match.

If the querystring, the part following the question mark in a URL exists and it has a key named client, the displayClient method is called, which returns the JavaScript to the browser. (An optional ability to compress the resulting JavaScript is disabled at this stage, as it needs some additional work to be used effectively.)

```
$PostOffice->displayClient();
```

You will be able to see the JavaScript created by this call once the business class is written. If the querystring does not contain the string client, first the page that handles any errors is included:

```
require_once JPSPAN . 'ErrorHandler.php';
```

(How errors are handled is discussed later in the chapter.)

Then, a call to the serve method is made:

```
$PostOffice->serve();
```

This processes the request and relays any arguments posted to the page to the appropriate class methods.

Creating the Business Class

So far you have seen the PHP code that will form a standard part of nearly all JPSpan projects. Next, you have to write the business class that will perform the core processing that the application needs.

For this example, the class is going to represent a customer. It has only one method, getAddressFromEmail(), which accepts an e-mail address and returns an array containing the customer's address details.

The idea behind the class is that when a customer is making an online purchase and needs to specify a delivery address, the details will be retrieved from a database and the form's elements will be pre-populated. As a call to a database can often take some time, this is an ideal scenario for an asynchronous operation. While the customer is specifying other parts of the order, the details are retrieved by a secondary request to the server.

The syntax for classes in PHP is very similar to that of C++, Java, and C#; they start with the class keyword and the name of the class:

```
class Customer
{
   public function getAddressFromEmail($email)
   {
     //Method implementation goes here
   }
}
```

The getAddressFromEmail() method will open a connection to a database and execute a simple SQL statement to retrieve the details.

In a production application, the code to access the database should be abstracted into separate classes and the database details should be retrieved from a configuration file. To demonstrate the principle, however, this class will be self contained.

In Chapter 2 you learned how to use library methods to connect to an instance of MySQL. In this example you'll see how to use ADO to connect to a database.

The database in question will be SQL Server, and the script to create it with the necessary tables is available in the chapter's code download along with the other necessary files. There is also an alternative version using a Microsoft Access database, which requires no server-side software to be running; simply copy Sales.mdb into the same folder as the web pages.

The Sales database has only one table: tblCustomer. The design is as shown in Figure 10-1.

The table has an integer identity field to provide a primary key, two string fields for the customer's forenames and surnames, and a string field for the customer's e-mail address. The other seven string fields contain the customer's address lines.

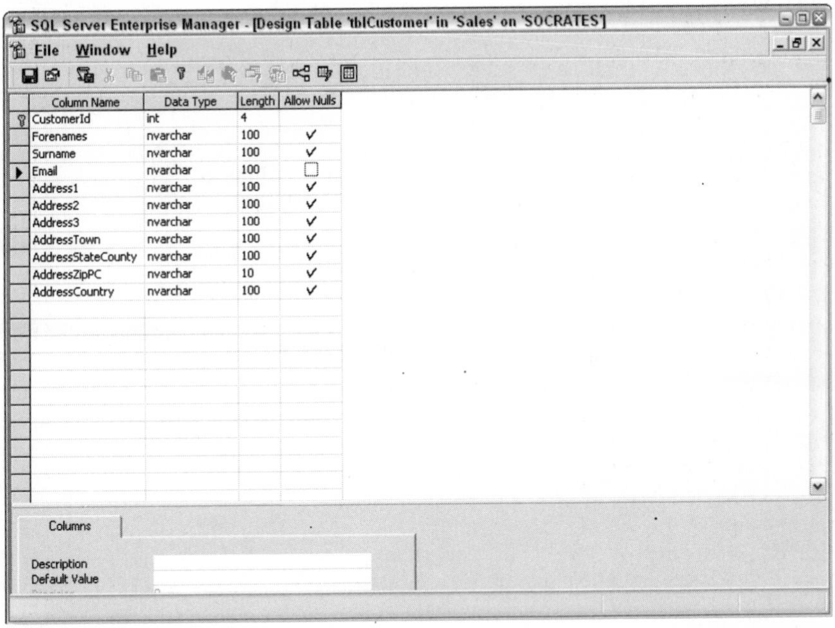

Figure 10-1

The code to retrieve the address begins by declaring an array, `$address`, to hold the result:

```
public function getAddressFromEmail($email)
{
    $address = array("success" => FALSE);
```

The array is given one member, success, which is used to indicate whether the details were found for the appropriate e-mail supplied. A built-in class named COM is then used to instantiate an Adodb.Connection:

```
public function getAddressFromEmail($email)
{
    $address = array("success" => FALSE);
    $conn = new COM("Adodb.Connection");
```

Because the database access involves using COM, it will work only on servers running Windows. For non-Windows devices, MySQL would be a suitable alternative.

To open the connection, you must know the location and type of the database. This is provided in the form of a connection string. The format of the connection string varies depending on the make of database being accessed. The string for SQL Server specifies the server on which the database resides; in this example, localhost is specificied because SQL Server is located on the web server itself. The other information needed is the name of the database or catalog as it is called and the user name and password. The user in this case need only have read access.

```
$dbConnString = "Provider=SQLOLEDB; Data Source='localhost'; "
              . "Initial Catalog='sales'; User Id='Test'; Password='test';";
$conn->connectionString = $dbConnString;
```

As an alternative to having the user name and password in the connection string, the account running the web server, usually IUSR_<machine name> in IIS, could be given access to the database and the following could be used:

```
"Provider=SQLOLEDB; Data Source='localhost'; Initial Catalog='sales'; Integrated
Security=SSPI;"
```

The next step is to open the connection and execute the simple SQL statement. First, the `str_replace()` function is used to make sure there are no single quote marks in the e-mail, which would produce an invalid SQL string. Each single quote is replaced by two single quotes and the modified string is stored in the variable `safeEmail`. Then, `safeEmail` is incorporated into the SQL string and the `execute` method is called on the connection object:

```
$conn->connectionString = $dbConnString;
$conn->open();
$safeEmail = str_replace('\'', '\'\'', $email);
$rs = $conn->execute("SELECT * FROM tblCustomer WHERE Email = '$safeEmail'");
```

Again, for the purposes of simplicity, a SQL string is built up at runtime. In a production standard application, a stored procedure would accept the e-mail address as a parameter and return the data.

The `execute` method returns an `Adodb.Recordset`, which is stored in `$rs`:

```
$rs = $conn->execute("SELECT * FROM tblCustomer WHERE Email = '$safeEmail'");
if (!$rs->EOF)
{
  $address['success'] = TRUE;
  $address['forenames'] = $rs->fields(1)->value;
  $address['surname'] = $rs->fields(2)->value;
  $address['address1'] = $rs->fields(4)->value;
  $address['address2'] = $rs->fields(5)->value;
  $address['address3'] = $rs->fields(6)->value;
  $address['addressTown'] = $rs->fields(7)->value;
  $address['addressStateCounty'] = $rs->fields(8)->value;
  $address['addressZipPC'] = $rs->fields(9)->value;
  $address['addressCountry'] = $rs->fields(10)->value;
}
```

An `Adodb.Recordset` is a class that holds the result of a SQL select query. It has methods that enable users to scroll through the rows returned as well as properties that allow the names, types, and values of the different fields returned to be retrieved.

The `Recordset` exposes a Boolean property, `EOF`, which stands for *End of File*. If this is not true, at least one row was returned; therefore, the `success` field of the `address` array is set to `TRUE`.

The various `fields` of the `recordset` are then added as named members of the `address` array.

> You can add named array members in PHP at will; you do not need to specify any other information. You also can add members indexed by integers, and you can specify the index or leave it blank in order to add the new value to the end of the array.

Both the `Recordset` and `Connection` are then closed to free up system resources, and `$address` is returned:

```
    $rs->close();
    $conn->close();
    return $address;
}
```

Once the server-side page is ready, it is saved as `CustomerServer-JPSpan.php` and placed in a folder named `JPSpanCustomer` underneath the web server's root folder.

Creating the Client-Side Page

Now that the `Customer` class is incorporated into the server-side page, you can construct the client-side page. As mentioned earlier, the idea is to simulate the stage when a logged-in user chooses an item and specifies a delivery address. Figure 10-2 shows the test page.

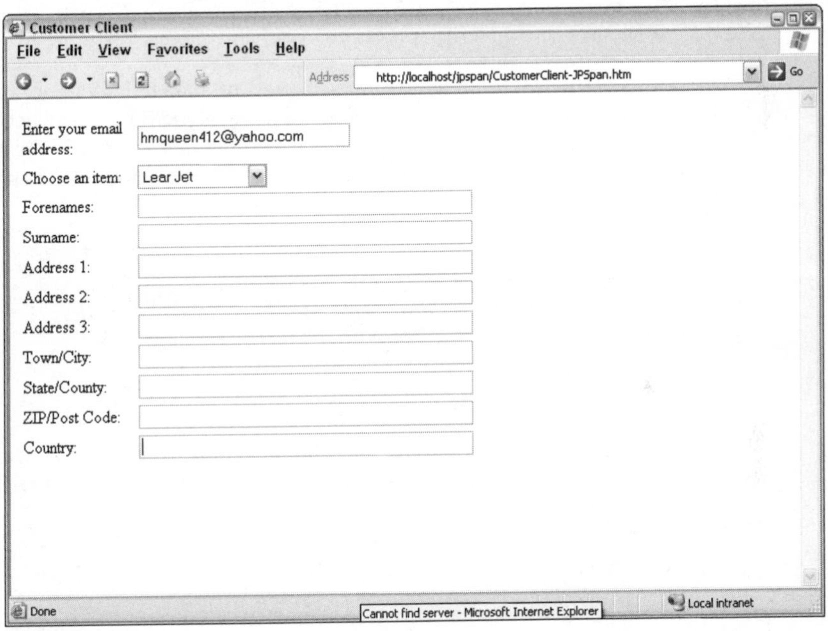

Figure 10-2

The HTML for the page is fairly standard: a number of `<input>` elements of type text with the appropriate labels embedded in a `<table>` element.

There are two `<script>` blocks in the page. The first retrieves the script via the customer-server.php page created earlier so its `src` is pointing to this, It also contains a query string value of `client` to instruct the page to return JavaScript:

```
<script type='text/javascript' src='customer-server.php?client'></script>
```

You will need this server generated JavaScript whenever you use `JPSpan`.

The second block contains inline code specific to this application, such as the `fetchAddress()` and `showAddress()` methods.

When the page has finished loading, the `init()` function is called by the `<body>` element's `onload` event firing:

```
<body onLoad="init();">
```

Inside `init()` a variable named `remoteCustomer` is initialized; there is no `var` preceding the statement, so this will be a global variable accessible to all code within the page:

```
function init()
{
   remoteCustomer = new customer(customerCallback);
}
```

The statement has two points of interest: first, the word `customer` appears in lowercase. This is because of a quirk in the PHP implementation of reflection. All class names and method names need to be in lowercase when used from JavaScript. Second, an argument, called the *callback object*, is passed to `customer`. It has its own methods that are called when the server-side processing finishes and a response is received on the client.

```
var customerCallback = {
                    getaddressfromemail: function(address)
                                        {
                                            showAddress(address);
                                        }
                    };
```

`customerCallback` is declared using the JavaScript object literal syntax. A property is declared with the name `getaddressfromemail`; as above, this is the lowercase version of the method in our `Customer` class.

For more information about using the JavaScript object literal syntax, refer to Chapter 7.

An anonymous function is assigned to this property. It has one parameter, `address`, which contains the details returned from the server. This function then passes the `address` argument to `showAddress()`, which displays the details on the page (see Figure 10-3).

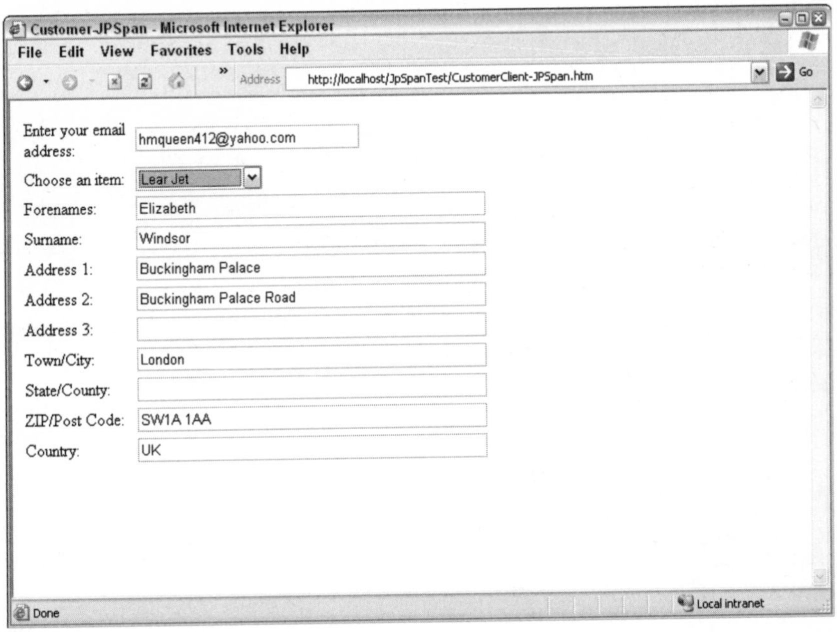

Figure 10-3

When the user leaves the e-mail text box by using the Tab key or by clicking the `<select>` element, the `onblur` event is fired, which calls the `fetchAddress()` function, which will use Ajax to fetch the corresponding address from the server-side database:

```
function fetchAddress(Email)
{
```

First, the value of `Email` is tested to make sure it is not empty:

```
function fetchAddress(Email)
{
  if (!Email)
  {
    alert("Please enter your email address before choosing an item.");
    document.getElementById("txtEmail").focus();
    return;
  }
```

If the e-mail address has not been filled in, `alert` is called and the focus returned to the requisite element; otherwise, `remoteCustomer` is used to call `getaddressfromemail()`, with the user's e-mail address as its argument:

```
remoteCustomer.getaddressfromemail(Email);
```

When the server-side processing is complete, the function named `getaddressfromemail()` defined on `customerCallback` is called, which in turn calls `showAddress()`:

```
function showAddress(Address)
{
    document.getElementById("txtForenames").value =
                            replaceIfNull(Address["forenames"], "");
    document.getElementById("txtSurname").value =
                            replaceIfNull(Address["surname"], "");
    //Other textboxes filled in...
```

The text fields on the page are populated with the values from the database. A small helper function, `replaceIfNull()`, is used to ensure the output is more user friendly if any of the fields are `null`; otherwise, the word "null" would appear in some of the boxes.

```
function replaceIfNull(Value, ReplaceWith)
{
    if (Value == null)
    {
        return ReplaceWith;
    }
    return Value;
}
```

`replaceIfNull()` checks the value of the first argument and, if it is `null`, returns the second arument, `ReplaceWith`. If it is not `null`, the value is returned unchanged.

If no values were present, because the e-mail address was not found in `tblCustomer`, this has the effect of clearing all the fields.

Then, the value of `success` is tested. If it equates to `false`, a message appears informing the user that he or she must fill in the address themselves. The focus is then set to the `Forenames` text field.

```
    if (!Address["success"])
    {
        alert("Address not registered, please fill in details.");
        document.getElementById("txtForenames").focus();
    }
}
```

The client page is saved as `CustomerClient-JPSpan.htm` in the same folder as `CustomerServer.php`. A successful search for the user's details should resemble Figure 10-4.

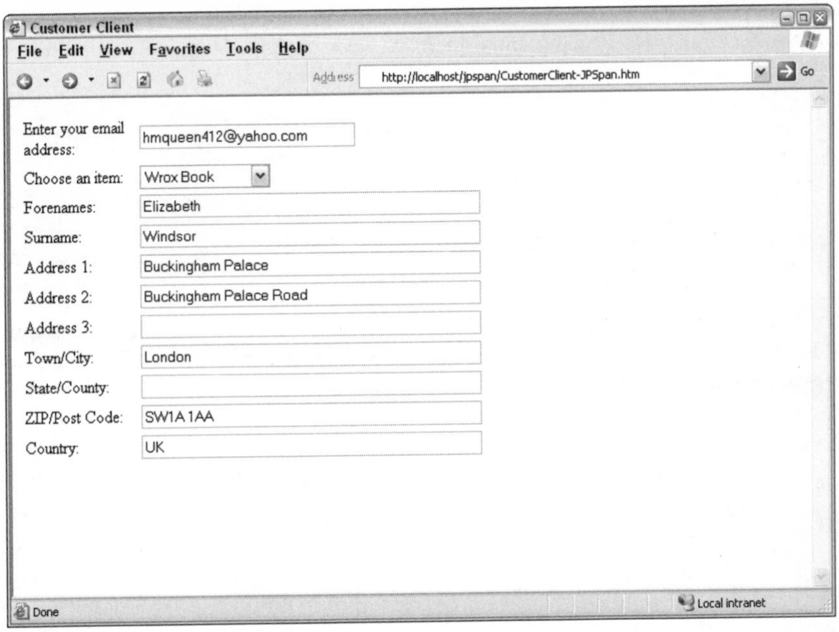

Figure 10-4

Error Handling

Errors can occur with any application, especially when communication between separate machines is involved. JPSpan has a means of trapping non-fatal errors that occur when processing the request server-side and having them appear as standard client-side exceptions.

The server-side page contains the following line:

```
require_once JPSPAN . 'ErrorHandler.php';
```

ErrorHandler.php is a generic handler that can propagate non-fatal errors to the client; it can handle general PHP errors as well as those caused specifically by JPSpan.

It allows for two basic configuration settings. The first defines how much information to give to the client when an error occurs directly as the result of PHP, not because of a JPSpan method causing an exception:

```
if (!defined('JPSPAN_ERROR_MESSAGES') )
{
    define ('JPSPAN_ERROR_MESSAGES', TRUE);
}
```

When defined as TRUE, as in the line above, a PHP error will simply show as "Server unable to respond." JPSpan errors will contain detailed information in the error object's message, code, and name properties. If defined as FALSE, extra information is available for all errors.

The second configuration option allows even more information to be sent to the client:

```
if (!defined('JPSPAN_ERROR_DEBUG') )
{
    define ('JPSPAN_ERROR_DEBUG', FALSE);
}
```

When JPSPAN_ERROR_DEBUG is defined as TRUE, two additional properties are added to the error: file and line. These properties carry the name of the PHP file from which the error was thrown and line number where it occurred, respectively. This information could be used in an attack against the web site, so the default value of FALSE causes these two pieces of information to be withheld. It is extremely useful, however, to have it set to TRUE in a development environment.

Type Translation

Any Ajax framework has to cope with the problem of representing types from the server-side language in JavaScript, and vice versa. Three main PHP pages, found in the JPSpan subfolder, deal specifically with converting types between the two languages: Serializer.php, Types.php, and Unserializer.php.

Serializer.php contains code that defines a global array named _JPSPAN_SERIALIZER_MAP. This contains an element for each PHP type that can be represented in JavaScript. As you can see, there are entries for all the standard types as well as ways of representing null and jpspan_error:

```
$GLOBALS['_JPSPAN_SERIALIZER_MAP'] = array(
    'string'=>array(
        'class'=>'JPSpan_SerializedString',
        'file'=>NULL
        ),
    'integer'=>array(
        'class'=>'JPSpan_SerializedInteger',
        'file'=>NULL
        ),
    'boolean'=>array(
        'class'=>'JPSpan_SerializedBoolean',
        'file'=>NULL
        ),
    'double'=>array(
        'class'=>'JPSpan_SerializedFloat',
        'file'=>NULL
        ),
    'null'=>array(
        'class'=>'JPSpan_SerializedNull',
        'file'=>NULL
        ),
    'array'=>array(
        'class'=>'JPSpan_SerializedArray',
        'file'=>NULL
        ),
```

```
        'object'=>array(
            'class'=>'JPSpan_SerializedObject',
            'file'=>NULL
            ),
        'jpspan_error'=>array(
            'class'=>'JPSpan_SerializedError',
            'file'=>NULL
            ),
    );
```

Each type uses a specific class to translate it into a function that returns the given data. The code for each class can reside in the page itself or can exist in a separate file. With the default JPSpan set up all the classes are defined in the page so the $file property is set to null.

Each serializer class has a method named generate that produces the JavaScript representation. For example, if a Boolean value of true was serialized to the client, the representation would be similar to the following:

```
    var data_serialized = 'new Function("var t1 = true;return t1;");';
    var data_func = eval(data_serialized);
    var data = data_func();
```

Unserializer.php and Types.php are used for conversion between JavaScript and PHP.

Types.php just contains definitions for two base types: JPSpan_Object and JPSpan_Error. (All JavaScript objects are converted into instances of one of these Although JPSpan_Error has the properties code, name, and message discussed in the section on errors, JPSpan_Object is simply an empty class that serves as a base for more specific implementations.

Unserializer.php uses one of two other classes for deserialization, both of which are found in the unserializer folder: JPSpan_Unserializer_XML in XML.php or JPSpan_Unserializer_PHP in PHP.php. Unless the PHP version is requested specifically, the XML version is used.

In the JPSpan representation, each argument to a method is represented by an element in an XML document; for example, the Boolean value is a <b> element with an attribute named v holding the value:

```
    <b v="1"/>
```

A value of false would be shown as v=0.

The complete document representing the call to getAddressFromEmail(), which accepts a string representing an e-mail address and returns the customer's full address details, is as follows:

```
    <r><a><e k="0"><s>hmqueen412@yahoo.com</s></e></a></r>
```

The <r> element is the root of the document, and <a> represents an array of the method's parameters. The first argument, contained by <e k="0">, represents a string, so the element consists of the actual data in an <s> element.

Summary of JPSpan

JPSpan is easy to use and integrates well with PHP. It can cope with classes that use the built-in types and more complex ones if they themselves are built from these. If JPSpan has one main failing, it is that the online documentation is somewhat sparse. Although PHP is covered extensively by numerous sites, if you need to customize JPSpan itself, you will need to dig into the source files and examples included in the basic installation.

DWR

Direct Web Remoting (DWR) is designed to be used with Java, one of the most widely used object-oriented languages. Java is not limited to any particular platform, but its main use has been server-side rather than desktop applications.

Remember that the similarity in names between Java and JavaScript owes more to marketing methods than inherent relationships between the two languages. Although the syntax of both is identical in a lot of places, there are many differences, especially when it comes to data typing.

How It Works

DWR also uses reflection to examine any of the classes specified in its configuration files. It then dispatches JavaScript to the client in which each function resembles those on the class but has an extra parameter specifying a function to call when the data is returned. As with JPSpan, DWR uses a cross-browser library and the relevant version of XmlHttpRequest, the ActiveX version if running Internet Explorer or the native JavaScript version for the Mozilla-based browsers and others such as Safari and Konqueror.

Installing DWR

Although the actual installation of DWR is straightforward, there are a number of prerequisites that need to be taken care of first.

Installing the Java SDK

First, download the Java software development kit from http://java.sun.com. The following examples are based on the version 1.5 kit, so if you have an earlier version you will need to upgrade.

You have a number of options available at Sun's site that can be confusing at times. For development work, you basically have two choices: either the plain development kit (which will also install the runtime files necessary for all Java applications) or the one that includes the NetBeans IDE (Integrated Development Environment). All the examples in this chapter can be developed and run without the IDE. This can then be downloaded separately if you are moving on to more serious Java development.

You can then install the kit and the runtime and create or update any environment variables as detailed in the accompanying readme file.

Installing the Web Server

Next, you will need a web server that supports Java servlets and JSP. The most common one is Tomcat, part of the Apache Jakarta project. There are versions available for Windows and UNIX/Linux, and details of how to install and configure them can be found at www.coreservlets.com/Apache-Tomcat-Tutorial/.

> At the URL just given you will see that there is a ready-to-run version that has been pre-configured with a number of standard settings. That is the version that was used for this chapter's examples; other than modifying the server's port so that it didn't clash with IIS, it worked out of the box.

After the Java SDK and the Tomcat server are installed, you should be able to start up Tomcat as shown in the tutorial and navigate to the home page. This will give you access to the management pages as well as a number of test pages and samples that you can use to make sure everything is set up correctly.

Finally, obtain the DWR files from http://getahead.ltd.uk/dwr/. This is only a small download of about 150KB. The main file, dwr.jar, needs to be placed in a specific folder of your web application. Put these files aside until the basic folder structure has been created.

Setting Up a Test Site

To set up a test site for DWR, create the folder structure, headed by DwrTest, as shown in Figure 10-5.

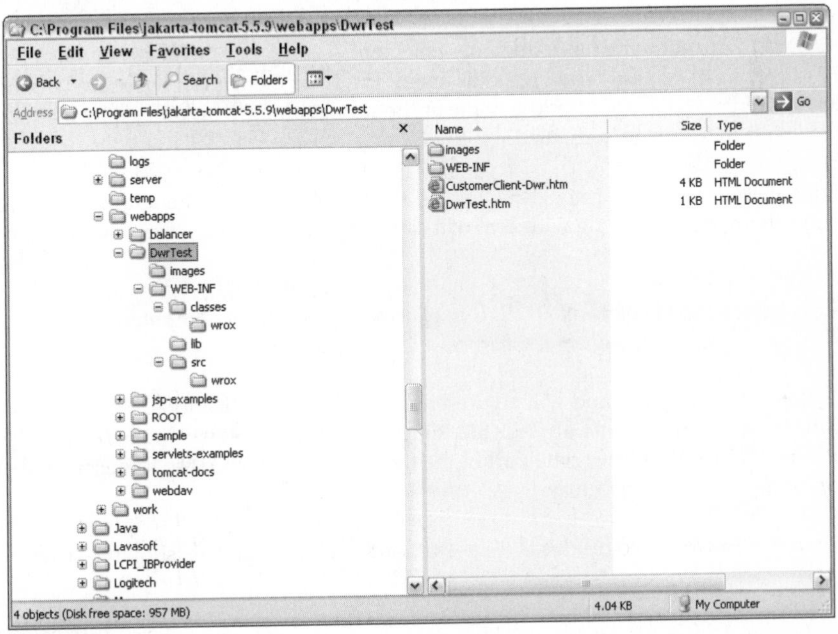

Figure 10-5

The next step is to create two XML configuration files: web.xml and dwr.xml. First, the basic structure of web.xml:

```
<web-app xmlns="http://java.sun.com/xml/ns/j2ee"
xmlns:xsi="http://www.w3.org/2001/XMLSchema-instance"
  xsi:schemaLocation="http://java.sun.com/xml/ns/j2ee
http://java.sun.com/xml/ns/j2ee/web-app_2_4.xsd"
  version="2.4">

  <servlet>
    <servlet-name>dwr-invoker</servlet-name>
    <display-name>DWR Servlet</display-name>
    <servlet-class>uk.ltd.getahead.dwr.DWRServlet</servlet-class>
    <init-param>
      <param-name>debug</param-name>
      <param-value>true</param-value>
    </init-param>
  </servlet>

  <servlet-mapping>
    <servlet-name>dwr-invoker</servlet-name>
    <url-pattern>/dwr/*</url-pattern>
  </servlet-mapping>
</web-app>
```

The preceding code shows a bare-bones web.xml *file. In addition to the XML prologue, there may also be sections showing the display name and description that appear in the Tomcat manager.*

The web.xml configuration file has a document element, <web-app>, which is in the default namespace of http://java.sun.com/xml/ns/j2ee (as are all the other elements). There are two main sections. The first block, <servlet>, specifies the name of the servlet along with other information, such as whether the built-in test page is enabled.

The second section, <servlet-mapping>, relates a URL to an entry in the <servlet> section. In this instance, specifying a URL ending with dwr will cause the dwr-invoker servlet to handle the client request.

> dwr-invoker *is the workhorse of DWR. It is a Java servlet responsible for providing all the basic functionality as well as the built-in test harness and other features.*

This file is not unique to DWR and will be present in all servlet applications. If you need to use DWR in an application that already has a web.xml file, simply add the necessary <servlet> and <servlet-mapping> elements to the appropriate part of the file. Save the file into the folder named WEB-INF directly under the DwrTest directory.

The second file, dwr.xml, also resides in WEB-INF. A minimal example is shown below.

```
<dwr>
  <allow>
    <create creator="new" javascript="JDate">
      <param name="class" value="java.util.Date" />
    </create>
  </allow>
</dwr>
```

This example dictates that an instance of the `java.util.Date` class will be made available to the client and will need to be referred to as `JDate`. The `creator` attribute is specified as `new`, meaning that the Java code to instantiate the object will use the `new` operator, as follows:

```
Date dt = new java.util.Date();
```

There are different ways of creating objects that you will see later and other `<create>` elements can also be added to expose more built-in Java classes or classes that you create yourself.

Finally, copy the `dwr.jar` file you downloaded earlier into the `WEB_INF\lib` directory.

You can now try out DWR by navigating to `http://localhost/DwrTest/dwr`. You should be presented with a link to JDate. On following this link, the full test page will be displayed, as shown in Figure 10-6.

Should you instead be greeted by an error message that seems to originate from one of the Java XML classes, you have two copies of the XML API on your system that are at loggerheads. You need to go to the installation folder of Tomcat, which is normally named `jakarta-tomcat-5.x.x`, and open the folder `common\endorsed`. Rename the file `xml-apis.jar` to `xml-apis.jar.bak`. You may also have to restart Tomcat.

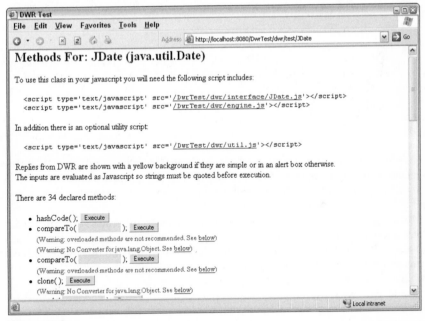

Figure 10-6

The test page lists all the methods exposed directly by the Java Date class and provides a way for you to run most them. There are also some tips about what not to do when creating your own classes that will be used via DWR. One of the main things to avoid is overloaded methods, a common feature of Java but which has no native support in JavaScript.

Methods are said to be overloaded when they have the same name but a different signature. This means that they can be differentiated by the type and number of arguments passed to the method. As JavaScript is a weakly typed language, it would not be able to differentiate between a method that accepted a string and one with the same name that accepted an integer, for example.

Creating the Client-Side Page

The following is a simple client-side page that shows how to use the DWR:

```html
<html>
<head>
  <title>DWR Test</title>
  <script type="text/javascript" src="/DwrTest/dwr/interface/JDate.js"></script>
  <script type="text/javascript" src="/DwrTest/dwr/engine.js"></script>
  <script type="text/javascript" src="/DwrTest/dwr/util.js"></script>
  <script type="text/javascript">

    function showDate()
    {
      JDate.toGMTString(callback);
    }

    var callback = function(Data)
                    {
                      alert(Data);
                    };
  </script>
</head>
<body>
  <input type="button" value="Show Date" onclick="showDate();">
</body>
</html>
```

The page has three included scripts, all of which are generated automatically by DWR. The first script, which is fetched from `/DwrTest/dwr/interface/JDate.js`, takes the name of the object you will use (this is the name defined in the `<create>` element in `dwr.xml`). This script has one JavaScript function for each of the methods implemented by `java.util.Date`. The second script, `engine.js`, contains the functions that use XMLHTTP to post to and receive from the server. The last script, `util.js`, contains a number of helper functions that, among other things, help format data returned from the server. In the example page above, the `toGMTString()` method returns a simple string, so none of these utility functions are needed. Many Java methods, however, return more complex types that need care when displaying or being passed on for further processing.

The page has one button that, when clicked, calls `showDate()`. This function in turn uses the `JDate` stub object and calls one of its methods, `toGMTString()`. Here you see a difference between the use of the JavaScript object and its Java counterpart.

```
function showDate()
{
  JDate.toGMTString(callback);
}
```

In Java, the `toGMTString()` method takes no arguments; in DWR's JavaScript, all methods have as their final parameter a function pointer that is called when the asynchronous return from the server is received.

```
var callback = function(Data)
                {
                    alert(Data);
                };
```

The `callback` function in this case is very simple. It has one argument representing the return value of `toGMTString()`, which in this case is displayed directly to the user.

You can try out this page by naming it `DwrTest.htm` and placing it in the `DwrTest` folder.

Using a Custom Class

Now that you've seen how to use one of the built-in Java classes, the next step is to create a custom class and access it via DWR.

The class in this example will be called `Customer` and will perform the same job as the one used to illustrate JPSpan. It will be a very simple representation of a customer and contain only one method, `getAddressFromEmail()`, which returns the address of the customer whose e-mail is passed as an argument.

In this class, you will use ODBC to connect to an Access database, so you will need to create a DSN that points to `Sales.mdb`. To create a DSN on Windows XP, go to Start⇨Administrative Tools⇨Data Sources (ODBC). Choose the tab specifying System DSN, and then click the Add button. After choosing the appropriate driver, SQL Server or Microsoft Access Driver (`.mdb`), you need to choose a name for the DSN and specify the location to `Sales.mdb`. In the example that follows, if you are using SQL Server, choose SQL Authentication, as opposed to Windows Authentication. You can now test the connection and if everything is working, just press OK continually to get out of the dialog boxes.

> You can read more about the Java database methods at `http://java.sun.com/j2se/1.4.2/docs/guide/jdbc/index.html`.

Next, create a text file named `Customer.java` and save it into the `WEB_INF\src\wrox` folder you created earlier.

The Java code starts by declaring the name of the package and then specifies two packages to be imported: `java.util` and `java.sql`. The classes in these packages can then be referenced by their short names rather than by the fully qualified names.

```
package wrox;
import java.util.*;
import java.sql.*;
```

Then follows the class header and the declaration of its solitary method:

```
public class Customer
{

  public HashMap getAddressFromEmail(String Email)
  {
    //Implementation goes here
  }
}
```

As before, the method accepts a string representation of an e-mail address and returns the details of the person's address. Whereas with PHP there was no need to specify the variable type, Java is a strongly typed language and so the return value of the function needs to be declared. A hashmap is similar to an array, but the values are retrieved by specifying a key, meaning that the client-side code written for the JPSpan client can be re-used with DWR.

The getAddressFromEmail() method begins with declaring the address hashmap and then sets the value of true to a key named success. A try...catch block then attempts to load the Java database driver that will be used to connect to the Sales database:

```
public HashMap getAddressFromEmail(String Email)
{
    HashMap address = new HashMap();
    address.put("success", false);
    try
    {
      Class.forName("sun.jdbc.odbc.JdbcOdbcDriver");
      //code continues here
    }
    catch (Exception e)
    {
      address.put("error", "Failed to load JDBC/ODBC driver.");
    }
```

Should the Class.forName fail, an error message will be added to the address details, which can help with debugging while the class is in the development stage.

```
    Class.forName("sun.jdbc.odbc.JdbcOdbcDriver");
    try
    {
      Connection con = DriverManager.getConnection("jdbc:odbc:sales","Test","test");
      //code continues here
    }
    catch (Exception e)
    {
      address.put("error", "Failed to connect.");
    }
```

A new Connection called con is declared, and the DriverManager from the JdbcOdbcDriver class attempts to connect to sales (the name of the DSN created earlier). If an error occurs here, a message is again added to the address hashmap.

```
Connection con = DriverManager.getConnection("jdbc:odbc:sales","Test","test");
try
{
  StringBuffer SQL = new StringBuffer("SELECT * FROM tblCustomer WHERE Email = '");
  String safeEmail = Email.replaceAll("'", "''");
  SQL.append(safeEmail);
  SQL.append("'");
  Statement stmt = con.createStatement();
```

The SQL statement is built up, again single quotes are duplicated, and then a `java.sql.Statement` is returned by using a factory method of the `con` object:

```
Statement stmt = con.createStatement();
ResultSet rs = stmt.executeQuery(SQL.toString());
boolean found = rs.next();
if (found)
{
  address.put("success", true);
  address.put("forenames", rs.getString(2));
  address.put("surname", rs.getString(3));
  address.put("address1", rs.getString(5));
  address.put("address2", rs.getString(6));
  address.put("address3", rs.getString(7));
  address.put("addressTown", rs.getString(8));
  address.put("addressStateCounty", rs.getString(9));
  address.put("addressZipPC", rs.getString(10));
  address.put("addressCountry", rs.getString(11));
}
```

A `ResultSet` is created by using the `executeQuery()` method against the SQL string.

The `ResultSet` class encapsulates the data returned by a SQL Select query. It has methods that allow the the user to move through the rows and to access the value of any particular field.

When an attempt is made to move to the next available row, a Boolean value, `found`, is returned, indicating success or failure. If successful, the values are added to the address hashmap; if not, the address details are left empty and the value of `success` is set to `false`.

Next, the `ResultSet` and `Connection` are closed to free resources:

```
rs.close();
con.close();
```

Finally, the details are returned:

```
return address;
```

After saving the `Customer.java` file, you need to compile it. Assuming you have set up your folders as illustrated in Figure 10-5, open a command prompt, navigate to the folder where `Customer.java` is saved, and run the following:

```
javac -d ..\..\classes Customer.java
```

You may get a warning about an unchecked method, which you can ignore.

To make the class accessible via DWR, you need to modify the `dwr.xml` file created earlier. Add the following `<create>` element to the `<allow>` section:

```
<create creator="new" javascript="Customer">
  <param name="class" value="wrox.Customer" />
</create>
```

You may need to use the management application, available from the Tomcat home page, to restart the DwrTest application. You can now navigate to `http://localhost/DwrTest/dwr` and verify that the Customer class appears with its `getAddressFromEmail()` method.

Once you have verified that the Customer class is available, you can re-use most of the `CustomerClient-JPSpan` page as your client. All the HTML can remain, but you need to change the script sections to include the DWR files, as shown previously, and you need to remove the `onload` attribute from the `<body>` element. One further change is to make use of some utility functions that DWR provides. These include procedures to set and retrieve element values, add options to select boxes, and display wait messages when operations that might take some time are executing.

```
<script type="text/javascript" src="/DwrTest/dwr/interface/Customer.js"></script>
<script type="text/javascript" src="/DwrTest/dwr/engine.js"></script>
<script type="text/javascript" src="/DwrTest/dwr/util.js"></script>
<script type="text/javascript">

function fetchAddress(Email)
{
  if (!Email)
  {
    alert("Please enter your email address before choosing an item.");
    $("txtEmail").focus();
    return;
  }
  Customer.getAddressFromEmail(Email, callback);
}

var callback = function (Address)
                {
                    showAddress(Address);
                };
```

The biggest change is that whereas with JPSpan you passed a callback object to the `remoteCustomer` constructor, here you pass a callback function to the `getAddressFrom Email()` method.

The calls to `document.getElementById()` have been replaced with one of the `util.js` functions, `$`. This is more flexible in that it takes one or more element IDs and returns either a specific element or, if there is more than one argument, an array of elements.

From the end user's point of view, the functionality of the page is identical to before. This page is available as `CustomerClient-DWR.htm` in the code download.

Error Handling

Any errors raised on the server are, by default, passed back to the client-side code as standard JavaScript errors. These can be handled with `try...catch` blocks if you don't want the default action, a message box showing the details, to appear. The error-handling procedures are customizable but the way of doing this is version-specific and is due to be changed in the next release.

More about dwr.xml

The `dwr.xml` file used so far has always used `<create>` elements, within the `<allow>` section, with the following structure:

```
<create creator="new" javascript="Customer">
  <param name="class" value="wrox.Customer" />
</create>
```

These have all specified `new` for the `creator` attribute and a class in the `<param>` element that equates to a new instance of the class being created. The `new` creator can also be used with static methods (those which can be called directly from a class rather than from an instance). DWR will examine a class to check whether a method is static before creating an instance.

The following sections discuss some of the other options available with `<create>`.

Excluding Methods

If you want to provide access to a class but limit which methods can be called, use the `<exclude>` element. For example, the following excludes the `toGMTString()` method from being called on the `Date` class:

```
<create creator="new" javascript="JDate">
  <param name="class" value="java.util.Date"/>
  <exclude method="toGMTString"/>
</create>
```

The Script Creator

Some objects cannot be set up by a simple call to a default constructor; they may be accessible only via the methods on another class or from a call to a static `getInstance()` method. An example of this is the `EmailValidator` class from the `org.apache.commons.validator` package. This does not have a public constructor, but an instance can be obtained by using the static method `getInstance()` on the class itself.

To create an instance of `EmailValidator`, use the following version of the `<create>` element:

```
<create creator="script" javascript="EmailValidator">
  <param name="language" value="beanshell"/>
  <param name="script">
    import org.apache.commons.validator.EmailValidator;
    return EmailValidator.getInstance();
  </param>
</create>
```

The scripting language used here is BeanShell, one of the Bean Scripted Framework (BSF) languages.

> **You can read more on BeanShell at** `www.beanshell.org/` **and see other languages supported by BSF at** `http://jakarta.apache.org/bsf/index.html`.

The Spring Creator

The Spring framework (`www.springframework.org`) is designed to bring together a number of different Java technologies as well as enable practical code re-use and sophisticated management of JavaBeans. It is a lightweight replacement for parts of the Java 2 Enterprise Edition (J2EE), which is used to create highly scalable applications where high numbers of users are expected to be using the system simultaneously. In these situations, resources such as memory need to be carefully managed.

You can make use of these enterprise beans by using the `spring` creator:

```
<create creator="spring" javascript="MyBean">
  <param name="beanName" value="MyBean"/>
  <param name="location" value="beans.xml"/>
</create>
```

The Spring framework and associated techniques are a huge topic. In addition to visiting the preceding URL, you can read more about integration of DWR and Spring at `http://getahead.ltd.uk/dwr/server/spring`.

The scope Parameter

The `<create>` element can also take an attribute named `scope`, which can be `page`, `session`, `request`, or `application`. This enables you to specify the lifetime of a bean; if no `scope` is specified, it defaults to `request`.

If you wanted to use the `Customer` class across a session, for example (which is not that helpful since it doesn't have any properties), the syntax would be as follows:

```
<create creator="new" javascript="Customer">
  <param name="class" value="wrox.Customer" scope="session"/>
</create>
```

Converters

Because Java has more data types than JavaScript, you may be wondering what would happen if DWR encountered a value that can't be translated directly. When no default translation is available, DWR uses converters to bridge the gap. *Converters* simply translate types between Java and JavaScript. There are a number of predefined converters that ship with DWR, such as the `DateConverter`, which marshalls between the `java.util.Date` and the JavaScript `Date` object. Other converters include the `ArrayConverter`, the `StringConverter`, and the `BeanConverter`.

In theory, it is possible to build your own converter; in practice, however, this is extremely unlikely and would be necessary only if your method required or returned a particularly unusual type.

There is, however, one aspect of converters that you should consider: security. It may be possible in certain circumstances to run malignant code through a converter; this is not possible with primitive types, but it could happen with a JavaBean. To safeguard against this, the bean converter is disabled by default. You can allow it, however, by adding an entry to the `<allow>` section of dwr.xml.

To allow everything in the bean, add the following line:

```
<dwr>
  <allow>
    <convert converter="bean" match="your.full.package.BeanName"/>
    <!-- other allowed converters and creators -->
  </allow>
</dwr>
```

The match specifies which bean to allow. You can expand it to your entire package by using an asterisk as a wild card:

```
<convert converter="bean" match="your.full.package.*"/>
```

You can exclude certain properties from being converted if you add a child element to the `<convert>`:

```
<convert converter="bean" match="your.full.package.BeanName">
  <param name="exclude" value="property1, property2"/>
</convert>
```

Alternatively, and more safely, you can specify which properties can be converted (all others are ignored):

```
<convert converter="bean" match="your.full.package.BeanName">
  <param name="include" value="property1, property2"/>
</convert>
```

> For more information on which converters are available and which need allowing specifically before they can be used by your code, see http://getahead.ltd.uk/dwr/server/dwrxml/converters.

Summary of DWR

DWR is an excellent way to harness the power of Java for use in client-side web pages. The hundreds of Java packages already available make it almost a certainty that, whatever your need, there will be something that fits the bill. There is also the advantage that there is no shortage of information, tutorials, and experts willing to share their knowledge about the Java platform.

Ajax.NET

Ajax.NET is designed to allow remote calling of classes written in a .NET language, specifically those accessed through ASP.NET. The .NET Framework has been around since 1999, and one of its aims is to enable code written in different languages to integrate with each other seamlessly. The main .NET languages are Visual Basic .NET and C#, but there are also many others, ranging from J#, a .NET port of Java, to COBOL .NET.

How It Works

As with the other frameworks discussed in this chapter, Ajax.NET uses a cross-browser, client-side library to post function calls to the server via the platform-specific version of XmlHttpRequest. It also uses reflection to analyze the server-side code in the ASP.NET page. Unlike the other frameworks, however, Ajax.NET takes advantage of a .NET feature called *attributes*, which is used to mark the methods that will be available from the client.

Installing Ajax.NET

To use Ajax.NET, you need to be running IIS version 5 or greater and have the .NET Framework installed. Although creating web sites that use ASP.NET can be done easily via Visual Studio .NET, this is not essential and can be done using a standard editor.

> *Chapter 6 discusses how to set up a new virtual folder for IIS and create an ASP.NET web project.*

Download the Ajax DLL from http://ajax.schwarz-interactive.de/. At the time of this writing, two releases are available: any one with a version number of 5.7.25.1 or greater is for use with version 2 of .NET; if you are not running this, download one of the earlier DLLs, such as 5.7.22.2.

Next, you need to add a reference to this DLL to each project in which you use Ajax.NET.

Adding the Ajax.dll Reference

You need to create your project before setting up Ajax.NET, so start Visual Studio .NET and add a new ASP.NET web application named *AjaxTest*.

> *The project can be in C#, Visual Basic .NET, or any other option available on your machine.*

Right-click the project name, *AjaxTest*, and then choose Add⇔New Folder. Name the new folder *ref*. Add the Ajax.dll downloaded earlier to this folder, and then add a reference to it by right-clicking the References folder, browsing to *ref*, and double-clicking Ajax.dll. Finally, rename the WebForm1.aspx page as Index.aspx. The layout of the project in the Solution Explorer on the right-hand side of Visual Studio will now look similar to Figure 10-7.

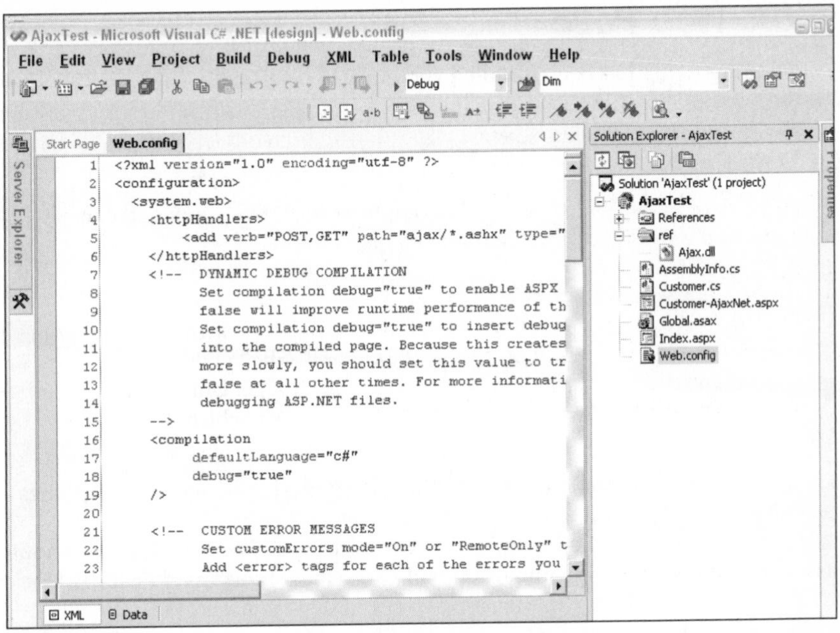

Figure 10-7

Adding a New HttpHandlers Element

You also need to modify the project's web configuration file. Open `Web.config` and add a new `<httpHandlers>` element underneath `<system.web>`.

```
<configuration>
  <system.web>
    <httpHandlers>
        <add verb="POST,GET" path="ajax/*.ashx"
             type="Ajax.PageHandlerFactory, Ajax" />
    </httpHandlers>
```

This tells IIS that any POST or GET request that is directed to ajax/*.ashx , where * means *any*, should be serviced by the `Ajax.PageHandlerFactory` instead of the built-in one that handles all other requests.

An `HttpHandler` handles a client request, either a GET request as a simple URL or a more complicated POST request containing additional data from an HTML form. It is responsible for any action taken, such as specialized business logic that must be followed. The built-in handler deals with .aspx, .asmx, and other similar ASP.NET files. `Ajax.PageHandlerFactory` processes requests with Ajax in the path and uses the information in the URL to generate the necessary client-side JavaScript based on the business object specified.

The initial setup is now complete and it's time to build the web page that will take advantage of Ajax.NET.

Creating the Web Page

To make sure that Ajax.NET has been installed and registered correctly, a simple test of the system is made using the `Index.aspx` file.

Creating a Test Page

From the Solution Explorer in Visual Studio .NET, right-click `Index.aspx` and choose View Code. Add the following line to the `Page_Load` procedure:

```
public class Index : System.Web.UI.Page
{
  private void Page_Load(object sender, System.EventArgs e)
  {
    Ajax.Utility.RegisterTypeForAjax(typeof(Index));
  }
```

The purpose of this line is to inject into the resulting HTML the necessary JavaScript files.

You are now in a position to test the set up. Start the project by pressing F5 and you should be greeted with a blank page. On viewing the source, you will notice the following two `<script>` elements:

```
<script type="text/javascript" src="/AjaxTest/ajax/common.ashx"></script>
<script type="text/javascript"
        src="/AjaxTest/ajax/AjaxTest.Index,AjaxTest.ashx"></script>
```

The first script provides the `XmlHttpRequest` functionality; the second is specific to the page and contains a few helper functions along with any server-side methods that have been made available.

Adding a Simple Method

To make a method available from the client, first add it to `Index.aspx` within the definition of the `Index` class:

```
public class Index : System.Web.UI.Page
{

  public int Add(int firstNumber, int secondNumber)
  {
    return firstNumber + secondNumber;
  }
```

To inform the Ajax.NET handler that this method needs a client-side JavaScript implementation, it is decorated with a .NET attribute:

```
[Ajax.AjaxMethod()]
public int Add(int firstNumber, int secondNumber)
{
  return firstNumber + secondNumber;
}
```

Access is then available client-side using the syntax `PageClass.Method(Arg1, Arg2, . . .)`. So, in this case the code would be:

```
var response = Index.Add(6, 8);
alert(response.value);
```

The response returned by `Index.Add` has three properties: `value` (as seen above), `error`, and `request`. To make your code more robust, you should check the `error` property to see if it is `true` before proceeding:

```
var response = Index.Add(6, 8);
if (response.error)
{
   alert(response.error);
}
else
{
   alert(response.value);
}
```

The `request` property provides access to the underlying `XmlHttpRequest` object and in more complicated scenarios can be helpful while debugging as the raw XML can be accessed.

The preceding example shows a synchronous call where, after the call to `Index.Add()`, the script waited while the method was being processed on the server. To start an asynchronous call, whereby the script continues after the method call, pass a function pointer as the last argument of the method:

```
var callback = function (response)
              {
                 if (response.error)
                 {
                    alert(response.error);
                 }
                 else
                 {
                    alert(response.value);
                 }
              }
Index.Add(6, 8, callback);
```

When using the asynchronous call, you can also pass in a context parameter immediately after the callback function. This is returned in the `response.context` property and enables you to use the same callback procedure for multiple calls while differentiating on return which each applied to:

```
var callback = function (response)
              {
                 if (response.error)
                 {
                    alert(response.error);
                 }
                 else
                 {
```

```
                        alert(response.context + response.value);
                }
        }
    Index.Add(6, 8, callback, "6 + 8 = ");
    Index.Add(9, 2, callback, "9 + 2 = ");
```

The preceding code would display the original sum as well as the result in two separate alert boxes.

Creating Customer-AjaxNET.aspx

Unlike the other two projects demonstrating JPSpan and DWR, there is only one page used with Ajax.NET: Customer-AjaxNET.aspx.

From the Solution Explorer in Visual Studio .NET, add a new web form to the project called Customer-AjaxNET.aspx. Before you make any further modifications to this page, the business class needs to be created; otherwise, Visual Studio .NET will complain that you are referencing an object that doesn't exist.

Implementing the Customer Class

In addition to accessing methods directly embedded in an .aspx page, you can make accessible the methods of any external class, provided that the types returned can be converted to a JavaScript format. Instead of using the current page class in the Ajax.Utility.RegisterTypeForAjax method, you need to pass the custom class.

Add a new class to the AjaxTest project and save it as Customer.cs. This implements the same functionality as in the other examples in this chapter—namely a single method, GetAddressFromEmail().

> As before, the following class is intended to aid the demonstration of using Ajax; it is certainly not a model of how to write a business class.

The class begins with a number of using statements to provide easier access to the needed types:

```
using System;
using System.Collections;
using System.Data.OleDb;
using System.Text;
```

The System namespace contains all the basic functionality and primitive data types, and System.Collections uses the Hashtable class that is used to store the address details. This is very similar to the hashmap from the DWR example. System.Data.OleDb contains classes to connect to and retrieve data from an OleDb datasource (SQL Server or Microsoft Access, for example). The System.Text class contains methods to manipulate strings and is needed for adding the extra quotation marks to the user-supplied e-mail address when necessary and also to provide access to the StringBuilder class used to construct the SQL statement.

Next comes the namespace and class declaration itself:

```
namespace AjaxTest
{
    public class Customer
    {
```

The `GetAddressFromEmail()` method is then implemented:

```
public Hashtable GetAddressFromEmail(string Email)
{
  Hashtable address = new Hashtable();
  address["success"] = false;
```

The return value is a hashtable, which stores data items that can be accessed through a unique key in a similar way to the hashmap used in the DWR example. A key named success is assigned a value of false, which will be modified to true if the call to the database is successful.

The next step is to create a connection to the Sales database. As mentioned earlier, the connection details for the database would be stored in a configuration file:

```
string sConnString = "Provider=SQLOLEDB; Data Source='localhost'; "
                  + "Initial Catalog='sales'; User Id='Test'; Password='test';";
OleDbConnection conn = new OleDbConnection(sConnString);
      conn.Open();
```

If you want to improve performance using SQL Server but are prepared to forgo the advantage of changing databases by altering your connection string, you can use the SQL Server–specific SqlConnection *instead of* OleDbConnection.

The SQL statement is then built up, using a `StringBuilder`, taking care to replace any single quotes that might be in the `Email` string:

In the .NET Framework, a String *object is immutable; once created it cannot be changed and any alterations, such as appending characters, are affected by creating a completely new string. The older version still remains in memory but is inaccessible. This is obviously wasteful from a memory point of view. To overcome this problem, a separate class named* StringBuilder *is used. This can be changed without replication, and when all changes are complete it can be converted to a fully fledged* String *object by calling its* ToString() *method.*

```
StringBuilder SQL = new StringBuilder("SELECT * FROM tblCustomer WHERE Email = '");
string safeEmail = Email.Replace("'", "''");
SQL.Append(safeEmail + "'");
```

An `OleDbCommand` object is used to execute the SQL and the results are returned in the form of an `OleDbDataReader`.

OleDbDataReader *is an ADO.NET class that is used to provide connected read-only access to the results of a Select query. It can traverse through the results only in a forward direction and provides methods to retrieve the values from any field either by using the field's name or its position.*

```
OleDbCommand cmd = new OleDbCommand(SQL.ToString(), conn);
OleDbDataReader dr = cmd.ExecuteReader();
```

As you can see, the code is extremely similar to its Java equivalent.

The rows are accessed one-by-one by calling the `read()` method, the return value of `dr.Read()` will be true only if the row exists. In this case, the hashtable is populated, and the `success` key set to `true`; otherwise it will be set to `false` and the address details will be left empty.

```
Boolean found = dr.Read();
if (found)
{
  address["success"] = true;
  address["forenames"] = (dr.IsDBNull(1) ? "" : dr.GetString(1));
  address["surname"] =(dr.IsDBNull(2) ? "" : dr.GetString(2));
  address["address1"] =(dr.IsDBNull(4) ? "" : dr.GetString(4));
  address["address2"] =(dr.IsDBNull(5) ? "" : dr.GetString(5));
  address["address3"] =(dr.IsDBNull(6) ? "" : dr.GetString(6));
  address["addressTown"] =(dr.IsDBNull(7) ? "" : dr.GetString(7));
  address["addressStateCounty"] =(dr.IsDBNull(8) ? "" : dr.GetString(8));
  address["addressZipPC"] =(dr.IsDBNull(9) ? "" : dr.GetString(9));
  address["addressCountry"] =(dr.IsDBNull(10) ? "" : dr.GetString(10));
}
```

The built-in method of the data reader, `IsDBNull()`, is used to avoid any problems with null values.

Finally, the data reader and the connection are closed and the hashtable is returned.

```
dr.Close();
conn.Close();
return address;
```

The one thing that remains is to add the custom attribute:

```
[Ajax.AjaxMethod()]
public Hashtable GetAddressFromEmail(string Email)
```

This completes the creation of the `Customer` class. It exists as a standalone class, so it can be used by other applications, not just the web page. The next stage is to register it for use via `Customer-AjaxNET.aspx` so that it is available client-side.

Adding the Customer Class as a Remote Object

To register the `Customer` class, return to the code view of the `Customer-AjaxNET.aspx` page and add the following to the `Page_Load()` event handler.

```
private void Page_Load(object sender, System.EventArgs e)
{
    Ajax.Utility.RegisterTypeForAjax(typeof(Customer));
}
```

As before in `Index.aspx`, this adds into the HTML the two JavaScript includes, which provide the client-side functionality necessary to relay the method calls to the server-side object.

Creating the Client-Side Code

There is little difference between this code and the other examples in the chapter. The `fetchAddress()` function is the same as the one using DWR, except for the slight capitalization difference in the method name:

```
function fetchAddress(Email)
{
  if (!Email)
  {
    alert("Please enter your email address before choosing an item.");
    document.getElementById("txtEmail").focus();
    return;
  }
  Customer.GetAddressFromEmail(Email, callback);
}
```

`fetchAddress()` accepts a string representing the customer's e-mail address. It first tests whether a value has been supplied, and if not, the user is prompted to supply one and the focus is returned to the appropriate text box.

If a value was supplied the `GetAddressFromEmail()` method is called on the `Customer` object. The second parameter to the method is the name of the function that will handle the response.

The callback function passes on the server response:

```
var callback = function (Response)
              {
                  showAddress(Response);
              };
```

There is a slight change to showAddress() to utilize the `Response.error` property that Ajax.NET provides. If the value is empty, no error has occurred; otherwise, the error message is displayed.

```
function showAddress(Response)
{
  if (Response.error)
  {
    alert("Unable to retrieve address.\n(" + Response.error + ")");
    return;
  }
```

Then comes the only significant change. Because of how Ajax.NET serializes the hashtable, it appears to JavaScript as an array, with each member holding an object with a key and a value. To enable re-using the code from before, the hashtable is converted by being passed to a helper function named `getAddressFromResponse()`:

```
var Address = getAddressFromResponse(Response);
```

getAddressFromResponse() iterates through the array and creates a simplified hashtable of the data that is easier to deal with:

```
function getAddressFromResponse(Response)
{
  var address = new Object();
  var data = Response.value;
  for (var i = 0; i < data.length; i++)
  {
    address[data[i].Key] = data[i].Value;
  }
  return address;
}
```

This completes the creation of the web page. To try it out, navigate to `http://localhost/AjaxTest/Customer-AjaxNet.aspx`, enter an e-mail address, and exit the text box. The result should be similar to Figure 10-8.

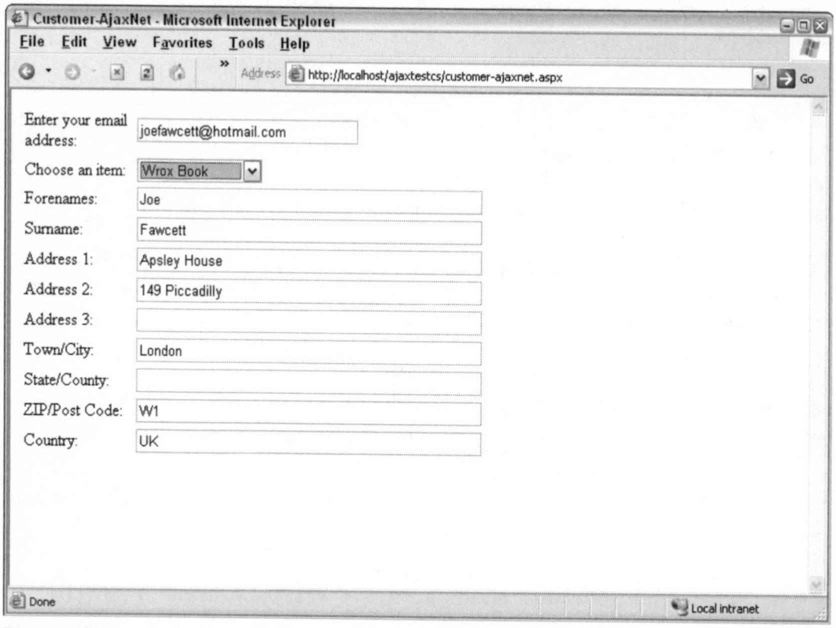

Figure 10-8

Simple and Complex Types

The Ajax.NET framework uses JavaScript Object Notation (JSON), which you have seen in Chapter 7, to pass objects to the client. It can cope with all the primitive types, such as integers, strings, and Boolean values, and also has built-in support for some of the common .NET complex types, such as an ADO.NET dataset or datatable.

As an example of manipulating a dataset on the client, imagine you have called a function on your server-side class that returns a dataset:

```
MyClass.GetDataSet(callback);
```

Your callback function could then read values from the dataset in much the same manner as using it from within .NET:

```
function callback(Response)
{
  if (Response.error)
  {
    alert(Response.error);
    return;
  }
  var tblNames = Response.value.Tables[0];
  var sTable = "<table><th>Forenames</td><td>Surname</td></tr>";
  for (var i = 0 ; i < tblNames.Rows.length; i++)
  {
    var oRow = tblNames.Rows[i];
    sTable += "<tr><td>" + oRow.Forenames + "</td>";
    sTable += "<td>" + oRow.Surname + "</td></tr>";
  }
  sTable += "</table>";
  document.getElementById("divNames").innerHTML = sTable;
}
```

If you want to return a custom class of your own from a method and have it serialized correctly by `Ajax.NET`, you need to mark it with the `Serializable` attribute. For example, consider a class that represents a web site user:

```
[Serializable()]
public class User
{
  private string _userName = "";
  private string _userEmail = "";

  public string UserName
  {
    get
    {
      return _userName;
    }
  }

  public string UserEmail
  {
    get
    {
      return _userEmail;
```

```
    }
  }
  public User(string Name, string Email)
  {
    _userName = Name;
    _userEmail = Email;
  }
}
```

Assuming a User object was returned by a method named GetUserFromId(), the properties would be available in JavaScript.

```
MyClass.GetUserFromId(6, callback);

function callback(Response)
{
  var oUser = Response.value;
  alert(oUser.UserName + "\n" + oUser.UserEmail);
}
```

Session State

Ajax.NET can also handle cases where you need access to session variables. When declaring the AjaxMethod attribute, you can pass a parameter specifying whether you need read, write, or read and write access.

```
[Ajax.AjaxMethod(HttpSessionStateRequirement.Read)]
public string MyMethod()
{
```

The other two options are HttpSessionStateRequirement.Write and HttpSessionStateRequirement.ReadWrite.

Suppose, for example, that the user has initiated a number of transactions on a site and wants to know which have been completed. In traditional web applications, he or she would need to revisit a specific page to see the status, but with an Ajax approach this is not necessary.

The ID of each transaction waiting to be completed is held in a session variable named WaitingTransactions.

```
[Ajax.AjaxMethod(HttpSessionStateRequirement.Read)]
public ArrayList FetchCompletedTransactions()
{
  if (HttpContext.Current.Session["WaitingTransactions"] == null)
  {
    return null;
  }
  ArrayList completedTransactions = new ArrayList();
  int[]transactions = (int[])HttpContext.Current.Session["WaitingTransactions"];
  for (int i = 0; i < transactions.Length; i++)
  {
```

```
      Transaction tx = Transaction.GetFromId(transactions[i]);
      if (tx != null && tx.Status == TransactionStatus.Ready)
      {
        completedTransactions.Add(tx);
      }
    }
  }
  return completedTransactions;
}
```

The session variable is checked; if found not to be `null`, it is cast to an array of integers. Each integer is fed to a method that retrieves details of the transaction and if it is ready then adds it to the `ArrayList` to be returned to the caller.

Now you can use the `window.setTimeout` method to poll the state of the transactions:

```
<script type="text/javascript">
  function transactionsCompleteCallback(response)
  {
    if (response.error != null)
    {
      alert(response.error);
      return;
    }
    var data = response.value;
    if (!data || !data.length) return;
    var sResult = "";
    for (var i = 0; i < data.length; i++)
    {
      sResult += "Transaction Id: " + data[i].TransactionId;
      sResult += " (" + data[i].TransactionName + ") Status: ";
      sResult += data[i].Status + "<br>";
    }
    document.getElementById("divTransactionStatus").innerHTML = sResult;
    setTimeout("MyPage.FetchCompletedTransactions(transactionsCompleteCallback)"
               , 10000);
  }
</script>
<body onload=
"setTimeout('MyPage.FetchCompletedTransactions(transactionsCompleteCallback)',
5000">
```

After a delay of 5 seconds, `FetchCompletedTransactions` is called and the results returned to the `transactionsCompleteCallback` function. If there is no error and some data available, HTML is built up detailing the transaction's ID, name, and status, and displayed to the user. The function then uses `setTimeout` again, ensuring that the results are repopulated every 10 seconds.

Summary of Ajax.NET

Provided that you are using IIS already, Ajax.NET is extremely simple to set up. It can handle most data types that you will need. And if you don't like some aspect of it, it is an open source framework, so you are free to examine how it works and suggest or even write you own improvements.

Summary

All three of the frameworks examined in this chapter have their strengths; the main factor in deciding which to use is almost certainly governed by what your web server is running at the moment. All three languages—PHP, Java, and .NET—have myriad web-based resources and books devoted to them (although Java probably comes slightly ahead of the others on this point). Ajax.NET probably scores highest for ease of use when it comes to making methods available; adding one line to an existing procedure and one line in the page load handler is certainly very simple, although with DWR there is no internal modification of the class at all, enabling you to re-use classes from elsewhere more easily. JPSpan's strength lies in the fact that, because both it and JavaScript are weakly typed, there is less effort involved in coercing types between the two languages.

Having completed this chapter, which covered a lot of ground on three different Ajax frameworks, you have accomplished a number of different tasks.

For JPSpan, you have installed PHP, created a class, and connected to a database.

With DWR, you set up a new web server that could handle Java servlets and JSP pages, and then created a Java class using a basic text editor before compiling it using command-line tools. You also learned how to modify the XML config files to allow the class to be used from the client.

For Ajax.NET, you learned how to modify the `web.config` file to override the built-in page handler and how to install `Ajax.dll` and add a reference to it. You then created a class that could retrieve information from a database and utilized this class using JavaScript on the client.

Index

B

Bean Scripted Framework (BSF) language, 372
BeanShell scripting language, 372
Beginning PHP, Apache, MySQL Web Development (Wiley Publishing), 24
Beginning XML, 3rd Edition (Wiley Publishing), 163
behavior, web service, 177
Berkman Center for the Internet & Society, 126
Bitflux
  Blog web site, 11–12
  LiveSearch technology, 11–12, 64, 266
BlogSearch Beta web site, 256
bookContainer class, 99
bookContainer-odd class, 99
bookstore application Best Picks feature, 96–102, 121–123
books.xml file, 96–97, 103, 106–107, 109, 111–113
books.xsl file, 111
braces ({ })
  JSON object literal delimiters, 192, 194
  XSLT variable delimiters, 113
brackets, square ([ ])
  JSON array literal delimiters, 191–192
  XPath condition delimiters, 103
Broken-Notebook.com web site, 68
browser. *See specific browser*
BSF (Bean Scripted Framework) language, 372
business class, 347, 349, 352–355

C

C# language
  getter, 145
  JSON library, 199, 267, 268
  MSSQL database, connecting to using, 271
callback object, 356
callService method, 178
cancelReply method, 340
cascading style sheets. *See CSS*
CDF (Channel Definition Format), 125
CFJSON library, 199
changeList function, 122
checkComments function, 71–72, 76, 77–78
CheckComments.php file, 68–69, 72
checkIFrame function, 30, 32
checkMail method, 287, 291, 292
childNodes collection, 85, 86, 98, 99

class. *See also specific class*
  Ajax.NET, returning custom class from method in, 383
  DWR
    calling method in another class, 371–372
    creating custom class in, 367–370
    method in class, excluding, 371
  web service, marking as, 171, 172
class.phpmailer.php file, 312
class.smtp.php file, 312
cleanupEmail function, 325, 334
clearAll method, 286–287
clearResults method, 275
clearTimeout function, 230
cloneNode method, 334
close method, 259, 261, 262
code-behind web page authoring, 140
Coggeshall, John ("E-mail validation with PHP 4"), 61
comment notification using communication pattern, 68–72
CompareTo method, 247
config.inc.php file, 284–285, 303, 308, 312
ConfigurationSettings object, 272
config.xml file, 241
confirm function, 338
connect method, 286, 287
contains function, 103
coreservlets.com web site, 363
count function, 293
CPAN web site, 199
Create method, 142
createDocument
  function, 82–83
  method, 91, 92, 95
createDropDown method, 210, 219
createElement method
  autosuggest text box, 210
  DOM, 89, 100, 148, 150, 248
  iframe object, creating using, 29
  input element, creating hidden using, 31
  weather widget, 248
  web search widget, 258
createIFrame function, 29, 30
createProcessor method, 116
createRequest function, 35, 53
createTextNode method, 100, 151, 334
createTextRange method, 205, 206
createXMLHttp function, 34–35
crockford.com web site, 195, 199
cross-site scripting (XSS), 184
csc.exe file, 172